Math Workbook for ISEE, SSAT, & HSPT Prep

Middle & High School Entrance Exams

2nd Edition

Allen Koh

Copyright information:

Math Workbook for ISEE, SSAT, & HSPT Prep

Middle & High School Entrance Exams
2nd Edition

Published by:

 CARDINAL
EDUCATION

P O Box 51594
Palo Alto CA, 94303
(650) 391-9814
info@CardinalEducation.com

ISBN-13: 978-1475143225
ISBN-10: 1475143222
LCCN: 2012906130

Visit us at online at www.CardinalEducation.com.

*ISEE, SSAT, and HSPT are registered trademarks, and this book is not officially endorsed by those respective trademark holders. Moreover, the "Cardinal" in Cardinal Education reflects the Stanford pedigree of over 90% of our staff, but does not constitute an official endorsement by Stanford University.

Guide to the High School Entrance Exams

ISEE and SSAT

The ISEE is a test for students seeking admission to private middle schools and high schools. There are three different levels of the ISEE: the Lower Level ISEE (for students currently in grades 4-5), the Middle Level ISEE (for students currently in grades 6-7), and the Upper Level ISEE (for students currently in grades 8-11). The ISEE is generally offered between November and February. Students may only take the ISEE once every six months.

The SSAT is a test for students seeking admission to private middle schools and high schools. There are two levels of the SSAT: the Lower Level SSAT (for students currently in grades 5-7) and the Upper Level SSAT (for students currently in grades 8-11). The SSAT is generally offered every month from October to June. Students may take the SSAT multiple times.

Most secular private schools will require students to take either the ISEE or SSAT. Some schools will accept both tests, while others may have a particular preference for one test over the other. Consult the admissions policies at every school for which you plan on applying in order to see which test(s) you will need to take.

The ISEE and SSAT are structured similarly. They each consist exclusively of multiple choice questions, divided into a verbal section, a reading comprehension section, and two math sections. Each test also contains an essay section, which is not scored, but is sent to schools along with the test scores.

The primary difference between the ISEE and SSAT is the difficulty level of their respective math sections. The SSAT is challenging but reasonable for well-prepared 5th graders (Lower Level) and 8th graders (Upper Level) who perform strongly in their school math classes. The Middle Level and Upper Level ISEE tests, on the other hand, are extremely difficult for even the strongest and most well-prepared math students, and require intense preparation. Students taking the Middle Level and Upper Level ISEE tests should be proficient in all of the concepts covered in this book, and 8th grade students should expect to see even more advanced material on the Upper Level ISEE.

There is one other major difference between the math sections of the ISEE and SSAT. The Middle and Upper Level ISEE exams contain a special type of question, called Quantitative Comparisons. This book covers Quantitative Comparison questions in Chapter 15.

HSPT

The HSPT is a test for 8th grade students seeking admission to Catholic high schools. The HSPT is generally administered in January, and students may only take it one time. The basic structure of the HSPT includes a verbal section, a reading comprehension section, two math sections, and a language section that is a test of grammar. The HSPT also contains supplemental sections—science, religion, and an essay—that schools may or may not require students to take.

The first math section of the HSPT is very different from the second math section. While the second math section contains a wide variety of questions, the first is made up almost entirely of the three unique types of HSPT questions covered in Chapter 14. The math on the HSPT is of roughly the same difficulty level as the math on the Upper Level SSAT and is significantly easier than the math on the Upper Level ISEE.

Changes from the First Edition

This second edition of the *Math Workbook for Middle School and High School Entrance Exams* has been overhauled from the first edition to reflect the most up-to-date knowledge of the private school admissions exams, as well as to incorporate new insights gleaned by our experts as they used the first edition to prepare students for these exams.

Here are some new features you will find in the second edition:

- A more logical progression of concepts and exercises

- Over 60 new practice sets covering basic arithmetic, algebra, geometry, and advanced topics

- Expanded sections specific to the ISEE and HSPT

- An assignment planner to help students track their practice sets and measure scores

- A formula sheet containing the most vital math rules and information

- A thorough explanation of the major differences between the ISEE, SSAT, and HSPT

- Updated answer key with easier navigation

Due date	Assignment	Complete		Due date	Assignment	Complete
_____	_____	☐		_____	_____	☐
_____	_____	☐		_____	_____	☐
_____	_____	☐		_____	_____	☐
_____	_____	☐		_____	_____	☐
_____	_____	☐		_____	_____	☐
_____	_____	☐		_____	_____	☐
_____	_____	☐		_____	_____	☐
_____	_____	☐		_____	_____	☐
_____	_____	☐		_____	_____	☐
_____	_____	☐		_____	_____	☐
_____	_____	☐		_____	_____	☐
_____	_____	☐		_____	_____	☐
_____	_____	☐		_____	_____	☐
_____	_____	☐		_____	_____	☐
_____	_____	☐		_____	_____	☐
_____	_____	☐		_____	_____	☐
_____	_____	☐		_____	_____	☐
_____	_____	☐		_____	_____	☐
_____	_____	☐		_____	_____	☐
_____	_____	☐		_____	_____	☐
_____	_____	☐		_____	_____	☐
_____	_____	☐		_____	_____	☐
_____	_____	☐		_____	_____	☐
_____	_____	☐		_____	_____	☐
_____	_____	☐		_____	_____	☐
_____	_____	☐		_____	_____	☐
_____	_____	☐		_____	_____	☐
_____	_____	☐		_____	_____	☐
_____	_____	☐		_____	_____	☐
_____	_____	☐		_____	_____	☐
_____	_____	☐		_____	_____	☐
_____	_____	☐		_____	_____	☐
_____	_____	☐		_____	_____	☐
_____	_____	☐		_____	_____	☐

Due date	Assignment	Complete		Due date	Assignment	Complete
_____	_____	☐		_____	_____	☐
_____	_____	☐		_____	_____	☐
_____	_____	☐		_____	_____	☐
_____	_____	☐		_____	_____	☐
_____	_____	☐		_____	_____	☐
_____	_____	☐		_____	_____	☐
_____	_____	☐		_____	_____	☐
_____	_____	☐		_____	_____	☐
_____	_____	☐		_____	_____	☐
_____	_____	☐		_____	_____	☐
_____	_____	☐		_____	_____	☐
_____	_____	☐		_____	_____	☐
_____	_____	☐		_____	_____	☐
_____	_____	☐		_____	_____	☐
_____	_____	☐		_____	_____	☐
_____	_____	☐		_____	_____	☐
_____	_____	☐		_____	_____	☐
_____	_____	☐		_____	_____	☐
_____	_____	☐		_____	_____	☐
_____	_____	☐		_____	_____	☐
_____	_____	☐		_____	_____	☐
_____	_____	☐		_____	_____	☐
_____	_____	☐		_____	_____	☐
_____	_____	☐		_____	_____	☐
_____	_____	☐		_____	_____	☐
_____	_____	☐		_____	_____	☐
_____	_____	☐		_____	_____	☐
_____	_____	☐		_____	_____	☐
_____	_____	☐		_____	_____	☐
_____	_____	☐		_____	_____	☐
_____	_____	☐		_____	_____	☐
_____	_____	☐		_____	_____	☐

Due date	Assignment	Complete		Due date	Assignment	Complete
_____	_____	☐		_____	_____	☐
_____	_____	☐		_____	_____	☐
_____	_____	☐		_____	_____	☐
_____	_____	☐		_____	_____	☐
_____	_____	☐		_____	_____	☐
_____	_____	☐		_____	_____	☐
_____	_____	☐		_____	_____	☐
_____	_____	☐		_____	_____	☐
_____	_____	☐		_____	_____	☐
_____	_____	☐		_____	_____	☐
_____	_____	☐		_____	_____	☐
_____	_____	☐		_____	_____	☐
_____	_____	☐		_____	_____	☐
_____	_____	☐		_____	_____	☐
_____	_____	☐		_____	_____	☐
_____	_____	☐		_____	_____	☐
_____	_____	☐		_____	_____	☐
_____	_____	☐		_____	_____	☐
_____	_____	☐		_____	_____	☐
_____	_____	☐		_____	_____	☐
_____	_____	☐		_____	_____	☐
_____	_____	☐		_____	_____	☐
_____	_____	☐		_____	_____	☐
_____	_____	☐		_____	_____	☐
_____	_____	☐		_____	_____	☐
_____	_____	☐		_____	_____	☐
_____	_____	☐		_____	_____	☐
_____	_____	☐		_____	_____	☐
_____	_____	☐		_____	_____	☐
_____	_____	☐		_____	_____	☐
_____	_____	☐		_____	_____	☐
_____	_____	☐		_____	_____	☐
_____	_____	☐		_____	_____	☐

Due date	Assignment	Complete		Due date	Assignment	Complete
_____	_____	☐		_____	_____	☐
_____	_____	☐		_____	_____	☐
_____	_____	☐		_____	_____	☐
_____	_____	☐		_____	_____	☐
_____	_____	☐		_____	_____	☐
_____	_____	☐		_____	_____	☐
_____	_____	☐		_____	_____	☐
_____	_____	☐		_____	_____	☐
_____	_____	☐		_____	_____	☐
_____	_____	☐		_____	_____	☐
_____	_____	☐		_____	_____	☐
_____	_____	☐		_____	_____	☐
_____	_____	☐		_____	_____	☐
_____	_____	☐		_____	_____	☐
_____	_____	☐		_____	_____	☐
_____	_____	☐		_____	_____	☐
_____	_____	☐		_____	_____	☐
_____	_____	☐		_____	_____	☐
_____	_____	☐		_____	_____	☐
_____	_____	☐		_____	_____	☐
_____	_____	☐		_____	_____	☐
_____	_____	☐		_____	_____	☐
_____	_____	☐		_____	_____	☐
_____	_____	☐		_____	_____	☐
_____	_____	☐		_____	_____	☐
_____	_____	☐		_____	_____	☐
_____	_____	☐		_____	_____	☐
_____	_____	☐		_____	_____	☐
_____	_____	☐		_____	_____	☐
_____	_____	☐		_____	_____	☐
_____	_____	☐		_____	_____	☐
_____	_____	☐		_____	_____	☐

ADDITION Practice Set 2

1. $6 + 188 =$

2. $295 + 8 =$

3. $314 + 6 =$

4. $69 + 567 =$

5. $55 + 719 =$

6. $367 + 434 =$

7. $188 + 565 =$

8. $567 + 609 =$

9. $788 + 656 =$

10. $945 + 266 =$

11. $6 + 25 + 9 =$

12. $11 + 4 + 47 + 7 =$

13. $28 + 132 + 21 =$

14. $15 + 179 + 42 + 7 =$

15. $83 + 16 + 5 =$

16. $23 + 87 + 41 =$

17. $32 + 19 + 78 =$

18. $25 + 36 + 49 =$

19. $97 + 58 + 69 =$

20. $43 + 53 + 72 + 18 =$

21. $1,472 + 59 + 8 + 76 =$

22. $2,418 + 396 + 72 + 431 =$

23. $584 + 219 + 34 + 87 =$

24. $3,429 + 87 + 523 + 90 =$

25. $857 + 489 + 301 =$

26. $419 + 9,475 + 1,056 =$

27. $938 + 4,710 + 293 + 28 =$

28. $892 + 416 + 58 + 2,946 =$

29. $461 + 2,847 + 5,082 + 3,264 =$

30. $4,910 + 1,749 + 6,235 + 904 =$

<u>SUBTRACTION Practice Set 1</u>

1. $33 - 17 =$

2. $67 - 58 =$

3. $81 - 29 =$

4. $123 - 9 =$

5. $104 - 25 =$

6. $302 - 36 =$

7. $521 - 74 =$

8. $124 - 98 =$

9. $562 - 184 =$

10. $712 - 586 =$

11. $223 - 199 =$

12. $901 - 632 =$

13. $653 - 207 =$

14. $847 - 358 =$

15. $2,786 - 99 =$

16. $10,234 - 75 =$

17. $7,825 - 39 =$

18. $1,087 - 97 =$

19. $7,830 - 392 =$

20. $12,050 - 567 =$

21. 1,005 − 126 =

22. 7,001 − 237 =

23. 7,862 − 5,974 =

24. 12,723 − 9,377 =

25. 9,200 − 5,009 =

26. 2,103 − 1,288 =

27. 5,086 − 1,234 − 378 =

28. 7,237 − 307 − 864 =

29. 1,086 − 788 − 82 =

30. 12,082 − 1,072 − 509 =

SUBTRACTION Practice Set 2

1. $51 - 34 =$

2. $66 - 18 =$

3. $86 - 27 =$

4. $98 - 13 =$

5. $131 - 76 =$

6. $257 - 49 =$

7. $419 - 92 =$

8. $142 - 113 =$

9. $879 - 455 =$

10. $384 - 237 =$

11. $313 - 143 =$

12. $679 - 197 =$

13. $626 - 413 =$

14. $992 - 746 =$

15. $784 - 229 =$

16. $1,585 - 94 =$

17. $11,400 - 87 =$

18. $3,110 - 58 =$

19. $708 - 48 =$

20. $4,120 - 757 =$

21. $11{,}290 - 927 =$

22. $835 - 216 =$

23. $5{,}999 - 451 =$

24. $15{,}393 - 8{,}392 =$

25. $7{,}800 - 7{,}352 =$

26. $1{,}927 - 1{,}899 =$

27. $6{,}878 - 1{,}116 - 692 =$

28. $9{,}844 - 867 - 447 =$

29. $1{,}559 - 583 - 94 =$

30. $13{,}473 - 1{,}152 - 401 =$

ADDITION/SUBTRACTION MISSING NUMBERS Practice Set 1

1. $96 - 5\square = 37$

2. $1,5\square8 + 359 = 1,927$

3. $10,247 - 8,\square28 = 2,119$

4. $28 + 36 + \square6 = 120$

5. $20\square - 14 - 67 = 127$

6. $54 + 2\square = \square3$

7. $3\square\square + 45 = \square45$

8. $93 - 7 = 8\square$

9. $\square3\square - 50 = \square4$

10. $1,\square\square\square - 372 = 628$

ADDITION/SUBTRACTION MISSING NUMBERS Practice Set 2

1. $3\square2 - 87 = 215$

2. $1\square + 829 = 847$

3. $1\square + 22 - 8 = 29$

4. $1\square6 + 34 + 156 = 316$

5. $3,147 + 14 - 2\square8 = 2,953$

6. $\square4 + 7 = 71$

7. $75 + \square7 = \square6\square$

8. $\square,26\square + 759 = 5,\square\square7$

9. $\square6 - 38 = 1\square$

10. $5\square0 - 295 = \square7\square$

MULTIPLICATION Practice Set 1

1. $56 \times 7 =$

2. $9 \times 78 =$

3. $121 \times 8 =$

4. $215 \times 7 =$

5. 3×338

6. $12 \times 15 =$

7. $14 \times 22 =$

8. $37 \times 12 =$

9. $75 \times 38 =$

10. $88 \times 56 =$

11. $22 \times 108 =$

12. $15 \times 226 =$

13. $372 \times 24 =$

14. $418 \times 37 =$

15. $512 \times 57 =$

16. $432 \times 186 =$

17. $518 \times 253 =$

18. $314 \times 194 =$

19. $762 \times 545 =$

20. $820 \times 613 =$

MULTIPLICATION Practice Set 2

1. $48 \times 4 =$

2. $9 \times 56 =$

3. $7 \times 189 =$

4. $413 \times 8 =$

5. $4 \times 742 =$

6. $23 \times 16 =$

7. $34 \times 16 =$

8. $33 \times 26 =$

9. $51 \times 32 =$

10. $86 \times 78 =$

11. $17 \times 287 =$

12. $553 \times 23 =$

13. $25 \times 682 =$

14. $932 \times 31 =$

15. $51 \times 624 =$

16. $405 \times 657 =$

17. $291 \times 306 =$

18. $712 \times 463 =$

19. $371 \times 902 =$

20. $711 \times 853 =$

MULTIPLICATION Practice Set 3

1. $23 \times 4 =$

2. $6 \times 39 =$

3. $263 \times 8 =$

4. $9 \times 516 =$

5. $575 \times 7 =$

6. $17 \times 28 =$

7. $15 \times 41 =$

8. $46 \times 22 =$

9. $37 \times 53 =$

10. $83 \times 57 =$

11. $398 \times 18 =$

12. $39 \times 218 =$

13. $749 \times 28 =$

14. $46 \times 447 =$

15. $718 \times 56 =$

16. $654 \times 172 =$

17. $393 \times 426 =$

18. $769 \times 521 =$

19. $933 \times 782 =$

20. $539 \times 604 =$

MULTIPLICATION Practice Set 4

1. $3 \times 24 =$

2. 42×7

3. $364 \times 5 =$

4. $4 \times 944 =$

5. $328 \times 7 =$

6. $25 \times 19 =$

7. $14 \times 31 =$

8. $27 \times 23 =$

9. $13 \times 59 =$

10. $61 \times 38 =$

11. $19 \times 407 =$

12. $332 \times 42 =$

13. $29 \times 813 =$

14. $504 \times 48 =$

15. $59 \times 354 =$

16. $337 \times 268 =$

17. $820 \times 457 =$

18. $308 \times 591 =$

19. $627 \times 783 =$

20. $935 \times 146 =$

3 NUMBER MULTIPLICATION Practice Set 1

1. $2 \times 8 \times 3 =$

2. $7 \times 4 \times 3 =$

3. $6 \times 5 \times 4 =$

4. $2 \times 9 \times 8 =$

5. $6 \times 7 \times 7 =$

6. $11 \times 3 \times 4 =$

7. $12 \times 6 \times 5 =$

8. $2 \times 26 \times 4 =$

9. $9 \times 13 \times 12 =$

10. $22 \times 7 \times 11 =$

11. $8 \times 36 \times 4 =$

12. $52 \times 7 \times 5 =$

13. $72 \times 8 \times 6 =$

14. $88 \times 3 \times 11 =$

15. $27 \times 23 \times 4 =$

16. $34 \times 6 \times 37 =$

17. $10 \times 17 \times 18 =$

18. $22 \times 13 \times 20 =$

19. $42 \times 30 \times 9 =$

20. $56 \times 26 \times 11 =$

3 NUMBER MULTIPLICATION Practice Set 2

1. $4 \times 7 \times 4 =$

2. $6 \times 3 \times 7 =$

3. $8 \times 9 \times 5 =$

4. $9 \times 6 \times 8 =$

5. $13 \times 2 \times 7 =$

6. $8 \times 15 \times 2 =$

7. $17 \times 3 \times 4 =$

8. $8 \times 17 \times 14 =$

9. $13 \times 19 \times 6 =$

10. $4 \times 13 \times 24 =$

11. $7 \times 4 \times 29 =$

12. $43 \times 7 \times 4 =$

13. $5 \times 61 \times 8 =$

14. $14 \times 17 \times 8 =$

15. $21 \times 18 \times 5 =$

16. $9 \times 19 \times 20 =$

17. $41 \times 63 \times 8 =$

18. $31 \times 10 \times 15 =$

19. $16 \times 20 \times 11 =$

20. $45 \times 12 \times 17 =$

MULTIPLICATION MISSING DIGITS Practice Set 1

1.
```
      1 8
   ×    □
   ────────
    1 □ 6
```

2.
```
      □ 8
   ×   9
   ────────
    3 □ 2
```

3.
```
      5 □
   ×   4
   ────────
    □ 2 4
```

4.
```
      8 5
   ×    □
   ────────
    □ 1 0
```

5.
```
       2 □
   ×  1 4
   ────────
      8 8
    2 □ 0
   ────────
    □ 0 8
```

6.
```
       □ 4
   ×  □ 2
   ────────
      6 8
    1,0 2 0
   ─────────
    1,□ □ 8
```

7.
```
       8 □
   ×   □ 2
   ────────
      6 8
    3,3 6 0
   ─────────
    3,5 □ 8
```

8.
```
       1 □ 6
   ×    2 □
   ──────────
      7 5 6
    2,□ 2 0
   ──────────
    □,2 7 6
```

9.
```
       □ 2 4
   ×    □ 6
   ──────────
    1,9 4 4
    1□,9 □ 0
   ──────────
    □ 4,9 0 4
```

10.
```
        □ 3 6
   ×     7 □
   ───────────
      □,2 8 8
    3 7,5 □ 0
   ───────────
    4 1,□ 0 8
```

33

MULTIPLICATION MISSING DIGITS Practice Set 2

1.
```
    1 7
  × □
  1 □ 2
```

2.
```
    □ 3
  ×   8
  3 □ 4
```

3.
```
    7 □
  ×   6
  □ 3 8
```

4.
```
    9 2
  ×   □
  □ 6 0
```

5.
```
    3 □
  × 1 8
  2 7 2
  3 □ 0
  □ 1 2
```

6.
```
      □ 2
  ×   □ 8
    4 1 6
  1,5 6 0
  1,□ □ 6
```

7.
```
      7 □
  ×   □ 2
    □ 5 6
  3,9 0 0
  4,0 □ 6
```

8.
```
      1 □ 2
  ×     3 □
      3 0 4
    4,□ 6 0
    □,8 6 4
```

9.
```
      □ 8 1
  ×     □ 4
    1,9 2 4
  1 □,4 □ 0
  □ 6,3 5 4
```

10.
```
      □ 8 2
  ×     6 □
    □,3 6 4
  4 0,9 □ 0
  4 2,□ 8 4
```

34

DIVISION Practice Set 1

1. $105 \div 7 =$

2. $261 \div 3 =$

3. $369 \div 9 =$

4. $252 \div 6 =$

5. $198 \div 22 =$

6. $273 \div 13 =$

7. $315 \div 45 =$

8. $323 \div 323 =$

9. $715 \div 65 =$

10. $1{,}638 \div 7 =$

11. $2{,}900 \div 4 =$

12. $2{,}868 \div 6 =$

13. $5{,}229 \div 9 =$

14. $1{,}157 \div 13 =$

15. $4{,}104 \div 76 =$

16. $3{,}034 \div 0 =$

17. $2{,}773 \div 59 =$

18. $1{,}488 \div 124 =$

19. $7{,}072 \div 416 =$

20. $9{,}828 \div 378 =$

DIVISION Practice Set 2

1. 108 ÷ 9 =

2. 132 ÷ 3 =

3. 264 ÷ 8 =

4. 222 ÷ 6 =

5. 184 ÷ 23 =

6. 218 ÷ 218 =

7. 361 ÷ 19 =

8. 245 ÷ 35 =

9. 507 ÷ 39 =

10. 1,568 ÷ 8 =

11. 2,898 ÷ 6 =

12. 6,192 ÷ 9 =

13. 6,881 ÷ 7 =

14. 1,458 ÷ 18 =

15. 3,087 ÷ 63 =

16. 2,262 ÷ 78 =

17. 2,565 ÷ 45 =

18. 0 ÷ 176 =

19. 6,642 ÷ 369 =

20. 9,683 ÷ 421 =

DIVISION Practice Set 3

1. 108 ÷ 6 =

2. 188 ÷ 4 =

3. 342 ÷ 9 =

4. 287 ÷ 7 =

5. 189 ÷ 27 =

6. 288 ÷ 16 =

7. 376 ÷ 47 =

8. 756 ÷ 54 =

9. 1,998 ÷ 3 =

10. 0 ÷ 5 =

11. 5,016 ÷ 8 =

12. 8,811 ÷ 9 =

13. 1,587 ÷ 23 =

14. 4,872 ÷ 84 =

15. 4,232 ÷ 92 =

16. 4,752 ÷ 72 =

17. 2,197 ÷ 169 =

18. 6,403 ÷ 337 =

19. 9,828 ÷ 364 =

20. 9,979 ÷ 0 =

DIVISION Practice Set 4

1. $104 \div 8 =$

2. $138 \div 6 =$

3. $203 \div 203 =$

4. $234 \div 9 =$

5. $174 \div 29 =$

6. $442 \div 17 =$

7. $351 \div 39 =$

8. $833 \div 49 =$

9. $1,404 \div 6 =$

10. $2,076 \div 4 =$

11. $5,439 \div 7 =$

12. $4,985 \div 5 =$

13. $1,302 \div 0 =$

14. $3,003 \div 77 =$

15. $3,264 \div 48 =$

16. $2,752 \div 64 =$

17. $3,376 \div 211 =$

18. $6,944 \div 496 =$

19. $8,976 \div 374 =$

20. $9,503 \div 731 =$

REMAINDERS Practice Set 1

Find the quotient and remainder for each problem.

1. $58 \div 9 =$

2. $97 \div 5 =$

3. $85 \div 16 =$

4. $74 \div 11 =$

5. $92 \div 22 =$

6. $186 \div 7 =$

7. $487 \div 6 =$

8. $229 \div 8 =$

9. $546 \div 22 =$

10. $871 \div 55 =$

11. $927 \div 88 =$

12. $456 \div 121 =$

13. $872 \div 201 =$

14. $746 \div 187 =$

15. $1{,}576 \div 45 =$

16. $5{,}234 \div 77 =$

17. $8{,}974 \div 86 =$

18. $5{,}643 \div 207 =$

19. $8{,}945 \div 456 =$

20. $7{,}568 \div 824 =$

REMAINDERS Practice Set 2

Find the quotient and remainder for each problem.

1. $53 \div 8 =$

2. $74 \div 4 =$

3. $99 \div 15 =$

4. $79 \div 12 =$

5. $82 \div 21 =$

6. $172 \div 6 =$

7. $306 \div 4 =$

8. $439 \div 9 =$

9. $721 \div 26 =$

10. $935 \div 66 =$

11. $798 \div 66 =$

12. $656 \div 189 =$

13. $800 \div 174 =$

14. $897 \div 123 =$

15. $1,535 \div 33 =$

16. $3,803 \div 61 =$

17. $7,600 \div 75 =$

18. $5,605 \div 317 =$

19. $6,885 \div 487 =$

20. $9,707 \div 999 =$

40

POWERS OF 10 Practice Set 1

1. $11 \times 20 =$

2. $17 \times 100 =$

3. $130 \div 10 =$

4. $8 \times 300 =$

5. $700 \div 20 =$

6. $600 \div 15 =$

7. $3,600 \div 18 =$

8. $420 \times 9 =$

9. $8,000 \div 50 =$

10. $2,300 \times 7 =$

11. $32,000 \div 40 =$

12. $31 \times 300 =$

13. $900 \times 50 =$

14. $84,000 \div 70 =$

15. $220 \times 60 =$

16. $121,000 \div 1,100 =$

17. $64,000 \div 400 =$

18. $30 \times 430 =$

19. $96,000 \div 80 =$

20. $1,900 \times 120 =$

POWERS OF 10 Practice Set 2

1. $8 \times 10 =$

2. $12 \times 100 =$

3. $80 \div 20 =$

4. $7 \times 200 =$

5. $200 \div 10 =$

6. $500 \div 25 =$

7. $240 \div 20 =$

8. $330 \times 11 =$

9. $2,000 \div 40 =$

10. $1,500 \times 8 =$

11. $15,000 \div 30 =$

12. $22 \times 100 =$

13. $700 \times 80 =$

14. $22,000 \div 110 =$

15. $160 \times 40 =$

16. $169,000 \div 1,300 =$

17. $81,000 \div 300 =$

18. $50 \times 150 =$

19. $64,000 \div 160 =$

20. $2,200 \times 110 =$

BASIC ORDER OF OPERATIONS Practice Set 1

1. $22 - 16 + 5 - 7 =$

2. $5 - 4 + 8 =$

3. $5 + 27 - 32 + 16 - 8 + 22 =$

4. $5 - 2 \times 2 =$

5. $9 - (20 - 12) =$

6. $22 \times 3 - 4 + 7 =$

7. $34 - 30 \div 3 \times 2 =$

8. $4(7 + 1) =$

9. $48 \div 12 \times 4 - 18 \div 3 =$

10. $84 - 7 \times 8 \div 4 - 50 =$

11. $3 + 4 * 2 =$

12. $4(121 \div 11 \times 11 - 89) - 4 \times 12 =$

13. $5 + 10(200 \div 40 - 3) + 2(18 \div 9 + 4) =$

14. $8 + 1(4) =$

15. $2 + 5(8 \times 2 - 15) + 144 \div 24 - 2 \times 3 =$

16. $5 \times 8 \div 4 =$

17. $20 - 16 \div 4 =$

18. $15 - 3(2 + 1) =$

19. $(2)9 + 5 =$

20. $20 \times 2 + 8 \div 4 - 1 =$

BASIC ORDER OF OPERATIONS Practice Set 2

1. $18 - 7 + 2 =$

2. $7 - 2 + 3 =$

3. $60 + 6 - 6 \times 3 - 30 =$

4. $13 - (3 + 5) =$

5. $3 \times 8 + 6 =$

6. $5 \times 2 + 5 =$

7. $8 + 4 \div 2 - 2 =$

8. $18 - 2(3) =$

9. $18 \div 2 - 4 \times 2 =$

10. $8 + 6 \times 3 =$

11. $6 - 15 \div 3 + 2 \times 4 =$

12. $10(7 + 6) =$

13. $3(6 - 2 \times 2) - 4(18 - 2 \times 9) =$

14. $3 * (24 \div 3) =$

15. $15 \times 6 \div 2 - 20 \div 4 - 22 =$

16. $25 - 10/5 + 5 =$

17. $18 - 2(22 - 10 \times 2 + 4) + 3 \times 6 - 4 =$

18. $(14 + 7 * 2 - 4) \div 6 =$

19. $44 \div 11 \times 2(22 \div 2 - 10) + 5(32 \div 8 - 3) =$

20. $14 - 12 \div 4 + 2 \times 3 =$

CHAPTER 2: NEGATIVE NUMBERS

Experts in Test Prep, Tutoring, & Admissions Counseling

www.CardinalEducation.com

BASIC NEGATIVE NUMBER ADDITION/SUBTRACTION Practice Set 1

1. $-8 + 12 =$

2. $-7 + 13 =$

3. $-15 + 7 =$

4. $22 - (-6) =$

5. $25 - (-27) =$

6. $19 - (-19) =$

7. $-32 - (-13) =$

8. $-19 - (-27) =$

9. $-15 - (-36) =$

10. $14 + (-5) =$

11. $17 + (-8) =$

12. $22 + (-25) =$

13. $31 - 42 =$

14. $8 - 13 =$

15. $-18 + (-5) =$

16. $-17 + (-1) =$

17. $-7 + (-26) =$

18. $-6 - 4 =$

19. $-17 - 21 =$

20. $-13 - 20 =$

BASIC NEGATIVE NUMBER ADDITION/SUBTRACTION Practice Set 2

1. $8 - 23 =$

2. $26 - 34 =$

3. $-41 - (-14) =$

4. $-22 - (-31) =$

5. $-12 - (-13) =$

6. $5 + (-16) =$

7. $17 + (-11) =$

8. $26 + (-4) =$

9. $9 - (-13) =$

10. $20 - (-7) =$

11. $32 - (-12) =$

12. $-6 + 12 =$

13. $-15 + 10 =$

14. $-50 + 15 =$

15. $-3 + (-5) =$

16. $-1 + (-43) =$

17. $-62 + (-14) =$

18. $-9 - 7 =$

19. $-11 - 21 =$

20. $-28 - 4 =$

BASIC NEGATIVE NUMBER ADDITION/SUBTRACTION Practice Set 3

1. $18 - (-23) =$

2. $6 - (-3) =$

3. $15 - (-15) =$

4. $25 + (-7) =$

5. $30 + (-16) =$

6. $19 + (-27) =$

7. $14 - 23 =$

8. $61 - 72 =$

9. $-8 - (-6) =$

10. $-17 - (-17) =$

11. $-28 - (-33) =$

12. $-36 + 12 =$

13. $-24 + 18 =$

14. $-27 + 45 =$

15. $-9 + (-21) =$

16. $-23 + (-17) =$

17. $-15 + (-30) =$

18. $-14 - 26 =$

19. $-8 - 35 =$

20. $-43 - 13 =$

BASIC NEGATIVE NUMBER ADDITION/SUBTRACTION Practice Set 4

1. $-3 - (-7) =$

2. $-6 - (-13) =$

3. $-15 - (-8) =$

4. $-7 - 25 =$

5. $-16 - 4 =$

6. $-22 - 18 =$

7. $-17 + (-4) =$

8. $-26 + (-15) =$

9. $-2 + (-31) =$

10. $9 - (-15) =$

11. $12 - (-17) =$

12. $34 - (-27) =$

13. $29 - 37 =$

14. $42 - 56 =$

15. $-5 + 19 =$

16. $-29 + 11 =$

17. $-34 + 13 =$

18. $31 + (-15) =$

19. $46 + (-55) =$

20. $51 + (-70) =$

CHALLENGING NEGATIVE NUMBER ADDITION/SUBTRACTION Practice
Set 1

1. $-53 + 5{,}930 =$

2. $-69 - (-10{,}536) =$

3. $-72 + 4{,}035 =$

4. $-57 - (-997) =$

5. $2{,}480 + (-562) =$

6. $-453 - (-9{,}940) =$

7. $-331 + 920 =$

8. $-884 - (-2{,}849) =$

9. $-309 - 5{,}156 =$

10. $8{,}354 + (-6{,}455) =$

11. $13{,}882 + (-9{,}305) =$

12. $-5{,}927 + 8{,}100 =$

13. $-2{,}151 - (-3{,}798) =$

14. $7{,}194 - 2{,}009 + (-751) =$

15. $6 - 539 - 714 + (-6{,}077) =$

16. $1{,}273 + (-641) - 77 =$

17. $-747 + (-682) - 1{,}783 =$

18. $-1{,}637 + (-579) - (-12{,}648) =$

19. $-698 - (-3{,}434) + (-9{,}172) =$

20. $-8{,}225 + 4{,}032 - (-2{,}153) - 6{,}258 =$

CHALLENGING NEGATIVE NUMBER ADDITION/SUBTRACTION Practice
Set 2

1. $4,070 + (-88) =$

2. $-93 - (-12,680) =$

3. $-61 + 5,155 =$

4. $-66 - (-1,046) =$

5. $6,190 + (-208) =$

6. $-565 + 10,050 =$

7. $-286 + 1,115 =$

8. $-367 - (-4,404) =$

9. $-279 - 7,797 =$

10. $6,196 - 7,159 =$

11. $11,975 + (-9,441) =$

12. $-4,471 + 5,660 =$

13. $-2,201 - (-3,058) =$

14. $-1,452 + (-544) - (-7,381) =$

15. $-673 - 759 + 8,127 =$

16. $1,144 + (-846) - 85 =$

17. $-836 + (-552) - 1,319 =$

18. $-1,724 + (-476) - (-16,512) =$

19. $-605 - (-1,526) + (-9,939) =$

20. $-9,846 + 3,372 - (-1,468) - 6,477 =$

CHALLENGING NEGATIVE NUMBER ADDITION/SUBTRACTION Practice
Set 3

1. $-390 + 2{,}038 =$

2. $-7{,}810 + 361 =$

3. $-105 + 1{,}273 =$

4. $404 - 738 =$

5. $-146 - (-1{,}289) =$

6. $911 + (-586) =$

7. $-3{,}532 + 1{,}523 =$

8. $-2{,}185 - (-3{,}791) =$

9. $2{,}493 + (-3{,}944) =$

10. $-8{,}810 + 9{,}740 =$

11. $-7{,}437 - (-6{,}999) =$

12. $-372 - 5{,}298 =$

13. $-228 - 4{,}206 =$

14. $4{,}627 - 6{,}231 =$

15. $-862 + (-623) - 1{,}208 =$

16. $-912 + (-881) - 1{,}697 =$

17. $-539 - (-2{,}805) + (-8{,}719) =$

18. $-799 - (-2{,}078) + (-9{,}824) =$

19. $-7{,}864 + 3{,}258 - (-1{,}255) - 6{,}081 =$

20. $-7{,}678 + 3{,}967 - (-2{,}419) - 5{,}869 =$

CHALLENGING NEGATIVE NUMBER ADDITION/SUBTRACTION Practice
Set 4

1. $-108 + 1{,}343 =$

2. $-6{,}075 + 511 =$

3. $-566 + 2{,}327 =$

4. $681 - 943 =$

5. $-208 - (-785) =$

6. $1{,}123 + (-2{,}045) =$

7. $-4{,}189 + 6{,}516 =$

8. $-3{,}817 - (-5{,}630) =$

9. $2{,}809 + (-3{,}523) =$

10. $-8{,}917 + 9{,}056 =$

11. $-6{,}382 - (-4{,}101) =$

12. $-418 - 6{,}276 =$

13. $-112 - 3{,}716 =$

14. $5{,}763 - 8{,}909 =$

15. $-761 + (-413) - 1{,}508 =$

16. $-792 + (-604) - 1{,}314 =$

17. $-522 - (-1{,}954) + (-7{,}308) =$

18. $-900 - (-2{,}463) + (-8{,}149) =$

19. $-8{,}116 + 4{,}537 - (-2{,}066) - 5{,}967 =$

20. $-9{,}111 + 2{,}453 - (-3{,}871) - 5{,}212 =$

NEGATIVE NUMBER MULTIPLICATION/DIVISION Practice Set 1

1. $(-4) \times 8 =$

2. $(-8) \times (-9) =$

3. $30 \div (-6) =$

4. $(-21) \div 3 =$

5. $(-32) \div (-8) =$

6. $12 \times (-9) =$

7. $(-65) \div 5 =$

8. $(-280) \div (-20) =$

9. $(-15) \times 6 =$

10. $22 \times (-16) =$

11. $(-52) \times 18 =$

12. $(-1,386) \div (-42) =$

13. $26 \times (-29) =$

14. $12 \times (-30) \div (-15) =$

15. $(-56) \div (-14) \times (-20) =$

16. $(-29) \times 41 \times (-19) =$

17. $(-25) \times 37 \times 3 =$

18. $(-120) \div (-4) \div (-6) =$

19. $22 \times (-16) \times (-28) \times 4 =$

20. $(-117) \times (-13) \times (-5) \times (-2) =$

54

NEGATIVE NUMBER MULTIPLICATION/DIVISION Practice Set 2

1. $(-56) \div 8 =$

2. $(-4) \times (-9) =$

3. $55 \div (-5) =$

4. $(-6) \times 7 =$

5. $(-8) \times (-8) =$

6. $96 \div (-8) =$

7. $(-75) \div 5 =$

8. $(-23) \times (-17) =$

9. $(-26) \times 5 =$

10. $112 \div (-16) =$

11. $(-44) \times 12 =$

12. $(-286) \div (-22) =$

13. $494 \div (-19) =$

14. $120 \div (-15) \times (-16) =$

15. $(-16) \times (-21) \times (-6) =$

16. $(-612) \div 9 \div (-17) =$

17. $(-33) \times 18 \div 11 =$

18. $(-13) \times (-20) \times (-7) =$

19. $1{,}680 \div 5 \div (-8) \div 6 =$

20. $(-480) \div 30 \times (-7) \div (-8) =$

CHAPTER 3: BASIC WORD PROBLEMS

Experts in Test Prep, Tutoring, & Admissions Counseling

www.CardinalEducation.com

ADDITION/SUBTRACTION WORD PROBLEMS Practice Set 1

1. What is the sum of 128 and 1,387?

2. What is the difference between 1,782 and 877?

3. The temperature at Heavenly Ski Resort on a Saturday morning was -3°C. If there was an 8°C increase in temperature by noon, what was the temperature at noon?

4. The students at Woodside Elementary collected cans of food for the food drive. On the first day they collected 523 cans. On the second and third days they collected 876 and 254 cans respectively. How many cans did they collect in total?

5. If 7 is added to a number, the sum is 39. If 2,098 is added to the same number, the sum is?

6. Fifty-five thousand, six hundred ninety-nine people attend a concert at the HP Pavilion. If the Pavilion can hold a maximum of 62,122 people, how many empty seats were there at the concert?

7. $200 + 62,503 + \boxtimes = 73,006$. What is $\boxtimes$?

8. Eddie is 12 years old. His brother is twice as old as he is. His mother and father have a combined age of 84. What is the combined age of Eddie's family?

9. 20,156 competitors started the San Francisco marathon. If officials counted only 9,768 competitors finishing the race, how many competitors did not finish the race?

10. A skydiver jumps from a plane flying at an altitude of 30,222 feet. If he lands on top of the Empire State Building which is 1,454 feet high, how long was his dive?

11. Susan has $52 saved in her piggy bank. John has saved $5 more than Susan, while Cameron has saved $18 less than Susan. What is the total amount of savings that the three of them have?

12. The Palo Alto Daily printed 1,345 newspapers on Monday. On Tuesday, they print 500 more copies than they printed on Monday. How many newspapers did they print on the two days?

13. What is the sum of twenty-one thousand, eight hundred seventy-three and five thousand, eight hundred ninety-seven?

14. What is the difference between -13 and 52?
    A. -39
    B. 29
    C. 39
    D. -65

15. A bus has 54 passengers. At the next stop, half of the passengers get off and 18 new passengers get on. How many passengers are now in the bus?

16. In 2002 Queen Elizabeth celebrated her Golden Jubilee. The Golden Jubilee is celebrated 50 years after coronation. In what year did Elizabeth become queen?

17. $5 + 17 + ■ = 2 + 27 + 29$. What is ■?

18. $5 + ⊠ - 13 = 56 - 22$. What is ⊠?

19. Lucy is 17 years old. Her brother Andrew is 24 years old. What was the sum of their ages ten years ago?

20. The difference between 12 and a number is 57. What is the difference between the number and 145?

1. $19 - \forall = 68$. What is $\forall - 172$?

2. John has two hundred fifty-six thousand, eight hundred nine dollars. Tim has one hundred thirty-two thousand, three hundred twenty-seven dollars. How much more money does John have than Tim?

3. $-57 + (-37) + \blacksquare = 628 - 512$. What is $\blacksquare$?

4. Bonnie is travelling 20,732 miles to see Clyde, but he travels 4,659 miles in her direction to surprise her. How many miles will Bonnie have travelled by the time she sees Clyde? A termite colony is comprised of 483,291 before a giant anteater finds it. Afterward, only 195,837 termites remain. How many termites were eaten?

5. What is the sum of 185 and 1,538?

6. Jordan is an author who took three years to complete his novel. He wrote 412 pages in his first year, 703 pages in his second year, and 559 pages in the last. How many pages total did Jordan write for his novel?

7. If 19 is added to a number, the sum is 33. If 3,096 is added to the same number, the sum is?

8. $700 + 34,297 + \boxtimes = 45,003$. What is $\boxtimes$?

9. Chester owes Digby $17. After mowing his neighbor's lawn for $45, how much money does Chester have left over after paying Digby?

10. What is the difference between -27 and 44?

11. Dewey is preparing to sell his button collection but has to sort and count them first. He counts 2,050 buttons his first day. He counts 785 more buttons on his second day than on his first day. How many buttons has Dewey counted in his first two days?

12. Paula orders 18,472 caterpillars for her farm. If she counts only 9,536 butterflies after their metamorphoses, how many caterpillars died before their transformation?

13. $21 + 5 + 28 = \blacksquare + 16 + 9$. What is $\blacksquare$?

14. Kahn's room is at a comfortable 74°F. Kahn accidentally leaves his window open during his absence. When he returns, the room temperature has dropped 16°F. He turns the heat higher up, and over the next hour, the temperature creeps 7°F warmer. What temperature is Kahn's room now?

15. Nikola Tesla was 86 when he died in 1943. What year was he born?

16. There are five hundred thirty-seven thousand, six hundred eighty-one redwood trees in a patch of forest. If in one year a logging company cuts down ninety-six thousand, three hundred seventy-seven trees, how many trees are left in the forest?

17. $9 + \boxtimes - 16 = 66 - 29$. What is $\boxtimes$?

18. Sarah's house is worth $673,829. If in ten years the value of the house increases to $915,405, what is the value difference in ten years?

19. Farmer Stan can produce 124 boxes of vegetables for the farmers' market. Farmer Eric can produce 40 boxes less than Farmer Stan, but 14 more boxes than Farmer Kyle. What is the total number of boxes that all three farmers can bring to the market?

20. At the end of the half, the home team and the away team have scored 37 points and 51 points, respectively. If fifteen minutes prior, both teams had exactly 15 points less, what is the sum of the two scores?

ADDITION/SUBTRACTION WORD PROBLEMS Practice Set 3

1. What is the difference between 1,526 and 793?

2. George wins the class election against John and Paul. John received 53 votes more than Paul but 17 votes less than George. If John received 89 votes, how many people voted in the class election?

3. $-28 + (-49) + \blacksquare = 677 - 546$. What is $\blacksquare$?

4. What is the sum of 356 and 1,408?

5. A total of one hundred five thousand, seven hundred sixty-one spectators attended a soccer game in Barcelona, during which the home team suffered a loss. During the next game, thirteen thousand, eight hundred twenty-five less spectators attended the soccer match. What is the total number of spectators who attended both games?

6. Marcus begins a mass download of 21,739 songs onto his hard drive. When he checks back a few hours later, 7,377 have downloaded. How many more songs does he have left to download?

7. If 9 is added to a number, the sum is 41. If 2,989 is added to the same number, the sum is?

8. $800 + 53,029 + \boxtimes = 64,004$. What is $\boxtimes$?

9. What is the difference between 1,497 and 816?

10. $24 + 8 + 27 = 17 + \blacksquare + 22$. What is $\blacksquare$?

11. A semi-truck loads 10,000 pounds of cargo in Texas. When it arrives in Kansas, it unloads 4,280 pounds of fruits but also picks up 2,934 pounds of vegetables. When the semi-truck leaves Kansas, how many pounds of cargo is it carrying?

12. Mary brags to Joe that her home in Georgia is 18°F warmer than his home in Tennessee. If it is -6°F in Tennessee, what is the temperature in Georgia?

13. $21 - \forall = 72$. What is $\forall - 145$?

14. 2011 marks the 148th anniversary of the first Medal of Honor issued by the United States government. If the recipient was 24 when he received his award, what year was he born?

15. Reviewing the family cell phone bill, Roger notices he used the most minutes. His wife used half the amount of minutes that Roger did, while each of his two children used 100 more minutes than his wife. If Roger used 900 minutes, how many minutes did the whole family use together?

16. Austin checks his bank account at the beginning of the month to see a balance of $25,982. At the end of the month, his balance is $7,376. How much did he spend in the month?

17. An airline pilot flies 4,250 miles on Thursday. On Friday, he flies 2,555 more miles than he did on Thursday. What is the total distance the pilot travelled over those two days?

18. What is the difference between -17 and 42?

19. The local nature center has a butterfly garden capable of supporting 48,555 butterflies. When the population spirals to 52,109, how many butterflies will have to find homes elsewhere?

20. Active stamp-collector Sammy is selling his three most prized pieces. He manages to sell his stamps for $298, $475, and $763. How much total did Sammy make by selling his stamps?

ADDITION/SUBTRACTION WORD PROBLEMS Practice Set 4

1. $6 + \boxtimes - 9 = 70 - 21$. What is $\boxtimes$?

2. Doc and Marty decide to travel to the West together in the car and drive 847 miles their first day. On the second and third days, they drive 376 and 659 miles respectively. How many total miles did they drive over those three days?

3. In 2007, the United States consumed 101,527 trillion btu of energy. In 1987, energy consumption was 79,173 trillion btu. What is the increase in energy consumption over the 20 year period?

4. $-62 + \blacksquare + (-17) = 455 - 358$. What is $\blacksquare$?

5. What is the sum of 249 and 1,786?

6. What is the difference between 1,751 and 743?

7. In her first year of Latin, Lily learns 3,528 words. At the end of her second year Lily knows 7,931 words, how many words did she learn her second year?

8. $4 + \blacksquare + 23 = 6 + 18 + 21$. What is $\blacksquare$?

9. If 13 is added to a number, the sum is 52. If 2,072 is added to the same number, the sum is?

10. The Apollo 11 mission celebrated its 40th anniversary in 2009. If Buzz Aldrin was born in 1930, how old was he when he landed on the moon?

11. $400 + 48,111 + \boxtimes = 58,001$. What is $\boxtimes$?

12. Elisa, Jen, and Kathryn are competitive rock climbers. Elisa has climbed 19 mountains, Kathryn has conquered 13 mountains less than Elisa, and Jen has climbed twice as many mountains as Kathryn. Given that each climber has never climbed the same mountain, what is the total number of mountains the three women have climbed?

13. Millie is working on her family quilt. Millie makes 985 stitches on Tuesday. On Wednesday, she makes 725 more stitches than she did on Tuesday. How many stitches has she made over those two days?

14. Checking her debit account, Debbie realizes she has overdrawn her account, and her account balance now stands at −$37.50. After depositing her paycheck of $225, how much will Debbie have left in her bank account?

15. Gordo's fridge holds 19 cans of soda. Over the next three days, Gordo drinks 2 cans each day and then buys a 24-pack of sodas. How many cans of soda are now in Gordo's refrigerator?

16. Jenna, Tracey, and Liz are playing marbles for keeps. Jenna has twice as many marbles as Tracey but 8 marbles less than Liz. If Liz has 56 marbles, what is the total number of marbles between the four players?

17. Rusty has $27, and Nancy has $43. If their aunt takes away $8 each, how much money do they have now?

18. Darby climbs a mountain 43,092 feet above the sea level. If the town at the base of the mountain is 6,853 feet above sea level, how far is the peak of the mountain from the town relative to the sea level?

19. What is the difference between -24 and 53?

20. A music album is able to sell to sell three hundred eighty-six thousand, nine hundred forty-two copies in its first week of release. The following week, the album sells one hundred thirty-six thousand, one hundred sixty-two less copies than it did in its first week. How many copies did the album sell in the two week span?

MULTIPLICATION/DIVISION WORD PROBLEMS Practice Set 1

1. What is the product of 12 and 7?

2. $3 \times 7 \times 8 \times 2$ is equal to the product of 28 and what number?

3. $8{,}722 \div 29$ is approximately
   - A. 200
   - B. 240
   - C. 270
   - D. 300

4. What is the quotient of 85 and 17?

5. If 60 is divided by the product of 4 and 5, what is the result?

6. When a number is divided by 7, the remainder is 3. Which of the following could be the number?
   - A. 21
   - B. 33
   - C. 59
   - D. 75

7. Which of the following is the product of two consecutive integers?
   - A. 20
   - B. 24
   - C. 35
   - D. 48

8. All of the following are multiples of 3 except
   - A. 87
   - B. 91
   - C. 342
   - D. 726

9. If x is an integer that is divisible by both 4 and 5, which of the following is a possible value of x?
   - A. 250
   - B. 300
   - C. 350
   - D. 410

10. In the number 427, the sum of the digits is how much less than the product of the digits?

11. In the division problem below, what digit does A represent?

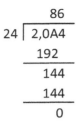

```
          86
    24 ⟌ 2,0A4
         192
         ‾‾‾‾‾
         144
         144
         ‾‾‾‾‾
           0
```

    A. 2
    B. 4
    C. 0
    D. 6

12. What is the remainder when 84,200 is divided by 4,021?

13. On a bookstore bookshelf, there are equal numbers of fiction novels, non-fiction novels, and autobiography books. Which of the following could be the number of books on the shelf?
    A. 251 books
    B. 308 books
    C. 456 books
    D. 799 books

14. Mallory needs 200 wine glasses for a dinner party she is hosting. She goes to a store which sells wine glasses in packs of 12. How many packs will Mallory have to buy in order to have enough wine glasses for her dinner party?

15. In the multiplication below, A represents which digit?

```
       8A
    x  56
    ‾‾‾‾‾‾
    4,872
```

    A. 2
    B. 5
    C. 7
    D. 8

16. The remainder when 82 is divided by y, is less than 8. Which of the following could NOT be y?
    A. 11
    B. 12
    C. 13
    D. 15

17. 150 students are going on a skiing trip. The students are taking the school buses, which according to the school rules must have a minimum of 10 students and a maximum of 40 students. What is the smallest number of buses required to accommodate the 150 students?

18. $9,600 was collected at a charity event. If each person at the event contributed the same amount, which of the following CANNOT be the amount that each person gave?
    A. $16
    B. $24
    C. $25
    D. $36

19. The Burj Khalifa in Dubai is the world's tallest skyscraper in the world, standing at a height of 2,087 feet. If each floor is approximately 16 feet tall, how many floors does the skyscraper have?
    A. 129
    B. 130
    C. 131
    D. 132

20. In the problem below, $X - Y =$

$$26 \overline{\smash{\big)}\ Y} \quad 14\ R\ 2 \qquad 26 \overline{\smash{\big)}\ X} \quad 23\ R\ 7$$

    A. 234
    B. 239
    C. 364
    D. 605

MULTIPLICATION/DIVISION WORD PROBLEMS Practice Set 2

1. What is the product of 19 and 6?

2. $5 \times 9 \times 2 \times 3$ is equal to the product of 5 and what integer?

3. $7,981 \div 42$ is approximately
    - A. 150
    - B. 200
    - C. 250
    - D. 300

4. What is the quotient of 96 and 16?

5. What is the remainder when 89 is divided by 17?

6. δ has a remainder of 2 when divided by 8. Which of the following could not be δ?
    - A. 66
    - B. 74
    - C. 83
    - D. 90

7. Which of the following is not a multiple of 8?
    - A. 72
    - B. 88
    - C. 92
    - D. 96

8. η is an integer that has less than 4 prime factors total. Which of the following is η?
    - A. 48
    - B. 72
    - C. 90
    - D. 105

9. β is an integer divisible by both 5 and 6. Which of the following is a possible value for β?
    - A. 220
    - B. 320
    - C. 440
    - D. 540

10. What is the quotient, when the product of 26 and 12 is divided by 4?

11. If 72 is divided by the product of 4 and 6, what is the result?

68

12. In the division problem below, find the value of A.

```
          36
      _____
   7A | 2,664
        222
        _____
        444
        444
        _____
          0
```

    A. 0
    B. 2
    C. 4
    D. 6

13. To draw a tree, Scott counts the number of leaves and notes it is divisible by 7. What is the possible number of leaves on this tree?
    A. 1,549 leaves
    B. 1,687 leaves
    C. 1,716 leaves
    D. 1,836 leaves

14. In regards to integer 563, what is the difference of the sum of the digits from the product of the digits?

15. Martin is making a tower of cupcakes for his grandmothers' birthdays which are on the same day. He needs 181 cupcakes, one for each year they have lived. If cupcakes only come in packs of 12, how many packs did Martin buy?

16. Working at an ice cream store, Billie is only allowed to scoop 3 to 5 ounces of ice cream per scoop. If he has 67 ounces of ice cream, what is the maximum number of scoops Billie can serve?

17. Mandy has a comprehensive online photo album of her travels around the world. She includes the same number of pictures from each country she visited. If she has 7,200 pictures in her album, which of the following cannot be the number of countries Mandy has visited?
    A. 15 countries
    B. 18 countries
    C. 28 countries
    D. 32 countries

18. The quotient of 109 and θ leaves a remainder of 14.
    Which of the following could be θ?
    A. 16
    B. 17
    C. 18
    D. 19

19. In the multiplication below, find the value of B.

$$
\begin{array}{r}
9B \\
\times\ 58 \\
\hline
5{,}394
\end{array}
$$

    A. 3
    B. 4
    C. 7
    D. 8

20. Use the problems below to find each value for x and y.
    Then solve for $X - Y =$

    $$34\,\overline{)\,X} \quad 26\text{ R }6 \qquad 34\,\overline{)\,Y} \quad 18\text{ R }2$$

    A. 262
    B. 268
    C. 272
    D. 276

70

MULTIPLICATION/DIVISION WORD PROBLEMS Practice Set 3

1. What is the quotient of 78 and 13?

2. What is the product of 16 and 9?

3. $4 \times 3 \times 8 \times 3$ is equal to the product of 18 and what integer?

4. What is the remainder when 95 is divided by 12?

5. $6,789 \div 23$ is approximately
    A. 250
    B. 300
    C. 350
    D. 400

6. Which of the following is not a multiple of 4?
    A. 52
    B. 64
    C. 76
    D. 82

7. δ has a remainder of 6 when divided by 11. Which of the following could not be δ?
    A. 50
    B. 61
    C. 73
    D. 94

8. η is an integer that has less than 4 prime factors total. Which of the following is η?
    A. 66
    B. 84
    C. 108
    D. 135

9. β is an integer divisible by both 6 and 9. Which of the following is a possible value for β?
    A. 225
    B. 324
    C. 433
    D. 536

10. What is 75 is divided by the product of 5 and 3?

11. What is the quotient when the product of 24 and 18 is divided by 9?

12. In the multiplication below, find the value of *A*.

$$\begin{array}{r} 4A \\ \times\ \ 72 \\ \hline 3,528 \end{array}$$

    A. 6
    B. 7
    C. 8
    D. 9

13. In the division problem below, find the value of *A*.

$$\begin{array}{r} 7A \\ 47\overline{)3,619} \\ \underline{329}\ \ \ \ \\ 329 \\ \underline{329} \\ 0 \end{array}$$

    A. 1
    B. 7
    C. 8
    D. 9

14. The quotient of 97 and θ leaves a remainder of 9. Which of the following could be θ?

    A. 9
    B. 11
    C. 15
    D. 17

15. Marsha eats equal calories of carbs, fats, and protein. How many calories could she have possibly eaten?

    A. 1,782 calories
    B. 1,912 calories
    C. 2,021 calories
    D. 2,156 calories

16. A poker tournament collects the same amount of money from each player to trade in for chips. The lump sum is $11,000. Which of the following cannot be the amount each player traded in to play?

    A. $440
    B. $450
    C. $500
    D. $550

17. Sasha is buying pizza for the entire freshmen class of 517 students. If everyone is having one slice, and 8 slices come in a pie, how many pies of pizza should Sasha buy?

18. In regards to integer 687, what is the difference of the product of the digits and the sum of the digits?

19. Josh hopes to read at least 25 pages a day, but no more than 58. If Josh's book is 729 pages long, what is the fewest number of days it will take to finish his book?

20. Use the problems below to find each value for x and y. Then solve for $X - Y =$

$$
\begin{array}{r}
16\ R\ 9 \\
29\overline{)\,Y}
\end{array}
\qquad
\begin{array}{r}
28\ R\ 4 \\
29\overline{)\,X}
\end{array}
$$

    A. 323
    B. 343
    C. 423
    D. 473

MULTIPLICATION/DIVISION WORD PROBLEMS Practice Set 4

1. What is the remainder when 93 is divided by 13?

2. What is the quotient of 108 and 12?

3. What is the product of 14 and 8?

4. $9,124 \div 19$ is approximately
   - A. 400
   - B. 500
   - C. 550
   - D. 600

5. $3 \times 4 \times 9 \times 4$ is equal to the product of 6 and what integer?

6. Which of the following is not a multiple of 6?
   - A. 66
   - B. 72
   - C. 82
   - D. 96

7. If 90 is divided by the product of 2 and 3, what is the result?

8. δ has a remainder of 5 when divided by 9. Which of the following could not be δ?
   - A. 23
   - B. 40
   - C. 50
   - D. 68

9. β is an integer divisible by both 4 and 6. Which of the following is a possible value for β?
   - A. 264
   - B. 316
   - C. 364
   - D. 502

10. η is an integer that has less than 4 prime factors total. Which of the following is η?
    - A. 60
    - B. 81
    - C. 75
    - D. 120

11. What is the product of 16 and 21 divided by 6?

12. Kate needs to travel 634 miles. If her car uses 43 miles per gallon, how many gallons will Kate need for her trip?

13. What is the difference between the product of the digits and the sum of the digits in the number 845?

14. In the division problem below, find the value of A.

```
            59
    82 | 4,A38
         410
         ‾‾‾‾
         738
         738
         ‾‾‾‾
           0
```

    A. 6
    B. 7
    C. 8
    D. 9

15. A book is separated into 6 equal chapters with the same number of pages. Which of the following could be the total number of pages?
    A. 1,226 pages
    B. 1,312 pages
    C. 1,452 pages
    D. 1,576 pages

16. In the multiplication below, find the value of W.

```
        83
    x   W7
    ‾‾‾‾‾‾
    5,561
```

    A. 2
    B. 6
    C. 7
    D. 9

17. After breaking up his piggy bank, Justin realizes that he has equal number of quarters, dimes, nickels, and pennies. Which of the following cannot be the total number of coins in Justin's piggy bank?
    A. 212 coins
    B. 316 coins
    C. 474 coins
    D. 508 coins

18. The quotient of 119 and θ leaves a remainder of 2. Which
of the following could be θ?
    A. 13
    B. 14
    C. 15
    D. 16

19. Jack has bought a bag of 300 assorted feathers to make
into cat toys for sale. If every cat toy has at least 15
feathers but no more than 22, what is the smallest number
of cat toys that Jack can make using every feather?

20. Use the problems below to find each value for x and y.
Then solve for $X - Y =$

$$32 \overline{)Y} \quad 21 \text{ R } 8 \qquad 32 \overline{)X} \quad 36 \text{ R } 3$$

    A. 470
    B. 475
    C. 480
    D. 485

MIXED WORD PROBLEMS Practice Set 1

1. What is the sum of all the even numbers between -7 and 9?

2. Sarah gives Heather $3. Tricia gives Heather the same amount as Sarah, plus $8. Molly gives Heather the same amount that Sarah and Tricia (combined) gave to Heather. How much money did Heather receive?

3. What is he difference between 89,232 and 7,898?

4. What is the sum of seventy-two thousand, nine hundred forty-five and five thousand, one hundred eighty-nine?

5. A city gym has 29,307 members. If 21,654 members went to the gym in the past month, how many people wasted the membership fee for the past month?

6. $15 - \forall = 49$. What is $\forall - 163$?

7. 12 bands enter a battle of the bands competition. 6 bands are eliminated in the first round, and 2 bands are eliminated in the second round. How many bands make it to the third round?

8. In a baseball league, there are 11 teams. Each team has 17 players. How many total baseball players are in the league?

9. Cyrus makes a cake, using equal amounts of water, sugar, chocolate, and flour. The total weight of the cake is 48 ounces. How much combined water and sugar is in the cake?

10. Thomas studies vocab for 8 weeks, and learns 50 new vocab words every week. If he forgets 5 new words the first week, forgets 10 new words the second week, forgets 15 new words the third week and so on, how many total new words will he know at the end of 8 weeks?

11. An orchard produces 20,000 apples. If each tree produced 40 apples, how many trees are in the orchard?

12. What is the sum of 345 and 1,489?

13. Scott buys a new pair of shoes every month. He throws out a pair of shoes once every three months. If he has 10 pairs of shoes at the start of 2012, how many pairs will he have at the start of 2013?

14. When Ben goes running, he passes through 5 different neighborhoods. He runs for 1 mile in each neighborhood except the last neighborhood, where he runs for 3 miles. How many total miles did Ben run?

15. If Jeremy scores 25 points in each of his first five games and 20 points in each of his next five games, how many total points did he score?

16. What is the product of 78 and 18?

17. 84 students are going on a school trip to Washington. If these students are split into 7 equal groups, and each group has 2 chaperones, how many total chaperones will go on the trip?

18. Rosemary has 12 pencils, Terry has 4 pencils and Angelina has no pencils. Rosemary gives half of her pencils to Terry. Terry then gives half of her pencils to Angelina. How many pencils does Angelina have now?

19. What is the difference between 2,052,187 and 1,594,876?

20. A fruit basket contains apples, oranges, bananas and peaches. If there are equal number of each type of fruit, which of the following cannot be the total number of fruit in the basket?
    A. 84 fruits
    B. 136 fruits
    C. 182 fruits
    D. 212 fruits

MIXED WORD PROBLEMS Practice Set 2

1. What is the sum of all odd numbers between -8 and 6?

2. What is the difference between 3,087,512 and 2,746,095?

3. What is the sum of one thousand, eight hundred seventy-nine and thirty-two thousand, one hundred ninety-five?

4. Chelsea gives Dave 10 chocolates for Valentine's Day. Leah gives Dave 20 more chocolates than Chelsea did. How many total chocolates did Dave receive on Valentine's Day?

5. A pound of apple seeds is 284,309 seeds. A pound of kiwi seeds contains 709,351 seeds. How many more seeds comprise a pound of kiwi than apple?

6. Jenna has $127. She gives $1 to the first person who says hello to her, $2 to the second person who says hello to her, $4 to the third person who says hello to her, and so on, giving twice as much money to each new person who says hello to her. If Jenna keeps doing this until her $127 is gone, how many people will she give money to?

7. Robert and Beth are waiting in line to go watch a movie. Robert is 17th in line while Beth is 54th in line. If three new people decide to cut in line between where Beth and Robert are standing, how many people will now be between Robert and Beth?

8. What is the sum of 243 and 1,293?

9. The high temperature on the first day of the month is 70°F. Every day after the first, the high temperature drops by 5°F. What will be the high temperature on the 6th day of the month?

10. A desk has 6 drawers, and each drawer is divided into 8 sections. How many total sections does the desk have?

11. Darcy cooks 3 meals every day for 6 weeks, including weekends. How many meals does she cook?

12. What is the difference between 67,681 and 8,519?

13. In the 1987 basketball season, Fat Lever played in 82 games and scored 1,558 points. If he scored the same number of points in each game, how many points did he score in each game?

14. Justin gets his hair cut only on months that correspond to even numbers (January=1, February=2, March=3, etc.). He only gets his hair cut on days of the month whose digits have a sum greater than 10. On which of the following days could Justin get a haircut?
    A. May 29
    B. May 30
    C. June 29
    D. June 30

15. Colby rolls a six-sided dice. If it lands on an even number, he gives Benjy twice as many dollars as the number on the dice shows. For example, if it lands on a 4, Colby gives Benjy $8. If Colby rolls the dice three times, what is the largest amount of money that he could possibly give to Benjy?

16. What is the quotient of 2,728 and 22?

17. A zoo buys one new dolphin in the middle of every year. On January 1, 2005, the zoo had 2 dolphins. In 2007, three dolphins were born at the zoo. In 2009, one dolphin died at the zoo. How many dolphins did the zoo have on December 31, 2010?

18. Perfect ski conditions occur when the temperature is -7°C. On a certain day, the temperature was 12°C. By how much does the temperature need to drop on that day to get perfect ski conditions?
    A. 5°C
    B. 7°C
    C. 12°C
    D. 19°C

19. The sum of Lori's and Randi's ages in 2012 is 94 years. What will be the sum of their ages in 2015?

20. In a warehouse, there are 84 crates each of which can hold 20 boxes. If each box contains 25 toys, what is the maximum number of toys that can be stored in the warehouse?

MIXED WORD PROBLEMS Practice Set 3

1. $-57 + (-38) + \blacksquare = 619 - 495$. What is $\blacksquare$?

2. The yoga room can only hold 14 people, but 63 people sign up for the yoga class. If each group has to fit inside the yoga room, what is the smallest number of groups that those 63 people can be split into?

3. An ant colony is comprised of four hundred eighty-seven thousand, nine hundred thirteen ants. If one hundred nine thousand, five hundred fifty-two worker ants leave the colony, how many ants will be left in the colony?

4. What is the sum of four thousand, two hundred ninety-two and fifty-seven thousand, two hundred thirty-nine?

5. Michael Jordan scored 29 points per game in his career. If there are 82 games in a typical NBA season, and Michael Jordan played for 17 seasons, how many total points did he score in his career?

6. A lemonade stand makes $20 on Monday. It makes $10 more on Tuesday than it did on Monday. It makes $10 more on Wednesday than it did on Tuesday. How much money does the lemonade stand make from Monday to Wednesday?

7. What is the sum of all even numbers between -9 and 5?

8. Kevin spent $168 on 27 cupcakes and 38 sodas for his birthday party. If each cupcake cost $2, what was the cost of each soda?

9. What is the difference between 4,019,935 and 3,426,821?

10. A school started the year with 20 school buses. One school bus broke in each month of the 9-month school year. Also, 5 more school buses broke at various times throughout the school year. If none of the buses were repaired, how many working buses were left at the end of the year?

11. A snack food company makes 5 different types of cookies. In one day at their factory, they make 1,000 boxes of each cookie flavor. Each box has 20 cookies. How many cookies does the factory make in 3 days?

12. What is the difference between 1,957,384 and 1,249,783?

13. What is the product of 339 and 3,851?

14. The 4th, 5th, and 6th grade students at Woodside Elementary are going on a field trip. If each grade has 63 students, and all the students are to be divided equally into seven buses, how many students will be in each bus?

    A. 21 students
    B. 27 students
    C. 29 students
    D. 36 students

15. Manny has 323 baseball cards. If it took him 17 years to collect all his baseball cards, what is the average number of baseball cards he collected each year?

16. The city of Palo Alto has 42,303 voters. If in a recent election 32,128 people voted "YES", and 7,895 people voted "NO", how many people did not vote?

17. The "Eleven Cities Tour", is a 120-mile speed skating race held during cold winters in the Netherlands when the ice is at least 6-inches thick. If 16,000 skaters started and finished the last race, what is the total mileage covered by all the skaters combined?

18. 54,048 cars go in and out of San Francisco in a single day (24 hours). How many cars are going in and out of San Francisco in an hour?

19. John is typing an 11-page paper for his history final. Each page contains an average of 544 words. If John types 32 words per minute, how long will it take him to type out the entire paper?

    A. 187 minutes
    B. 192 minutes
    C. 196 minutes
    D. 197 minutes

20. In 2011, a scientist counted 200,000 breeding pairs of Emperor penguins in Antarctica. Each breeding pair had a newborn penguin. If 15,809 newborn penguins are killed by predators, what was the population of Emperor penguins?
    A. 184,809 penguins
    B. 284,191 penguins
    C. 315,809 penguins
    D. 384,191 penguins

MIXED WORD PROBLEMS Practice Set 4

1. There are 30 students in Mrs. Klotz's class. Mrs. Klotz wants to divide the students into groups with an equal number of students in each group. If she wants each group to have at least 4 students in it, what is the largest number of groups that Mrs. Klotz can divide the students into?

2. What is the product of 824 and 519?

3. What is the difference between 74,712 and 8,933?

4. Each month Ronnie spends 15 hours volunteering at a local dog shelter, 25 hours playing sports, and 18 hours painting. How much time does he spend participating in the three activities during a year?

5. An ice creams store charges $6 for an ice cream with three toppings and $3 for each additional topping. If Susan wants an ice cream with 6 toppings, how much will she pay?

6. A science experiment begins with a tank of 40 flies. If the number of flies doubles every day, how many flies will there be after 5 days?

7. Twelve students sold candy bars to raise money for their debate team. If each student sold 86 pieces of candy, and each piece of candy cost $4, how much money did they raise?

8. What is the quotient of 51,770 and 167?

9. Mr. Severin goes to the store to buy one pair of shoes and two pairs of socks for each of his four children. If each pair of shoes costs $55 and each pair of socks cost $9, how much money did Mr. Severin spend?

10. What is the sum of seventy-two thousand, nine hundred forty-five and five thousand, one hundred eighty-nine?

11. Three hundred eighteen Stanford students go to see the new Harry Potter movie. If the total cost of all their movie tickets was $2,544, what was the price of each movie ticket?

12. The Iditarod is an annual sled dog race that takes place in Alaska. If each team uses 16 dogs, and the race is 1,049 miles long, what is the combined total distance covered by the dogs in each team?

13. $11 + \boxtimes - 23 = 57 - 16$. What is $\boxtimes$?

14. Ms. Callaghan makes a science test which has 30 multiple choice questions. To prevent students from guessing, she awards five points for each correct problem but subtracts 2 points for each incorrect problem. If Serena gets 21 problems correct and skips 5 problems, how many points did she get in the test?
    A. 95 points
    B. 97 points
    C. 101 points
    D. 105 points

15. 13,000 people were asked what their favorite kind of food was. Half the people said they prefer Italian food, 3,893 said they prefer Chinese food and the rest chose Mexican food. How many people chose Mexican food?

16. A survey of households in a small city showed that there was an average of 3 persons per household, and an average of 2 televisions per households. If there are 36,000 people in the city, estimate the total number of televisions in the city?
    A. 12,000 televisions
    B. 20,000 televisions
    C. 24,000 televisions
    D. 36,000 television

17. Terry is eight times the age of his 6-year old daughter. How old will he be in five years?
    A. 48 years old
    B. 53 years old
    C. 55 years old
    D. 63 years old

18. The Wikipedia for San Francisco lists the population of the city as 805,236. If there was a typing error when the pages was being created, and the digit '5' was supposed to be a '9', by how many people does Wikipedia underestimate the population of San Francisco?
    A. 400 people
    B. 4,000 people
    C. 40,000 people
    D. 400,000 people

84

19. The varsity volleyball team at Menlo School is flying to Las Vegas for a tournament. There are fifteen players in the team and three adult coaches accompanying the group on the trip. If the airfare for each student is $237 and the airfare for an adult is $314, how much was the total cost for flying the team to Las Vegas?

20. The temperature at 10 am was 45°C. If the temperature increased at a constant rate of 2°C degrees every hour, what was the temperature at 3 pm?

CHAPTER 4: NUMBER PROPERTIES

Experts in Test Prep, Tutoring, & Admissions Counseling

www.CardinalEducation.com

ROUNDING AND PLACE VALUES Practice Set 1

1. Which is sixty-four thousand, three hundred eight?
    - A. 64,380
    - B. 604,308
    - C. 64,308
    - D. 640,308

2. Write 50,033 in words.

3. What is the place value of 3 in 234,897?

4. Write 3,564,267 in words.

5. Which number shows 4 in the thousands place?
    - A. 2,403
    - B. 84,275
    - C. 43,817
    - D. 125,487

6. What is two hundred seven thousand, three hundred forty-two?

7. Which number shows 6 in the thousands place?
    - A. 764,714
    - B. 297,645
    - C. 645,129
    - D. 126,894

8. Which number shows 2 in the hundred thousands place?
    - A. 210,788
    - B. 124,490
    - C. 29,465
    - D. 82,789

9. What is two million, forty-three thousand, six hundred three?

10. In the number below, the "2" in the x place has a value how many times the value of the "2" in the y place?

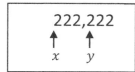

    - A. 10
    - B. 100
    - C. 1,000
    - D. 10,000

Round each of the following to the respective digits

11. 54 to the nearest tens

12. 27,048 to the nearest hundreds

13. 3,029 to the nearest hundreds

14. 6,999 to the nearest tens

15. 10,997 to the nearest tens

16. 100,898 to the nearest thousands

17. 12,384 to the nearest thousands

18. 1,024,999 to the nearest ten thousands

19. 88,123 to the nearest ten thousands

20. 3,279,999 to the nearest hundred

ROUNDING AND PLACE VALUES Practice Set 2

1. Which is seventy-three thousand, two hundred nine?
   A. 7,329
   B. 703,290
   C. 73,209
   D. 73,290

2. Write 20,244 in words.

3. What is the place value of 8 in 122,087?

4. Write 4,109,234 in words.

5. Which number shows 5 in the thousands place?
   A. 25,305
   B. 2,935
   C. 159,345
   D. 253

6. What is three hundred nineteen thousand, two hundred twenty-two?
   A. 319,222
   B. 31,922
   C. 1,392
   D. 3,190,222

7. Which number shows 3 in the ten thousands place?
   A. 34,678
   B. 2,635
   C. 634
   D. 63,789

8. Which number shows 4 in the hundreds and hundred thousands place?
   A. 4,564,564
   B. 143,143
   C. 432,432
   D. 1,104,104

9. What is three million, twenty-three thousand, eight hundred two?
   A. 3,023,802
   B. 3,230,802
   C. 3,230,820
   D. 3,023,820

10. In the number below, the "1" in the X place has a value how many times the value of the "1" in the Y place?

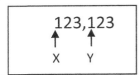

   A. 10
   B. 100
   C. 1,000
   D. 10,000

Round each of the following to the respective digits

11. 27 to the nearest tens.

12. 7,088 to the nearest tens

13. 3,149 to the nearest hundreds

14. 38,932 to the nearest hundreds

15. 23,088 to the nearest thousands

16. 679,726 to the nearest thousands

17. 99,789 to the nearest thousands.

18. 3,016,954 to the nearest ten thousands

19. 404,945 to the nearest ten thousands

20. 4,859,983 to the nearest hundreds

BASIC NUMBER PROPERTIES Practice Set 1

1. Which of the following is an integer?
   - A. −25
   - B. $\frac{1}{4}$
   - C. 0.25
   - D. 2.5

2. Which of the following is NOT an integer?
   - A. 7 ÷ 1
   - B. 28 ÷ 7
   - C. 15 ÷ 5
   - D. 18 ÷ 4

3. Circle all of the integers: -8, 12.2, 40/3, 0, 543

4. Circle all of the even numbers:
   -4; 0; 1; 19; 60.6; 8,641

5. All even numbers are divisible by what number?

6. Circle all of the odd numbers:
   -7.7; -1; 0; 2; 9; 25; 3,570

7. Which of the following is the largest?
   - A. 1,000
   - B. 25 × 39
   - C. 1,001 − 2
   - D. 999

8. Which of the following is smallest?
   - A. 3,737
   - B. 7,337
   - C. 3,773
   - D. 3,733

9. List three numbers that are multiples of 5:

10. List three numbers that are factors of 24:

11. Which of the following numbers is divisible by 3?
   - A. 25
   - B. 29
   - C. 32
   - D. 42

12. Which of the following numbers is divisible by 4?
   - A. 82
   - B. 126
   - C. 401
   - D. 1,200

13. Which of the following is a factor of 28?
   - A. 3
   - B. 7
   - C. 8
   - D. 56

14. Which of the following is a factor of 132?
   - A. 7
   - B. 10
   - C. 11
   - D. 14

15. Which of the following is a multiple of 6?
   - A. 3
   - B. 10
   - C. 16
   - D. 60

16. Which of the following is a multiple of 13?
   - A. 6.5
   - B. 31
   - C. 39
   - D. 100

17. Which of the following is a prime number?
   - A. 5
   - B. 6
   - C. 8
   - D. 12

18. Which of the following is a prime number?
   - A. 9
   - B. 11
   - C. 15
   - D. 39

19. What is the smallest prime number?

20. How many odd numbers are between 10 and 20?

BASIC NUMBER PROPERTIES Practice Set 2

1. Circle all of the even numbers:
   5, 8, 22, 17, -20, 102, 23

2. Circle all of the prime numbers:
   9, 4, 15, 3, 27, 11, -17

3. Circle all of the odd numbers:
   -12, 13, 7, 101, 22, -23

4. Which of the following statements is true?
   A. The number 2 is both a prime and odd
   B. The number 3 is odd but not prime
   C. 0 is a prime number
   D. 0 is an even number

5. Which of the following is the prime factorization of 24?
   A. 4×6
   B. $2 \times 2 \times 2 \times 3$
   C. $3 \times 2 \times 4$
   D. $2 \times 3 \times 3 \times 3$

6. List all the prime numbers less than 10.

7. Give an example of a number that is both prime and even.

8. All of the following are multiples of 6 except
   A. 42
   B. 54
   C. 60
   D. 63

9. List all the prime numbers greater than 20 but less than 30.

10. True or false: the sum of two even numbers is even.

11. How many integers are there between 5 and 22?

12. True or false: the sum of two odd numbers is odd.

13. Write the prime factorization of 30.

14. All of the following are factors of 120 except?
    A. 8
    B. 9
    C. 15
    D. 24

15. The sum of an odd number and an even number is always
    A. 0
    B. Prime
    C. Odd
    D. Even

16. True or false: 2 is a factor of 20.

17. True or false: 20 is a factor of 5.

18. List all the factors of 30.

19. What is the largest even number less than 100?

20. Write the prime factorization of 180.

NUMBER PROPERTIES Practice Set 1

1. Which of the following numbers are even?
   8; 21; -51; 0; 27; 7.4; 2,002; 6; -72; 0.4

2. List all the prime numbers between 10 and 30.

3. How many odd numbers are there between -6 and 11 inclusive?

4. What is the product of two smallest prime numbers?

5. Which of the following numbers are prime?
   9, 22, 33, 0, 29, 17, -5, 79, -15, 1

6. Write the prime factorization of 48?

7. All of the following are multiples of 2 except?
   A. 44
   B. 0
   C. -18
   D. 29

8. What is the sum of all the prime factors of 76?

9. How many integers are there from 2,225 to 2,345?

10. What is the greatest prime factor of 42?

11. How many distinct prime factors does 484 have?

12. What is the LCM of 5, 15, and 20?

13. What is the GCF of 24, 36, and 42?

14. Which of the following is divisible only by itself and 1?
    A. 27
    B. 51
    C. 89
    D. 121

15. What are the three smallest multiples of 2 and 3?

16. Which of the following is an odd negative integer that lies between -5 and 8?
    A. -7
    B. -3
    C. 1
    D. 5

17. What is the LCM of 24, 48, and 72?

18. If n is a negative number and p is a positive number, which of the following statements is true?
    A. $\frac{n}{p} < 0$
    B. $\frac{p}{n} > 0$
    C. $np > 0$
    D. $p^2 < 0$

19. If x is an odd number, which of the following must be even?
    A. $3x + 2$
    B. $-2x - 1$
    C. $2x + 1$
    D. $-3x - 1$

20. If a is a negative number and b is a positive number, which of the following statements is true?
    A. $a - b > 0$
    B. $b - a > 0$
    C. $ab > 0$
    D. $a^2 < 0$

NUMBER PROPERTIES Practice Set 2

1. Which of the following numbers are even?
   9; 16; -31; 0; 36; 3.1; 2,063; 1; -9.8; 2.3

2. List all the prime numbers between 0 and 38.

3. How many even numbers are there between -12 and 4 inclusive?

4. What is the product of 12 and the largest single digit prime number?

5. Which of the following numbers are prime?
   8, 21, 37, 0, -5, 41, -3, 83, -11, 2

6. Write the prime factorization of 36.

7. All of the following are multiples of 3 except?
   A. 45
   B. 10
   C. -18
   D. 27

8. What is the sum of all the prime factors of 96?

9. How many integers are there from 3,167 to 3,227?

10. What is the greatest prime factor of 84?

11. How many distinct prime factors does 396 have?

12. What is the LCM of 4, 16, and 20?

13. What is the GCF of 32, 48, and 96?

14. Which of the following is divisible only by itself and 1?
    A. 9
    B. 12
    C. 97
    D. 4

15. What are the three smallest multiples of 4 and 5?

16. Which of the following is an even negative integer that lies between -12 and 9?
    A. 13
    B. -4
    C. 2
    D. -14

17. What is the LCM of 36, 48, and 96?

18. If x and y are negative, which statements is true?
    A. $xy < 0$
    B. $xy > 0$
    C. $xy = 0$
    D. $2x > 0$

19. If x is odd, which of the following must be even?
    A. $5x + 4$
    B. $-5x - 4$
    C. $4x + 3$
    D. $-5x - 3$

20. If x is a negative number and y is a positive number, which of the following statements is true?
    A. $x - y < 0$
    B. $\frac{x}{y} > 0$
    C. $xy > 0$
    D. $2y < 0$

NUMBER PROPERTIES Practice Set 3

1. What is the sum of the prime factors of 36?

2. All of the following are factors of 48 EXCEPT
   A. 12
   B. 24
   C. 3
   D. 7

3. Which of the following is a factor of 60 but not 75?
   A. 15
   B. 3
   C. 6
   D. 5

4. What are the common factors of 12 and 48?
   A. 1, 2, 3, 4, 6
   B. 1, 2, 3, 4, 6, 12
   C. 1, 2, 3, 4, 6, 8, 12
   D. 1, 2, 3, 4, 12

5. How many prime numbers are between 30 and 49?

6. What is the greatest prime factor of 72?

7. Least common multiple of 6, 12, and 30?

8. Write the prime factorization of 56.

9. What is the greatest prime factor of 48?

10. Which of the following pairs of numbers are two different prime factors of 36?
    A. 2 and 3
    B. 3 and 4
    C. 3 and 12
    D. 4 and 9

11. What is the sum of the factors of 36?
    A. 53
    B. 91
    C. 90
    D. 54

12. What is the greatest common factor of 36, 48, and 96?

13. Which of the following numbers are odd?

    3, 6, 8, 11, 15, -6, -9, 2.5

14. If x, y, and z are consecutive odd integers, what is the difference between x and z?

15. Sum of the prime factors of 42?

16. All of the following are multiples of 4 except
    A. 90
    B. 96
    C. 48
    D. 36

17. How many integers are there between -3 and 4 inclusive?

18. How many distinct prime factors does 75 have?

19. How many even numbers are between 11 and 21?

20. Which of these are odd integers?
    3.6, -2, 4, 5, -1, 0, 7.8

NUMBER PROPERTIES Practice Set 4

1. How many prime numbers are there between 5 and 24 inclusive?

2. What is the greatest prime factor of 30?

3. What is the LCM of 3, 12, and 20?

4. Write the prime factorization of 66.

5. What is the greatest prime factor of 91?

6. Which of the following pairs of numbers are the two different prime factors of 24?
   A. 2 and 3
   B. 3 and 4
   C. 3 and 12
   D. 3 and 8

7. What is the sum of the factors of 24?
   A. 35
   B. 64
   C. 60
   D. 56

8. What is the GCF of 16, 32, and 72?

9. Which of the following numbers are even?
   3, 6, 8, 11, 15, -6, -9, 2.5, -8

10. If $x, y,$ and z are consecutive even integers, what is the difference between x and z?

11. What is the sum of the prime factors of 40?

12. All of the following are multiples of 12 except
    A. 96
    B. 80
    C. 48
    D. 36

13. All of the following are factors of 36 EXCEPT
    A. 12
    B. 24
    C. 3
    D. 9

14. Which of the following is a factor of 24 but not 32?
    A. 8
    B. 12
    C. 4
    D. 2

15. What are the common factors of 14 and 56?
    A. 1, 2, 4, 7, 14
    B. 1, 2, 14, 52
    C. 1, 2, 7
    D. 1, 2, 7, 14

16. How many integers are there between -7 and 2 inclusive?

17. How many distinct prime factors does 24 have?

18. How many even numbers are there between 9 and 23?

19. Which of these are even integers?
    3.6, -2, 4, 5, -1, 0, 7.8, -6

20. What is the sum of the prime factors of 24?

CHALLENGING NUMBER PROPERTIES Practice Set 1

1. What is the greatest odd number less than 200 that is divisible by 3?

2. What is the sum of all the distinct prime factors of 88?

3. How many odd numbers are there between 11 and 201 inclusive?
   A. 94
   B. 95
   C. 96
   D. 97

4. Zoë is x feet tall. She has an older brother who is 2 feet taller than she is. Which of the following could not be the sum of their heights?
   A. 6 ft
   B. 8 ft
   C. 9 ft
   D. 10 ft

5. If $a, b,$ and c are distinct prime numbers, what is the least value of abc?

6. Mary can run around a track in 60 seconds. Hillary can run around the same track in 80 seconds. If they both start from the same point on the track, how long will it be before they meet at the same point again?

7. The product of two consecutive even integers is 168. What is the sum of the two numbers?

8. There are 480 9th graders at Palo Alto High School and 600 9th graders at Gun High School. At each school, the students are divided into classes with each class having an equal number of students. Which of the following could not be the number of students in a class at both schools?
   A. 20 students
   B. 24 students
   C. 40 students
   D. 50 students

9. Which of the following would be the greatest common factor of $9x$ and $12xy$?
   A. $2x$
   B. $3x$
   C. $3y$
   D. $6xy$

10. If the sum of all integers from 1 to 1,500 inclusive is x, then which expression represents the sum of all integers from 1 to 1,498 inclusive?
    A. $x - 2,999$
    B. $2x - 3,000$
    C. $x - 1,500$
    D. $2x - 3,000$

11. If a is a factor of 12 and b is a factor of 49, what is the least value that ab must be a factor of?
    A. 2
    B. 14
    C. 21
    D. 42

12. The sum of 4 consecutive integers is 122. What is the largest of the four integers?

13. If x and y are prime numbers, what is the least common multiple of $9x$, $4y^2$ and $15xy$?
    A. $60xy^2$
    B. $120xy$
    C. $180xy^2$
    D. $240xy^2$

14. If p and q are distinct odd numbers, which of the following must be even?
    A. $2p - 3q$
    B. $q^2 + 6p$
    C. $2p^2 + 1$
    D. $4pq - 2p^2$

15. The product of three consecutive integers is 210. If one of the integers is 6, what is the sum of the three integers?

16. If d, e, and f are prime numbers, which of the following could represent the least common multiple of the three numbers.

    A. def

    B. $\frac{de}{f}$

    C. d^2ef

    D. $\frac{df}{3}$

17. If w is an even number, which of the following must be true?

    A. $2w - 2 > 0$

    B. $3w + 5$ is even

    C. $\frac{w}{2}$ is even

    D. $10w - 1$ is odd

18. 20 planes take off from the San Francisco International Airport every hour. The number of planes taking off per hour from the San Jose Airport and Oakland Airport is 12 and 16 respectively. Which of the following cannot be the total number of planes taking off from the three airports in one day?

    A. 120 planes

    B. 240 planes

    C. 480 planes

    D. 720 planes

19. The number p can be divided by 10 and 12 without any remainders. Which of the following numbers can p also be divided by without any remainders?

    A. 24

    B. 40

    C. 36

    D. 60

20. If a, b and c are prime numbers, what is the least common factor of $12ab, 30c^2$ and $24a^2c$?

    A. $60abc$

    B. $120abc^2$

    C. $120a^2bc$

    D. $120a^2bc^2$

CHALLENGING NUMBER PROPERTIES Practice Set 2

1. Chris goes bowling every three days, starting on January 3rd. Lisa goes bowling every seven days, starting on January 7th. What is the first day on which both Chris and Lisa will go bowling?
   A. January 7th
   B. January 15th
   C. January 21st
   D. February 2nd

2. Tom and Blaine are trying to arrange a time to meet between classes. Both have their first class at 9 am. Tom's classes are a half hour long. Blaine's classes are 45 minutes long. There is a ten minute break between each class. When is the earliest that Tom and Blaine will be able to meet?
   A. 9:40 am
   B. 10:30 am
   C. 11:20 am
   D. 12:10 pm

3. Leah wrote down a prime number greater than 25 and less than 35. When Dave guessed a prime number between 25 and 35, Leah told him that if he increased his guess by 2, he would have the correct number. What number did Leah write down?
   A. 27
   B. 29
   C. 31
   D. 37

4. There are 24 students in Mr. Brewer's class. Mr. Brewer wants to split his class up into groups. All groups must have an equal number of students, and there must be at least 2 students in each group. How many different arrangements of groups are possible?
   A. 2 arrangements
   B. 4 arrangements
   C. 6 arrangements
   D. 24 arrangements

5. Assume that each letter of the alphabet corresponds to an integer, starting with A=1, B=2, etc. Justin only dates girls whose names begin with odd letters. Which of the following girls would he not date?
   A. Cassie
   B. Lauren
   C. Kristina
   D. Sarah

6. If you start counting down from 100, what are the first three prime numbers that you would count?
   A. 97, 89, 83
   B. 97, 91, 89
   C. 99, 98, 97
   D. 99, 97, 95

7. How many even numbers are between 0 and 1,000 inclusive?
   A. 499
   B. 500
   C. 501
   D. 502

8. Starting with the first home game of the season (Game 1), a minor-league baseball team gives away free bobblehead dolls at every prime numbered home game and free t-shirts at every home game that is a multiple of 3. If there are 32 home games in the season, will there be more bobblehead giveaways or more t-shirt giveaways?

9. The product of 3 consecutive integers is 1,320. What is the largest integer?

10. The sum of 5 consecutive integers is 100. What is the middle integer?

11. The sum of 4 consecutive even numbers is 68. What is the smallest number?

12. m can be divided by both 6 and 8 with no remainders. Which of the following numbers can m also be divided by without any remainder?
    A. 14
    B. 24
    C. 42
    D. 60

13. k is a factor of 16, 24, and 52. Which of the following numbers could be k?
    A. 4
    B. 6
    C. 8
    D. 12

14. Carl has $10 more than Brett. Dave has $5 more than Carl. Together, Brett, Carl, and Dave have $85. How much money does Carl have?
    A. $10
    B. $20
    C. $30
    D. $35

15. Matt has twice as many toys as Harris. Harris has twice as many toys as Derek. Together, Matt, Harris, and Derek have 42 toys. How many toys does Matt have?
    A. 4 toys
    B. 6 toys
    C. 24 toys
    D. 42 toys

16. New York is in a time zone three hours ahead of Los Angeles. For example, when it is 5pm in Los Angeles, it is 8pm in New York. If it is 1pm in New York, what time is it in Los Angeles?

17. London is in a time zone five hours ahead of Boston. For example, when it is 2pm in Boston, it is 7pm in London. A plane leaves Boston at 8am (Boston time) and lands in London 6 hours later. What was the time (in London) when the plane landed?

18. If p represents the sum of all integers from 1 to 200 inclusive, which of the following represents the sum of all consecutive integers from 1 to 202 inclusive?
    A. $p + 2$
    B. $p + 3$
    C. $p - 3$
    D. $p + 403$

19. The sum of all integers from 1 to 100 inclusive, is represented by q. Which of the following is equal to $2q$?
    A. The sum of all even integers from 1 to 200 inclusive
    B. The sum of all integers from 1 to 200 inclusive
    C. 202
    D. 2,000

20. If x and y are prime numbers, what is the least common multiple of $5xy$, $15xy^2$, and $10y$?
    A. $15y$
    B. $30xy^2$
    C. $30x^2y^4$
    D. $750x^2y^4$

PATTERNS Practice Set 1

1. Find the next number in this sequence: 10, 9, 7, 4, 0, ___
   - A. 4
   - B. -4
   - C. -5
   - D. -10

2. Use the pattern to answer the question.

   $81 \div 9 = 9$

   $64 \div 8 = 8$

   _____

   $36 \div 6 = 6$

   Which of the following fits in the missing line?
   - A. $49 \div 7 = 7$
   - B. $56 \div 7 = 7$
   - C. $50 \div 7 = 7$
   - D. $25 \div 5 = 5$

3. Use the table to determine the rule for the function.
   - A. $j + 24 = k$
   - B. $13j = k$
   - C. $10j + 9 = k$
   - D. $k \div 12 = j$

j	k
2	26
3	39
5	65
10	130

4. Karen's plant grows 1 inch in its first week of life, 2 inches in its second week, and 3 inches in its third. If it keeps growing at this rate, how tall will the plant be after 7 weeks?
   - A. 1 foot, 9 inches
   - B. 2 feet, 4 inches
   - C. 2 feet, 8 inches
   - D. 3 feet, 3 inches

5. The amount of money in Becca's bank account doubles every year. If her bank account had x dollars in her first year, how much money will it have in the fourth year?
   - A. 8 dollars
   - B. $8x$ dollars
   - C. 16 dollars
   - D. $16x$ dollars

6. Use the table to determine the rule for the function.
   - A. $s + 4 = t$
   - B. $2s - 1 = t$
   - C. $(s - 1) \times 2 = t$
   - D. $(s \div 2) + 1 = t$

s	t
5	9
10	19
12	23
20	39

7. A swim team is keeping track of how many of each type of races it wins each year. If the pattern continues, how many butterfly races will the swim team win in Year 5?

	Freestyle	Backstroke	Butterfly
Year 1	0	0	10
Year 2	1	0	8
Year 3	2	1	6
Year 4	3	1	4

   A. 0 races
   B. 1 race
   C. 2 races
   D. 4 races

8. On his first day of training, Holden runs 200 meters. On his second day of training, he runs 300 meters. On his third day, he runs 500 meters. On his fourth day, he runs 800 meters. How many meters does he run on the sixth day?

   A. 1,000 meters
   B. 1,100 meters
   C. 1,200 meters
   D. 1,700 meters

9. When he was 12 years old, Devon could eat 4 slices of pizza. At age 15, he could eat 6 slices of pizza. At age 21, he could eat 10 slices of pizza. What is the difference between the number of slices of pizza Devon could eat at age 18 and the number of slices he could eat at age 9?

   A. 2 slices
   B. 4 slices
   C. 6 slices
   D. 8 slices

10. A drill sergeant is issuing marching orders to his troops. He shouts out: Left, Right, Left, Left, Right, Left, Left, Left, Right, Left, Left, _____. What will be the next three orders that he shouts?

   A. Left, Left, Right
   B. Left, Right, Left
   C. Right, Left, Left
   D. Left, Right, Right

PATTERNS Practice Set 2

1. Find the next number in this sequence:

   3, 5, -5, -3, 3, 5, -5, _____
   - A. 3
   - B. -3
   - C. 5
   - D. -5

2. The number of fish that Sandra can catch while ice fishing is dependent on the temperature. The chart below shows how many fish Sandra can catch at various temperatures. If Sandra caught 64 fish, what was the temperature?
   - A. -20°F
   - B. -25°F
   - C. -30°F
   - D. -45°F

Temperature	Fish Caught
0°F	1
-5°F	2
-10°F	4
-15°F	8

3. The amount of money Brian owes to the bank is halved every year. If he owed $256 in his first year, how much money will he owe in the fifth year?
   - A. $16
   - B. $32
   - C. $512
   - D. $1,280

4. Sparky the dog weighs 3 pounds in his first week of life, 6 pounds in his second week, and 11 pounds in his third week. If he keeps growing at this rate, how much will Sparky weigh after 5 weeks?
   - A. 14 pounds
   - B. 17 pounds
   - C. 21 pounds
   - D. 27 pounds

5. Use the table to determine the rule for the function.
   - A. $m + 7 = n$
   - B. $m = n + 7$
   - C. $m \times 0 = n$
   - D. $m + n = 7$

m	n
10	3
7	0
4	-3
1	-6

6. Find the next two numbers in this sequence:

   0, 0, 0, 0, 2, 0, 0, 0, 2, 0, ___
   - A. 0, 0
   - B. 0, 2
   - C. 2, 0
   - D. 2, 2

7. When he was 12 years old, Steve could run a mile in 8 minutes. At age 14, he could run a mile in 7 minutes. At age 18, he could run a mile in 5 minutes. What is the difference between the time it took Steve to run a mile at age 10 and the time it took him to run a mile at age 16?
    A. 3 minutes
    B. 4 minutes
    C. 5 minutes 30 seconds
    D. 9 minutes

8. The chart below shows the types of works an artist has produced each year. If the pattern continues, what will be the relationship between the artist's amounts of work in Year 4?

	Portraits	Landscapes	Sculptures
Year 1	10	0	2
Year 2	8	3	3
Year 3	6	6	4

    A. Portraits = Landscapes + Sculptures
    B. Portraits = Sculptures - Landscapes
    C. Sculptures = Landscapes - Portraits
    D. Portraits + Landscapes + Sculptures = 17

9. If Ruben starts with x dollars and adds $6 each day, how many dollars will he have after five days?
    A. $6x$ dollars
    B. $30x$ dollars
    C. $6 + x$ dollars
    D. $30 + x$ dollars

10. Use the table to determine the rule for the function.
    A. $y \div 9 = z$
    B. $10y - 1 = z$
    C. $y \div 10 + 1 = z$
    D. $y - 62 = z$

y	z
70	8
50	6
40	5
0	1

PATTERNS Practice Set 3

1. Find the next number in this sequence:

    3, 12, 48, 192, ___
    -   A. 206
    -   B. 384
    -   C. 576
    -   D. 768

2. Use the pattern to help answer the question

    $1 + 2 = 3$
    $1 + 4 = 5$
    $1 + 6 = 7$

    What would the sixth line in this pattern be?
    -   A. $1 + 7 = 8$
    -   B. $1 + 9 = 10$
    -   C. $1 + 12 = 13$
    -   D. $1 + 14 = 15$

3. Use the table to determine the rule for the function.
    -   A. $w + 4 = z$
    -   B. $(2 \times w) - 1 = z$
    -   C. $w + 6 = z$
    -   D. $w + 9 = z$

Input w	Output z
5	9
7	13
10	19
15	29

4. Use the pattern to answer the question

    $2^2 - 1^2 = 3$
    $3^2 - 2^1 = 5$
    $4^2 - 3^2 = 7$
    $5^2 - 4^2 = 9$

    Which of the following will be a solution to 17?
    -   A. $8^2 - 7^2$
    -   B. $9^2 - 8^2$
    -   C. $10^2 - 9^2$
    -   D. $11^2 - 10^2$

5. What is the next number in the following sequence?

    1, 3, 6, 10, 15, 21, 28, ___
    -   A. 32
    -   B. 34
    -   C. 36
    -   D. 40

6. The table below shows the height of the tide at Half Moon Bay at different times of the day. What would be the entry in the last row according to the pattern of the data presented?
    A. 6 am; 5 ft
    B. 6 am; 3 ft
    C. 4 am; 5 ft
    D. 10 am; 3 ft

Time	Height in feet of tide
6 am	5 ft
10 am	8 ft
2 pm	5 ft
6 pm	3 ft
10 pm	5 ft
2 am	8 ft
?	?

7. Use the table to determine the rule for the function.
    A. $\otimes - 7 = \bowtie$
    B. $(\otimes \times 2) + 3 = \bowtie$
    C. $\otimes \div 2 - 3 = \bowtie$
    D. $\otimes \div 4 - 1 = \bowtie$

$\otimes$	$\bowtie$
8	1
10	2
18	6
20	7

8. Aurelia deposits $10 in her piggy bank one day. The next day she deposits $15, and the day after $20. If she continues this trend for five straight days, and she initial had $10 dollars in the piggy bank, how much money will she have in her piggy bank?
    A. $55
    B. $90
    C. $100
    D. $110

9. What is the missing number in the following sequence?
    1, 9, 25, __, 81
    A. 47
    B. 49
    C. 57
    D. 59

10. The table below shows the average number of whales, seals and seagulls counted in a particular area in the last five years. Which of the following could be the expected number of whales, seals and seagulls in 2013?
    A. 20 whales, 205 seals, 4,720 seagulls
    B. 16 whales, 245 seals, 4,510 seagulls
    C. 14 whales, 225 seals, 4,720 seagulls
    D. 15 whales, 224 seals, 4,220 seagulls

Year	Whales	Seals	Seagulls
2008	15	120	2,200
2009	14	140	2,705
2010	16	159	3,211
2011	13	182	3,701
2012	15	203	4,201

PATTERNS Practice Set 4

1. A class put three cans full of water in the sun. Each can was covered and had a thermometer in it to measure the temperature of the water in degrees Fahrenheit. One can was painted red, one can was painted blue, and the third can was painted yellow. The class collected the data shown below. According to the pattern from the data, what would be the predicted temperature of the water in the blue can at 5 hours?

	Red Can	Blue Can	Yellow Can
Start	40°F	40°F	40°F
1 hour	43°F	42°F	40°F
2 hours	47°F	46°F	41°F
3 hours	52°F	52°F	41°F
4 hours	58°F	60°F	42°F

   A. 42°F
   B. 65°F
   C. 68°F
   D. 70°F

2. A class has 3 tanks with animals in them. One tank has 2 guppies, another tank has 2 turtles, and the last tank has 2 mice. The class measures the reproduction rates of the animals by counting how many animals are in each tank every month. According to the pattern from these data, how many mice will there be after 5 months?

	Guppies	Turtles	Mice
Start	2	2	2
1 month	20	2	4
2 months	200	2	8
3 months	2,000	2	16

   A. 2 mice
   B. 24 mice
   C. 32 mice
   D. 64 mice

3. Janie has a pool in her backyard, filled with 5 feet of water. Every day, an inch of water evaporates. How much water will be in Janie's pool after two weeks?

   A. 3 feet, 8 inches
   B. 3 feet, 10 inches
   C. 4 feet
   D. 6 feet, 2 inches

4. At the start of 3rd grade, Carrie was 4 feet tall. In 3rd grade, she grew 2 inches. In 4th grade, she grew 3 inches. In 5th grade, she grew 4 inches. If this pattern continues, how tall will she be at the END of the 6th grade?

   A. 4 feet, 9 inches
   B. 4 feet, 14 inches
   C. 5 feet, 2 inches
   D. 5 feet, 5 inches

5. Use the table to determine the rule for the function.

   A. $m + 5 = k$
   B. $k + 5 = m$
   C. $(k \times 2) + 1 = m$
   D. $k + 4 = m$

k	m
4	9
6	11
13	18
22	27

6. Use the table to determine the rule for the function.
    A. $a - 21 = b$
    B. $4a = b$
    C. $a \div 4 = b$
    D. $a \div 5 = b$

a	b
28	7
20	5
17	4.25
8	2

7. Use the table to determine the rule for the function.
    A. $r + 3 = s$
    B. $r \times 4 = s$
    C. $r \times 4 - 1 = s$
    D. $r \times 3 + 1 = s$

r	s
1	4
3	10
4	13
10	31

8. Use the pattern to help answer the question.

$4^2 = 1 + 3 + 5 + 7$
$3^2 = 1 + 3 + 5$
$2^2 = 1 + 3$
$1^2 = 1$

Which of the following is a solution to 5^2?
    A. $1 + 3 + 5 + 7 + 9$
    B. $1 \times 3 \times 5 \times 7 \times 9$
    C. $1 + 3 + 5 + 7$
    D. 36

9. Use the pattern to help answer the question. In this triangle, each number comes from adding together the two numbers located diagonally above it. For example, the 3's in the fourth row come from adding the 1's and the 2 in the third row. Which of the following could be the next (7th) row of the triangle?
    A. 1 5 10 10 5 1
    B. 1 6 15 20 15 6 1
    C. 1 6 15 20 5 2 1
    D. 1 4 5 0 5 4 1

```
        1
       1  1
      1  2  1
     1  3  3  1
    1  4  6  4  1
  1  5  10  10  5  1
```

10. In the sequence below, each number is the sum of the two previous numbers. What is the missing number?

0, 1, 1, 2, 3, 5, __, 13, 21, 32

    A. 8
    B. 9
    C. 10
    D. 11

CHAPTER 5: FRACTIONS

Experts in Test Prep, Tutoring, & Admissions Counseling

www.CardinalEducation.com

SIMPLIFYING FRACTIONS Practice Set 1

1. $\frac{3}{6} =$

2. $\frac{2}{6} =$

3. $\frac{5}{10} =$

4. $\frac{3}{12} =$

5. $\frac{5}{30} =$

6. $\frac{7}{35} =$

7. $\frac{8}{-56} =$

8. $\frac{9}{90} =$

9. $\frac{8}{72} =$

10. $\frac{4}{28} =$

11. $\frac{9}{6} =$

12. $-\frac{28}{8} =$

13. $\frac{25}{10} =$

14. $\frac{48}{112} =$

15. $\frac{52}{78} =$

16. $\frac{-88}{96} =$

17. $\frac{84}{60} =$

18. $\frac{36}{270} =$

19. $\frac{176}{110} =$

20. $-\frac{99}{143} =$

SIMPLIFYING FRACTIONS Practice Set 2

1. $\frac{3}{6} =$

2. $\frac{6}{9} =$

3. $\frac{6}{10} =$

4. $\frac{6}{12} =$

5. $\frac{4}{20} =$

6. $\frac{8}{24} =$

7. $\frac{4}{32} =$

8. $\frac{7}{49} =$

9. $\frac{7}{56} =$

10. $\frac{9}{81} =$

11. $-\frac{6}{4} =$

12. $\frac{20}{12} =$

13. $-\frac{36}{12} =$

14. $\frac{98}{42} =$

15. $-\frac{104}{64} =$

16. $\frac{136}{51} =$

17. $-\frac{210}{84} =$

18. $-\frac{300}{135} =$

19. $\frac{198}{77} =$

20. $-\frac{126}{70} =$

SIMPLIFYING FRACTIONS Practice Set 3

1. $\frac{3}{9} =$

2. $\frac{6}{8} =$

3. $\frac{4}{10} =$

4. $\frac{9}{12} =$

5. $\frac{3}{15} =$

6. $\frac{7}{21} =$

7. $\frac{9}{36} =$

8. $\frac{8}{48} =$

9. $\frac{5}{45} =$

10. $\frac{9}{63} =$

11. $-\frac{12}{8} =$

12. $\frac{26}{6} =$

13. $-\frac{28}{7} =$

14. $\frac{80}{32} =$

15. $-\frac{110}{44} =$

16. $\frac{136}{48} =$

17. $-\frac{117}{26} =$

18. $\frac{228}{96} =$

19. $-\frac{156}{91} =$

20. $\frac{95}{57} =$

SIMPLIFYING FRACTIONS Practice Set 4

1. $\frac{2}{8} =$

2. $\frac{8}{10} =$

3. $\frac{4}{12} =$

4. $\frac{8}{12} =$

5. $\frac{6}{18} =$

6. $\frac{6}{24} =$

7. $\frac{6}{36} =$

8. $\frac{6}{42} =$

9. $\frac{8}{64} =$

10. $\frac{9}{72} =$

11. $\frac{20}{5} =$

12. $-\frac{22}{4} =$

13. $\frac{39}{9} =$

14. $-\frac{192}{72} =$

15. $\frac{190}{60} =$

16. $-\frac{324}{72} =$

17. $-\frac{104}{39} =$

18. $\frac{154}{66} =$

19. $-\frac{57}{38} =$

20. $\frac{221}{78} =$

CONCEPTUAL FRACTIONS Practice Set 1

1. A cake has 20 pieces. Which of the following fractions represents 5 pieces of the cake?
   A. $\frac{1}{2}$
   B. $\frac{1}{3}$
   C. $\frac{1}{4}$
   D. $\frac{15}{20}$

2. There are 12 boys and 6 girls in a class. Girls represent what fraction of the class?
   A. $\frac{1}{2}$
   B. $\frac{1}{3}$
   C. $\frac{1}{4}$
   D. $\frac{2}{3}$

3. 36 students are trying out for the 12 spots on the basketball team. What fraction of students trying out will NOT make the team?
   A. $\frac{1}{2}$
   B. $\frac{1}{3}$
   C. $\frac{1}{4}$
   D. $\frac{2}{3}$

4. What fraction of the diagram below is shaded?
   A. $\frac{1}{4}$
   B. $\frac{2}{3}$
   C. $\frac{3}{4}$
   D. $\frac{6}{12}$

5. Mr. Johnson weighs 200 pounds. His wife weighs 120 pounds, his son weighs 100 pounds, and his daughter weighs 80 pounds. Mr. Johnson has what fraction of the family's total weight?
   A. $\frac{1}{2}$
   B. $\frac{2}{5}$
   C. $\frac{1}{3}$
   D. $\frac{3}{4}$

6. The circle graph below shows the favorite ice cream flavors of the students in Mrs. Justice's class. Approximately what fraction of the students chose vanilla?
   A. $\frac{1}{3}$
   B. $\frac{1}{4}$
   C. $\frac{1}{2}$
   D. $\frac{3}{4}$

7. 1,000 people entered the raffle, but only 3 people won. Which of the following shows the fraction of people who won the raffle?
   A. $\frac{3}{1,000}$
   B. $\frac{1}{333}$
   C. $\frac{1}{250}$
   D. $\frac{3}{997}$

8. If the column on the far right were removed, what fraction of the boxes would be shaded?
   A. $\frac{1}{2}$
   B. $\frac{1}{3}$
   C. $\frac{2}{3}$
   D. $\frac{5}{9}$

9. On a recent math test, 10 students scored below a 70, 8 students scored between 70 and 89, and 6 students scored between 90 and 100. What fraction of the class scored below a 70?
   A. $\frac{5}{12}$
   B. $\frac{5}{6}$
   C. $\frac{1}{4}$
   D. $\frac{1}{3}$

10. There are 10 goldfish in a pond. If 20 guppies are added to the pond, goldfish will represent what fraction of the fish in the pond?
    A. $\frac{1}{3}$
    B. $\frac{2}{3}$
    C. $\frac{1}{2}$
    D. 2

CONCEPTUAL FRACTIONS Practice Set 2

1. Johnny bought a pizza which has a total of 8 slices. If Johnny eats 4 slices, and his younger sister eats 2 slices, what fraction of the pizza is left?

2. The list shown below represents the numbers generated by a lottery machine. What fraction of the numbers in the list is odd?
   22, 15, 67, 5, 108, 19, 34, 11, 203
   A. $\frac{3}{4}$
   B. $\frac{1}{3}$
   C. $\frac{6}{8}$
   D. $\frac{2}{3}$

3. The jar shown below can hold 1 cup of liquid when filled to the top. How much liquid is in the jar?
   A. $\frac{1}{3}$ cup
   B. $\frac{2}{3}$ cup
   C. $\frac{3}{4}$ cup
   D. $\frac{4}{5}$ cup

   Jar 1

4. What fraction of the diagram is shaded?
   A. $\frac{3}{16}$
   B. $\frac{1}{4}$
   C. $\frac{3}{12}$
   D. $\frac{3}{8}$

5. A survey of 60 student's favorite subjects is displayed in circle graph shown below. About what fraction of students prefers Science?
   A. $\frac{1}{4}$
   B. $\frac{1}{2}$
   C. $\frac{1}{8}$
   D. $\frac{1}{6}$

   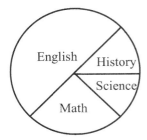

6. There are 8 yellow and 16 green marbles in a bag. What fraction of the marbles is green?

7. What fraction of the figure is shaded?
   A. $\frac{1}{4}$
   B. $\frac{1}{3}$
   C. $\frac{1}{2}$
   D. $\frac{2}{3}$

   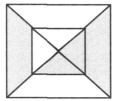

8. 700 students voted in a school election. If 400 of the voters were girls, what fraction of the voters were boys?

9. How many more boxes have to be colored in order for $\frac{2}{3}$ of the figure to be colored?

   A. 1 box
   B. 2 boxes
   C. 3 boxes
   D. 4 boxes

10. Avery enters an elevator which already has four people in it. If Avery weighs 90 lbs, and the weight of the four people in the elevator is 450 lbs, what fraction of the total weight will be Avery's?
    A. $\frac{1}{6}$
    B. $\frac{1}{5}$
    C. $\frac{1}{4}$
    D. $\frac{1}{3}$

MIXED NUMBERS TO IMPROPER FRACTIONS Practice Set 1

Write as an improper fraction in simplest form.

1. $1\frac{1}{4} =$

2. $2\frac{1}{2} =$

3. $1\frac{3}{5} =$

4. $1\frac{4}{9} =$

5. $2\frac{2}{3} =$

6. $2\frac{5}{6} =$

7. $3\frac{5}{8} =$

8. $4\frac{3}{8} =$

9. $8\frac{4}{7} =$

10. $10\frac{1}{10} =$

11. $2\frac{3}{6} =$

12. $2\frac{6}{10} =$

13. $3\frac{6}{14} =$

14. $5\frac{6}{9} =$

15. $4\frac{28}{36} =$

16. $4\frac{12}{24} =$

17. $7\frac{30}{50} =$

18. $5\frac{15}{60} =$

19. $8\frac{48}{72} =$

20. $9\frac{33}{99} =$

114

MIXED NUMBERS TO IMPROPER FRACTIONS Practice Set 2

Write as an improper fraction in simplest form.

1. $1\frac{1}{3} =$

2. $2\frac{1}{4} =$

3. $1\frac{3}{4} =$

4. $1\frac{5}{8} =$

5. $2\frac{3}{5} =$

6. $2\frac{2}{7} =$

7. $3\frac{5}{6} =$

8. $4\frac{2}{9} =$

9. $5\frac{3}{8} =$

10. $7\frac{1}{7} =$

11. $2\frac{4}{6} =$

12. $4\frac{6}{8} =$

13. $3\frac{4}{12} =$

14. $2\frac{8}{10} =$

15. $6\frac{14}{49} =$

16. $5\frac{15}{25} =$

17. $7\frac{40}{60} =$

18. $5\frac{35}{45} =$

19. $8\frac{18}{45} =$

20. $9\frac{24}{96} =$

115

IMPROPER FRACTIONS TO MIXED NUMBERS Practice Set 1

Write as a mixed number in simplest form.

1. $\frac{5}{4} =$

2. $\frac{9}{8} =$

3. $\frac{5}{2} =$

4. $\frac{5}{3} =$

5. $\frac{15}{4} =$

6. $\frac{33}{6} =$

7. $\frac{60}{7} =$

8. $\frac{97}{10} =$

9. $\frac{52}{5} =$

10. $\frac{77}{9} =$

11. $\frac{16}{6} =$

12. $\frac{6}{4} =$

13. $\frac{11}{5} =$

14. $\frac{13}{5} =$

15. $\frac{36}{8} =$

16. $\frac{34}{6} =$

17. $\frac{42}{4} =$

18. $\frac{108}{10} =$

19. $\frac{68}{7} =$

20. $\frac{80}{18} =$

IMPROPER FRACTIONS TO MIXED NUMBERS Practice Set 2

Write as a mixed number in simplest form.

1. $\frac{3}{2} =$

2. $\frac{6}{5} =$

3. $\frac{7}{3} =$

4. $\frac{9}{7} =$

5. $\frac{45}{10} =$

6. $\frac{69}{9} =$

7. $\frac{71}{8} =$

8. $\frac{100}{11} =$

9. $\frac{65}{6} =$

10. $\frac{80}{9} =$

11. $\frac{18}{4} =$

12. $\frac{12}{5} =$

13. $\frac{19}{7} =$

14. $\frac{16}{5} =$

15. $\frac{40}{6} =$

16. $\frac{60}{8} =$

17. $\frac{50}{4} =$

18. $\frac{96}{9} =$

19. $\frac{73}{8} =$

20. $\frac{65}{15} =$

ADDITION/SUBTRACTION OF FRACTIONS WITH COMMON DENOMINATORS Practice Set 1

Write answer in simplest form.

1. $\frac{1}{4} + \frac{2}{4} =$

2. $\frac{3}{4} - \frac{1}{4} =$

3. $\frac{3}{5} + \frac{1}{5} =$

4. $\frac{2}{5} - \frac{1}{5} =$

5. $\frac{2}{6} + \frac{3}{6} =$

6. $\frac{4}{6} - \frac{2}{6} =$

7. $\frac{2}{7} + \frac{3}{7} =$

8. $\frac{6}{7} - \frac{3}{7} =$

9. $\frac{4}{8} + \frac{1}{8} =$

10. $\frac{3}{8} - \frac{7}{8} =$

11. $\frac{3}{9} + \frac{5}{9} =$

12. $\frac{7}{9} - \frac{6}{9} =$

13. $\frac{2}{10} + \frac{5}{10} =$

14. $\frac{3}{10} - \frac{9}{10} =$

15. $\frac{1}{6} + \frac{3}{6} =$

16. $\frac{5}{8} - \frac{3}{8} =$

17. $\frac{4}{9} + \frac{2}{9} =$

18. $\frac{3}{8} - \frac{5}{8} =$

19. $\frac{5}{8} + \frac{2}{8} =$

20. $\frac{7}{10} - \frac{2}{10} =$

ADDITION/SUBTRACTION OF FRACTIONS WITH COMMON DENOMINATORS Practice Set 2

Write answer in simplest form.

1. $\frac{1}{6} + \frac{2}{6} =$

2. $\frac{5}{6} - \frac{1}{6} =$

3. $\frac{2}{6} + \frac{2}{6} =$

4. $\frac{4}{7} - \frac{2}{7} =$

5. $\frac{1}{7} + \frac{4}{7} =$

6. $\frac{5}{7} - \frac{3}{7} =$

7. $\frac{1}{7} + \frac{2}{7} =$

8. $\frac{4}{7} - \frac{2}{7} =$

9. $\frac{1}{8} + \frac{5}{8} =$

10. $\frac{7}{8} - \frac{6}{8} =$

11. $\frac{2}{8} + \frac{2}{8} =$

12. $\frac{7}{8} - \frac{3}{8} =$

13. $\frac{2}{8} + \frac{5}{8} =$

14. $\frac{6}{8} - \frac{3}{8} =$

15. $\frac{4}{9} + \frac{4}{9} =$

16. $\frac{2}{8} - \frac{6}{8} =$

17. $\frac{5}{9} + \frac{2}{9} =$

18. $\frac{5}{9} - \frac{1}{9} =$

19. $\frac{3}{9} + \frac{3}{9} =$

20. $\frac{1}{9} - \frac{5}{9} =$

ADDITION/SUBTRACTION OF FRACTIONS WITH DIFFERENT DENOMINATORS Practice Set 1

Write answer in simplest form.

1. $\frac{1}{2} + \frac{1}{4} =$

2. $\frac{1}{2} - \frac{1}{4} =$

3. $\frac{1}{3} + \frac{2}{6} =$

4. $\frac{1}{4} - \frac{1}{8} =$

5. $\frac{1}{3} + \frac{1}{4} =$

6. $\frac{1}{3} - \frac{1}{5} =$

7. $\frac{2}{5} + \frac{1}{2} =$

8. $\frac{2}{3} - \frac{3}{6} =$

9. $\frac{2}{4} + \frac{1}{6} =$

10. $\frac{4}{5} - \frac{4}{8} =$

120

11. $\frac{2}{5} + \frac{2}{6} =$

12. $\frac{4}{6} - \frac{5}{9} =$

13. $\frac{3}{5} + \frac{2}{10} =$

14. $\frac{1}{6} - \frac{1}{9} =$

15. $\frac{2}{6} + \frac{5}{8} =$

16. $\frac{5}{9} - \frac{3}{8} =$

17. $\frac{2}{3} + \frac{3}{9} =$

18. $\frac{8}{10} - \frac{3}{5} =$

19. $\frac{3}{4} + \frac{1}{8} =$

20. $\frac{6}{7} - \frac{3}{14} =$

ADDITION/SUBTRACTION OF FRACTIONS WITH DIFFERENT DENOMINATORS Practice Set 2

Write answer in simplest form.

1. $\frac{1}{5} + \frac{1}{10} =$

2. $\frac{1}{2} - \frac{1}{4} =$

3. $\frac{1}{4} + \frac{3}{8} =$

4. $\frac{1}{8} - \frac{1}{16} =$

5. $\frac{1}{7} + \frac{1}{3} =$

6. $\frac{1}{2} - \frac{1}{6} =$

7. $\frac{1}{4} + \frac{2}{9} =$

8. $\frac{4}{5} - \frac{3}{10} =$

9. $\frac{5}{6} + \frac{1}{8} =$

10. $\frac{2}{3} - \frac{3}{8} =$

122

11. $\frac{2}{5} + \frac{5}{9} =$

16. $\frac{7}{8} - \frac{3}{7} =$

12. $\frac{7}{10} - \frac{3}{15} =$

17. $\frac{2}{3} + \frac{2}{12} =$

13. $\frac{1}{4} + \frac{3}{8} =$

18. $\frac{6}{9} - \frac{2}{3} =$

14. $\frac{10}{12} - \frac{6}{16} =$

19. $\frac{5}{12} + \frac{6}{15} =$

15. $\frac{2}{6} + \frac{4}{7} =$

20. $\frac{10}{12} - \frac{12}{18} =$

ADDITION/SUBTRACTION OF FRACTIONS WITH DIFFERENT DENOMINATORS Practice Set 3

Write answer in simplest form.

1. $\frac{1}{3} + \frac{1}{6} =$

2. $\frac{1}{2} - \frac{1}{8} =$

3. $\frac{1}{5} + \frac{1}{10} =$

4. $\frac{1}{7} - \frac{1}{14} =$

5. $\frac{1}{2} + \frac{1}{5} =$

6. $\frac{1}{3} - \frac{1}{6} =$

7. $\frac{1}{3} + \frac{2}{7} =$

8. $\frac{3}{4} - \frac{3}{8} =$

9. $\frac{1}{3} + \frac{5}{9} =$

10. $\frac{6}{7} - \frac{2}{4} =$

11. $\frac{2}{4} + \frac{2}{6} =$

12. $\frac{6}{9} - \frac{5}{12} =$

13. $\frac{2}{6} + \frac{5}{12} =$

14. $\frac{12}{18} - \frac{3}{12} =$

15. $\frac{3}{7} + \frac{3}{8} =$

16. $\frac{7}{9} - \frac{3}{10} =$

17. $\frac{3}{15} - \frac{3}{18} =$

18. $\frac{6}{9} + \frac{3}{10} =$

19. $\frac{6}{7} - \frac{5}{6} =$

20. $\frac{8}{9} - \frac{12}{15} =$

ADDITION/SUBTRACTION OF FRACTIONS WITH DIFFERENT DENOMINATORS Practice Set 4

Write answer in simplest form.

1. $\frac{1}{4} + \frac{1}{8} =$

2. $\frac{1}{3} + \frac{3}{6} =$

3. $\frac{1}{5} + \frac{4}{10} =$

4. $\frac{1}{9} - \frac{1}{18} =$

5. $\frac{1}{4} + \frac{1}{9} =$

6. $\frac{1}{4} - \frac{1}{7} =$

7. $\frac{1}{5} + \frac{4}{6} =$

8. $\frac{5}{6} - \frac{7}{12} =$

9. $\frac{2}{5} + \frac{3}{7} =$

10. $\frac{7}{9} - \frac{3}{5} =$

11. $\frac{4}{8} + \frac{1}{3} =$

12. $\frac{5}{8} - \frac{5}{12} =$

13. $\frac{4}{7} + \frac{6}{14} =$

14. $\frac{1}{2} + \frac{3}{8} =$

15. $\frac{10}{12} - \frac{3}{4} =$

16. $\frac{3}{4} + \frac{3}{16} =$

17. $\frac{3}{4} + \frac{3}{20} =$

18. $\frac{20}{25} - \frac{3}{10} =$

19. $\frac{4}{6} + \frac{5}{16} =$

20. $\frac{7}{14} - \frac{6}{21} =$

ADDITION/SUBTRACTION OF MIXED NUMBERS Practice Set 1

Write answer as a mixed number in simplest form.

1. $\frac{2}{3} + \frac{5}{6} =$

2. $1\frac{1}{3} - \frac{5}{6} =$

3. $\frac{2}{4} + \frac{6}{8} =$

4. $1\frac{7}{8} - 1\frac{3}{4} =$

5. $\frac{8}{5} + \frac{14}{10} =$

6. $1\frac{2}{5} - \frac{8}{10} =$

7. $\frac{4}{3} - \frac{10}{12} =$

8. $2\frac{7}{9} - 1\frac{2}{6} =$

9. $\frac{10}{4} + \frac{15}{8} =$

10. $2\frac{2}{7} - 1\frac{1}{4} =$

11. $1\frac{1}{3} + 1\frac{2}{4} =$

16. $3\frac{2}{3} - 1\frac{3}{4} =$

12. $1\frac{1}{2} - 1\frac{1}{4} =$

17. $1\frac{2}{6} + 2\frac{1}{3} =$

13. $1\frac{2}{3} + \frac{2}{5} =$

18. $4\frac{3}{5} - 4\frac{1}{2} =$

14. $2\frac{1}{3} - 1\frac{1}{5} =$

19. $2\frac{1}{4} + 1\frac{2}{8} =$

15. $1\frac{1}{4} + 1\frac{1}{5} =$

20. $2\frac{4}{8} - 2\frac{2}{6}$

ADDITION/SUBTRACTION OF MIXED NUMBERS Practice Set 2

Write answer as a mixed number in simplest form.

1. $\frac{2}{3} + \frac{4}{9} =$

2. $\frac{7}{5} - \frac{3}{10} =$

3. $\frac{7}{4} + \frac{3}{8} =$

4. $1\frac{2}{3} - \frac{7}{9} =$

5. $\frac{7}{8} + 1\frac{1}{2} =$

6. $\frac{5}{4} - \frac{9}{8} =$

7. $\frac{5}{4} + \frac{18}{12} =$

8. $\frac{3}{4} + \frac{2}{3} =$

9. $\frac{7}{5} - \frac{2}{3} =$

10. $\frac{1}{2} + \frac{8}{5} =$

11. $1\frac{1}{2} - \frac{5}{9} =$

12. $\frac{3}{8} + 1\frac{2}{3} =$

13. $\frac{5}{4} - \frac{8}{7} =$

14. $\frac{7}{6} + \frac{9}{8} =$

15. $\frac{9}{5} - 1\frac{2}{3} =$

16. $1\frac{2}{3} + \frac{12}{8} =$

17. $\frac{22}{12} - 1\frac{3}{4} =$

18. $\frac{14}{9} - 1\frac{1}{2} =$

19. $2\frac{3}{4} + 1\frac{1}{6} =$

20. $\frac{10}{4} - 2\frac{1}{7} =$

131

ADDITION/SUBTRACTION OF MIXED NUMBERS Practice Set 3

Write answer as a mixed number in simplest form.

1. $\frac{3}{4} + \frac{5}{8} =$

2. $\frac{3}{2} - \frac{3}{4} =$

3. $\frac{5}{3} + \frac{4}{6} =$

4. $1\frac{1}{2} - \frac{5}{6} =$

5. $1\frac{3}{4} + \frac{7}{12} =$

6. $\frac{5}{3} - \frac{11}{9} =$

7. $\frac{3}{2} + \frac{12}{8} =$

8. $\frac{2}{3} + \frac{3}{5} =$

9. $\frac{3}{2} - \frac{4}{5} =$

10. $\frac{5}{4} + \frac{3}{5} =$

11. $1\frac{1}{2} - \frac{5}{7} =$

12. $\frac{5}{6} + 1\frac{3}{4} =$

13. $\frac{10}{6} - \frac{8}{5} =$

14. $\frac{10}{7} + \frac{5}{4} =$

15. $1\frac{5}{6} - \frac{3}{2} =$

16. $\frac{7}{5} + 1\frac{3}{4} =$

17. $1\frac{2}{3} - \frac{7}{5} =$

18. $\frac{9}{7} - 1\frac{1}{4} =$

19. $2\frac{1}{5} + 1\frac{3}{4} =$

20. $\frac{12}{5} - 2\frac{1}{8} =$

ADDITION/SUBTRACTION OF MIXED NUMBERS Practice Set 4

Write answer as a mixed number in simplest form.

1. $\frac{3}{5} + \frac{7}{10} =$

2. $\frac{7}{4} - \frac{3}{8} =$

3. $\frac{9}{6} + \frac{2}{3} =$

4. $1\frac{1}{4} - \frac{5}{12} =$

5. $\frac{8}{9} + 1\frac{1}{3} =$

6. $\frac{8}{5} - \frac{13}{10} =$

7. $\frac{5}{3} + \frac{15}{12} =$

8. $\frac{1}{2} + \frac{4}{5} =$

9. $\frac{6}{4} - \frac{1}{3} =$

10. $\frac{2}{3} + \frac{5}{2} =$

11. $1\frac{1}{3} - \frac{5}{8} =$

16. $1\frac{1}{4} + \frac{9}{6} =$

12. $1\frac{1}{5} + \frac{2}{7} =$

17. $1\frac{1}{6} - \frac{9}{8} =$

13. $\frac{5}{3} - \frac{6}{5} =$

18. $2\frac{1}{5} - \frac{3}{8} =$

14. $\frac{7}{5} + \frac{5}{4} =$

19. $1\frac{2}{3} + 1\frac{2}{10} =$

15. $\frac{13}{9} - 1\frac{1}{3} =$

20. $1\frac{1}{6} - \frac{11}{10} =$

MULTIPLICATION OF FRACTIONS Practice Set 1

Write answer in simplest form.

1. $\frac{1}{5} \times \frac{1}{4} =$

2. $\frac{1}{6} \times \frac{1}{9} =$

3. $\frac{1}{7} \times \frac{3}{10} =$

4. $\frac{2}{5} \times \frac{1}{10} =$

5. $\frac{2}{3} \times \frac{1}{8} =$

6. $\frac{1}{3} \times \frac{4}{7} =$

7. $\frac{1}{4} \times \frac{4}{9} =$

8. $\frac{3}{5} \times \frac{6}{7} =$

9. $\frac{5}{6} \times \frac{2}{9} =$

10. $\frac{3}{8} \times \frac{8}{9} =$

11. $\frac{3}{4} \times \frac{2}{5} =$

12. $\frac{4}{5} \times \frac{7}{9} =$

13. $\frac{2}{3} \times \frac{4}{5} =$

14. $\frac{5}{7} \times \frac{3}{4} =$

15. $\frac{6}{9} \times \frac{3}{7} =$

16. $\left(-\frac{2}{6}\right) \times \frac{5}{8} =$

17. $\frac{2}{3} \times \frac{6}{8} =$

18. $\frac{2}{7} \times \frac{7}{8} =$

19. $\frac{4}{8} \times \left(-\frac{5}{9}\right) =$

20. $\frac{4}{6} \times \frac{6}{7} =$

MULTIPLICATION OF FRACTIONS Practice Set 2

Write answer in simplest form.

1. $\frac{1}{4} \times \frac{1}{7} =$ $\frac{1}{28}$

2. $\frac{1}{2} \times \frac{1}{8} =$ $\frac{1}{16}$

3. $\frac{5}{6} \times \frac{3}{4} =$ $\frac{5}{8}$

4. $\frac{1}{6} \times \frac{4}{12} =$ $\frac{2}{36} = \frac{1}{18}$

5. $\frac{1}{2} \times \frac{5}{6} =$ $\frac{5}{12}$

6. $\frac{2}{5} \times \frac{5}{6} =$

7. $\frac{1}{2} \times \frac{4}{7} =$

8. $\frac{8}{9} \times \frac{3}{5} =$

9. $\frac{4}{6} \times \frac{7}{8} =$ $\frac{7}{12}$

10. $\frac{2}{9} \times \frac{5}{6} =$ $\frac{5}{27}$

11. $\frac{2}{5} \times \frac{3}{4} =$

12. $\frac{3}{5} \times \frac{3}{8} =$

13. $\frac{4}{7} \times \frac{5}{6} =$

14. $\frac{2}{4} \times \frac{3}{9} =$

15. $\frac{2}{9} \times \frac{3}{6} =$

16. $\frac{6}{8} \times \frac{5}{9} =$

17. $\frac{2}{5} \times \frac{5}{8} =$

18. $\frac{3}{7} \times \left(-\frac{8}{9}\right) = \frac{3}{7} \times -\frac{8}{9}$ $\left(-\frac{8}{21}\right)$

19. $\left(-\frac{5}{6}\right) \times \frac{4}{10} = -\frac{5}{6} \times \frac{4}{10} = -\frac{2}{6} = -\frac{1}{3}$

20. $\frac{7}{10} \times \frac{5}{9} =$

137

MULTIPLICATION OF MIXED/IMPROPER/WHOLE Practice Set 1

Write answer as a mixed number in simplest form.

1. $1\frac{1}{5} \times 1\frac{1}{9} =$

6. $3\frac{1}{3} \times 2\frac{2}{5} =$

2. $1\frac{1}{2} \times 4 =$

7. $1\frac{3}{7} \times 2\frac{7}{9} =$

3. $2\frac{2}{8} \times 1\frac{4}{6} =$

8. $2\frac{8}{10} \times 6 = \frac{28}{10} \times \frac{6}{1} = \frac{54}{5}$

5 $10\frac{4}{5}$

4. $\frac{13}{6} \times 1\frac{2}{3} =$

9. $3\frac{1}{8} \times 2\frac{2}{4} =$

5. $3\frac{1}{5} \times \frac{10}{7} =$

10. $\frac{7}{4} \times \frac{16}{7} =$

11. $3\frac{2}{6} \times 2\frac{4}{8} =$

16. $1\frac{1}{2} \times 3 = \frac{3}{2} \times \frac{3}{1} = \frac{9}{2} = \boxed{4\frac{1}{2}}$

12. $\frac{20}{8} \times 3\frac{3}{4} =$

17. $\frac{18}{5} \times \frac{10}{4} =$

13. $1\frac{2}{3} \times 3\frac{3}{9} = \frac{5}{3} \times \frac{30}{9} = \frac{50}{9} = \boxed{5\frac{5}{9}}$

18. $3\frac{1}{8} \times 3\frac{3}{4} = \frac{25}{8} \times \frac{15}{4} =$

14. $1\frac{3}{5} \times \frac{25}{10} = \frac{8}{5} \times \frac{25}{10} = \frac{20}{5} = 4$

19. $2\frac{3}{6} \times 1\frac{4}{5} =$

15. $2\frac{6}{7} \times 1\frac{6}{9} = \frac{20}{7} \times \frac{15}{9} = \frac{300}{63}$

20. $10\frac{5}{6} \times 1\frac{2}{10} =$

139

MULTIPLICATION OF MIXED/IMPROPER/WHOLE Practice Set 2

Write answer as a mixed number in simplest form.

1. $1\frac{1}{8} \times 1\frac{1}{5} =$

2. $\frac{4}{3} \times 2\frac{5}{8} =$

3. $1\frac{6}{8} \times 2 =$

4. $2\frac{2}{10} \times \frac{8}{5} =$

5. $3\frac{2}{6} \times 1\frac{3}{20} =$

6. $3\frac{1}{5} \times 5$

7. $1\frac{6}{8} \times 2\frac{2}{5} =$

8. $\frac{15}{6} \times \frac{21}{9} =$

9. $3\frac{5}{10} \times 2\frac{4}{5} =$

10. $\frac{9}{5} \times 2\frac{6}{7} =$

11. $3\frac{5}{6} \times 2\frac{1}{4} =$

16. $\frac{11}{5} \times 1\frac{3}{15} =$

12. $2\frac{4}{6} \times \frac{11}{3} =$

17. $2\frac{2}{3} \times 3\frac{3}{4} =$

13. $1\frac{4}{10} \times 3\frac{2}{8} =$

18. $\frac{15}{4} \times \frac{20}{6} =$

14. $1\frac{4}{6} \times 2 =$

19. $2\frac{2}{6} \times 1\frac{7}{8} =$

15. $1\frac{3}{5} \times 2\frac{2}{7} =$

20. $\frac{64}{6} \times 1\frac{8}{10} =$

MULTIPLICATION OF MIXED/IMPROPER/WHOLE Practice Set 3

Write answer as a mixed number in simplest form.

1. $\frac{7}{6} \times \frac{8}{7} =$

2. $1\frac{1}{4} \times 2\frac{2}{7} =$

3. $2 \times 1\frac{3}{5} =$

4. $1\frac{1}{2} \times 2\frac{2}{6} =$

5. $3\frac{3}{4} \times \frac{6}{5} =$

6. $3\frac{2}{6} \times 2\frac{4}{10} =$

7. $\frac{11}{6} \times 2\frac{4}{9} =$

8. $2\frac{1}{10} \times 2 =$

9. $3\frac{5}{6} \times 2\frac{2}{3} =$

10. $\frac{23}{8} \times \frac{5}{3} =$

11. $2\frac{7}{9} \times 3\frac{4}{5} =$

12. $\frac{18}{8} \times 3\frac{3}{6} =$

13. $1\frac{4}{6} \times 3 =$

14. $1\frac{1}{2} \times 2\frac{6}{8} =$

15. $1\frac{7}{8} \times \frac{20}{7} =$

16. $1\frac{1}{4} \times 2\frac{5}{20} =$

17. $\frac{15}{6} \times \frac{16}{5} =$

18. $3\frac{1}{3} \times 3\frac{3}{6} =$

19. $2\frac{2}{6} \times 1\frac{5}{7} =$

20. $10\frac{5}{8} \times \frac{12}{10} =$

MULTIPLICATION OF MIXED/IMPROPER/WHOLE Practice Set 4

Write answer as a mixed number in simplest form.

1. $1\frac{1}{8} \times 0 =$

6. $3 \times 2\frac{2}{5} =$

2. $\frac{6}{5} \times 2\frac{5}{6} =$

7. $2\frac{1}{10} \times 1\frac{3}{7} =$

3. $1\frac{3}{9} \times 2\frac{2}{6} =$

8. $2\frac{4}{8} \times \frac{12}{5} =$

4. $2\frac{4}{8} \times 1\frac{1}{4} =$

9. $2\frac{1}{6} \times 3\frac{3}{8} =$

5. $\frac{8}{7} \times \frac{14}{4} =$

10. $\frac{7}{4} \times \frac{17}{6} =$

11. $3\frac{2}{3} \times 2 =$

16. $2\frac{1}{3} \times \frac{16}{12} =$

12. $3\frac{3}{5} \times 2\frac{1}{10} =$

17. $3\frac{3}{5} \times 2\frac{2}{3} =$

13. $3\frac{6}{8} \times 1\frac{5}{6} =$

18. $3\frac{1}{2} \times 3\frac{1}{5} =$

14. $\frac{11}{4} \times 1\frac{1}{10} =$

19. $\frac{9}{5} \times \frac{15}{6} =$

15. $2\frac{4}{6} \times 1\frac{4}{7} =$

20. $10\frac{4}{9} \times 1\frac{5}{10} =$

DIVISION OF FRACTIONS Practice Set 1

Write answer as a mixed number in simplest form.

1. $\frac{3}{8} \div \frac{1}{4} =$

2. $\frac{4}{5} \div \frac{4}{7} =$

3. $\frac{2}{5} \div \frac{4}{9} =$

4. $\frac{8}{9} \div \frac{2}{3} =$

5. $\frac{1}{8} \div \frac{1}{5} =$

6. $\frac{15}{18} \div \frac{5}{6} =$

7. $\frac{1}{9} \div \frac{3}{10} =$

8. $\frac{4}{7} \div \frac{4}{5} =$

9. $\frac{8}{12} \div \frac{4}{18} =$

10. $\frac{3}{8} \div \frac{9}{10} =$

11. $\frac{2}{9} \div \frac{1}{3} =$

12. $\frac{3}{4} \div \frac{5}{20} =$

13. $\frac{2}{6} \div \frac{2}{5} =$

14. $\frac{15}{16} \div \frac{3}{6} =$

15. $\frac{15}{18} \div \frac{2}{3} =$

16. $\frac{2}{6} \div \frac{5}{15} =$

17. $\frac{20}{60} \div \frac{40}{80} =$

18. $\frac{24}{30} \div \frac{5}{6} =$

19. $\frac{4}{7} \div \frac{35}{49} =$

20. $\frac{15}{45} \div \frac{2}{3} =$

DIVISION OF FRACTIONS Practice Set 2

Write answer as a mixed number in simplest form.

1. $\frac{3}{4} \div \frac{1}{2} =$

2. $\frac{6}{7} \div \frac{6}{9} =$

3. $\frac{2}{6} \div \frac{8}{9} =$

4. $\frac{9}{10} \div \frac{3}{8} =$

5. $\frac{1}{7} \div \frac{1}{3} =$

6. $\frac{12}{16} \div \frac{4}{12} =$

7. $\frac{1}{8} \div \frac{3}{5} =$

8. $\frac{5}{6} \div \frac{7}{10} =$

9. $\frac{3}{5} \div \frac{5}{15} =$

10. $\frac{5}{6} \div \frac{10}{18} =$

11. $\frac{1}{2} \div \frac{5}{6} =$

12. $\frac{2}{3} \div \frac{7}{12} =$

13. $\frac{5}{8} \div \frac{5}{7} =$

14. $\frac{18}{20} \div \frac{3}{8} =$

15. $\frac{14}{16} \div \frac{4}{6} =$

16. $\frac{3}{8} \div \frac{5}{12} =$

17. $\frac{30}{90} \div \frac{40}{60} =$

18. $\frac{39}{45} \div \frac{3}{9} =$

19. $\frac{3}{6} \div \frac{48}{54} =$

20. $\frac{36}{48} \div \frac{3}{4} =$

DIVISION OF MIXED/IMPROPER/WHOLE Practice Set 1

Write answer as a mixed number in simplest form.

1. $2\frac{7}{10} \div \frac{2}{5} =$

6. $1\frac{2}{3} \div 1\frac{3}{6} =$

2. $1\frac{2}{5} \div \frac{1}{4} =$

7. $\frac{6}{10} \div 2\frac{1}{3} = \frac{6}{10} \times \frac{3}{9} = \frac{18}{90} = \frac{9}{35}$

3. $2\frac{5}{8} \div 1\frac{1}{2} =$

8. $2\frac{6}{9} \div 3\frac{1}{2} = \frac{24}{9} \times \frac{2}{7} = \frac{48}{63} = \frac{16}{21}$

4. $1\frac{2}{6} \div \frac{1}{9} =$

9. $1\frac{3}{4} \div 1\frac{2}{7} = \frac{7}{4} \times \frac{7}{9} = \frac{49}{36} = 1\frac{13}{36}$

5. $\frac{4}{9} \div 2\frac{1}{3} =$

10. $4\frac{1}{2} \div 4\frac{7}{9} = \frac{9}{2} \times \frac{9}{43} = \frac{81}{86}$

11. $12 \div \frac{10}{12} =$

16. $20 \div \frac{20}{25} =$

12. $14 \div \frac{20}{7} =$

17. $5 \div \frac{20}{25} =$

13. $\frac{4}{10} \div 5 =$

18. $8 \div \frac{4}{7} =$

14. $\frac{6}{9} \div 3 =$ $\frac{6}{9} \times \frac{1}{3} = \frac{2}{9}$

$$\begin{array}{r} 49 \\ \times 5 \\ \hline 95 \\ 19 \\ \hline 285 \end{array}$$

19. $19 \div \frac{10}{15} =$ $\frac{19}{1} \times \frac{15}{10} = \frac{57}{2} = 28\frac{1}{2}$

15. $12 \div \frac{3}{4} =$ $\frac{12}{1} \times \frac{4}{3} = \frac{16}{1}$

20. $\frac{6}{7} \div 42 =$ $\frac{6}{7} \times \frac{1}{42} = \frac{1}{49}$

DIVISION OF MIXED/IMPROPER/WHOLE Practice Set 2

Write answer as a mixed number in simplest form.

1. $\frac{2}{9} \div 4 =$

2. $\frac{2}{3} \div 2 =$

3. $3 \div \frac{4}{6} =$

4. $\frac{4}{5} \div 5 =$

5. $\frac{7}{10} \div 3 =$

6. $4 \div \frac{3}{8} =$

7. $3 \div \frac{7}{8} =$

8. $5 \div \frac{2}{9} =$

9. $8 \div \frac{4}{6} =$

10. $\frac{3}{7} \div 6 =$

150

11. $3\frac{2}{6} \div 2\frac{4}{10} =$

12. $4\frac{1}{8} \div 3\frac{2}{3} =$

13. $5\frac{2}{10} \div 5\frac{2}{4} =$

14. $9\frac{2}{4} \div 6\frac{5}{15} =$

15. $39\frac{1}{2} \div 2\frac{3}{9} =$

16. $7\frac{1}{3} \div 1\frac{4}{12} =$

17. $7\frac{2}{3} \div 4\frac{6}{9} =$

18. $22\frac{2}{4} \div 2\frac{3}{12} =$

19. $16\frac{1}{2} \div 1\frac{3}{8} =$

20. $9\frac{2}{3} \div 6\frac{11}{12} =$

DIVISION OF MIXED/IMPROPER/WHOLE Practice Set 3

Write answer as a mixed number in simplest form.

1. $1\frac{5}{8} \div \frac{3}{4} =$

2. $2\frac{2}{9} \div \frac{5}{7} =$

3. $2\frac{5}{6} \div 1\frac{2}{3} =$

4. $1\frac{1}{8} \div \frac{9}{10} =$

5. $\frac{3}{12} \div 2\frac{1}{4} =$

6. $1\frac{3}{4} \div 1\frac{3}{8} =$

7. $3\frac{2}{8} \div 4\frac{1}{3} =$

8. $4\frac{1}{7} \div 5\frac{4}{5} =$

9. $5\frac{4}{8} \div 5\frac{1}{2} =$

10. $\frac{5}{6} \div 2\frac{2}{5} =$

11. $10 \div \frac{9}{10} =$

12. $4 \div \frac{6}{8} =$

13. $\frac{10}{12} \div 5 =$

14. $\frac{3}{18} \div 9 =$

15. $15 \div \frac{3}{5} =$

16. $25 \div \frac{25}{30} =$

17. $6 \div \frac{24}{36} =$

18. $8 \div \frac{3}{5} =$

19. $\frac{8}{9} \div 72 =$

20. $23 \div \frac{13}{52} =$

DIVISION OF MIXED/IMPROPER/WHOLE Practice Set 4

Write answer as a mixed number in simplest form.

1. $\frac{3}{8} \div 3 =$

2. $\frac{1}{3} \div 4 =$

3. $2 \div \frac{3}{4} =$

4. $\frac{3}{4} \div 4 =$

5. $\frac{5}{8} \div 3 =$

6. $5 \div \frac{7}{10} =$

7. $2 \div \frac{6}{7} =$

8. $7 \div \frac{3}{8} =$

9. $6 \div \frac{3}{5} =$

10. $\frac{4}{7} \div 8 =$

11. $2\frac{5}{8} \div 3\frac{3}{5} =$

12. $3\frac{3}{4} \div 2\frac{3}{6} =$

13. $2\frac{3}{4} \div 2\frac{6}{7} =$

14. $9\frac{1}{3} \div 2\frac{3}{9} =$

15. $21\frac{1}{4} \div 2\frac{4}{8} =$

16. $6\frac{6}{9} \div 1\frac{5}{15} =$

17. $8\frac{1}{2} \div 5\frac{4}{6} =$

18. $15\frac{1}{3} \div 3\frac{10}{12} =$

19. $12\frac{1}{4} \div 2\frac{3}{16} =$

20. $7\frac{1}{7} \div 3\frac{7}{21} =$

COMPARING FRACTIONS Practice Set 1

For each pair of fractions, circle which is greater.

1. $\frac{1}{6}$ or $\frac{1}{5}$

2. $\frac{3}{10}$ or $\frac{1}{5}$

3. $\frac{4}{8}$ or $\frac{4}{6}$

4. $\frac{3}{4}$ or $\frac{5}{6}$

5. $\frac{7}{10}$ or $\frac{10}{15}$

6. $\frac{2}{11}$ or $\frac{3}{12}$

7. $\frac{7}{12}$ or $\frac{3}{5}$

8. $1\frac{1}{2}$ or $\frac{6}{3}$

9. $1\frac{7}{8}$ or $\frac{7}{4}$

10. $1\frac{3}{6}$ or $\frac{10}{6}$

11. $\frac{4}{3}$ or $1\frac{2}{8}$

12. $\frac{11}{5}$ or $2\frac{1}{10}$

13. $\frac{10}{8}$ or $1\frac{1}{5}$

14. $\frac{16}{5}$ or $\frac{19}{6}$

15. $\frac{8}{7}$ or $\frac{11}{9}$

16. $\frac{16}{7}$ or $\frac{9}{4}$

17. $\frac{16}{3}$ or $\frac{11}{2}$

18. $\frac{13}{4}$ or $\frac{20}{6}$

19. $\frac{22}{18}$ or $\frac{24}{20}$

20. $\frac{27}{5}$ or $\frac{38}{7}$

COMPARING FRACTIONS Practice Set 2

For each pair of fractions, circle which is greater.

1. $\frac{1}{4}$ or $\frac{1}{5}$

2. $\frac{1}{4}$ or $\frac{3}{8}$

3. $\frac{5}{7}$ or $\frac{5}{9}$

4. $\frac{8}{9}$ or $\frac{7}{8}$

5. $\frac{13}{16}$ or $\frac{10}{12}$

6. $\frac{3}{13}$ or $\frac{4}{14}$

7. $\frac{1}{7}$ or $\frac{2}{15}$

8. $\frac{16}{9}$ or $1\frac{5}{7}$

9. $\frac{5}{3}$ or $1\frac{5}{6}$

10. $\frac{17}{9}$ or $1\frac{7}{9}$

11. $\frac{8}{5}$ or $1\frac{4}{6}$

12. $\frac{15}{6}$ or $2\frac{5}{12}$

13. $1\frac{1}{3}$ or $\frac{11}{8}$

14. $\frac{22}{7}$ or $\frac{25}{8}$

15. $\frac{13}{10}$ or $\frac{11}{8}$

16. $\frac{11}{8}$ or $\frac{4}{3}$

17. $\frac{24}{5}$ or $\frac{29}{6}$

18. $\frac{26}{7}$ or $\frac{31}{9}$

19. $\frac{22}{12}$ or $\frac{18}{10}$

20. $\frac{35}{6}$ or $\frac{41}{7}$

COMPARING FRACTIONS Practice Set 3

For each pair of fractions, circle which is greater.

1. $\frac{1}{7}$ *or* $\frac{1}{8}$

2. $\frac{3}{12}$ *or* $\frac{1}{6}$

3. $\frac{2}{5}$ *or* $\frac{2}{3}$

4. $\frac{6}{7}$ *or* $\frac{7}{8}$

5. $\frac{7}{9}$ *or* $\frac{9}{12}$

6. $\frac{9}{15}$ *or* $\frac{8}{14}$

7. $\frac{4}{9}$ *or* $\frac{2}{5}$

8. $1\frac{3}{4}$ *or* $\frac{11}{6}$

9. $1\frac{9}{10}$ *or* $\frac{9}{5}$

10. $\frac{12}{8}$ *or* $1\frac{3}{8}$

11. $\frac{7}{4}$ *or* $1\frac{5}{7}$

12. $\frac{8}{3}$ *or* $2\frac{5}{6}$

13. $1\frac{1}{4}$ *or* $\frac{12}{10}$

14. $\frac{19}{6}$ *or* $\frac{22}{7}$

15. $\frac{10}{8}$ *or* $\frac{7}{6}$

16. $\frac{9}{5}$ *or* $\frac{16}{9}$

17. $\frac{19}{3}$ *or* $\frac{25}{4}$

18. $\frac{31}{10}$ *or* $\frac{25}{8}$

19. $\frac{26}{14}$ *or* $\frac{42}{24}$

20. $\frac{41}{7}$ *or* $\frac{53}{9}$

COMPARING FRACTIONS Practice Set 4

For each pair of fractions, circle which is greater.

1. $\frac{1}{9}$ *or* $\frac{1}{8}$

2. $\frac{3}{14}$ *or* $\frac{1}{7}$

3. $\frac{3}{4}$ *or* $\frac{3}{6}$

4. $\frac{4}{5}$ *or* $\frac{5}{6}$

5. $\frac{5}{6}$ *or* $\frac{6}{8}$

6. $\frac{5}{12}$ *or* $\frac{6}{13}$

7. $\frac{6}{11}$ *or* $\frac{5}{9}$

8. $1\frac{2}{3}$ *or* $\frac{8}{5}$

9. $1\frac{8}{12}$ *or* $1\frac{8}{16}$

10. $1\frac{5}{7}$ *or* $\frac{13}{7}$

11. $\frac{9}{6}$ *or* $1\frac{5}{9}$

12. $\frac{11}{4}$ *or* $2\frac{7}{8}$

13. $\frac{6}{5}$ *or* $1\frac{1}{6}$

14. $\frac{25}{8}$ *or* $\frac{28}{9}$

15. $\frac{8}{7}$ *or* $\frac{6}{5}$

16. $\frac{18}{10}$ *or* $\frac{11}{6}$

17. $\frac{21}{4}$ *or* $\frac{26}{5}$

18. $\frac{19}{5}$ *or* $\frac{27}{7}$

19. $\frac{38}{22}$ *or* $\frac{28}{16}$

20. $\frac{45}{8}$ *or* $\frac{28}{5}$

ORDERING FRACTIONS Practice Set 1

1. Order from least to greatest. $\frac{1}{6}, \frac{2}{3}, \frac{1}{2}, \frac{3}{4}$

2. Circle the largest fraction. $\frac{1}{4}, \frac{2}{5}, \frac{5}{8}, \frac{4}{7}$

3. Order from least to greatest. $\frac{2}{6}, \frac{2}{9}, \frac{3}{7}, \frac{5}{10}$

4. Circle the largest fraction. $\frac{1}{9}, \frac{4}{6}, \frac{6}{12}, \frac{1}{3}$

5. Circle the smallest fraction. $\frac{7}{8}, \frac{1}{3}, \frac{4}{6}, \frac{1}{2}$

6. Which fraction is in between $\frac{1}{2}$ and $\frac{7}{10}$?
   A. $\frac{1}{4}$
   B. $\frac{3}{6}$
   C. $\frac{5}{8}$
   D. $\frac{8}{10}$

7. Order from least to greatest. $\frac{6}{8}, \frac{8}{9}, \frac{2}{5}, \frac{3}{10}$

8. Circle the largest fraction. $\frac{7}{9}, \frac{2}{3}, \frac{11}{12}, \frac{5}{6}$

9. Order from least to greatest. $\frac{5}{6}, \frac{7}{8}, \frac{6}{7}, \frac{4}{5}$

10. Circle the smallest fraction. $\frac{6}{5}, \frac{4}{3}, 1\frac{1}{7}, 1\frac{1}{2}$

11. Order from least to greatest. $2\frac{1}{4}, \frac{11}{5}, 2, \frac{21}{10}$

12. Circle the smallest fraction. $\frac{7}{4}, \frac{8}{7}, 1\frac{3}{14}, \frac{15}{8}$

13. Order from least to greatest. $\frac{22}{9}, \frac{26}{9}, \frac{7}{3}, 2\frac{5}{6}$

14. Circle the largest fraction. $2\frac{3}{4}, \frac{22}{10}, 2\frac{1}{2}, \frac{12}{5}$

15. Which fraction is in between $\frac{16}{5}$ and $\frac{33}{10}$?
    A. $3\frac{1}{5}$
    B. $3\frac{1}{3}$
    C. $\frac{19}{6}$
    D. $\frac{13}{4}$

16. Circle the largest fraction. $4\frac{1}{3}, \frac{29}{7}, \frac{41}{10}, 4\frac{1}{5},$

17. Order from least to greatest. $-\frac{17}{5}, -\frac{23}{6}, -3\frac{5}{8}, -\frac{34}{9}$

18. Circle the smallest fraction. $-4\frac{1}{6}, -\frac{33}{8}, -4\frac{1}{9}, -\frac{17}{4}$

19. Order from least to greatest. $\frac{34}{6}, \frac{43}{8}, 5\frac{2}{9}, 5\frac{6}{7}$

20. Circle the largest fraction. $\frac{77}{10}, \frac{37}{5}, \frac{68}{9}, 7\frac{3}{8}$

ORDERING FRACTIONS Practice Set 2

1. Order from least to greatest. $\frac{1}{3}, \frac{1}{2}, \frac{1}{4}, \frac{2}{5}$

2. Which fraction is between $\frac{1}{8}$ and $\frac{3}{8}$?
   - A. $\frac{1}{5}$
   - B. $\frac{3}{7}$
   - C. $\frac{3}{4}$
   - D. $\frac{5}{6}$

3. Circle the largest fraction. $\frac{2}{7}, \frac{4}{6}, \frac{3}{5}, \frac{4}{9}$

4. Circle the smallest fraction. $\frac{5}{12}, \frac{2}{9}, \frac{1}{3}, \frac{1}{6}$

5. Order from least to greatest. $\frac{2}{8}, \frac{3}{5}, \frac{3}{4}, \frac{2}{6}$

6. Circle the largest fraction. $\frac{3}{9}, \frac{2}{7}, \frac{2}{10}, \frac{2}{8}$

7. Order from least to greatest. $\frac{3}{8}, \frac{1}{2}, \frac{2}{9}, \frac{1}{5}$

8. Circle the smallest fraction. $\frac{2}{7}, \frac{1}{4}, \frac{3}{8}, \frac{2}{6}$

9. Order from least to greatest. $\frac{3}{5}, \frac{4}{8}, \frac{4}{6}, \frac{3}{7}$

10. Circle the largest fraction. $\frac{6}{5}, \frac{10}{9}, 1\frac{1}{6}, 1\frac{1}{7}$

11. Order from least to greatest. $\frac{11}{9}, 2, \frac{11}{4}, 2\frac{1}{6}$

12. Circle the smallest fraction. $-\frac{8}{7}, \frac{11}{9}, -1\frac{2}{12}, \frac{7}{5}$

13. Which fraction is between $2\frac{2}{5}$ and $\frac{13}{5}$?
    A. $\frac{14}{6}$
    B. $\frac{23}{9}$
    C. $\frac{8}{3}$
    D. $2\frac{7}{9}$

14. Order from least to greatest. $\frac{16}{6}, 2\frac{1}{9}, \frac{18}{8}, 2\frac{4}{5}$

15. Order from least to greatest. $-3\frac{2}{4}, -3\frac{3}{5}, -\frac{19}{6}, -\frac{11}{3}$

16. Circle the largest fraction. $4\frac{1}{6}, \frac{35}{9}, \frac{31}{8}, 4\frac{1}{4}$

17. Circle the smallest fraction. $\frac{28}{9}, \frac{25}{7}, 3\frac{2}{8}, \frac{29}{6}$

18. Circle the smallest fraction. $4\frac{3}{4}, 4\frac{3}{7}, \frac{27}{6}, \frac{34}{8}$

19. Order from least to greatest. $5\frac{8}{10}, \frac{23}{4}, 5\frac{7}{8}, \frac{35}{6}$

20. Circle the largest fraction. $\frac{34}{5}, \frac{66}{9}, 7\frac{2}{9}, 7\frac{3}{8}$

ORDERING FRACTIONS Practice Set 3

1. Order from least to greatest. $\frac{3}{4}, \frac{3}{6}, \frac{2}{5}, \frac{5}{7}$

2. Circle the largest fraction. $\frac{2}{5}, \frac{5}{6}, \frac{3}{4}, \frac{1}{3}$

3. Order from least to greatest. $\frac{6}{9}, \frac{3}{10}, \frac{4}{5}, \frac{4}{8}$

4. Circle the largest fraction. $\frac{2}{12}, \frac{2}{3}, \frac{5}{9}, \frac{3}{6}$

5. Order from least to greatest. $\frac{6}{8}, \frac{4}{7}, \frac{4}{5}, \frac{2}{6}$

6. Circle the smallest fraction. $\frac{1}{2}, \frac{4}{10}, \frac{5}{6}, \frac{6}{9}$

7. Order from least to greatest. $\frac{3}{4}, \frac{2}{7}, \frac{3}{6}, \frac{1}{3}$

8. Circle the smallest fraction. $\frac{4}{9}, \frac{2}{3}, \frac{5}{6}, \frac{6}{12}$

9. Which fraction is between $\frac{7}{10}$ and $\frac{4}{5}$?
    A. $\frac{5}{7}$
    B. $\frac{4}{6}$
    C. $\frac{6}{10}$
    D. $\frac{4}{9}$

10. Circle the largest fraction. $1\frac{1}{6}, 1\frac{1}{10}, \frac{9}{8}, \frac{5}{4}$

164

11. Order from least to greatest. $2, \frac{14}{5}, \frac{17}{9}, 2\frac{2}{8}$

12. Circle the smallest fraction. $1\frac{6}{8}, \frac{11}{6}, \frac{15}{9}, 1\frac{4}{10}$

13. Which fraction is between $\frac{23}{10}$ and $2\frac{2}{5}$?

    A. $2\frac{1}{10}$

    B. $\frac{9}{4}$

    C. $\frac{19}{8}$

    D. $\frac{15}{6}$

14. Circle the largest fraction. $\frac{16}{6}, 2\frac{1}{3}, \frac{19}{9}, 2\frac{4}{7}$

15. Order from least to greatest. $\frac{22}{7}, \frac{13}{4}, 3\frac{1}{5}, 3\frac{5}{6}$

16. Circle the smallest fraction. $\frac{14}{3}, \frac{34}{7}, 4\frac{3}{8}, 4\frac{3}{5}$

17. Order from least to greatest. $-\frac{15}{4}, -3\frac{7}{10}, -\frac{18}{5}, -\frac{11}{3}$

18. Circle the smallest fraction. $\frac{14}{3}, 4\frac{2}{9}, \frac{24}{6}, 4\frac{1}{2}$

19. Order from least to greatest. $5\frac{3}{9}, \frac{38}{7}, 5\frac{2}{3}, \frac{27}{5}$

20. Circle the largest fraction. $-7\frac{5}{6}, -\frac{68}{9}, -\frac{30}{4}, -7\frac{4}{7}$

ORDERING FRACTIONS Practice Set 4

1. Order from least to greatest. $\frac{1}{2}, \frac{3}{4}, \frac{3}{5}, \frac{2}{6}$

2. Circle the smallest fraction. $\frac{2}{5}, \frac{1}{6}, \frac{3}{9}, \frac{2}{8}$

3. Order from least to greatest. $\frac{3}{4}, \frac{5}{6}, \frac{1}{3}, \frac{5}{9}$

4. Circle the largest fraction. $\frac{7}{10}, \frac{4}{6}, \frac{6}{8}, \frac{6}{10}$

5. Which fraction is between $\frac{1}{2}$ and $\frac{7}{10}$?
   A. $\frac{2}{8}$
   B. $\frac{2}{6}$
   C. $\frac{2}{3}$
   D. $\frac{3}{4}$

6. Circle the smallest fraction. $\frac{3}{5}, \frac{4}{8}, \frac{2}{6}, \frac{7}{9}$

7. Order from least to greatest. $\frac{2}{4}, \frac{6}{8}, \frac{4}{10}, \frac{7}{9}$

8. Circle the largest fraction. $\frac{4}{6}, \frac{2}{9}, \frac{1}{3}, \frac{9}{12}$

9. Order from least to greatest. $\frac{3}{7}, \frac{6}{9}, \frac{4}{10}, \frac{5}{8}$

10. Circle the smallest fraction. $1\frac{1}{5}, \frac{9}{8}, \frac{7}{6}, 1\frac{1}{9}$

11. Order from least to greatest. $\frac{14}{8}, 2, \frac{11}{6}, \frac{19}{9}$

12. Circle the largest fraction. $1\frac{6}{8}, \frac{11}{6}, \frac{15}{9}, \frac{19}{15}$

13. Order from least to greatest. $\frac{13}{6}, 1\frac{4}{12}, \frac{13}{12}, \frac{17}{8}$

14. Circle the smallest fraction. $\frac{27}{10}, 2\frac{3}{5}, 2\frac{3}{4}, \frac{23}{8}$

15. Which fraction is between $-\frac{15}{4}$ and $-3\frac{1}{4}$?
    A. $-3\frac{1}{9}$
    B. $-\frac{25}{8}$
    C. $-\frac{22}{6}$
    D. $-3\frac{6}{7}$

16. Circle the largest fraction. $\frac{33}{7}, \frac{39}{9}, 4\frac{4}{6}, 4\frac{3}{4}$

17. Order from least to greatest. $\frac{27}{8}, \frac{10}{3}, 3\frac{3}{6}, \frac{17}{5}$

18. Circle the smallest fraction. $\frac{29}{7}, 4\frac{1}{7}, \frac{13}{3}, 4\frac{2}{5}$

19. Circle the largest fraction. $-5\frac{3}{8}, -5\frac{4}{6}, -\frac{39}{7}, -\frac{45}{8}$

20. Order from least to greatest. $\frac{39}{5}, \frac{23}{3}, 7\frac{4}{8}, 7\frac{6}{10}$

FRACTION APPLICATIONS Practice Set 1

1. All of the following are equal to $\frac{2}{3}$ except?

   A. $\frac{6}{9}$
   B. $\frac{30}{60}$
   C. $\frac{24}{36}$
   D. $\frac{14}{21}$

2. If $\frac{3}{7}$ of a number is 42, what is the number?

   A. 18
   B. 24
   C. 84
   D. 98

3. Which of the following is NOT equal to a whole number?

   A. $\frac{36}{8}$
   B. $5 \times \frac{20}{50}$
   C. $\frac{24}{3} \div 8$
   D. $\frac{4}{7} \div \frac{2}{14}$

4. Simplify $\dfrac{9}{6\frac{2}{3}}$

5. Which is the largest fraction?

   A. $2\frac{5}{6}$
   B. $\frac{5}{3}$
   C. $\frac{23}{8}$
   D. $2\frac{5}{9}$

6. Maria donated $\frac{2}{5}$ of her savings to the American Red Cross and $\frac{1}{7}$ to the World Wildlife Fund. What fraction of her savings did she have left?

7. If two-thirds of a number is equal to 24, what is one-half of the number?

   A. 18
   B. 24
   C. 36
   D. 48

168

8. Shannon spent $\frac{3}{8}$ of the day at school and $\frac{2}{6}$ of the day sleeping. How much time did she spend on other activities?

    A. 4 hours
    B. 5 hours
    C. 7 hours
    D. 9 hours

9. What is the quotient of $3\frac{3}{7}$ and $2\frac{4}{7}$?

10. Jeffrey spent $1\frac{1}{6}$ hours Saturday morning mowing the lawn. If he spent another $2\frac{3}{5}$ hours in the afternoon finishing up, how many hours in total did spend mowing the lawn?

11. $\frac{7}{12}$ is less than?

    A. $\frac{1}{2}$
    B. $\frac{3}{8}$
    C. $\frac{5}{11}$
    D. $\frac{3}{5}$

12. What is one-third of two-sevenths?

13. There are three times as many children as parents at an amusement park. If one-third of the children are on the merry-go-round, and the total number of parents at the amusement park is 20, how many children are not on the merry-go-round?

    A. 20 children
    B. 40 children
    C. 60 children
    D. 80 children

14. A bus contains 18 passengers. If at the next stop two-thirds of the passengers get off, and ten more passengers get on the bus, how many passengers will now be in the bus?

    A. 16 passengers
    B. 18 passengers
    C. 22 passengers
    D. 24 passengers

15. Jocelyn wants to buy a new car which costs $30,000. Her parents contribute $\frac{1}{5}$ of the cost of the car, and she contributes $\frac{2}{3}$ of the cost of the car. The rest comes from a loan she takes from the bank. How much in loans did she get from the bank to cover the cost of the new car?
    A. $4,000
    B. $5,000
    C. $6,000
    D. $8,000

16. $7\frac{1}{5}$ gallons of milk are divided equally into 9 containers. How many gallons of milk are in each container?
    A. $\frac{4}{9}$ gallon
    B. $\frac{3}{5}$ gallon
    C. $\frac{4}{5}$ gallon
    D. $\frac{5}{9}$ gallon

17. At an elementary school, $\frac{4}{9}$ of the students are girls, and $\frac{3}{10}$ of the girls are in the drama club. If the school has a total of 450 students, how many girls are in the drama club?

18. Simplify $\dfrac{\frac{1}{5} + \frac{3}{10}}{\frac{5}{8} - \frac{1}{4}}$
    A. $\frac{1}{2}$
    B. $\frac{3}{8}$
    C. $\frac{3}{5}$
    D. $\frac{4}{3}$

19. If $\frac{a}{4} = \frac{b}{8} = 4$, what is the value of $a + b$?
    A. 16
    B. 48
    C. 56
    D. 64

20. Woodside Elementary needs to sell 300 raffle tickets for a charity event. In the first month, they manage to sell $\frac{2}{3}$ of the tickets. In the second month, they manage to sell $\frac{2}{5}$ of the remaining tickets. How many tickets are still unsold after the two months?
    A. 20 tickets
    B. 40 tickets
    C. 60 tickets
    D. 100 tickets

FRACTION APPLICATIONS Practice Set 2

1. All of the following are equal to $\frac{3}{4}$ except?
   - A. $\frac{12}{15}$
   - B. $\frac{45}{60}$
   - C. $\frac{66}{88}$
   - D. $\frac{75}{100}$

2. Which is the largest fraction?
   - A. $\frac{11}{3}$
   - B. $3\frac{3}{5}$
   - C. $3\frac{3}{4}$
   - D. $\frac{18}{7}$

3. Which of the following is NOT equal to a whole number?
   - A. $\frac{48}{6}$
   - B. $5 \times \frac{5}{10}$
   - C. $\frac{36}{4} \div 3$
   - D. $\frac{10}{3} \div \frac{5}{9}$

4. If $\frac{3}{8}$ of a number is 39, what is the number?
   - A. 104
   - B. 68
   - C. 52
   - D. 36

5. Simplify $\dfrac{7}{6\frac{1}{8}}$

6. If $\frac{3}{4} \times \theta = 48$, what is $\frac{3}{8} \times \theta$?
   - A. 16
   - B. 18
   - C. 24
   - D. 32

7. What is three-fourths of one-sixth?

8. Marcus is organizing his vinyl collection into alphabetical order. On the first day, he manages to finish $\frac{2}{5}$ of his collection and finishes another $\frac{3}{8}$ of his collection on the next. What fraction of Marcus' collection is still out of order?

9. Hanna receives $\frac{2}{5}$ of all her phone calls from her mother and $\frac{1}{4}$ from her best friend. If she receives 360 calls, how many of her phone calls are from everyone else?
   A. 90 calls
   B. 126 calls
   C. 144 calls
   D. 234 calls

10. $\frac{7}{9}$ is less than which of the following?
    A. $\frac{4}{5}$
    B. $\frac{3}{4}$
    C. $\frac{2}{3}$
    D. $\frac{5}{7}$

11. What is the quotient of $3\frac{5}{8}$ and $3\frac{2}{8}$?

12. Bill tutors for $1\frac{1}{4}$ hours on Monday and $2\frac{2}{9}$ hours on Thursday. How many hours total has he tutored this week?

13. The temperature in Charlottesville is 72°F. If the temperature drops by one-sixth overnight and then slowly rises again 16°F in the morning, what is the temperature now?
    A. 74°F
    B. 76°F
    C. 78°F
    D. 88°F

14. At Matoaka Elementary, there are four times as many right-handed students as left-handed students. If two-fifths of the right-handed students play an instrument, and the total number of left-handed children is 40, how many right-handed children do not play an instrument?
    A. 64 students
    B. 96 students
    C. 144 students
    D. 160 students

15. At the pretzel shop, $\frac{5}{8}$ of customers order pretzels, $\frac{2}{11}$ of which are cinnamon pretzels. If there are 440 customers, how many cinnamon pretzels will be sold?

172

16. A popular taco stand services 45,000 customers a year. One-third of the customers request extra condiments, while three-fifths ask for the removal of condiments. If the rest of the customers do not make any special requests, what is the exact number of those customers?
    A. 1,000 customers
    B. 3,000 customers
    C. 5,000 customers
    D. 15,000 customers

17. Simplify $\dfrac{\frac{1}{6}+\frac{5}{12}}{\frac{5}{6}-\frac{1}{3}}$
    A. $\dfrac{7}{24}$
    B. $1\dfrac{1}{4}$
    C. $1\dfrac{1}{6}$
    D. $1\dfrac{2}{3}$

18. Brooke has run for $9\dfrac{3}{8}$ miles in 15 equal parts over the week. How many miles does she run at one time?
    A. $\dfrac{5}{8}$ miles
    B. $\dfrac{3}{8}$ miles
    C. $\dfrac{6}{8}$ miles
    D. $\dfrac{3}{16}$ miles

19. If $\dfrac{a}{6}=\dfrac{b}{9}=5$, what is the value of $a+b$?
    A. 270
    B. 75
    C. 54
    D. 30

20. Percy received 420 grams of holiday chocolate. He eats $\dfrac{3}{5}$ of his total stash in the first week and $\dfrac{1}{6}$ of the remaining candy in the second week. How many grams of chocolate remain after the two weeks?
    A. 52 grams
    B. 70 gams
    C. 98 grams
    D. 140 grams

FRACTION APPLICATIONS Practice Set 3

1. Which of the following is NOT equal to a whole number?
   A. $\frac{63}{9}$
   B. $3 \times \frac{14}{42}$
   C. $\frac{45}{3} \div 5$
   D. $\frac{6}{8} \div \frac{3}{18}$

2. Which is the largest fraction?
   A. $\frac{11}{4}$
   B. $2\frac{4}{6}$
   C. $\frac{25}{9}$
   D. $2\frac{5}{8}$

3. All of the following are equal to $\frac{3}{6}$ except?
   A. $\frac{1}{2}$
   B. $\frac{9}{18}$
   C. $\frac{32}{64}$
   D. $\frac{75}{125}$

4. If $\frac{5}{9}$ of a number is 75, what is the number?
   A. 150
   B. 135
   C. 125
   D. 90

5. Simplify $\frac{8}{4\frac{4}{7}}$

6. Mr. Bogosian brings a large bag of candy for his students. He shares $\frac{1}{4}$ of the candy with his first class and $\frac{3}{5}$ of the candy with his second class. What fraction of the candy is left for Mr. Bogosian to take home?

7. What is the quotient of $2\frac{4}{6}$ and $3\frac{2}{6}$?

8. If $\frac{5}{6} \times \theta = 30$, what is $\frac{2}{9} \times \theta$?
   A. 6
   B. 8
   C. 12
   D. 36

9. A car collector leaves behind $\frac{1}{4}$ of her cars to her husband, $\frac{2}{5}$ to her friend, and the rest to her only child. If she has 40 cars in her collection, how many cars are for her child?
    A. 7 cars
    B. 13 cars
    C. 14 cars
    D. 26 cars

10. $\frac{8}{14}$ is greater than which of the following?
    A. $\frac{5}{8}$
    B. $\frac{3}{4}$
    C. $\frac{5}{9}$
    D. $\frac{6}{10}$

11. What is one-fourth of three-eighths?

12. Khan consumes $1\frac{1}{8}$ liters of water in the morning. If he drinks $2\frac{5}{6}$ liters in the afternoon, how many liters of water has he had to drink so far?

13. A party sandwich is $5\frac{3}{5}$ feet long and will be cut into 8 equal pieces. How long will each piece be?
    A. $\frac{7}{10}$ feet
    B. $\frac{3}{10}$ feet
    C. $\frac{3}{5}$ feet
    D. $\frac{3}{8}$ feet

14. Watching television, Barney calculates that $\frac{3}{7}$ of all the channels are broadcasted by cable networks, $\frac{5}{9}$ of which are playing commercials at any given time. If there are 315 channels, how many cable networks are playing commercials?

15. Martin's water bottle contains 560 mL of water. If he drinks three-fifths before he adds another 280 mL, how much water will be in the bottle?
    A. 224 mL
    B. 336 mL
    C. 504 mL
    D. 616 mL

16. If $\frac{a}{12} = \frac{b}{5} = 3$, what is the value of $a + b$?
    A. 17
    B. 20
    C. 51
    D. 72

17. In a peculiar book, there are six times as many words as there are punctuation marks. If one-fourth of the words start with a vowel, and the total number of punctuation marks is 14, how many words do not start with a vowel?
    A. 21 words
    B. 30 words
    C. 56 words
    D. 63 words

18. After following his diet for ten days, Steve notes that he has consumed 22,000 kilocalories. If $\frac{14}{40}$ of his total calories are from protein, $\frac{11}{20}$ from carbohydrates, and the rest from fats, how many kilocalories were from fats?
    A. 1,210 kcal
    B. 2,200 kcal
    C. 7,700 kcal
    D. 12,100 kcal

19. Gordon wins $420,000 from the local lottery. He spends $\frac{1}{6}$ of his fortune on a car the first month, invests $\frac{3}{4}$ of the remaining money in a new business, and decides to spend the rest on vacation. How much money does he have for vacation?
    A. $85,000
    B. $87,500
    C. $92,500
    D. $335,000

20. Simplify $\dfrac{\frac{1}{4}+\frac{3}{8}}{\frac{7}{9}-\frac{2}{3}}$
    A. $5\frac{5}{8}$
    B. $\frac{5}{18}$
    C. $\frac{5}{72}$
    D. $5\frac{5}{9}$

FRACTION APPLICATIONS Practice Set 4

1. If $\frac{5}{6}$ of a number is 80, what is the number?
   - A.   96
   - B.   92
   - C.   64
   - D.   48

2. Simplify $\dfrac{5}{4\frac{2}{7}}$

3. All of the following are equal to $\frac{3}{5}$ except?
   - A. $\frac{15}{25}$
   - B. $\frac{35}{75}$
   - C. $\frac{60}{100}$
   - D. $\frac{66}{110}$

4. Which is the largest fraction?
   - A. $2\frac{3}{5}$
   - B. $\frac{24}{9}$
   - C. $\frac{19}{7}$
   - D. $2\frac{5}{6}$

5. Which of the following is NOT equal to a whole number?
   - A. $\frac{42}{7}$
   - B. $4 \times \frac{9}{12}$
   - C. $\frac{20}{2} \div 4$
   - D. $\frac{8}{12} \div \frac{2}{6}$

6. On an exam, Alexi receives full credit on $\frac{6}{9}$ of the questions and partial credit for $\frac{2}{8}$ of the questions. If there are 84 questions on the exam, how many questions did Alexi receive no credit?
   - A.   3 questions
   - B.   7 questions
   - C.   21 questions
   - D.   28 questions

7. What is the quotient of $2\frac{8}{9}$ and $2\frac{3}{9}$?

8. Nonni only has one pound of flour left. He uses $\frac{1}{6}$ of the flour for cupcakes and $\frac{3}{10}$ for a cake. What fraction of the flour remains unused?

9. $\frac{9}{16}$ is greater than which of the following?

   A. $\frac{4}{7}$

   B. $\frac{5}{8}$

   C. $\frac{3}{5}$

   D. $\frac{5}{9}$

10. What is two-fifths of four-ninths?

11. If $\frac{3}{5} \times \theta = 27$, what is $\frac{2}{3} \times \theta$?

    A. 18
    B. 27
    C. 30
    D. 45

12. Marnie's bouquet contains 24 flowers. If one-fourth of the flowers die, and she adds 12 more flowers, how many flowers are now in her bouquet?

    A. 6 flowers
    B. 18 flowers
    C. 26 flowers
    D. 30 flowers

13. In a factory, $\frac{5}{7}$ of the production is widgets, $\frac{3}{8}$ of which are blue. If the factory produces 280 widgets, how many of them are blue?

14. Scott uses $1\frac{2}{3}$ gallons of gas on his drive to work and $2\frac{3}{5}$ gallons to meet his wife at a restaurant. How many gallons of gas did Scott use in those two trips?

15. If $\frac{a}{5} = \frac{b}{10} = 6$, what is the value of $a + b$?

    A. 50
    B. 60
    C. 80
    D. 90

16. In a small town, there are eight times as many people as books at the library. If two-thirds of the population never visit the library, and the total number of books at the library is 144, how many people in the town visit the library?

    A. 96 people
    B. 192 people
    C. 384 people
    D. 768 people

17. Simplify $\dfrac{\frac{4}{5}+\frac{1}{10}}{\frac{8}{9}-\frac{2}{3}}$

    A. $\frac{1}{5}$

    B. $\frac{1}{9}$

    C. $3\frac{1}{45}$

    D. $4\frac{1}{20}$

18. Farmer Fran has planted 540 crops. $\frac{1}{9}$ is killed during a frost, and $\frac{2}{5}$ of the remaining crops are eaten by pests. How many crops are left over after the season?

    A. 192 crops

    B. 216 crops

    C. 264 crops

    D. 288 crops

19. Ray has just scored 45,000 points on his pinball game. If he collected one-fourth of the points on his first life and two-fifths of his total score on his second life, how many points did he collect on his third and final life?

    A. 11,250 points

    B. 14,700 points

    C. 15,750 points

    D. 29,250 points

20. Martha has $18\frac{3}{4}$ inches of ribbon that she needs to cut into 20 pieces. How long will each piece of ribbon be?

    A. $\frac{3}{4}$ inches

    B. $\frac{13}{16}$ inches

    C. $\frac{7}{8}$ inches

    D. $\frac{15}{16}$ inches

CHAPTER 6: DECIMALS

Experts in Test Prep, Tutoring, & Admissions Counseling

www.CardinalEducation.com

ROUNDING DECIMALS Practice Set 1

Round each of the following to the respective digit unless instructed to do otherwise.

1. 1.87 to the nearest tenth

2. 11.8 to the nearest ones

3. 15.827 to the nearest hundredth

4. What is the place value of the 2 in 0.2333?

5. 1.36589 to the nearest ten thousandth

6. 0.08 to the nearest tenth

7. 3.09 to the nearest units

8. What is the place value of the 8 in 0.0789?

9. 16.59 to the nearest units

10. What is the place value of the 1 in 0.0109?

11. 5.96 to the nearest units

12. 18.98 to the nearest tenth

13. 0.0099 to the nearest thousandth

14. 129.987 to the nearest tenth

15. 0.989 to the nearest ones

16. What is the place value of the 1 in 15.0095?

17. What is the place value of the 7 in 0.019762?

18. 100.897 to the nearest thousandth

19. 299.984 to the nearest tenth

20. 0.89996 to the nearest ten thousandth

ROUNDING DECIMALS Practice Set 2

Round each of the following to the respective digit unless instructed to do otherwise.

1. 0.26 to the nearest tenth

2. 18.277 to the nearest hundredth

3. What is the place value of the 8 in 0.00682?

4. 122.56872 to the nearest ten thousandth

5. What is the place value of the 5 in 15.299?

6. 0.0799 to the nearest tenth

7. 129.098 to the nearest units

8. What is the place value of the 9 in 0.5494?

9. 0.10079 to the nearest ten thousandth

10. 17.99 to the nearest tenth

11. 5,892.0899 to the nearest thousandth

12. What is the place value of the 4 in 16.0499?

13. 29.979 to the nearest units

14. 0.86799 to the nearest thousandth

15. 0.10099 to the nearest ten thousandth

16. 60.7982 to the nearest hundredth

17. 0.406 to the nearest ones

18. What is the place value of the 2 in 16.28?

19. 22.8996 to the nearest thousandth

20. 299.99998 to the nearest ten thousandth

ADDITION OF DECIMALS Practice Set 1

1. $1.2 + 5.6 =$

2. $0.8 + 8.7 =$

3. $11.4 + 9.9 =$

4. $3.7 + 0.68 =$

5. $6.53 + 17.7 =$

6. $20.09 + 50.7 =$

7. $7.8 + 1.507 =$

8. $89.374 + 22.8 =$

9. $11.5 + 37.672 =$

10. $9.67 + 4.88 =$

11. $37.62 + 78.99 =$

12. $122.47 + 49.65 =$

13. $57.378 + 34.29 =$

14. $134.36 + 27.809 =$

15. $765.76 + 83.471 =$

16. $0.9 + 15.127 =$

17. $5.261 + 72.908 =$

18. $14.665 + 77.1 =$

19. $89.018 + 122.79 =$

20. $0.108 + 156.969 =$

ADDITION OF DECIMALS Practice Set 2

1. 1.7 + 4.8 =

2. 0.6 + 6.3 =

3. 10.9 + 9.2 =

4. 5.3 + 0.87 =

5. 6.64 + 18.5 =

6. 50.07 + 40.9 =

7. 7.1 + 1.382 =

8. 96.545 + 28.6 =

9. 17.3 + 22.837 =

10. 17.6 + 3.79 =

11. 88.78 + 26.87 =

12. 174.38 + 23.9 =

13. 49.938 + 38.51 =

14. 116.89 + 35.241 =

15. 758.49 + 72.673 =

16. 0.525 + 16.58 =

17. 4.7 + 63.912 =

18. 21.13 + 66.658 =

19. 59.006 + 142.898 =

20. 0.719 + 179.4 =

SUBTRACTION OF DECIMALS Practice Set 1

1. $6.8 - 3.5 =$

2. $12.5 - 8.7 =$

3. $56.3 - 29.6 =$

4. $16.23 - 11.7 =$

5. $25.2 - 19.83 =$

6. $37.6 - 19.17 =$

7. $1.68 - 0.87 =$

8. $22.23 - 9.44 =$

9. $5.12 - 4.67 =$

10. $89.61 - 67.58 =$

11. $18.6 - 5.183 =$

12. $2.9 - 1.905 =$

13. $33.182 - 29.7 =$

14. $-6.18 + 4.772 =$

15. $46.73 - 39.747 =$

16. $8.701 - 6.27 =$

17. $-1.072 + 0.289 =$

18. $48.021 - 37.355 =$

19. $-29.117 + 15.572 =$

20. $122.812 - 19.856 =$

SUBTRACTION OF DECIMALS Practice Set 2

1. $5.6 - 1.8 =$

2. $12.3 - 6.6 =$

3. $76.5 - 27.9 =$

4. $18.39 - 12.7 =$

5. $26.6 - 17.72 =$

6. $32.7 - 19.36 =$

7. $1.82 - 0.97 =$

8. $25.41 - 4.73 =$

9. $8.26 - 7.97 =$

10. $99.05 - 87.47 =$

11. $19.6 - 5.824 =$

12. $4.6 - 3.7 =$

13. $-58.512 + 49.6 =$

14. $8.369 - 6.953 =$

15. $-64.64 + 59.659 =$

16. $5.507 - 2.28 =$

17. $-1.037 + 0.692 =$

18. $46.058 - 33.581 =$

19. $34.413 - 19.964 =$

20. $-135.627 + 25.671 =$

SUBTRACTION OF DECIMALS Practice Set 3

1. $8.7 - 3.9 =$

2. $15.4 - 9.7 =$

3. $62.3 - 35.4 =$

4. $18.38 - 11.7 =$

5. $23.4 - 16.87 =$

6. $34.8 - 18.24 =$

7. $1.45 - 0.79 =$

8. $24.19 - 3.92 =$

9. $7.37 - 6.68 =$

10. $68.31 - 46.59 =$

11. $15.4 - 4.515 =$

12. $8.2 - 7.8 =$

13. $-44.264 + 39.8 =$

14. $9.472 - 7.638 =$

15. $56.78 - 49.791 =$

16. $3.54 - 6.809 =$

17. $1.043 - 0.867 =$

18. $-59.046 + 35.857 =$

19. $39.219 - 25.773 =$

20. $29.987 - 131.962 =$

SUBTRACTION OF DECIMALS Practice Set 4

1. $9.2 - 5.4 =$

2. $13.7 - 8.8 =$

3. $71.4 - 59.6 =$

4. $19.74 - 13.9 =$

5. $27.1 - 19.45 =$

6. $39.9 - 16.57 =$

7. $1.73 - 0.88 =$

8. $28.24 - 9.56 =$

9. $4.41 - 3.84 =$

10. $75.48 - 53.59 =$

11. $17.8 - 4.932 =$

12. $5.4 - 3.9 =$

13. $63.346 - 59.7 =$

14. $-7.541 + 5.839 =$

15. $38.64 - 29.658 =$

16. $9.604 - 6.19 =$

17. $-1.082 + 0.543 =$

18. $37.012 - 26.634 =$

19. $25.342 - 19.846 =$

20. $-125.736 + 19.758 =$

MULTIPLICATION OF DECIMALS Practice Set 1

1. $0.2 \times 8 =$

2. $0.7 \times 0.6 =$

3. $0.04 \times 0.3 =$

4. $0.5 \times 13.5 =$

5. $1.2 \times 1.7 =$

6. $0.08 \times 2.4 =$

7. $0.32 \times 0.07 =$

8. $0.005 \times 285 =$

9. $1.1 \times 9.99 =$

10. $18.3 \times 5.21 =$

11. $0.655 \times 0.12 =$

12. $0.024 \times 0.008 =$

13. $19.25 \times 0.31 =$

14. $2.15 \times 10.7 =$

15. $0.051 \times 500 =$

16. $10.4 \times 11.22 =$

17. $7.7 \times 0.88 =$

18. $150 \times 0.0025 =$

19. $13.78 \times 14.12 =$

20. $8.23 \times 6.17 =$

MULTIPLICATION OF DECIMALS Practice Set 2

1. $0.4 \times 7 =$

2. $0.5 \times 0.9 =$

3. $0.08 \times 0.2 =$

4. $0.8 \times 12.5 =$

5. $1.6 \times 1.5 =$

6. $0.06 \times 5.3 =$

7. $0.41 \times 0.08 =$

8. $0.009 \times 245 =$

9. $4.4 \times 3.33 =$

10. $21.3 \times 3.52 =$

11. $0.790 \times 0.23 =$

16. $7.9 \times 14.66 =$

12. $0.041 \times 0.004 =$

17. $6.6 \times 0.55 =$

13. $18.25 \times 0.37 =$

18. $225 \times 0.0045 =$

14. $5.30 \times 0.83 =$

19. $19.19 \times 11.74 =$

15. $0.039 \times 600 =$

20. $4.87 \times 8.74 =$

MULTIPLICATION OF DECIMALS Practice Set 3

1. $0.3 \times 6 =$

2. $0.4 \times 0.3 =$

3. $0.09 \times 0.6 =$

4. $0.7 \times 17 =$

5. $1.9 \times 1.4 =$

6. $0.03 \times 8.2 =$

7. $0.67 \times 0.05 =$

8. $0.003 \times 325 =$

9. $2.2 \times 5.55 =$

10. $15.7 \times 7.21 =$

11. 0.375 × 0.37 =

16. 9.6 × 13.11 =

12. 0.037 × 0.006 =

17. 5.5 × 0.33 =

13. 13.75 × 0.43 =

18. 125 × 0.0035 =

14. 4.70 × 9.7 =

19. 15.38 × 14.79 =

15. 0.067 × 450 =

20. 7.32 × 5.93 =

MULTIPLICATION OF DECIMALS Practice Set 4

1. $0.5 \times 10 =$

2. $0.8 \times 0.8 =$

3. $0.03 \times 0.7 =$

4. $0.4 \times 16.5 =$

5. $1.8 \times 1.3 =$

6. $0.07 \times 3.6 =$

7. $0.72 \times 0.03 =$

8. $0.007 \times 195 =$

9. $3.3 \times 8.88 =$

10. $12.9 \times 9.34 =$

11. $0.930 \times 0.11 =$

12. $0.019 \times 0.003 =$

13. $21.50 \times 0.27 =$

14. $3.45 \times 11.6 =$

15. $0.043 \times 560 =$

16. $8.7 \times 12.33 =$

17. $9.9 \times 0.66 =$

18. $175 \times 0.0045 =$

19. $16.96 \times 12.39 =$

20. $6.43 \times 9.18 =$

DIVISION OF DECIMALS Practice Set 1

1. $0.9 \div 0.3 =$

2. $1.2 \div 0.4 =$

3. $2.5 \div 0.5 =$

4. $1.52 \div 0.4 =$

5. $0.4 \div 0.5 =$

6. $1.68 \div 0.8 =$

7. $4 \div 0.5 =$

8. $3.75 \div 0.2 =$

9. $96 \div 1.2 =$

10. $4.032 \div 5 =$

11. 0.448 ÷ 4 =

16. 2.3958 ÷ 1.98 =

12. 1.215 ÷ 0.3 =

17. 52.224 ÷ 6.4 =

13. 9.779 ÷ 1.27 =

18. 395.38 ÷ 18.65 =

14. 1.6 ÷ 0.05 =

19. 0.14 ÷ 0.008 =

15. 47.656 ÷ 2.3 =

20. 0.00294 ÷ 0.35 =

DIVISION OF DECIMALS Practice Set 2

1. $0.2 \div 0.5 =$

2. $0.4 \div 0.2 =$

3. $24 \div 0.8 =$

4. $4.9 \div 0.7 =$

5. $1.62 \div 0.6 =$

6. $1.96 \div 0.4 =$

7. $10 \div 0.25 =$

8. $2.25 \div 0.6 =$

9. $68 \div 1.7 =$

10. $2.078 \div 5 =$

11. 0.798 ÷ 7 =

16. 3.7275 ÷ 1.75 =

12. 1.420 ÷ 0.8 =

17. 43.523 ÷ 7.1 =

13. 9.114 ÷ 1.86 =

18. 321.205 ÷ 14.15 =

14. 3.5 ÷ 0.07 =

19. 0.123 ÷ 0.006 =

15. 105.987 ÷ 4.9 =

20. 0.00246 ÷ 0.48 =

DIVISION OF DECIMALS Practice Set 3

1. $0.6 \div 0.8 =$

2. $0.6 \div 0.5 =$

3. $1.5 \div 0.3 =$

4. $1.6 \div 0.4 =$

5. $1.24 \div 0.8 =$

6. $1.72 \div 0.4 =$

7. $6 \div 0.25 =$

8. $6.5 \div 0.8 =$

9. $75 \div 1.5 =$

10. $3.021 \div 5 =$

11. $0.656 \div 4 =$

16. $2.0264 \div 1.49 =$

12. $1.635 \div 0.5 =$

17. $85.291 \div 6.7 =$

13. $9.636 \div 1.46 =$

18. $442.612 \div 15.64 =$

14. $2.2 \div 0.05 =$

19. $0.09 \div 0.004 =$

15. $53.822 \div 3.4 =$

20. $0.002015 \div 0.31 =$

DIVISION OF DECIMALS Practice Set 4

1. $0.3 \div 0.5 =$

2. $0.8 \div 0.4 =$

3. $1.8 \div 0.6 =$

4. $3.6 \div 0.6 =$

5. $1.86 \div 0.6 =$

6. $1.56 \div 0.6 =$

7. $8 \div 0.50 =$

8. $5.25 \div 0.5 =$

9. $126 \div 1.4 =$

10. $5.043 \div 10 =$

11. $0.976 \div 8 =$

12. $1.888 \div 0.4 =$

13. $7.425 \div 1.35 =$

14. $1.7 \div 0.04 =$

15. $52.136 \div 2.8 =$

16. $2.3247 \div 1.23 =$

17. $55.991 \div 5.9 =$

18. $231.15 \div 17.25 =$

19. $0.26 \div 0.016 =$

20. $0.00342 \div 0.45 =$

DECIMAL WORD PROBLEMS Practice Set 1

1. Which of the following numbers is greater than 1.5 but less than 1.8?
    - A. 1.49
    - B. 1.64
    - C. 1.82
    - D. 1.92

2. Rick has $7,125.67 in his checking account. He writes a check for $3,865.88 and another one for $189.72. How much is left in his account?

3. In which of the following numbers does the digit 7 represent $\frac{7}{100}$?
    - A. 2.70
    - B. 7.20
    - C. 2.07
    - D. 700.2

4. Elisa went to the store to buy some fruits. She spent $3.18 on oranges, $3.58 on mangoes, $4.27 on bananas, $5.34 on pineapples, and $1.79 on grapes. If she paid using a $20 bill, how much in change did she get back?

5. Which of the following is true?
    - A. $0.4 \times 0.4 = 1.6$
    - B. $\frac{0.4}{4} = 0.1$
    - C. $0.4 \times 4 = 0.16$
    - D. $\frac{0.4}{0.4} = 0.1$

6. Which of the following is closest in value to 8?
    - A. 8.1
    - B. 7.89
    - C. 7.99
    - D. 8.009

7. $0.083 =$
    - A. $\frac{8}{100} + \frac{3}{1,000}$
    - B. $\frac{8}{10} + \frac{3}{100}$
    - C. $\frac{8}{100} + \frac{7}{10}$
    - D. $\frac{80}{10} + \frac{700}{1,000}$

8. At a bookstore, a mechanical pencil costs 89 cents, and an eraser costs $1.26. Aaron buys six pencils and three erasers. How much money did he spend?

9. At a flower shop, a dozen roses cost $46.20. What is the cost of a single rose?

10. The product of 1.280 and 100 is approximately?
    A. 0.1280
    B. 1,300
    C. 12.8
    D. 130

11. Eleven times a certain number is 26.4. What is the result if the number is divided by 3?

12. Simplify the ratio $\frac{8.7}{60.9}$
    A. $\frac{1}{8}$
    B. $\frac{2}{11}$
    C. $\frac{1}{7}$
    D. $\frac{3}{8}$

13. Lois has been on a diet for the past eight months, losing 5.6 lbs per month. She currently weighs 176.5 lbs. What was her weight 8 months ago?

14. In the decimal 4.6738, the digit 7 is equivalent of which of the following?
    A. $\frac{7}{100}$
    B. $\frac{7}{10}$
    C. $\frac{7}{1,000}$
    D. $\frac{7}{700}$

15. The temperature at Lake Tahoe on one winter day was -3.5°C at 8:00 am. The temperature increased by 7.9°C at noon and then dropped by 10.3°C in the evening. What was the final temperature in the evening?

16. If 0.79 is about $\frac{x}{100}$, then x is closest to which of the following?
    A. 8
    B. 7.9
    C. 80
    D. 790

17. What is $\frac{1}{3}$ of 0.81?

18. 0.15 =
    A. $\frac{5}{10} + \frac{1}{100}$
    B. $\frac{1}{10} + \frac{5}{100}$
    C. $\frac{1}{100} + \frac{5}{1,000}$
    D. $\frac{9}{10} + \frac{5}{1,000}$

19. Angelina spent $\frac{3}{4}$ of her savings on a birthday gift for her brother. If she had $8.25 left after purchasing the gift, how much money did she originally have?

20. Christine has twice as much money as Jordan. Jordan has four times as much money as Joyce. If Joyce has $11.45, how much money do the three of them have combined?

DECIMAL WORD PROBLEMS Practice Set 2

1. Which digit represents the thousandths place in the number 1.3297?
   A. 1
   B. 9
   C. 2
   D. 7

2. Which number has the greater value, 17.38 or 17.378?

3. A cashier is given $5.12 for an item that costs $3.62. How much change will the customer receive?

4. What is the solution for $8.324 - 7.86 =$
   A. 0.464
   B. 0.46
   C. 0.47
   D. 1.46

5. 0.498 is equivalent to which fraction?
   A. $\frac{498}{100}$
   B. $\frac{498}{10,000}$
   C. $\frac{498}{10}$
   D. $\frac{498}{1,000}$

6. What is the fraction $\frac{223}{10}$ in decimal form?

7. Which of the following numbers is largest?
   A. 1.1
   B. 1
   C. 1.01
   D. 1.101

8. $0.205 =$
   A. $\frac{2}{1} + \frac{5}{10}$
   B. $\frac{2}{10} + \frac{5}{1,000}$
   C. $\frac{2}{10} + \frac{5}{100}$
   D. $\frac{2}{100} + \frac{5}{1,000}$

9. Johnny has $4.35 and Billy has twice as much as Johnny. Beth has a third of what Billy has. How much does Beth have?
   A. $2.78
   B. $3.23
   C. $2.94
   D. $2.90

208

10. James has \$483.78, he buys a new video game for \$63.94 and then puts half of the rest of his money into a bank. How much money does James have left?

11. Which number is next in order?
    1.02, 2.04, 4.08, 8.16 ...
    A. 9.18
    B. 12.24
    C. 10.2
    D. 16.32

12. 1.02 =
    A. $1 + \frac{2}{10}$
    B. $\frac{1}{10} + \frac{2}{10}$
    C. $\frac{1}{10} + \frac{2}{100}$
    D. $1 + \frac{2}{100}$

13. If $2.73 - x = 1.36$, what is $2x + 2.14$?

14. 0.32
    A. $3 + \frac{2}{10}$
    B. $\frac{3}{10} + \frac{2}{100}$
    C. $\frac{3}{100} + \frac{2}{1,000}$
    D. $\frac{2}{10} + \frac{3}{100}$

15. Justin can bake 3.5 cakes in one hour. Cindy can bake 4.4 cakes in one hour. If they both bake for 10 hours in their own kitchens, how many cakes will be baked?

16. It takes Greg 10.8 minutes to get to the pool from his house. Linda lives a quarter closer to the pool than Greg. How long should it take Linda to get to the pool? Round to the nearest tenth.
    A. 2.7 minutes
    B. 8.1 minutes
    C. 8.4 minutes
    D. 13.5 minutes

17. Wanda's fish eats 0.3 grams of food 4 times a day. A bottle of fish food has 15.6 grams of food inside. How many days will a bottle of food last Wanda?

18. Mt. Kilgore High has 44 students going on a trip by car. They need a group of parents equal to $\frac{1}{4}$ of the total number of students as chaperones. If each car can fit a maximum of 4 people, what is the minimum number of cars required for the trip?

19. Kahn the ape weighs 87.65 lbs. If three years ago he weighed $\frac{3}{5}$ of his current weight, what was his weight three years ago?

20. A steel bar that is 1 foot long weighs 5.53 pounds. Another bar that is proportionate is 5 feet long. How much does it weigh?
    A. 1.106 lbs
    B. 10.39 lbs
    C. 27.65 lbs
    D. 34.87 lbs

DECIMAL WORD PROBLEMS Practice Set 3

1. Round 12.3476 to the tenths place.
   A. 12.35
   B. 12.0
   C. 12.3
   D. 12.348

2. If you were to plot 1.68 and 1.3 on a number line, which number is closer to a whole number?

3. Frank can peel 35.2 apples in one hour, and Lucy can peel 17.3 in an hour. How many will they peel in four hours?

4. Put 0.232 in simplest fraction form.
   A. $\frac{232}{1,000}$
   B. $\frac{116}{500}$
   C. $\frac{29}{125}$
   D. $\frac{29}{1,000}$

5. If Courtney buys 3 books at $4.35 a book, 3 book markers for $0.35 each, and a pen for $1.95. How much did she spend?

6. If $12 - 5x = 2.65$ then what is $3x + 1.25 + x$?
   A. 7.48
   B. 8.73
   C. −7.48
   D. −8.73

7. Diego spends $44.52 on a brand new Blu-ray disc. A month later, Sam buys a similar Blu-ray disc for a quarter of the price. How much more did Diego pay for the disc than Sam?

8. The product of 0.102 and 2,000 is approximately?
   A. 10
   B. 20
   C. 100
   D. 200

9. Which of the following would make the statement
   $5x = x + 1.6$ true?
   A. $x = 0.2$
   B. $x = 0.4$
   C. $x = 2$
   D. $x = 0.6$

10. A dozen golf balls were priced at $7.20. If the price is reduced by a third, how much will be the price of each ball?
     A. $0.20
     B. $0.40
     C. $0.60
     D. $0.80

11. Billy runs 3 mph for 1.5 hours on Monday, 4 mph for 1.25 hours on Wednesday and 2 mph for 2.75 hours on Friday. How many miles did he run for the three days?

12. $5.608 = ?$
     A. $5 + \frac{6}{10} + \frac{8}{1,000}$
     B. $5 + \frac{6}{100} + \frac{8}{1,000}$
     C. $5 + \frac{8}{10} + \frac{6}{1,000}$
     D. $5 + \frac{8}{100} + \frac{6}{1,000}$

13. Winny skates a quarter mile in 1.53 minutes. Karen skates a quarter mile in 1.28 minutes. How much less time does it take Karen to skate a quarter mile?

14. Betty sees a dress in a store for $12.80. She figures she can buy it at Target for $\frac{3}{10}$ of the price. How much will she save by buying the dress at Target?
     A. $7.48
     B. $8.96
     C. $9.12
     D. $10.58

15. Hans earns $448 per week. He spends $\frac{4}{5}$ of his income on expenses and saves the rest. How much will he save in a 52 week year?
     A. $2,912.00
     B. $3,792.48
     C. $4,136.44
     D. $4,659.20

16. Ms. Choung had $1,200. She bought a desk for $158.98 and spent half of the rest on a used car. How much does she have left?
     A. $1,041.02
     B. $520.01
     C. $520.51
     D. $679.29

17. Tim's family took a trip for 12 days. If they spent a total of $579.84, how much did they spend on average each day?

212

18. A plane ticket from San Francisco to Los Angeles costs $68.40. If $\frac{1}{8}$ of the price is the sales tax, how much is the cost of the ticket before the tax?
    A. $58.45
    B. $59.85
    C. $60.85
    D. $62.45

19. Henry has seven goats and four cows. If a goat sells for $114.36 and a cow sells for $\frac{5}{3}$ the price of a goat, how much will Henry get if he sells all his cows and 3 goats?

20. It costs $14.44 per square foot to cement a new walkway. How much will it cost to put cement on 192 square feet of walkway?

DECIMAL WORD PROBLEMS Practice Set 4

1. Which of these numbers, if put on a number line, would be closest to 2.5?
   - A. 2.45
   - B. 2.54
   - C. 2.6
   - D. 2.551

2. What is $\frac{3}{8}$ of 0.64?
   - A. 0.24
   - B. 24
   - C. 8
   - D. 0.8

3. If $3.32 + x = 4.82$, then what is $x + 1.5x$?

4. Sonny has 43 baseball cards worth $5.37 per card, and Terry has 621 cards worth $0.29 a card. How much more valuable is Sonny's collection than Terry's?

5. Ashton can read 2.5 pages of a book in 1 minute. How many pages can she read in 18 minutes?

6. A painting costs $115.40. Each week the price of the painting decreases by a tenth. How much will the painting cost after 2 weeks?

7. $0.91 =$
   - A. $\frac{1}{10} + \frac{9}{100}$
   - B. $\frac{9}{10} + \frac{1}{100}$
   - C. $9 + \frac{1}{10}$
   - D. $\frac{9}{100} + \frac{1}{1,000}$

8. May and Suzy have a total of $22.75. They buy two movie tickets costing $7.38 each, a bag of popcorn for $3.18, and two sodas for $1.58 each? How much money do they have left?

9. The Whales are first in the league with a 28-10 win-loss record. What is the record of the third place team that has won half as many games as the Whales and has played the same number of games?
   - A. 28-5
   - B. 14-10
   - C. 14-24
   - D. 33-5

214

10. A puppy gains 0.24 lbs every week. If the puppy current weighs 12.37 lbs, what was the weight of the puppy 13 weeks ago?

11. A tree is 45.67 feet tall. It has been alive for 16 years. If the tree continues growing at the same rate, how tall will it be in 3 years?
    A. 55.32 feet
    B. 54.11 feet
    C. 54.67 feet
    D. 54.23 feet

12. Bob cuts a 16 inch ribbon into 2.75 inch pieces. What will be the length of the last and smallest piece?

13. Mannie bought a steak that weighed 5lbs for $3.20 a pound and bananas weighing 3 lbs for $0.68 a pound. Mannie paid with a $20 bill. How much change will he get back?

14. $6.705 =$
    A. $6 + \frac{70}{10} + \frac{5}{1,000}$
    B. $6 + \frac{7}{10} + \frac{5}{1,000}$
    C. $6 + \frac{7}{100} + \frac{5}{10,000}$
    D. $6 + \frac{5}{10} + \frac{7}{1,000}$

15. Huck worked six days this week. He averaged 7.2 hours a day. He makes $9.13 an hour until 40 hours and $13.49 every hour after the 40th. How much money did he make this week? Round to the nearest cent.

16. Jerome buys 8 gallons of gas for $1.29 per gallon. If he pays with a $20 bill, how much change did he receive?

17. Sam bought 3 dozen new shirts at a cost of $4.50 per shirt. How much will he make in profit if he sells all the shirts at $4.85 each?
    A. $0.35
    B. $4.20
    C. $10.60
    D. $12.60

18. Dennis has $783.39. Stephen has $40.56 less than Brent who has $\frac{1}{3}$ the amount of money that Dennis has. How much does Stephen have?

19. Marge goes to a grocery store to buy apples and oranges. Apples cost 87 cents each and each orange cost $\frac{2}{3}$ the price of an apple? How much will she pay for 5 apples and 6 oranges?
    A. $7.83
    B. $8.42
    C. $8.56
    D. $9.24

20. Katrina spent $\frac{2}{5}$ of her savings on a brand new iPod. If she had $112.50 left after purchasing the iPod, how much money did she have originally?
    A. $167.50
    B. $187.50
    C. $225.50
    D. $235.50

CHAPTER 7: FRACTION, DECIMAL, PERCENT CONVERSIONS

Experts in Test Prep, Tutoring, & Admissions Counseling

www.CardinalEducation.com

DECIMALS TO FRACTIONS Practice Set 1

Convert the following decimals into fractions. Write answer in simplest form.

1. 0.1

2. 0.2

3. 0.5

4. 0.8

5. 0.25

6. 0.03

7. 0.06

8. 0.09

9. 1.22

10. 0.32

11. 0.01

12. 0.75

13. 0.025

14. 0.070

15. 0.76

16. 12.5

17. 1.42

18. 4.08

19. 2.004

20. 0.088

DECIMALS TO FRACTIONS Practice Set 2

Convert the following decimals into fractions. Write answer in simplest form.

1. 0.3

2. 0.7

3. 0.12

4. 0.02

5. 0.05

6. 0.45

7. 0.24

8. 0.22

9. 0.38

10. 0.55

11. 0.76

12. 0.84

13. 1.26

14. 0.075

15. 0.090

16. 20.5

17. 1.68

18. 4.07

19. 4.002

20. 0.044

FRACTIONS TO DECIMALS Practice Set 1

Convert the following fractions into decimals.

1. $\frac{1}{2}$

2. $\frac{1}{4}$

3. $\frac{1}{3}$

4. $\frac{1}{5}$

5. $\frac{3}{10}$

6. $\frac{2}{5}$

7. $1\frac{1}{8}$

8. $2\frac{6}{10}$

9. $\frac{7}{8}$

10. $\frac{9}{5}$

11. $\frac{3}{20}$

12. $\frac{24}{36}$

13. $4\frac{15}{20}$

14. $\frac{19}{20}$

15. $\frac{11}{50}$

16. $6\frac{12}{40}$

17. $\frac{75}{20}$

18. $\frac{84}{50}$

19. $3\frac{7}{20}$

20. $5\frac{9}{30}$

FRACTIONS TO DECIMALS Practice Set 2

Convert the following fractions into decimals.

1. $\frac{2}{3}$

2. $\frac{1}{6}$

3. $\frac{4}{5}$

4. $\frac{3}{4}$

5. $\frac{7}{10}$

6. $\frac{5}{8}$

7. $1\frac{1}{6}$

8. $2\frac{6}{8}$

9. $\frac{11}{8}$

10. $\frac{15}{2}$

11. $\frac{3}{15}$

12. $\frac{2}{25}$

13. $\frac{45}{60}$

14. $\frac{24}{25}$

15. $\frac{17}{50}$

16. $8\frac{5}{20}$

17. $\frac{95}{40}$

18. $\frac{92}{50}$

19. $3\frac{21}{30}$

20. $4\frac{24}{40}$

DECIMALS TO PERCENTS Practice Set 1

Convert the following decimals into percentages.

1. 0.1

2. 0.5

3. 0.4

4. 0.7

5. 0.03

6. 0.08

7. 0.25

8. 0.006

9. 0.0008

10. 0.105

11. 0.780

12. 0.086

13. 0.022

14. 1.86

15. 2.05

16. 9.07

17. 3.002

18. 22.3

19. 17.88

20. 20.005

DECIMALS TO PERCENTS Practice Set 2

Convert the following decimals into percentages.

1. 0.2

2. 0.8

3. 0.7

4. 0.01

5. 0.04

6. 0.13

7. 0.22

8. 0.005

9. 0.0006

10. 0.112

11. 0.640

12. 0.077

13. 0.045

14. 1.24

15. 2.09

16. 8.88

17. 4.003

18. 21.5

19. 15.79

20. 30.003

PERCENTS TO DECIMALS Practice Set 1

Convert the following percentages into decimals.

1. 20%

2. 55%

3. 4%

4. 34%

5. 9%

6. 10.5%

7. 97.2%

8. 120%

9. 214%

10. $20\frac{1}{2}$%

11. $5\frac{3}{4}$%

12. 122.8%

13. $33\frac{1}{3}$%

14. 0.5%

15. 0.06%

16. 1.070%

17. $66\frac{2}{3}$%

18. 77.23%

19. 8.62%

20. 0.285%

PERCENTS TO DECIMALS Practice Set 2

Convert the following percentages into decimals.

1. 10%

2. 35%

3. 3%

4. 8%

5. 26%

6. 20.5%

7. 24.5%

8. 140%

9. 241%

10. $25\frac{1}{4}\%$

11. $4\frac{2}{3}\%$

12. 143.4%

13. $83\frac{1}{3}\%$

14. 0.8%

15. 0.05%

16. 6.060%

17. $8\frac{3}{8}\%$

18. 41.78%

19. 5.93%

20. 0.123%

FRACTIONS TO PERCENTS Practice Set 1

Convert the following fractions into percentages.

1. $\frac{1}{2}$

2. $\frac{1}{4}$

3. $\frac{1}{8}$

4. $\frac{1}{3}$

5. $\frac{3}{8}$

6. $\frac{3}{5}$

7. $\frac{9}{10}$

8. $\frac{6}{5}$

9. $1\frac{1}{2}$

10. $2\frac{1}{10}$

11. $\frac{2}{3}$

12. $\frac{7}{50}$

13. $\frac{21}{20}$

14. $\frac{11}{500}$

15. $3\frac{3}{20}$

16. $\frac{12}{200}$

17. $\frac{7}{400}$

18. $\frac{15}{6}$

19. $2\frac{5}{6}$

20. $\frac{30}{8}$

FRACTIONS TO PERCENTS Practice Set 2

Convert the following fractions into percentages.

1. $\frac{1}{5}$

2. $\frac{2}{3}$

3. $\frac{4}{5}$

4. $\frac{7}{10}$

5. $\frac{3}{4}$

6. $\frac{2}{8}$

7. $\frac{6}{9}$

8. $\frac{9}{8}$

9. $1\frac{1}{3}$

10. $2\frac{2}{10}$

11. $3\frac{2}{3}$

12. $\frac{23}{8}$

13. $\frac{8}{25}$

14. $\frac{51}{50}$

15. $\frac{7}{200}$

16. $4\frac{7}{20}$

17. $\frac{11}{500}$

18. $\frac{17}{250}$

19. $\frac{8}{125}$

20. $\frac{94}{400}$

PERCENTS TO FRACTIONS Practice Set 1

Convert the following percentages into fractions. Write answer in simplest form.

1. 20%

2. 60%

3. 75%

4. 5%

5. 9%

6. 120%

7. $20\frac{1}{2}$%

8. 3.5%

9. $33\frac{1}{3}$%

10. 0.8%

11. 0.7%

12. 1.34%

13. 225%

14. $66\frac{2}{3}\%$

15. 0.12%

16. 0.25%

17. 2.50%

18. $27\frac{1}{8}\%$

19. $6\frac{2}{5}\%$

20. $8\frac{1}{4}\%$

PERCENTS TO FRACTIONS Practice Set 2

Convert the following percentages into fractions. Write answer in simplest form.

1. 30%

2. 80%

3. 75%

4. 7%

5. 2%

6. 140%

7. 6.5%

8. $66\frac{2}{3}\%$

9. 0.4%

10. 0.9%

11. $10\frac{4}{5}\%$

12. 275%

13. $55\frac{5}{9}\%$

14. 0.16%

15. 0.50%

16. 1.64%

17. 5.25%

18. $5\frac{4}{5}\%$

19. $14\frac{3}{8}\%$

20. $67\frac{3}{4}\%$

CONVERSION CHART Practice Set 1

Fill in the chart. If necessary, round to the nearest hundredths.

	Fraction	Decimal	Percent
	$\frac{1}{4}$		
	$\frac{3}{5}$		
		0.2	
		0.7	
			80%
			45%
		1.4	
	$\frac{19}{6}$		
			5%
		0.01	
	$\frac{12}{12}$		
	$\frac{21}{3}$		
			200%
		2.08	
			115%
25 ÷ 4		6.25	
14 ÷ 42			33.33%
104 ÷ 12			
8 ÷ 36			
74 ÷ 7			

CONVERSION CHART Practice Set 2

Fill in the chart. If necessary, round to the nearest hundredths.

	Fraction	Decimal	Percent
	$\frac{2}{5}$		
	$\frac{1}{8}$		
		0.3	
		0.75	
			90%
			85%
		1.8	
	$\frac{14}{3}$		
			7%
		0.03	
	$\frac{0}{11}$		
	$\frac{20}{5}$		
			100%
		3.72	
			235%
27 ÷ 8		3.375	
2 ÷ 3			66.67%
50 ÷ 6			
35 ÷ 42			
43 ÷ 9			

CONVERSION CHART Practice Set 3

Fill in the chart. If necessary, round to the nearest hundredths.

	Fraction	Decimal	Percent
	$\dfrac{1}{4}$		
		0.6	
			12%
		0.8	
	$\dfrac{5}{8}$		
			8%
		0.275	
	$\dfrac{1}{3}$		
		2.5	
			22.5%
		0.85	
			120%
	$\dfrac{7}{2}$		
		0.02	
	$\dfrac{7}{4}$		
$18 \div 4 =$			
$34 \div 5 =$			
$18 \div 24 =$			
$78 \div 60 =$			
$9 \div 27 =$			

CONVERSION CHART Practice Set 4

Fill in the chart. If necessary, round to the nearest hundredths.

	Fraction	Decimal	Percent
		0.06	
			2%
		0.65	
	$\frac{4}{5}$		
			45%
	$\frac{1}{20}$		
		1.6	
	$\frac{3}{8}$		
			8.5%
		2.8	
			0.15%
	$\frac{2}{3}$		
		0.018	
	$\frac{9}{4}$		
			87.5%
$6 \div 5 =$			
$26 \div 4 =$			
$36 \div 48 =$			
$101 \div 10 =$			
$49 \div 8 =$			

CHAPTER 8: PERCENTAGES

Experts in Test Prep, Tutoring, & Admissions Counseling

www.CardinalEducation.com

PERCENTAGES Practice Set 1

1. 20% of 75 apples is how many apples?

2. 30 cars are 40% of how many cars?

3. A $24 toy is sold at a discounted price of $18. What is the percent discount?

4. $15 is what percent of $75?

5. 12 is 8% of what number?

6. 18 is what percent of 360?

7. 9% of 1,200 people is how many people?

8. What percent of 96 is 12?

9. 10% of 20% of 240 is?

10. 5% of 12.5 is approximately what number?
    A. 0.63
    B. 6.3
    C. 63
    D. 630

11. What percent of 18 is 72?

12. 30% of 80% of 60 is approximately?
    A. 0.14
    B. 1.4
    C. 14
    D. 140

13. What percent of 42 is 6.3?

14. 33 is approximately what percent of 200?
    A. 0.12%
    B. 2%
    C. 12%
    D. 17%

15. 16.5 is 20% of what number?

16. A pair of boots is listed at a price of $84. If there is a 25% tax on every purchase, what will be the cost of buying the boots?
    A. $90
    B. $105
    C. $120
    D. $130

17. 2% of 6% of 55 is?
    A. 0.066
    B. 0.66
    C. 6.6
    D. 66

18. 27 acres of land is what percent of 18 acres of land?

19. 16 is 0.5% of what number?

20. 22% of 30% of 120 is approximately?
    A. 6.8
    B. 6.9
    C. 7.6
    D. 7.9

PERCENTAGES Practice Set 2

1. 40% of 40 dolls is how many dolls?

2. $12 is 20% of what amount?

3. What percent of 35 is 7?

4. 32 is what percent of 128?

5. 8 crows are 16% of how many crows?

6. 7 is what percent of 175?

7. 8% of 1,900 trees is how many trees?

8. What percent of 112 is 14?

9. 25% of 20% of 360 is?

10. 70% of 13.5 is approximately what number?
    A. 0.95
    B. 9.5
    C. 95
    D. 950

11. What percent of 13 is 65?

12. 80% of 20% of 60 is approximately?
    A. 0.96
    B. 9.6
    C. 96
    D. 960

13. What percent of $38 is $5.32?

14. 44 is approximately what percent of 300?
    A. 0.14%
    B. 4%
    C. 12%
    D. 15%

15. 12.5 is 40% of what number?

16. 120% of 55 is closest to?
    A. 40
    B. 60
    C. 70
    D. 80

17. 2% of 5% of 48 is?
    A. 0.048
    B. 0.48
    C. 4.8
    D. 48

18. 36 is what percent of 12?

19. 12 airplanes is 0.75% of how many airplanes?

20. 15% of 26% of 140 is approximately?
    A. 5.1
    B. 5.5
    C. 6.6
    D. 6.9

PERCENTAGES Practice Set 3

1. 60% of 45 feet is how many feet?

2. 14 golf balls is 40% of how many golf balls?

3. What percent of $64 is $24?

4. 65 is what percent of 260?

5. 9 is 12% of what number?

6. 8 is what percent of 160?

7. 7% of 1,600 people is how many people?

8. What percent of 78 is 13?

9. 25% of 40% of 430 oranges is?

10. 60% of 14.5 is approximately what number?
    A. 0.87
    B. 8.7
    C. 87
    D. 870

11. What percent of 16 is 56?

12. 80% of 15% of 65 is approximately?
    A. 0.78
    B. 7.8
    C. 78
    D. 780

13. What percent of 43 is 9.89?

14. 52 is approximately what percent of 250?
    A. 0.19%
    B. 2%
    C. 16%
    D. 21%

15. 16.5 is 60% of what number?

16. 112% of 75 liters is closest to?
    A. 80 liters
    B. 90 liters
    C. 100 liters
    D. 110 liters

17. 3% of 5% of $26 is?
    A. $0.04
    B. $0.39
    C. $3.90
    D. $39

18. 65 is what percent of 13?

19. 15 is 0.6% of what number?

20. 17% of 24% of 162 is approximately?
    A. 5.3
    B. 6.2
    C. 6.6
    D. 7.1

PERCENTAGES Practice Set 4

1. 30% of 60 books is how many books?

2. $12 is 25% of what amount?

3. What percent of 68 inches is 51 inches?

4. 52 is what percent of 130?

5. 99 pencils is 30% of how many pencils?

6. 7 is what percent of 140?

7. 12% of 1,200 is what number?

8. What percent of 125 is 14?

9. 20% of 30% of 350 is?

10. 80% of 11.5 m is how many meters?
    A. 0.092 m
    B. 0.92 m
    C. 9.2 m
    D. 92 m

11. What percent of 12 is 33?

12. 20% of 90% of 54 ounces is approximately?
    A. 0.972 ounces
    B. 9.72 ounces
    C. 97.2 ounces
    D. 972 ounces

13. What percent of 55 is 9.9?

14. 72 is approximately what percent of 368?
    A. 0.19%
    B. 12%
    C. 20%
    D. 25%

15. 6.35 is 25% of what number?

16. 115% of 80 gallons is closest to?
    A. 80 gallons
    B. 90 gallons
    C. 100 gallons
    D. 110 gallons

17. 2% of 4% of 40 is?
    A. 0.032
    B. 0.32
    C. 3.2
    D. 32

18. 63 is what percent of 14?

19. 12 km is 0.3% of how many km?

20. 13% of 27% of $150 is approximately?
    A. $4.80
    B. $5.30
    C. $6.00
    D. $6.90

244

PERCENT WORD PROBLEMS Practice Set 1

1. A fruit basket contains a total of 24 fruits. If there are 6 pears in the basket, what percent of the fruits are pears?

2. A $200 coat goes on sale for $155. What was the percent discount?

3. Two-thirds of twenty percent of $180 is?

4. If 60% of a number equals 285, then 20% of the number equals?

5. During the summer, the price of a gallon of gas in California went up from $3.20 to $4.00. What was the percent increase in the price of a gallon of gas?

6. Jose deposited $12,000 in his savings account. If the money earns 2% interest annually, how much will be in Jose's account after 3 years?

7. What number is 20 less than 6% of 840?

8. The population of a town increased from 220,000 to 230,000 within a year. What was the approximate percent increase in population for the town?
   A. 4.3%
   B. 4.4%
   C. 4.5%
   D. 4.6%

9. Best Buy is having a sale during the month of December; all goods are on a 10% discount. What would be the price of an Xbox that was originally being sold for $275?

10. The sales tax on a car valued at $35,600 is $1,424. What is the tax rate?
    A. 4%
    B. 5%
    C. 6%
    D. 8%

11. Increased by 120%, the number 85 becomes?
    A. 102
    B. 120
    C. 170
    D. 187

12. Lauren receives a base salary of $1,200 plus a 9% commission on any sales over $4,000. If in one month she sold $15,500 worth of goods, what was her total salary?

13. During the recession, the cost of all real estate declines by 15%. What would be the cost of a house after the recession, if the house was originally valued at $1,250,000?

14. Phil spent 30% of his allowance on video games. He then spent 40% of what was left on comic books. What percent of his allowance was he left with?
    A. 30%
    B. 42%
    C. 58%
    D. 70%

15. How much larger than 40 is 80?
    A. 40%
    B. 50%
    C. 100%
    D. 200%

16. The price of a company's stock decreased by 8% on Monday. On Tuesday, the price increased by 10%. What was the percent change in the price of the company's stock over the two days?
    A. 1.2%
    B. 2%
    C. 10%
    D. 12%

17. A charity event raises $44,000. If this value is only $33\frac{1}{3}\%$ of their goal, what was their goal?

18. A dealer buys a car for $6,000. How much do you have to pay for the car if the dealer makes a 20% profit and there is a 10% sales tax?

19. The number of new students enrolling at St. Francis is 780. If this number is 30% greater than the number of students who enrolled the previous year, how many students enrolled in the previous year?
    A. 546 students
    B. 600 students
    C. 700 students
    D. 1,014 students

20. The price of a share of stock fell 5% on Monday. Then rose 20% on Tuesday to $228. What was the price of the share of stock before trading began on Monday?
    A. $180
    B. $190
    C. $200
    D. $210

PERCENT WORD PROBLEMS Practice Set 2

1. Joe bought a dozen eggs. When he got home, he saw that 3 of the eggs were broken. What percent were broken?

2. A car usually sells for $15,000 dollars, but it is on sale this month for $12,750. What was the percent discount?

3. Five-ninths of forty percent of $675 is?

4. If 50% of a number is 465, then 30% of the number is?

5. Right before Thanksgiving, the price of a plane flight from LA to San Francisco went up from $80 to $130. What was the percent increase in the price of the flight?

6. Jesse takes out a loan for $14,000. It accumulates 15% interest annually. How much will Jesse owe after 2 years if he makes no payments?

7. What number is 50 less than 12% of 675?

8. The number of deer living in a forest increased from 14,000 to 17,000 within a year. What was the approximate percent increase in the deer population?
    A. 2.0%
    B. 2.1%
    C. 2.2%
    D. 2.3%

9. Target is having an after Christmas sale with all goods on a 20% discount. What would be the price of a pair of skis that were originally being sold for $320?

10. The sales tax on a horse valued at $12,600 is $1,008. What is the tax rate?
    A. 4%
    B. 5%
    C. 6%
    D. 8%

11. Increased by 110%, the number 60 becomes?
    A. 66
    B. 86
    C. 126
    D. 170

12. Jessica sells knives and receives a base salary of $1,200 per month plus a 8% commission on any knives she sells over $500. If in one month she sold $1,300 worth of goods, what was her total salary?

13. During the recession, number of jobs decreased by 25%. What would be the number of jobs after the recession if there were initially 150 million jobs in the US?

14. 30% of Jack's paycheck went to taxes. He then spent 24% of what was left on his rent. What percent of his paycheck was he left with?
    A. 32%
    B. 46%
    C. 53%
    D. 70%

15. How much larger than 30 is 90?
    A. 33%
    B. 66%
    C. 100%
    D. 200%

16. The price of a company's stock decreased by 4% on Thursday. On Friday, the price increased by 12%. Approximately what was the percent change in the price of the company's stock over the two days?
    A. 1.2%
    B. 7.5%
    C. 8%
    D. 16%

17. The Relay for Life raises $76,000. If this value is only $16\frac{1}{6}\%$ of their goal, what was their goal?

18. A dealer buys a diamond ring for $2,000. How much do you have to pay for the ring if the dealer makes a 25% profit and there is a 10% sales tax?

19. The number of students admitted to Stanford is 2,080. If this number is 8% greater than the number of students who enrolled the previous year, how many students enrolled in the previous year?
    A. 1,802 students
    B. 1,913 students
    C. 1,926 students
    D. 2,246 students

20. The price of a share of stock fell 13% on Monday. Then the price rose 13% on Tuesday to $145. What was the price of the share of stock before trading began on Monday?
    A. $143
    B. $145
    C. $147
    D. $149

PERCENT WORD PROBLEMS Practice Set 3

1. Heather has 20 pairs of socks in her drawer. She usually only wears pink socks, of which she has 8 pairs. What percent of her socks are pink?

2. James owns 15 cars. He stores 3 of the cars in the garage on his house. What percent of the cars are in the garage?

3. Anne has 18 different keys on her key ring. She has labeled 6 keys on her key ring. What percent of her keys are NOT labeled?

4. A collection of football pads usually sells for $420 dollars, but it is on sale this month for $294. What was the percent discount?

5. Two-sevenths of fifteen percent of 1,400 is?

6. If 75% of a number equals 365, then 15% of the number equals?

7. Jeff was trying to take the train to his grandmother's house this weekend. When he checked the price last week it was $60, but when he went to buy it today the price had risen to $75. What was the percent increase in the price of the train fare?

8. Bobby puts $18,000 in a magic piggy bank. The money in the piggy bank accumulates 6.5% interest annually. How much will Bobby have in the piggy bank after 2 years?

9. What number is 12 less than 0.5% of 12,000?

10. The number of squirrels living in a forest decreased from 15,000 to 12,000 within a year because of increasing coyote populations. What was the approximate percent decrease in population of squirrels?
    A. 10%
    B. 11%
    C. 13%
    D. 20%

11. During the summer, barbeque grills are on a 15% discount. What would be the price of a barbeque grill that was originally being sold for $582.25?

12. The sales tax on a pair of pants valued at $140 is $9.80. What is the tax rate?

    A. 4%

    B. 5%

    C. 6%

    D. 7%

13. Increased by 150%, the number 30 becomes?

    A. 45

    B. 60

    C. 75

    D. 90

14. Alex sells vacuum cleaners and receives a base salary of $2,200 per month plus a 10% commission on any vacuum cleaners she sells over $1,000. If in one month she sold $4,300 worth of goods, what was her total salary?

15. During the recession, the number of jobs decreased by 25%. What would be the number of jobs after the recession if there were initially 150 million jobs in the US?

16. 25% of Angela's paycheck went to taxes. She then spent 48% of what was left on her rent. What percent of her paycheck was she left with?

    A. 27%

    B. 39%

    C. 52%

    D. 60%

17. How much larger than 25 is 62.5?

    A. 25%

    B. 37.5%

    C. 150%

    D. 250%

18. The price of a company's stock decreased by 11% on Thursday. On Friday, the price increased by 15%. What was the percent change in the price of the company's stock over the two days?

    A. 2.35%

    B. 3.40%

    C. 4.15%

    D. 6.25%

19. A bake sale raises $1,500. If this value is only $33\frac{1}{3}\%$ of their goal, what was their goal?

20. A dealer buys a jet ski for $3,500. How much do you have to pay for the jet ski if the dealer makes a 15% profit and there is a 8% sales tax?

PERCENT WORD PROBLEMS Practice Set 4

1. Jose bought a bag of M&M's that contained 36 pieces of candy. He only eats the blue ones, of which there are 9. What percent of the M&M's are blue?

2. A jar for writing utensils holds 42 pens and 18 pencils. What percent of the jars contents are pencils?

3. Allen owns a barn that has 56 stalls that can hold one animal each. There are 35 cows currently staying in the barn. What percent of the stalls are EMPTY?

4. A painting by a local artist usually sells for $1,200 dollars, but it is on sale this month for $1,104. What was the percent discount?

5. Five-fourths of twenty percent of 340 is?

6. If 35% of a number equals 445, then 7% of the number equals?

7. Last week, gas prices were about $4.00 per gallon in the Bay Area. This week, they rose to $4.20 per gallon. What was the percent increase in the gas price per gallon?

8. Anna puts $10,000 in a retirement account. The money in the retirement account accumulates 11% interest annually. How much will Anna have in the piggy bank after 2 years?

9. What number is 11 less than 26% of 200?

10. In the spring, the frog population decreases dramatically because cars hit them. The population before the spring was 18,000 and after the spring it was 3,000. What was the approximate percent decrease in population of frogs during the spring?
    A. 17%
    B. 21%
    C. 83%
    D. 600%

11. The early bird special on season tickets to the 49ers games offers a 5% discount. If the full price for season tickets was $745, what is the discounted price?

12. The sales tax on a pair of pants valued at $540 is $32.40. What is the tax rate?
    A. 4%
    B. 6%
    C. 8%
    D. 10%

13. Increased by 250%, the number 40 becomes?
    A. 100
    B. 120
    C. 140
    D. 160

14. Jude sells cars and receives a base salary of $1,600 per month plus a 6% commission on any car he sells over $50,000. If in one month he sold $80,000 worth of cars, what was his total salary?

15. During the school year, the number of minutes per day spent doing activities outside decreased by 40%. How much time do kids spend doing activities outside each day if they initially spent 240 minutes outside per day?

16. 20% of Ben's paycheck went to taxes. He then spent 40% of what was left on his rent. What percent of his paycheck was he left with?
    A. 23%
    B. 40%
    C. 48%
    D. 62%

17. How much larger than 18 is 81?
    A. 45%
    B. 63%
    C. 350%
    D. 450%

18. The price of a company's stock decreased by 7% on Thursday. On Friday, the price increased by 9%. Approximately what was the percent change in the price of the company's stock over the two days?
    A. -1.3%
    B. 0%
    C. 0.5%
    D. 1.4%

19. A garage sale raises $3,600. If this value is only $66\frac{2}{3}\%$ of their goal, what was their goal?

20. A dealer buys a motorcycle for $8,000. How much do you have to pay for the motorcycle if the dealer makes a 10% profit and there is a 10% sales tax?

COMPARING FRACTIONS, DECIMALS, & PERCENTS Practice Set 1

Determine the decimal, fraction or percent of greater value in each set.

1. 27% or 0.265

2. 1.178 or 1.18

3. $\frac{1}{3}$ or 0.30

4. 2.78 or 281%

5. 8.803 or 8.821

6. $\frac{3}{7}$ or 40.2%

7. 0.218 or $\frac{2}{9}$

Order each set from least to greatest.

8. $\frac{1}{2}, 0.37, \frac{2}{5}, 29\%$

9. $\frac{1}{3}, 0.35, 31\%, \frac{2}{8}$

10. $165\%, \frac{9}{5}, 1.605, \frac{5}{3}$

11. $2.64, 2.604, 2.619, 2.651$

12. $\frac{3}{8}, 0.357, \frac{4}{11}, 36\%$

13. $8.3, 819\%, 8.088, 8.42$

14. $6.012, 6.102, 6.021, 6.201$

15. $\frac{2}{7}, 27\%, 0.209, 29\%$

16. $-3.306, -3.360, -3.063, -3.036$

17. Which of the following is closest in value to 7?
   A. 7.080
   B. 680%
   C. $7\frac{6}{1,000}$
   D. $\frac{6,900}{1,000}$

18. Which of the following is less than 2.7 but greater than 2.6?
   A. 268.9%
   B. 2.067
   C. 270.1%
   D. 2.589

19. Which of the following is greater than $\frac{2}{5}$ but less than 0.45?
   A. 46.1%
   B. $\frac{3}{7}$
   C. 0.398
   D. $\frac{6}{13}$

20. Which of the following is closest in value to $\frac{2}{3}$?
   A. 67%
   B. $\frac{607}{1,000}$
   C. 0.766
   D. $\frac{668}{1,000}$

COMPARING FRACTIONS, DECIMALS, & PERCENTS Practice Set 2

Determine the decimal, fraction or percent of greater value in each set.

1. 85% or 0.849

2. 3.388 or 3.39

3. $\frac{2}{3}$ or 65%

4. 4.37 or 4.307

5. 7.485 or 7.484

6. $\frac{5}{8}$ or 0.6

7. 32% or $\frac{2}{7}$

8. 9.115 or $\frac{73}{8}$

Order each set from least to greatest.

9. $\frac{2}{9}, 0.22, \frac{1}{8}, 13\%$

10. $\frac{3}{8}, 0.44, 35\%, \frac{3}{7}$

11. $144\%, \frac{12}{8}, 1.41, \frac{10}{7}$

12. $493.1\%, 4.906, 4.963, 496.1\%$

13. $\frac{5}{9}, \frac{3}{7}, 0.419, 49\%$

14. $6.161, 6.616, 6.661, 6.116$

15. $5.282, 525.2\%, \frac{21}{4}, \frac{37}{7}$

16. $75.757, 75.775, 75.575, 75.557$

17. Which of the following is closest in value to 5?
   A. 499.6%
   B. 5.007
   C. $\frac{4,997}{1,000}$
   D. $5\frac{6}{1,000}$

18. Which of the following is less than 3.5 but greater than 3.4?
   A. 3.59
   B. 304%
   C. $3\frac{3}{8}$
   D. $\frac{24}{7}$

19. Which of the following is furthest in value from 8?
   A. 763.4%
   B. 8.467
   C. $\frac{8,476}{1,000}$
   D. $7\frac{643}{1,000}$

20. Which of the following is greater than 2.8 or less than 2.7?
   A. $2\frac{5}{7}$
   B. $\frac{15}{6}$
   C. 271%
   D. 2.701

COMPARING FRACTIONS, DECIMALS, & PERCENTS Practice Set 3

Determine the decimal, fraction or percent of greater value from each set.

1. 0.34 or 33.6%

2. 2.259 or 2.26

3. $\frac{1}{6}$ or 15%

4. 3.94 or 3.904

5. 6.693 or 696.3%

6. $\frac{1}{7}$ or 14%

7. 0.76 or $\frac{7}{9}$

8. 9.011 or $\frac{82}{9}$

Order each set from least to greatest.

9. $\frac{2}{10}, \frac{1}{6}$ 21%, 0.14

10. $0.33, \frac{1}{3}, \frac{1}{4}, 26\%$

11. $\frac{12}{7}, 177\%, 1.74, \frac{7}{4}$

12. 3.525, 3.510, 3.55, 3.505

13. $91.5\%, \frac{5}{6}, \frac{11}{12}, 0.834$

14. 9.101, 9.111, 9.110, 9.011

15. $\frac{78}{9}, 862\%, \frac{69}{8}, 8.67$

16. 10.101, 10.011, 10.110, 10.001

17. Which of the following is closest in value to 6?
    A. 5.992
    B. 600.9%
    C. $5\frac{993}{1,000}$
    D. $\frac{6,008}{1,000}$

18. Which of the following is less than 4.9 but great than 4.8?
    A. $\frac{29}{6}$
    B. $4\frac{7}{9}$
    C. 491%
    D. 4.09

19. Which of the following is furthest in value from 7?
    A. 651.8%
    B. 7.492
    C. $\frac{6,552}{1,000}$
    D. $7\frac{481}{1,000}$

20. Which of the following is greater than 3.7 or less than 3.6?
    A. $3\frac{5}{8}$
    B. $\frac{33}{9}$
    C. 3.71
    D. 369%

COMPARING FRACTIONS, DECIMALS, & PERCENTS Practice Set 4

Determine the decimal, fraction or percent of greater value from each set.

1. 67% or 0.667

2. 4.456 or 4.46

3. $\frac{2}{9}$ or 21%

4. 516% or 5.106

5. 8.764 or 8.674

6. $\frac{5}{6}$ or 0.83

7. 0.87 or $\frac{7}{8}$

8. 915.2% or $\frac{64}{7}$

Order each set from least to greatest.

9. $0.29, \frac{1}{5}, 19\%, \frac{2}{7}$

10. $49\%, \frac{4}{7}, 0.46, \frac{3}{5}$

11. $116.9\%, \frac{10}{9}, \frac{7}{6}, 1.113$

12. $5.212, 5.201, 5.221, 5.202$

13. $\frac{2}{5}, 0.39, \frac{4}{9}, 30.9\%$

14. $7.054, 7.045, 7.504, 7.405$

15. $7.566, 755.6\%, \frac{53}{7}, \frac{68}{9}$

16. $96.699, 96.696, 96.996, 96.969$

17. Which of the following is closest in value to 9?
    A. 8.914
    B. 908.5%
    C. $9\frac{96}{1,000}$
    D. $\frac{8,910}{1,000}$

18. Which of the following is less than 6.2 but greater than 6.1?
    A. $6\frac{1}{5}$
    B. 6.21
    C. $\frac{37}{6}$
    D. 601%

19. Which of the following is furthest in value from 10?
    A. 9.225
    B. 10.858
    C. $\frac{9525}{1,000}$
    D. $10\frac{885}{1,000}$

20. Which of the following is greater than 5.3 or less than 5.2?
    A. $5\frac{2}{7}$
    B. $\frac{42}{8}$
    C. 521%
    D. 5.39

CHAPTER 9: EXPONENTS AND ROOTS

Experts in Test Prep, Tutoring, & Admissions Counseling

www.CardinalEducation.com

BASIC EXPONENTS Practice Set 1

1. $5^2 =$

2. $15^2 =$

3. $23^2 =$

4. $4^3 =$

5. $2^5 =$

6. $45^1 =$

7. $8^3 =$

8. $(-7)^2 =$

9. $-7^2 =$

10. $(-5)^3 =$

11. $(-3)^4 =$

12. $-(2^3) =$

13. $3^2 + 8^2 =$

14. $3^4 - 4^3 =$

15. $11^2 - 5^3 =$

16. $(20 - 8)^2 =$

17. $3^3 \times 2^2 =$

18. $5^3 \div 5^1 =$

19. $2^3 \times 3^2 \times 4^1 =$

20. $6^2 \times 20^2 \div 6^2 =$

BASIC EXPONENTS Practice Set 2

1. $0^{10} - 1^{10}$

2. 14^2

3. 7^3

4. $(-6)^4$

5. 10^3

6. $\frac{3^4}{9^2}$

7. Which of the following is equal to 12^4?
   - A. 12×4
   - B. $12 + 12 + 12 + 12$
   - C. 4^{12}
   - D. $12 \times 12 \times 12 \times 12$

8. $(-11)^3$

9. $-15^2 + (-9)^2$

10. $\frac{10^4}{10^2}$

11. $-3^4 - (-3)^4$

12. $\frac{2^3 - 4^2}{3^3}$

13. $5^3 - (-3)^3$

14. $2^3(3^2 - 4)$

15. $\frac{4^2 - 3^3}{4^2 + 3^2}$

16. True or false?
    $2^3 + 3^3 = 5^3$

17. $-5(-3)^3$

18. $3^4 \times 6^2$

19. $\frac{9^3}{3^3}$

20. $0^4(2^2 - 4^3 + 3^4) - (-3)^3 =$

BASIC ROOTS Practice Set 1

1. $\sqrt{49} =$

2. $\sqrt{9} =$

3. $\sqrt{1} =$

4. $\sqrt{64} =$

5. $\sqrt{121} =$

6. $\sqrt{225} =$

7. $\sqrt{169} =$

8. $\sqrt{400} =$

9. $\sqrt{900} =$

10. $\sqrt{0} =$

11. $\sqrt{289} =$
    A. 12
    B. 15
    C. 17
    D. 20

12. $\sqrt{529} =$
    A. 20
    B. 23
    C. 25
    D. 27

13. $\sqrt{1,600} =$
    A. 4
    B. 40
    C. 50
    D. 160

14. $\sqrt{961} =$
    A. 26
    B. 31
    C. 33
    D. 92

15. $\sqrt{256} =$
    A. 14
    B. 16
    C. 17
    D. 26

16. $\sqrt{35}$ is approximately
    A. 5
    B. 6
    C. 9
    D. 1,225

17. $\sqrt{170}$ is approximately
    A. 13
    B. 14
    C. 17
    D. 21

18. $\sqrt{7}$ is between
    A. 0 and 1
    B. 1 and 2
    C. 2 and 3
    D. 6 and 8

19. $\sqrt{20}$ is between
    A. 4 and 5
    B. 7 and 8
    C. 9 and 12
    D. 399 and 401

20. $\sqrt{200}$ is between
    A. 4 and 8
    B. 12 and 13
    C. 14 and 15
    D. 19 and 21

BASIC ROOTS Practice Set 2

1. $\sqrt{0} =$

2. $\sqrt{36} =$

3. $\sqrt{16} =$

4. $\sqrt{81} =$

5. $\sqrt{225} =$

6. $\sqrt{196} =$

7. $\sqrt{144} =$

8. $\sqrt{100} =$

9. $\sqrt{625} =$

10. $\sqrt{147}$ is approximately
    A. 12
    B. 13
    C. 14
    D. 15

11. $\sqrt{289} =$
    A. 13
    B. 16
    C. 17
    D. 19

12. $\sqrt{576} =$

13. $\sqrt{625} =$

14. Which of the following is closest to $\sqrt{50} + \sqrt{17}$?
    A. 8
    B. 9
    C. 11
    D. 14

15. True or false? $\sqrt{36 + 64} = \sqrt{36} + \sqrt{64}$

16. Simplify $\frac{\sqrt{81}}{\sqrt{9}}$

17. $\sqrt{961} =$
    A. 25
    B. 27
    C. 31
    D. 39

18. Which of the following is not equal to $\sqrt{4} + \sqrt{4}$?
    A. 4
    B. $\sqrt{4} \times \sqrt{4}$
    C. $\sqrt{16}$
    D. $\sqrt{8}$

19. $\sqrt{1,849} =$
    A. 33
    B. 37
    C. 43
    D. 47

20. Which of the following statements is false?
    A. $\sqrt{17} > 4$
    B. $\sqrt{9} + \sqrt{16} > \sqrt{9 + 16}$
    C. $\sqrt{50} < 7$
    D. $3 < \sqrt{10}$

CHALLENGING EXPONENTS Practice Set 1

1. $2^0 =$

2. 5^{-3}

3. $\left(\frac{2}{3}\right)^2 =$

4. $3.2 \times 10^3 + 2.7 \times 10^2 =$

5. Evaluate $8^{\frac{2}{3}} \times 3$.

6. $10^4 =$
   A. 10×4
   B. $10 + 10 + 10 + 10$
   C. $10 \times 10 \times 10 \times 10$
   D. 4^{10}

7. $1.8 \times 10^{-3} =$

8. Write 9,723 in expanded form, using exponents
   A. $(9 \times 10^2) + (7 \times 10^3) + (2 \times 10) + 3$
   B. $(9 \times 10^3) + (7 \times 10^2) + (2 \times 10) + 3$
   C. $(9 \times 10^3) + (7 \times 10) + (2 \times 10^1) - 7$
   D. $(9 \times 10^2) + (7 \times 10^1) + (2 \times 10) - 3$

9. Which of the following is **NOT** equal to 4^6?
   A. $4 \times 4 \times 4 \times 4 \times 4 \times 4$
   B. $(4^3)^2$
   C. $4^5 + 4^1$
   D. $4^4 \times 4^2$

10. What is the value of $(-1)^{50}(-5)^2$?
    A. -25
    B. -10
    C. 25
    D. 500

11. Which of the following is the greatest?
    A. 1.2×10^4
    B. 20×10^1
    C. 30.0×10^1
    D. 9.7×10^3

266

12. Find the value of $7 \times 10^3 - 1.6 \times 10^3$
    A. 5.4
    B. 540
    C. 5,400
    D. 54,000

13. Which of the following equations is true?
    A. $3^2 + 4^2 = 7^2$
    B. $(3 + 4)^2 > 7^2$
    C. $3^2 + 4^2 < (3 + 4)^2$
    D. $7^2 = 2^7$

14. What is the value of $(3^2)^6 - (3^4)^3$?

15. $-6(-32)^{\frac{3}{5}} =$

16. $10^4 \times \left(\frac{1}{10}\right)^3 =$

17. Find the value of $\frac{8^7 \times 6^5}{6^3 \times 8^6}$
    A. $\frac{4}{3}$
    B. 48
    C. 234
    D. 288

18. Evaluate $(2.4 \times 10^2) + (70 \times 10^2) - (45 \times 10^2)$

19. $\frac{9 \times 6^9}{3 \times 6^7} =$

20. Simplify $\left(\frac{4}{9}\right)^{\frac{3}{2}} - \left(\frac{3}{5}\right)^{-3}$

CHALLENGING EXPONENTS Practice Set 2

1. What is the cube of 4?

2. Evaluate $\frac{7^9}{7^6}$

3. $5.6 \times 10^0 =$

4. $4^{\frac{5}{2}} \times 4 =$

5. $6^6 =$
   A. $6 + 6 + 6 + 6 + 6 + 6$
   B. $(6 + 6)^2$
   C. $6 \times 6 \times 6 \times 6 \times 6 \times 6$
   D. 6×6

6. Find the value of $2.1 \times 10^5 + 5.6 \times 10^6$

7. $7.2 \times 10^{-6} =$

8. Which of the following is **NOT** equal to 9^6?
   A. $9^3 \times 9^3$
   B. $9 \times 9 \times 9 \times 9 \times 9 \times 9$
   C. $9^3 + 9^2$
   D. $(9^3)^2$

9. Write 4,839 in expanded form using exponents.
   A. $(4 \times 10^4) + (8 \times 10^3) + (3 \times 10^2) + 9$
   B. $(4 \times 10^3) + (8 \times 10) + (3 \times 10^2) - 9$
   C. $(4 \times 10^3) + (8 \times 10^2) + (3 \times 10) + 9$
   D. $(4 \times 10^4) + (8 \times 10^2) + (3 \times 10) - 9$

10. What is the value of $(-1)^{30}(-2)^{-4}$?
    A. -40
    B. -16
    C. $\frac{1}{16}$
    D. 240

11. Find the value of $6 \times 10^2 - 2{,}100 \times 10^{-3}$
    A. 2,100,060
    B. -2,099,940
    C. 4,384.78
    D. 597.9

12. Which of the following is the greatest?
    A. 8.9×10^3
    B. 0.15×10^4
    C. 4.8×10^4
    D. 73.0×10^3

13. Which of the following equations is true?
    A. $5^2 + 5^2 = 10^2$
    B. $5^2 + 5^2 < (5+5)^2$
    C. $(5+5)^2 > 10^2$
    D. $5^{10} = 10^5$

14. What is the value of $(7^9)^3 \div (7^5)^5$?

15. Simplify $-12(-2)^3$

16. Evaluate $4^7 \times \left(\frac{1}{4}\right)^4$

17. What is the value of $\frac{7^5 \times 4^7}{4^9 \times 7^4}$?
    A. $\frac{16}{7}$
    B. $\frac{7}{16}$
    C. 16
    D. 49

18. Evaluate $(30 \times 10^3) + (8.6 \times 10^2) - (72 \times 10^1)$

19. $\frac{10 \times 5^5}{15 \times 5^7} =$

20. Simplify $\left(\frac{1}{4}\right)^{-2} \times \left(\frac{1}{49}\right)^{-\frac{3}{2}}$

CHALLENGING EXPONENTS Practice Set 3

1. $17^0 =$

2. Evaluate $\frac{8^7}{8^5}$

3. $81^{\frac{3}{4}} \times 6 =$

4. $2^8 =$
   A. 8^2
   B. 2×8
   C. $2 \times 2 \times 2 \times 2 \times 2 \times 2 \times 2 \times 2$
   D. $2 + 2 + 2 + 2 + 2 + 2 + 2 + 2$

5. Which of the following is **NOT** equal to 5^5?
   A. $5 \times 5 \times 5 \times 5 \times 5$
   B. $5^2 \times 5^3$
   C. 5×5
   D. $5^3 \times 25$

6. $128 \times 4^{-3} =$

7. Find the value of $\left(\frac{5}{2}\right)^{-3}$

8. $7.4 \times 10^{-5} =$

9. Write 8,113 in expanded form using exponents.
   A. $(8 \times 10^4) + (1 \times 10^3) + (1 \times 10^2) + 3$
   B. $(8 \times 10^4) + (1 \times 10^2) + (1 \times 10) - 3$
   C. $(8 \times 10^3) + (1 \times 10^1) + (1 \times 10) + 3$
   D. $(8 \times 10^3) + (1 \times 10^1) + (1 \times 10^2) + 3$

10. Which of the following is the greatest?
    A. 39×10^2
    B. 2.0×10^3
    C. 61×10^1
    D. 0.54×10^3

11. Find the value of $125^{\frac{4}{3}}$

270

12. What is the value of $(-1)^{85}(-6)^0$?

   A. -1
   B. 0
   C. 1
   D. 6

13. Which of the following equations is true?

   A. $1^2 + 2^2 = 3^2$
   B. $(1 + 2)^2 < 3^2$
   C. $(1 + 2)^2 > 1^2 + 2^2$
   D. $1^2 = 2^1$

14. What is the value of $(5^2)^9 - (5^3)^6$?

15. Simplify $8(-4)^3$

16. Evaluate $50,000 \times \left(\frac{1}{10}\right)^7$

17. Find the value of $\frac{9^3 \times 3^9}{3^8 \times 9^4}$

   A. $\frac{1}{3}$
   B. 3
   C. 9
   D. 27

18. Simplify $\left(\frac{2}{9}\right)^{-2} \times \left(\frac{64}{25}\right)^{\frac{1}{2}}$

19. Evaluate $(1.9 \times 10^3) + (47 \times 10^3) - (0.61 \times 10^3)$

20. Simplify $\frac{16 \times 8^8}{8 \times 8^5}$

CHALLENGING EXPONENTS Practice Set 4

1. $5^{-4} =$

2. Evaluate $\frac{9^5}{9^2}$

3. $100^{\frac{5}{2}}$

4. Find the value of $8.3 \times 10^3 + 1.7 \times 10^4$

5. $4^{-\frac{1}{2}} \times 3 =$

6. $3.8 \times 10^{-4} =$

7. $7^6 =$
    A. $7 + 7 + 7 + 7 + 7 + 7$
    B. 7×6
    C. 6^7
    D. $7 \times 7 \times 7 \times 7 \times 7 \times 7$

8. Which of the following is **NOT** equal to 8^4?
    A. $(8^2)^2$
    B. $8^2 + 8^2$
    C. $8 \times 8 \times 8 \times 8$
    D. $8^2 \times 8^2$

9. Write 2,833 in expanded form using exponents.
    A. $(2 \times 10^3) + (8 \times 10^2) + (3 \times 10) - 3$
    B. $(2 \times 10^3) + (8 \times 10^2) + (3 \times 10) + 3$
    C. $(2 \times 10^4) + (8 \times 10^3) + (3 \times 10^2) - 3$
    D. $(2 \times 10^4) + (8 \times 10^2) + (3 \times 10) + 3$

10. Which of the following is the greatest?
    A. 7.02×10^2
    B. 4.1×10^2
    C. 0.53×10^3
    D. 38.0×10^1

11. What is the value of $(-1)^{77}(-4)^3$?
    A. -12
    B. -64
    C. 12
    D. 64

272

12. Find the value of $9 \times 10^3 - 5.7 \times 10^2$
    A. 3.3×10^2
    B. $8,430$
    C. 330×10^2
    D. 8.43×10^2

13. Which of the following equations is true?
    A. $2^2 + 4^2 = 6^2$
    B. $(2 + 4)^2 < 6^2$
    C. $2^2 + 4^2 > (2 + 4)^2$
    D. $2^4 = 4^2$

14. Evaluate $\left(\frac{3}{2}\right)^4 \times \left(\frac{1}{3}\right)^3$

15. What is the value of $(6^4)^4 - (6^2)^8$?

16. Simplify $-20(-5)^{-3}$

17. Evaluate $(65 \times 10^2) + (55 \times 10^1) - (7.4 \times 10^2)$

18. Simplify $\frac{8 \times 4^8}{2 \times 4^5}$

19. Find the value of $\frac{8^6 \times 2^2}{2^8 \times 8^5}$
    A. $\frac{1}{8}$
    B. $\frac{1}{2}$
    C. 1
    D. 64

20. Simplify $256^{\frac{3}{4}} \div \left(\frac{1}{8}\right)^{-2}$

CHALLENGING ROOTS Practice Set 1

1. $\sqrt{3} + \sqrt{3} =$

2. $3\sqrt{2} + \sqrt{2} =$

3. $5\sqrt{3} - 2\sqrt{3} =$

4. $11\sqrt{7} + 4\sqrt{7} =$

5. $3\sqrt{5} + 2\sqrt{5} - \sqrt{5} =$

6. $21\sqrt{6} - 15\sqrt{6} - 8\sqrt{6} =$

7. $5\sqrt{5} - 11\sqrt{5} + 8\sqrt{5} =$

8. $2\sqrt{3} + 8\sqrt{2} - 4\sqrt{3} + 3\sqrt{2} =$

9. $7\sqrt{7} + 4\sqrt{6} - 3\sqrt{6} - 9\sqrt{7} =$

10. $16\sqrt{13} - 22\sqrt{23} - 11\sqrt{13} + 15\sqrt{23} =$

11. $\sqrt{5} \times \sqrt{5} =$

12. $2\sqrt{7} + 5\sqrt{7} =$

13. Evaluate $\frac{\sqrt{80}}{\sqrt{5}}$

14. $3\sqrt{16} \times 5\sqrt{25} =$

15. $\sqrt{50} + \sqrt{70}$ is approximately
    A. 12
    B. 13
    C. 15
    D. 20

16. $2\sqrt{3} - 5\sqrt{6} + 10\sqrt{3} - 7\sqrt{6} =$

17. $\sqrt{11} \times 2\sqrt{3} =$

18. $3\sqrt{6} \times 2\sqrt{6} =$

19. Which of the following is true?
    A. $\sqrt{4} > 3$
    B. $\sqrt{3} = 4$
    C. $3 + \sqrt{4} > 4$
    D. $4 + \sqrt{4} > 3\sqrt{4}$

20. Evaluate $2\sqrt{3} \times 4\sqrt{5} \times 3\sqrt{15}$

CHALLENGING ROOTS Practice Set 2

1. $\sqrt{7} + \sqrt{7} =$

2. $2\sqrt{11} + \sqrt{11} =$

3. $5\sqrt{6} - 3\sqrt{6} =$

4. $12\sqrt{3} + 7\sqrt{3} =$

5. $7\sqrt{5} + 2\sqrt{5} - 3\sqrt{5} =$

6. $4\sqrt{15} - 11\sqrt{15} - 8\sqrt{15} =$

7. $-5\sqrt{6} - 11\sqrt{6} + 4\sqrt{6} =$

8. $2\sqrt{2} + \sqrt{3} - 4\sqrt{2} - 3\sqrt{3} =$

9. $11\sqrt{11} - 12\sqrt{10} - 22\sqrt{10} + 17\sqrt{11} =$

10. $-2\sqrt{13} - 16\sqrt{17} + 9\sqrt{13} - 7\sqrt{17} =$

11. $3 \times \sqrt{9} =$

12. $\sqrt{2} - 3\sqrt{2} + 9\sqrt{2} =$

13. $\sqrt{3} \times \sqrt{7} =$

14. $4\sqrt{5} \times 3\sqrt{3} =$

15. Which of the following is true?
    A. $\sqrt{9} > 3$
    B. $\sqrt{15} < 4$
    C. $3 + 2 < \sqrt{10}$
    D. $2 > \sqrt{1} + \sqrt{1}$

16. $\frac{\sqrt{27}}{\sqrt{3}} =$

17. $8\sqrt{2} + 6\sqrt{7} - 3\sqrt{2} - 12\sqrt{7} =$

18. $\frac{\sqrt{54}}{\sqrt{24}} =$

19. $\sqrt{4} \times 2\sqrt{8} \times 4\sqrt{2} =$

20. $2\sqrt{8} \times \sqrt{18} =$

275

CHALLENGING ROOTS Practice Set 3

1. $\sqrt{5} + \sqrt{5} =$

2. $4\sqrt{7} + 2\sqrt{7} =$

3. $7\sqrt{11} - 4\sqrt{11} =$

4. $-5\sqrt{13} + 11\sqrt{13} =$

5. $2\sqrt{7} + 8\sqrt{7} - 6\sqrt{7} =$

6. $11\sqrt{22} - 2\sqrt{22} - 13\sqrt{22} =$

7. $-3\sqrt{15} - 7\sqrt{15} + 3\sqrt{15} =$

8. $\sqrt{6} + 4\sqrt{17} - 4\sqrt{6} + 2\sqrt{17} =$

9. $8\sqrt{5} - 19\sqrt{3} - 2\sqrt{5} + 22\sqrt{3} =$

10. $-5\sqrt{19} + 6\sqrt{43} - 11\sqrt{19} - 19\sqrt{43} =$

11. $4 \times \sqrt{16} =$

12. $\sqrt{6} \times \sqrt{7} =$

13. $\sqrt{17} + \sqrt{24}$ is approximately
    A. 7
    B. 9
    C. 11
    D. 12

14. $2\sqrt{9} + 3\sqrt{3} - 7\sqrt{3} =$

15. $\sqrt{9} \times 5\sqrt{6} =$

16. $2\sqrt{11} - 3\sqrt{17} + 8\sqrt{11} - 9\sqrt{17} =$

17. $2\sqrt{6} \times 11\sqrt{24} =$

18. $\frac{\sqrt{75}}{\sqrt{27}} =$

19. Which of the following is not true?
    A. $\sqrt{25} < 6$
    B. $\sqrt{7} \times \sqrt{7} = 7$
    C. $\sqrt{5} \times \sqrt{5} = 2\sqrt{5}$
    D. $\sqrt{8} \div \sqrt{2} = 2$

20. $\sqrt{31} \times \sqrt{3} =$

CHALLENGING ROOTS Practice Set 4

1. $\sqrt{9} + \sqrt{9} =$

2. $2\sqrt{14} + 3\sqrt{14} =$

3. $8\sqrt{11} - 5\sqrt{11} =$

4. $-6\sqrt{22} + 12\sqrt{22} =$

5. $7\sqrt{19} + 2\sqrt{19} - 6\sqrt{19} =$

6. $-3\sqrt{5} - 11\sqrt{5} - 2\sqrt{5} =$

7. $2\sqrt{17} - 5\sqrt{17} + 8\sqrt{17} =$

8. $8\sqrt{3} - 5\sqrt{7} + 11\sqrt{3} - 12\sqrt{7} =$

9. $3\sqrt{11} - 21\sqrt{22} - 5\sqrt{11} - 7\sqrt{11} =$

10. $-6\sqrt{13} + 4\sqrt{31} - 3\sqrt{13} - 2\sqrt{31} =$

11. $\sqrt{2} + 3\sqrt{2} =$

12. $\sqrt{6} \times \sqrt{6} =$

13. $\frac{\sqrt{32}}{\sqrt{2}} =$

14. $3\sqrt{7} - 2\sqrt{13} + 5\sqrt{7} - 4\sqrt{7} =$

15. $\sqrt{50} - \sqrt{37}$ is approximately?
    A. 1
    B. 3
    C. 13
    D. 16

16. $\sqrt{13} \times 3\sqrt{7} =$

17. $\sqrt{3} \times \sqrt{12} =$

18. $2\sqrt{80} \times 3\sqrt{5} =$

19. $4\sqrt{3} \times 2\sqrt{2} \times \sqrt{6} =$

20. Which of the following is true?
    A. $\sqrt{7} \times \sqrt{7} = 2\sqrt{7}$
    B. $\sqrt{7} + \sqrt{7} = \sqrt{14}$
    C. $\sqrt{7} \times \sqrt{7} = 7$
    D. $\sqrt{14} \times \sqrt{14} < 7$

CHALLENGING ORDER OF OPERATIONS Practice Set 1

1. $22 - 7 \times 4 + 8 =$

2. $36 - (-12) \div 6 - 18 =$

3. $-3(6 + 18 \div \sqrt{81} \times 5) =$

4. $2^2(20 \times 2 \div 5 + 12) =$

5. $3^2 + 8 - 3(2 + 15 \div \sqrt{9} \times 2) =$

6. $(8 - 5 \times 3) + 9^2 \div 27 - (-43) =$

7. $-3(54 \div 9) - 5(12 - 8 \times 3) =$

8. $(3^2)8 - 5(16 - 13) - (-42) =$

9. $6^2 \div 3(10 \times 2 \div 5) + 18 =$

10. $3 \times 4(2^4 + (-12) \div 6 \times 3^2) =$

278

11. $5^2 - 29 - 3(7^2 - 29 - 6 \times 5) =$

12. $10^2 - (3^2 \times 4 - 18) + 11^2 =$

13. $20 - 3^3(8 - 15 \div 3 \times 2) =$

14. $\left(\sqrt{49} \times 9 \div 21 + 18 \div 3^2 + 11\right)3 =$

15. $(8^2 - 2^3 \times 2^2 + 7^2) - 2(6^2 - 6 \times 3) =$

16. $-5^2 - 3^2\left(18 \div 9 \times \sqrt{16} - 12\right) =$

17. $\left(\sqrt{36} \times 3 - 6\right)^2 - 3(56 \div 8 - 3)^2 =$

18. $-5(2 - 22 \div 11 \times 2^3) + 3(72 \div 12 - 13) =$

19. $\left(128 \div \sqrt{64} - 3^2 \times 2\right)^3 + (36 - 11 \times 3)^3 =$

20. $\left(252 \div \sqrt{144} \times 3 \div 9\right)^2 - 4(3^2 - 28 \div 7)^2 + \left(221 \div 13 - 5 \times \sqrt[3]{27}\right) =$

CHALLENGING ORDER OF OPERATIONS Practice Set 2

1. $4 + \sqrt{64} \times \sqrt{49} - 2 =$

2. $5(2 + 21 \div \sqrt{9}) =$

3. $19 - 5 \times 3 + 3^2 =$

4. $4^2 - 4 \times 3 - (-7) =$

5. $-2(7 + \sqrt{225} \div 3 \times 4) =$

6. $5(2 \times 12 \div 2^3 - (-8)) =$

7. $2^2 + 4(9 \times 3 \div 6 - \sqrt{121}) =$

8. $3^3 + 7 - 5(2 - (-12) \div 4 \times 2) =$

9. $(6 + 7 \times (-2)) + 8^2 \div 2^4 - 27 =$

10. $-3(21 \div \sqrt{49}) + (14 - 6 \times 3) + 17 =$

280

11. $20 \div 5\left(\sqrt{100} \times 2 \div \sqrt{400} + 4\right) - 2\left(4 \times 8 \div 4^2\right) =$

12. $3 \times 2\left(10 \times 2^2 \div 5 - 5\right) + 4\left(4 \times \sqrt{36} \div 3\right) =$

13. $4^2 - 37 - \left(9^2 \div 27 + (-17)\right) =$

14. $-36 - \left(6^2 \times 2 \div 9\right) + 8^2 =$

15. $7 - \frac{1}{6}\left(8^2 \div 2^4 + 4 \times \sqrt{64}\right) - \frac{1}{5}(6 \times 7 - 12) =$

16. $\frac{1}{4}\left(9^2 \div 3^3 - 3^3\right) - \frac{1}{6}(8 \times 7 - 8) - 14 =$

17. $-2\left(2^3 + 6 - 4 \times 7\right) + \frac{1}{4}\left(63 \div 3^2 \times \sqrt{25} + 13\right) =$

18. $\frac{1}{5}\left(7^2 \div 7 \times 9 - 23\right) - \sqrt{25}\left(6 + 13 - 3 \times \sqrt{81}\right) =$

19. $\frac{2}{5}\left(40 - 8^2 \div 4^2 + 64 \div 2^4\right) - \frac{2}{3}\left(9^2 - 9 \times 6 + 3^3\right) =$

20. $\frac{3}{4}\left(4^2 + 12 \times 8 - 12\right) + \frac{3}{5}\left(\sqrt{121} - 12^2 \div 4 - 48 \div 8 \times 5\right) =$

CHALLENGING ORDER OF OPERATIONS Practice Set 3

1. $4^2 \div 2 + 8 + 6 \times (-2) =$

2. $(7 - 7 \times 2) - \sqrt{64} \div 2 + 5$

3. $8 \div 2 \times \left(20 \div \sqrt{100} + 5\right) + 4 \times 3 - 111^0 =$

4. $3^3 - 3\left(8 \div \sqrt{16} \times 7 - 5\right) =$

5. $(9 - 9 \times 3) + 9^2 \div 3 + (-22) =$

6. $\sqrt{144} \div 4(8 \times 2 \div 2^4 + 3) + 3((-6) \times 3 \div 9) =$

7. $7^2 - 29 - \left(8^2 \div 16 - \sqrt{400}\right) =$

8. $\frac{1}{3}\left(8 \times \sqrt{49} - 5\right) - \frac{1}{2}(4^2 - 3 \times 8) =$

9. $5^2 + 5 - (6^2 - 4^2) - (-12) =$

10. $-7 - 3\left(8 - \sqrt[3]{8} \times 3\right) - 12 + 2^2 \times 3 =$

11. $(2^2 \times 7 \div 4 - 2) \times (8^2 - \sqrt{64}) + 14 \div 2$

12. $\frac{1}{4}(\sqrt{25} \times 4 - 8) + 2^2 \times 3 - 7 =$

13. $(6 + 2)^2 \div 4 \times 2 - 3(2 + 1^5)^2$

14. $(9 \times 3^3 \div 3 + 15) - 2 \times (8 + 5^2 + 1)$

15. $5 - \frac{1}{4}(4^3 \div 2^3 + 5 \times 4) - \frac{1}{5}(\sqrt{49} \times 10 - 15) =$

16. $-3(9 + 3 - \sqrt{25} \times 7) + \frac{1}{2}(4^2 \div 2 \times 3 + 10) =$

17. $5^2 + 8 - (6^2 - 4^2 \times 2) + 12 \div (3^2 \div 9^{\frac{1}{2}})$

18. $-8(2 + 2^3 - 7 \times 2) - \frac{1}{3}(3^2 + 16^{\frac{1}{2}} \times 9) =$

19. $(4^3 \div 2^3 - 3 \times 2) - 2(8 + \sqrt{144} \div 4 + 5) + \frac{1}{2}(-3 \times 4 - 2) =$

20. $\frac{2}{3}(17 + 6^2 \div 9 + 36 \div 2^2) - \frac{2}{5}(5^2 - 10 \times 2 + 175) =$

CHALLENGING ORDER OF OPERATIONS Practice Set 4

1. $34 - \sqrt{64} \times 3 + (-12) =$

2. $44 + 18 \div 3^2 + (-29) =$

3. $84 \div \sqrt{49} - 10 \times 3 - 3 =$

4. $-4\left(5 + 28 \div (-7) \times \sqrt{9}\right) =$

5. $2\left(\sqrt{144} \times 4 \div 2^4 + 8\right) =$

6. $4^2 - 11 - 2(3 - 21 \div 7 \times (-2)) =$

7. $(11 - 6 \times 3) + 8^2 \div 4 + \sqrt{36} =$

8. $-3\left(72 \div 4\sqrt{36} + 2\right) - 2\left(18 - \sqrt{49} \times 3\right) =$

9. $(3^2)4 - 6\left(22 \times 2 \div 11 - \sqrt{81}\right) - 12 =$

10. $54 \div 9((-18) \times 3 \div (-27)) + 11 =$

11. $\sqrt{4} \times 7(22 - 3^3 \div 3 \times 2^2) =$

12. $6^2 + 13 - (9^2 - 32 - 8 \times 4) =$

13. $11^2 - (2^2 \times 8 - 31) - 10^2 =$

14. $30 - 4^2(9 - 22 \div \sqrt{121} \times 4) =$

15. $\left(13 \times \sqrt[3]{27} - 56 \div 8 \times 3 + 2\right)4 =$

16. $(7^2 - 7 \times 5 + 7^2) - 3\left(5^2 - \sqrt{25} \times 4\right) =$

17. $-8^2 - 4^2\left(24 \div (-8) \times \sqrt{100} \div (-5)\right) =$

18. $(13 \times 5 - 56)^2 - \sqrt[3]{8}\left(54 \div \sqrt{81} - 2^4\right) =$

19. $-\frac{1}{3}(176 \div 16 + 13) + \frac{2}{3}\left(42 - 8 \times 5 + 100^{\frac{1}{2}}\right) =$

20. $\frac{1}{4}\left(5^2 + 18 \times \sqrt[3]{27} - 3\right) + \frac{2}{5}\left(13 - 11^2 \div 11 + 56 \div 64^{\frac{1}{2}} - (-6)\right) =$

CHAPTER 10: ALGEBRA

Experts in Test Prep, Tutoring, & Admissions Counseling

www.CardinalEducation.com

CONCEPTUAL ALGEBRA Practice Set 1

1. Jack is j years old. Write an expression for how old Jack was five years ago.

2. There are thirty students who each have p pencils. Write an expression for the total number of pencils.

3. Kyla is 12 years old. Lizzi is y years younger than Kyla. Write an expression for Lizzi's age.

4. Owen's team wins first prize in a debate contest. The first prize of $200 is to be shared equally among the members of the debate team. If there are d members in the team, write an expression for how much each member received.

5. There are d donuts which are divided evenly among c children. Which of the following expresses the number of donuts that each child ate?
   - A. $\frac{c}{d}$
   - B. cd
   - C. $\frac{d}{c}$
   - D. $d - c$

6. Miles is m years old. His younger brother Ilan is i years old. Which of the following expressions represents how much older Miles is than his younger brother?
   - A. $i - m$
   - B. $i + m$
   - C. $m - i$
   - D. $2m - i$

7. The perimeter of a square is x. Which of the following represents the length of one side of the square?
   - A. $4x$
   - B. $\frac{x}{4}$
   - C. $2x$
   - D. $x - 4$

8. Katrina runs x miles on Monday. On Tuesday, she runs twice the distance that she ran on Monday. Which expression represents the total distance that Katrina ran?
   - A. $2x$
   - B. $x + 2$
   - C. $\frac{x}{2} + 2$
   - D. $3x$

9. Which expression represents "five less than three times a number?" Let n represent the number.
    A. $3n - 5$
    B. $5 - 3n$
    C. $\frac{3n}{5}$
    D. $5n - 3$

10. There are s students at Jordan. There are 200 more students at Woodside than there are at Jordan. Which expression represents the total number of students?
    A. $s + 200$
    B. $2s + 200$
    C. $s + 400$
    D. $2s - 200$

11. Roscoe has six less than two times the number of toys that Abby has. If Abby has b toys, which one of the following represents the number of toys that Roscoe has?
    A. $2b - 6$
    B. $\frac{1}{2}b - 6$
    C. $b - 12$
    D. $6 - 2b$

12. Which equation can be read as "3 more than 8 times a number is equal to 5 less than the number'?
    A. $8x + 3 = 5 - x$
    B. $8x + 3 = x - 5$
    C. $3x - 8 = x + 5$
    D. $3x + 8 = 5 - x$

13. The population of Palo Alto is 2,000 more than 3 times the population of Woodside. If the population of Woodside is w, which of the following represents the population of Palo Alto?
    A. $3w$
    B. $w + 2,000$
    C. $2,000 - w$
    D. $3w + 2,000$

14. Playing basketball, Aurelia scored a points, while Chloe scored c points. If Chloe scored seven more than half the points that Aurelia scored, which statement is true?
    A. $c = \frac{1}{2}a + 7$
    B. $a = 2c - 7$
    C. $c = 7 - 2a$
    D. $a = \frac{1}{2}c + 7$

288

15. Which of the following statements describes the equation $3x - 7 = y$ in words?
    A. y is seven more than three times x
    B. x is seven more than three times y
    C. y is seven less than three times x
    D. x is three more than seven times y

16. The amount of snow falling in Tahoe was s inches. The next day, twice the amount of snow was received. On the third day, the amount of snow was 2 inches less than the amount of snow received on the second day. Which of the following expressions shows the total amount of snow?
    A. $3s - 2$
    B. $3s$
    C. $4s - 2$
    D. $5s - 2$

17. Which equation can be read as "2 less than half of a number is equal to 7 more than five times the number"?
    A. $\frac{1}{2}n - 2 = 5n + 7$
    B. $\frac{1}{2}n - 7 = 5n - 2$
    C. $5n + 2 = 7n - 1$
    D. $2n - \frac{1}{2} = 5n + 7$

18. May and Ellie are counting the number of red cars driving by. May counts m cars and Ellie counts e cars. If Ellie counted 8 less cars than May, which equation is correct?
    A. $e - m = 8$
    B. $m - e = 8$
    C. $m + e = 8$
    D. $8 - e = m$

19. Which of the following statements describes the equation $x = \frac{1}{2}y + 17$ in words?
    A. x is half more than seventeen y
    B. y is seventeen less than half of x
    C. x is seventeen more than half of y
    D. y is half more than seventeen x

20. Eve has e dollars. She spends $8 on a new toy, and gives half of the remaining amount to her younger sister. Which expression shows the amount she gave to her sister?
    A. $\frac{e}{2} - 8$
    B. $e - 4$
    C. $\frac{e-8}{2}$
    D. $8 - \frac{e}{2}$

CONCEPTUAL ALGEBRA Practice Set 2

1. Roy has r shoes. He receives four more shoes this week. Write an expression for how many shoes he has now.

2. Five kids played foosball, and each scored p points. Write an expression for the total points that they scored.

3. Simon's iguana is 2 feet long. Jeff's snake is m feet longer than the iguana. Write an expression for the snake's length.

4. George's group wins $500 in the lottery. The money is to be shared equally among the u group members. Write an expression for how much each member receives.

5. A cake costs c dollars. If the cake has p slices, which of the following expresses the price of a single slice?
    A. c
    B. $\frac{c}{p}$
    C. $\frac{p}{c}$
    D. $c - p$

6. Vince is v years old. His older brother is j years old. Which expression shows how much younger Vince is than his brother?
    A. $v - j$
    B. $j - v$
    C. $j + v$
    D. $2v - j$

7. Elaine makes 100 holiday cards and splits the cards into m equal groups. How many cards are in each group?
    A. $100 - m$
    B. $100m$
    C. $\frac{100}{m}$
    D. $\frac{m}{100}$

8. The side of a square has a length of x. Which of the following represents the perimeter of the square?
    A. x^2
    B. $2x + 2y$
    C. $4x$
    D. $\frac{x}{4}$

9. Which expression represents "eight less than one-third of a number?" Let n represent the number.

    A. $8 - \frac{n}{3}$

    B. $\frac{n}{3} - 8$

    C. $8 - 3n$

    D. $5n$

10. Claire spends t hours doing homework on Monday. On Tuesday, she spends twice as long on homework as she did on Monday. Which expression represents the total time that Claire spent doing homework?

    A. $2t$

    B. $t + 2$

    C. $2t + 2$

    D. $3t$

11. Liz answers one more than five times the number of questions that Kyra answers. If Kyra answers k questions, how many questions does Liz answer?

    A. 6

    B. $6k$

    C. $5k + 1$

    D. $5k - 1$

12. The equation $4h - 12 = g$, shows the relationship between g and h. Which of the following statements describes the equation in words?

    A. g is 12 more than four times h

    B. h is 12 more than four times g

    C. h is 12 less than four times g

    D. g is 12 less than four times h

13. Which of the following statements describes the equation $y = \frac{2}{3}x + 4$ in words?

    A. y is four less than two-thirds of x

    B. x is four less than two-thirds of y

    C. y is four more than two-thirds of x

    D. x is four more than two-thirds of y

14. Tina gets 10 tries to beat the first level of a videogame. If she beats the level on try number x, which of the following represents the number of tries she had remaining when she beat the level?

    A. $10 - x$

    B. $10x$

    C. x

    D. $10 + x$

15. In the line below, the distance from point X to point Z is
    a. The distance from point Y to point Z is b. Which of the
    following gives the distance from X to Y?

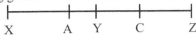

    X   A   Y   C   Z

    A. b

    B. $a + b$

    C. $a - b$

    D. $b - a$

16. Which story best fits the expression $a - 4 = j$?
    A. Jon has four more CDs than Andy.
    B. Jon and Andy together have 4 CDs.
    C. If Andy gave Jon four CDs, they would have an
       equal number of CDs.
    D. If Andy gave Jon two CDs, they would have an
       equal number of CDs.

17. If the perimeter of an octagon is $48z$, what is the length
    of one side of the octagon?
    A. 6
    B. 6z
    C. 8
    D. 8z

18. Jane made 10 less than four times as much as Ari. If Jane
    made j and Ari made a, which equation shows this?
    A. $a = 4j - 10$
    B. $j = 4a + 10$
    C. $j = 4a - 10$
    D. $j = 10 - 4a$

19. A small number is 7 more than half of x, a large number.
    Which expression represents the small number?
    A. $\frac{x}{2} + 7$
    B. $2x - 7$
    C. $2x - 14$
    D. $\frac{x}{2} - 7$

20. In a city, the number of men's teams is twelve more than
    one-fourth the number of women's teams. Which is true?
    A. $m = \frac{w}{16}$
    B. $m = \frac{w}{4} + 12$
    C. $m + 12 = 4w$
    D. $m + 12 = \frac{w}{4}$

CONCEPTUAL ALGEBRA Practice Set 3

1. Malik is h years old. Write an expression for how old Malik will be in ten years.

2. There are thirty-one flavors at the ice cream shop. The shop has c cartons of each flavor. Write an expression for the total number of cartons in the store.

3. Neil is 52 years old. Lanny is k years older than Neil. Write an expression for Lanny's age.

4. There are d dollars of tips to be split evenly among w waiters. Which of the following expresses the number of dollars each waiter receives?
   A. dw
   B. $d \div w$
   C. $d - w$
   D. $2w$

5. If Sean has j pieces of candy and he gives k pieces of candy to Gavin, how many pieces will Sean have left?
   A. j
   B. $k - j$
   C. $j - k$
   D. $k + j$

6. Dennis has f dollars, and Mac has no money. Dennis gives g dollars to Mac. How much money does Mac have now?
   A. f
   B. g
   C. $f + g$
   D. $f - g$

7. Charlie and Frank each have h slices of pizza. If Charlie eats half of his pizza, how much pizza will Frank and Charlie have together?
   A. h
   B. $2h$
   C. $0.5h$
   D. $1.5h$

8. Hank has $3r$ apples. Walter has $5r$ apples. How many apples do they have together?
   A. $2r$
   B. $8r$
   C. $15r$
   D. $15r^2$

9. From her house, Cindy has to drive y miles due east to get to the grocery store and z miles due west to get to the movie theatre. Which of the following represents the distance between the grocery store and the movie theatre?
    A. $y + z$
    B. $2y$
    C. yz
    D. $y - z$

10. Oswald has s groups of baseball cards, with t cards in each group. How many total baseball cards does he have?
    A. $s + t$
    B. $s - t$
    C. st
    D. $s \div t$

11. If the side of a square is a, which of the following represents the perimeter of the square?
    A. $2a$
    B. $4a$
    C. $8a$
    D. a^2

12. If the perimeter of a hexagon is $2b$, what is the length of one side of the hexagon?
    A. $12b$
    B. $6b$
    C. b
    D. $\frac{b}{3}$

13. In the line below, the distance from point A to point B is x. The distance from point A to point C is y. Which of the following gives the distance from B to C?
    A. y
    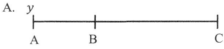
    B. $x + y$
    C. $x - y$
    D. $y - x$

14. The area of the rectangle below is 50. Which of the following equations correctly shows how to find the
    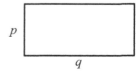
length of side p?
    A. $p = 50 - q$
    B. $p = 50 \div q$
    C. $p = 50q$
    D. $p = 50 - 2q$

294

15. Barbara won three times as many medals as Claire. If Barbara won b medals, and Claire won c medals, then which equation accurately represents this relationship?
  A. $3b = c$
  B. $3c = b$
  C. $c + 3 = b$
  D. $bc = 3$

16. Three less than five times a number is equal to eight more than the same number. This relationship is represented by which of the following equations?
  A. $3 - 5n = 8 + n$
  B. $5n - 3 = 8 - n$
  C. $(5 - 3)n = n + 8$
  D. $5n - 3 = n + 8$

17. A smaller number is 6 less than one-third of a larger number. If x represents the larger number, which of the following represents the smaller number?
  A. $\frac{x}{3} - 6$
  B. $\frac{3}{x} + 6$
  C. $3x - 6$
  D. $6 - \frac{3}{x}$

18. Which story best fits the expression $\frac{a+j}{5}$?
  A. Alex and Jim combine their marbles and divide the all the marbles into 5 smaller groups.
  B. Alex gave one-fifth of his marbles to Jim.
  C. Jim has five times as many marbles as Alex.
  D. Alex and Jim each received 10 more marbles and split their combined marbles in half.

19. Jason's weight is 50 pounds less than twice Phil's weight. If Phil's weighs p pounds, which of the following represents the sum of Jason's weight and Phil's weight?
  A. $3p - 50$
  B. $2p - 50$
  C. $p - 100$
  D. $2p + 50$

20. In the figure below, the area of the triangle is a. The sides of the rectangle are x and y. Which of the following equations is true?

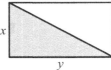

  A. $a = xy$
  B. $\frac{a}{2} = xy$
  C. $a = \frac{xy}{2}$
  D. $2ax = y$

CONCEPTUAL ALGEBRA Practice Set 4

1. Anna has t toys. She received two more toys today. Write an expression for how many toys she now has.

2. Twelve kids went trick-or-treating on Halloween, and each one of them received c candies. Write an expression for total amount of candy that they collected.

3. Haley is 4 feet tall. Her older brother is h feet taller than she is. Write an expression for her brother's height.

4. The sum of two numbers is 18. If one of the numbers is f, then the other number is?

5. A pizza costs p dollars. If the pizza has s slices, which of the following expresses the price of a single slice?
    A. ps
    B. $\frac{s}{p}$
    C. $\frac{p}{s}$
    D. $p - s$

6. Virginia spent v dollars at the village fair. Julia spent j dollars. Which of the following represents how much more Julia spent at the village fair than Virginia spent?
    A. $\frac{v}{j}$
    B. $j + v$
    C. $\frac{j}{v}$
    D. $j - v$

7. The Woodside boys' soccer team won g games in 2011. They won two more games in 2012 than they did the previous year. Which expression represents the total number of games they won in the two years?
    A. $g + 2$
    B. $2g + 2$
    C. $3g$
    D. $3g - 2$

8. Which expression represents "eleven less than twice a number"? Let the number be n.
    A. $2n - 11$
    B. $11 - 2n$
    C. $n - 22$
    D. $11n - 2$

296

9. A bookstore sells b fiction books. If the bookstore sold 15 more non-fiction books than fiction books, what is the total number of books sold by the bookstore?

    A. $2b$

    B. $b + 15$

    C. $2b + 15$

    D. $16b$

10. Zak answered two more than three times the number of questions that Mark answered. If Mark answered m questions, how many questions did Zak answer?

    A. $m + 3$

    B. $3m + 2$

    C. $2m + 3$

    D. $4m + 2$

11. Which expression represents "2 less than four-fifths of a number"? Let n be the number.

    A. $\frac{4}{5}n - 2$

    B. $\frac{5}{4}n + 2$

    C. $2 - \frac{5}{4}n$

    D. $2 - \frac{4}{5}n$

12. A wooden rod is cut into two pieces. The longer piece is w inches long and the shorter piece is 4 less than a half of the longer piece. Which of the following represents the length of the shorter piece?

    A. $w - 4$

    B. $\frac{1}{2}w - 2$

    C. $w - 2$

    D. $\frac{1}{2}w - 4$

13. Zak cycles for z kilometers and Julia cycles for j kilometers. If Julia cycled 10 less kilometers than Zak, which of the following equations is correct?

    A. $j - z = 10$

    B. $j + z = 10$

    C. $z - j = 10$

    D. $10 - j = z$

14. Which equation can be read as "5 less than 4 times a number equals 8 less the number"? Let the number be n.

    A. $5 - 4n = 8 - n$

    B. $4n - 5 = n - 8$

    C. $n - 5 = 4n - 8$

    D. $5 - 4n = n - 8$

15. Lisa walked l miles and Tim walked t miles. If Tim walked twice the distanced that Lisa walked, which of the following equations is correct?

    A. $l = \frac{1}{2}t$

    B. $2t = l$

    C. $l = 2 + t$

    D. $t = 2 + l$

16. The equation $p = 2q + 3$, shows the relationship between p and q. Which of the following statements describes the equation in words?

    A. p is two more than three times q

    B. q is three more than two times p

    C. q is two more than three times p

    D. p is three more than two times q

17. Kat has k dollars saved. Serena has three times as much savings as Kat, and Drew has \$15 more in savings than Serena. How much money does Drew have saved?

    A. $k + 15$

    B. $15 - k$

    C. $3k + 15$

    D. $15k + 3$

18. Which of the following statements describes the equation $\frac{1}{3}a - 7 = b$ in words?

    A. a is seven more than one-third of b

    B. b is seven less than one-third of a

    C. a is seven less than one-third of b

    D. b is seven more than one-third of a

19. Brett weighs 5 lbs more than Joey. Jack weighs 2 lbs less than Joey. If Joey weighs x lbs, what is their total weight?

    A. $x + 3$

    B. $2x + 3$

    C. $x + 8$

    D. $3x + 3$

20. A car rental company has r red cars and b blue cars. If the number of red cars is 8 less than two-thirds the number of blue cars, which of the following equations is correct?

    A. $r = \frac{2}{3}b - 8$

    B. $b = 8 - \frac{3}{2}r$

    C. $r = 8 - \frac{2}{3}r$

    D. $b = 8 - \frac{2}{3}r$

BASIC ALGEBRA Practice Set 1

Find the value of x.

1. $19 = x + 7$

2. $4x = 20$

3. $2x - 8 = 28$

4. $\frac{1}{4}x = 7$

5. $25 - 3x = 7$

6. If $2x = 8$, what must $2x + 5$ equal?

7. If $4a - 4 = 24$, what must $a - 1$ equal?

8. If $12 + 4y = 24$, what must $3 + y$ equal?

9. If $m + 2 = 10$, what must $3m + 6$ equal?

10. If $6a - 3 = 27$, what must $2a - 1$ equal?

11. Use the equations to answer the question.
    $a + 4 = 7$
    $b + 2 = 3$
    What is $a + b$?

12. Use the equations to answer the question.
    $x + 2 = 6$
    $3 + y = 3$
    What is $x + y$?

13. Use the equations to answer the question.
    $11 - m = 8$
    $n + 2 = 4$
    What is $m - n$?

14. Use the equations to answer the question.
    $3 + 3a = 15$
    $12 - 2b = 8$
    What is the value of $a - b$?

15. Simplify the expression
    $2x + 4x - 3$

16. Simplify the expression
    $5a - 3 + a + 4$

17. Simplify the expression
    $2a - 3b - a + 5b$

18. If $x + 2 = y$, which expression is equal to x?
    A. $y - 2$
    B. $y + 2$
    C. $-2 - y$
    D. $2 - y$

19. If $j + k = 9$, which expression is equal to j?
    A. $k - 9$
    B. $-9 - k$
    C. $9 + k$
    D. $9 - k$

20. If $5 - c = d$, which expressions is equal to c?
    A. $5 + d$
    B. $d - 5$
    C. $-d + 5$
    D. $-5 - d$

BASIC ALGEBRA Practice Set 2

Find the value of x.

1. $20 = 2x - 8$

2. $3x + 5 = 38$

3. $12 + 5x = 52$

4. $\frac{1}{2}x - 1 = 5$

5. $18 - 2x = 4$

6. If $2x - 1 = 8$, what must $4x - 2$ equal?

7. If $3x - 7 = 12$, what must $9x - 21$ equal?

8. If $2x + 4y = 6$, what must $x + 2y$ equal?

9. If $y - 5x = 2$, what must $3y - 15x$ equal?

10. If $2a + 3b = c$, what must $4a + 6b$ equal?

11. Use the equations to answer the question.
    $4 + a = 8$
    $5 + b = 3$
    What is the sum of $a + b$?

12. Use the equations to answer the question.
    $x + 5 = 2$
    $2 + y = 5$
    What is the sum of $x + y$?

13. Use the equations to answer the question.
    $14 + m = 8$
    $n + 2 = 13$
    What is the sum of $m - n$?

14. Use the equations to answer the question.
    $1 + 2a = 11$
    $5 + 3b = 23$
    What is the value of of $a - b$?

15. Simplify the expression
    $2x - 3xy - 7y + 8xy - 2x$

16. Simplify the expression
    $5ab + 3b - 2a - 11ab + 11b$

17. Simplify the expression
    $2m - 3n - 7mn - 8n + 4m$

18. If $a - b = 5$, which expression is equal to b?
    A. $a + 5$
    B. $a - 5$
    C. $5 - a$
    D. $-5 - a$

19. If $m + n = 1$, which expression is equal to m?
    A. $1 + n$
    B. $n - 1$
    C. $-1 - n$
    D. $1 - n$

20. If $2 - x = y$, which expression is equal to x?
    A. $-y + 2$
    B. $2 + y$
    C. $y - 2$
    D. $-2 - y$

BASIC ALGEBRA Practice Set 3

Find the value of x.

1. $10 = x + 6$

2. $15 - x = 7$

3. $3x - 5 = 25$

4. $\frac{1}{5}x - 4 = 1$

5. $20 - 4x = 12$

6. If $3x = 33$, what must $3x + 5$ equal?

7. If $5a - 7 = 23$, what must $5a - 6$ equal?

8. If $1 + 2y = 7$, what must $2 + 4y$ equal?

9. If $2m + 6 = 10$, what must $m + 3$ equal?

10. If $4a - 12 = 16$, what must $a - 3$ equal?

11. Use the equations to answer the question.
    $a + 8 = 10$
    $b + 1 = 7$
    What is $a + b$?

12. Use the equations to answer the question.
    $x + 4 = 4$
    $5 + y = 9$
    What is $x + y$?

13. Use the equations to answer the question.
    $10 - m = 7$
    $n + 5 = 6$
    What is $m - n$?

14. Use the equations to answer the question.
    $2 + 2a = 16$
    $8 - 3b = 2$
    What is the value of $a - b$?

15. Simplify the expression
    $3x + 9 - 5$

16. Simplify the expression
    $4a + 5 + a - 3$

17. Simplify the expression
    $6a + 2b - a - 4b$

18. If $x + 9 = y$, then which expression is equal to x?
    A. $y + 9$
    B. $y - 9$
    C. $9 - y$
    D. $-9 - y$

19. If $j + k = 4$, then which expression is equal to j?
    A. $4 + k$
    B. $4 - k$
    C. $k - 4$
    D. $-4 - k$

20. If $6 - c = d$, then which expressions is equal to c?
    A. $-d + 6$
    B. $6 + d$
    C. $d - 6$
    D. $-6 - d$

BASIC ALGEBRA Practice Set 4

Find the value of x.

1. $3x + 7 = 28$

2. $54 = 4x + 6$

3. $18 + 2x = 14$

4. $\frac{1}{3}x - 8 = 7$

5. $5 - 3x = 23$

6. If $x + 3y = 19$, what must $2x + 6y$ equal?

7. If $6a - 3 = 21$, what must $2a - 1$ equal?

8. If $12x - 8y = 24$, what must $3x - 2y$ equal?

9. If $14m + 7n = 56$, what must $2m + n$ equal?

10. If $9a - 3 = 33$, what must $3a - 1$ equal?

11. Use the equations to answer the question.
    $x + 3 = 11$
    $2 + y = 22$
    What is the sum of $x + y$?

12. Use the equations to answer the question.
    $3 + m = 7$
    $n + 11 = 4$
    What is the sum of $m - n$?

13. Use the equations to answer the question.
    $2 + 4a = 22$
    $7 + 2b = 43$
    What is the value of of $b - a$?

14. Simplify the expression
    $18x - 7xy - 11y + 8xy - 22x$

15. Simplify the expression
    $13y + 2x - 9xy - 7y - 2xy - 6x$

16. Simplify the expression
    $42mn - 3m - 17n - 8n + 32mn - 17m$

17. If $w - z = 11$, then which expression is equal to z?
    A. $11 - w$
    B. $w + 11$
    C. $-w + 11$
    D. $w - 11$

18. If $g + h = -2$, then which expression is equal to h?
    A. $g - 2$
    B. $-2 - g$
    C. $2 - g$
    D. $g + 2$

19. If $7 - c = d$, then which expression is equal to c?
    A. $7 + d$
    B. $7 - d$
    C. $d - 7$
    D. $-7 - d$

20. If $x - y = z$, then which expression is equal to y?
    A. $z - x$
    B. $x + z$
    C. $x - z$
    D. $-z - x$

ALGEBRAIC EXPRESSIONS Practice Set 1

Simplify each expression.

1. $2c + c^2 + 5 - 3c + 3c^2$

2. $11a^2b - 5a^4b^2 - 7a^4b^2 - a^2b$

3. $xy^4 - (7xy^3 - xy^4) + xy^4$

4. $20r^2st^3 - 5rst - 4(5r^2st^3 - 6rst)$

5. Which expressions is equivalent to $(x - 4)(x + 4)$?
   A. 0
   B. $2x - 8$
   C. $x^2 - 16$
   D. $x^2 - 8x - 16$

6. Which expression is equivalent to $(x - 7)(x + 1)$?
   A. $x^2 - 6x - 7$
   B. $x^2 - 7$
   C. $2x - 6$
   D. $x^2 - 6$

7. If $(x - 6)^2 = x^2 - kx + 36$, what is the value of k?
   A. 6
   B. 12
   C. 18
   D. 36

8. If $(x - 3)(x + 4) = x^2 + x - f$, what is the value of f?
   A. -1
   B. 1
   C. 7
   D. 12

9. If $3p - 3 = xp - x$ and $p \neq 1$, what is the value of x?
   A. 1
   B. 3
   C. 6
   D. 9

10. If $4jk - k = 20j - 5$, what is the value of k?
    A. 4
    B. 5
    C. 9
    D. 29

11. For what value(s) of x does $\frac{x^2 - 4}{(x+1)(x-2)} = 0$?
    A. -2
    B. 2 and -1
    C. ± 2
    D. ± 16

12. Given $4 + ay = z$, find the value of a.
    A. $x = z - 4y$
    B. $a = 4z - y$
    C. $a = \frac{z - 4}{y}$
    D. $a = \frac{z}{4y}$

13. Given $-4a + 2bc = 12$, find the value of c.
  - A. $c = 12 + 4a - 2b$
  - B. $c = 2a - 6 + b$
  - C. $c = \dfrac{6+2a}{b}$
  - D. $c = \dfrac{b}{2+6a}$

17. Solve for x:
  $$3x^2 - 12 = 36$$
  - A. 1
  - B. ± 3
  - C. ± 4
  - D. 6

14. Given $x = \dfrac{y}{2-y}$, find the value of $3x$.
  - A. $\dfrac{3y}{6-y}$
  - B. $\dfrac{3y}{2-y}$
  - C. $\dfrac{-3y}{6+y}$
  - D. $\dfrac{3y}{6-3y}$

18. Solve for x:
  $$\frac{1}{4}x - 2 = 4$$
  - A. 12
  - B. 18
  - C. 24
  - D. 32

15. If $(5 + 12)m = m$, then what is the value of m?
  - A. 0
  - B. 7
  - C. 12
  - D. 16

19. Find the value of x:
  $$2x - y = -3$$
  $$2x + y = 7$$
  - A. -2
  - B. 0
  - C. 1
  - D. 2

16. Solve for x:
  $$2(x + 7) + 5x + 14 = 0$$
  - A. -4
  - B. -5
  - C. -7
  - D. 7

20. Find the value of $a + b$:
  $$2a + 5b = 19$$
  $$a + 2b = 8$$
  - A. 2
  - B. 3
  - C. 5
  - D. 6

ALGEBRAIC EXPRESSIONS Practice Set 2

Simplify each expression.

1. $6x - 2x^2 - 18 - 7x^2 - 18x + 22$

2. $3a^4b^2 - 2a^2b^4 + 4a^4b^2 - 3a^2b^4$

3. $m^3n^5 - (2m^2n^3 - 4m^3n^5) + 5m^2n^3$

4. $-4xy^2z^3 - 3(2x^2y^3 - 2xy^2z^3) - 5x^2y^3$

5. Which expression is equivalent to $(x - 4)(x - 5)$?
   A. $2x - 9$
   B. $x^2 - 20$
   C. $x^2 - x - 20$
   D. $x^2 - 9x - 20$

6. Which expression is equivalent to $(x + 3)(x - 2)$?
   A. $x^2 + x - 6$
   B. $x^2 - x$
   C. $x^2 - 6$
   D. $x^2 + 5x - 6$

7. If $(x + 8)^2 = x^2 + mx + 64$, what is the value of m?
   A. 8
   B. 16
   C. 24
   D. 64

8. If $(x - 6)^2 = x^2 - 12x + n$, what is the value of n?
   A. 3
   B. 12
   C. 36
   D. 72

9. If $4a - 4 = ab - b$ and $a \neq 1$, what is the value of b?
   A. 0
   B. 1
   C. 4
   D. 8

10. If $2xy - 4y = 8x - 16$ and $x \neq 2$, what is the value of y?
    A. 2
    B. 4
    C. 8
    D. 16

11. For what value(s) of x does $\frac{x^2 - 16}{(x-2)(x+3)} = 0$?
    A. 2
    B. 2 and -3
    C. ± 4
    D. 2 and 4

12. Given $xy - 8 = z$, find the value of y.
    A. $y = \frac{z+8}{x}$
    B. $y = z - x + 8$
    C. $y = \frac{z}{x} + 8$
    D. $y = \frac{x-8}{z}$

13. Given $4p + pq - 8 = 0$, find the value of q.
    - A. $q = 2 + 4p$
    - B. $q = \dfrac{8}{4p}$
    - C. $q = 2 - p$
    - D. $q = \dfrac{8 - 4p}{p}$

14. Given $a = \dfrac{5}{3-b}$, find the value of $\dfrac{1}{2}a$.
    - A. $\dfrac{10}{3-b}$
    - B. $\dfrac{5}{6-2b}$
    - C. $\dfrac{5}{6-b}$
    - D. $\dfrac{5}{3-2b}$

15. If $(2.25 + 1.75)d = d$, then what is the value of d?
    - A. 0
    - B. 1
    - C. 2
    - D. 3

16. Solve for x:
    $4(x - 4) - 2(x + 1) = 6$
    - A. 4
    - B. 8
    - C. 12
    - D. 16

17. Solve for x:
    $4x^2 - 2 = 98$
    - A. 4
    - B. ± 5
    - C. 5
    - D. ± 25

18. Solve for x:
    $\dfrac{x}{4} + 3 = 18$
    - A. 60
    - B. 64
    - C. 72
    - D. 84

19. Find the value of n:
    $2n - 3m = 1$
    $3n + 3m = 24$
    - A. -3
    - B. 3
    - C. 5
    - D. 9

20. Find the value of a:
    $b - a = 3$
    $2b - 5a = 9$
    - A. -4
    - B. -3
    - C. -2
    - D. -1

ALGEBRAIC EXPRESSIONS Practice Set 3

Simplify each expression.

1. $7a + 4a^2 - 11 - 5a + 6a^2$

2. $2x^2y - 4x^4y^2 + 8x^4y^2 - 2x^2y$

3. $pq^3 - 2(3p^2q^5 - pq^3) - 7p^2q^5$

4. $11r^2st^5 - 5rst^3 - 2(4r^2st^5 - 4rst^3)$

5. Which expressions is equivalent to $(x - 5)(x + 5)$?
   A. 0
   B. $2x - 10$
   C. $x^2 - 10$
   D. $x^2 - 25$

6. Which expression is equivalent to $(x + 9)(x - 1)$?
   A. $2x + 8$
   B. $x^2 + 8$
   C. $x^2 + 8x - 9$
   D. $x^2 + 9x + 8$

7. If $(x - 11)^2 = x^2 - px + 121$, what is the value of p?
   A. 11
   B. 22
   C. 44
   D. -22

8. If $(x - 4)(x + 7) = x^2 + 3x + d$, what is the value of d?
   A. -28
   B. 28
   C. 42
   D. 49

9. If $9w - 9 = wz - z$ and $w \neq 1$, what is the value of z?
   A. 1
   B. 3
   C. 9
   D. 12

10. If $3mn - n = 15m - 5$, what is the value of n?
    A. 3
    B. 5
    C. 9
    D. 15

11. For what value(s) of x does $\frac{x^2 - 9}{(x+5)(x-4)} = 0$
    A. ± 3
    B. 4 and -5
    C. -4 and 5
    D. ± 9

12. Given $6 + ab = c$, find the value of a.
    A. $a = c - 6b$
    B. $a = 6c - b$
    C. $a = \frac{c}{6b}$
    D. $a = \frac{c-6}{b}$

13. Given $-3r + st = 4$, find the value of t.
    - A. $t = 4 + 3r - s$
    - B. $t = \frac{4+3r}{s}$
    - C. $t = 3r - 4 + s$
    - D. $t = \frac{s}{4+3r}$

17. Solve for x:
    $2x^2 + 12 = 30$
    - A. 1
    - B. ± 2
    - C. ± 3
    - D. 9

14. Given $x = \frac{8-y}{5+y}$, find the value of $\frac{1}{3}x$.
    - A. $\frac{8-y}{15+3y}$
    - B. $\frac{8-y}{15+y}$
    - C. $\frac{24-3y}{5+y}$
    - D. $\frac{8-y}{5+3y}$

18. Solve for x:
    $\frac{2}{3}x - 13 = 5$
    - A. 12
    - B. 18
    - C. 21
    - D. 27

15. If $(22 - 19)a = a$, then what is the value of a?
    - A. 0
    - B. 3
    - C. 19
    - D. 22

19. Find the value of m:
    $2m - n = -3$
    $2m + n = -9$
    - A. -4
    - B. -3
    - C. -1
    - D. 2

16. Solve for x:
    $-3(x - 7) + 8x + 9 = 0$
    - A. -8
    - B. -7
    - C. -6
    - D. 5

20. Find the value of a:
    $4b + 3a = 7$
    $b + 2a = 8$
    - A. -2
    - B. 3
    - C. 4
    - D. 5

ALGEBRAIC EXPRESSIONS Practice Set 4

Simplify each expression.

1. $c^2 + 2 - 6c - 5c$

2. $10ab - 5a^4 - 15ab - 20a^4$

3. $2x^3y - (3xy - 5x^3y) + 8xy$

4. $6r^2st^3 - 12rst - 2(10r^2st^3 - 4rst)$

5. Which expressions is equivalent to $(x + 6)(x - 6)$?
   A. $2x$
   B. $2x - 12$
   C. $x^2 - 12x - 36$
   D. $x^2 - 36$

6. Which expression is equivalent to $(x - 5)(x + 2)$?
   A. $x^2 - 3x - 10$
   B. $x^2 - 10$
   C. $2x - 3x - 3$
   D. $x^2 - 7$

7. If $(x + 5)^2 = x^2 + kx + 25$, what is the value of k?
   A. 5
   B. 10
   C. 30
   D. 125

8. If $(x - 2)(x + 4) = x^2 + 2x - f$, what is the value of f?
   A. -2
   B. 2
   C. 8
   D. 12

9. If $5p + 5 = xp + x$ and $p \neq -1$, what is the value of x?
   A. 1
   B. 2
   C. 5
   D. 10

10. If $7gh - g = 21h - 3$, what is the value of g?
    A. 3
    B. 4
    C. 7
    D. 21

11. For what value(s) of x does $\frac{(x-3)(x+4)}{(x+1)(x-2)} = 0$?
    A. -1 and 2
    B. -2 and 1
    C. -3 and 4
    D. -4 and 3

12. Given $xy = z$, find the value of y.
    A. $y = z - x$
    B. $y = z + y$
    C. $y = \frac{z}{x}$
    D. $y = \frac{x}{z}$

13. Given $-2 + bc = 7$, find the value of c.
    A. $c = 9 - 2b$
    B. $c = 5 + b$
    C. $c = \frac{b}{5}$
    D. $c = \frac{9}{b}$

14. Given $x = 7y$, find the value of $3x$.
    A. $\frac{7y}{3}$
    B. $\frac{7}{3y}$
    C. $21y$
    D. $10y$

15. If $(3 - 8)m = m$, then what is the value of m?
    A. -24
    B. -5
    C. -4
    D. 0

16. Solve for x:
    $-1(x - 7) + 2x - 10 = 0$
    A. -3
    B. -5
    C. 5
    D. 3

17. Solve for x:
    $4x^2 - 4 = 0$
    A. ± 1
    B. ± 2
    C. ± 4
    D. 0

18. Solve for x:
    $\frac{3}{4}x - 5 = 4$
    A. 3
    B. 9
    C. 12
    D. 24

19. Find the value of x:
    $x - y = -3$
    $2x + y = 3$
    A. -2
    B. 0
    C. 1
    D. 3

20. Find the value of $a + b$:
    $a + 2b = 6$
    $a + 3b = 7$
    A. 2
    B. 3
    C. 5
    D. 6

ALGEBRAIC WORD PROBLEMS Practice Set 1

1. Eight times a certain number is 89.6. What is the result if we divide the original number by 4?
   - A. 2.8
   - B. 5.6
   - C. 11.6
   - D. 22.4

2. Luis scored 74%, 77% and 92% in his first algebra tests. What does he need on his fourth test to maintain an average of 80%?

3. The quotient of 42 and a number is equal to the product of three-fourths and 36 reduced by 21. Find the number.
   - A. 4
   - B. 5
   - C. 6
   - D. 7

4. The length of a rectangle is 6 more than twice its width. If the width is represented by x, find the perimeter of the rectangle in terms of x.
   - A. $4x + 6$
   - B. $6x + 12$
   - C. $6x + 6$
   - D. $4x + 12$

5. If $\frac{17}{2} = \frac{102}{a}$, then what is the value of a?

6. If the average of 8 and x is equal to the average of 11, 2, and x, what is the value of x?
   - A. 2
   - B. 3
   - C. 7
   - D. 8

7. Peter is p years old and Andrew is twice as old as Peter. What was the sum of their ages 7 years ago?
   - A. $p - 7$
   - B. $2p - 7$
   - C. $3p - 7$
   - D. $3p - 14$

8. For all real numbers m and n, $m \boxtimes n = n^2 - m^2 - n$. Find the value of $3 \boxtimes 5$.
   - A. 11
   - B. 12
   - C. 15
   - D. 22

9. Roger has b baseball cards. Mark has 4 less than three times the number of baseball cards that Roger has. If Mark loses 5 of his baseball cards, in terms of b, how many cards does he have left?
   A. $3b - 5$
   B. $b - 5$
   C. $3b - 9$
   D. $b - 1$

10. On a hike, Gloria saw five times as many sunflowers as dandelions. If the number of sunflowers she saw was s, and the total number of flowers was 54, which of the following equations can be used to find out how many flowers of each type Gloria saw?
    A. $s + \frac{s}{5} = 54$
    B. $s + 5s = 54$
    C. $s - 5s = 54$
    D. $\frac{5s}{54} = s$

11. Byron is b years old. Leon is l years old. Byron is 4 more than three times Leon's age. Which of the following equations represents the relationship between Byron's and Leon's ages?
    A. $b = 3l$
    B. $l = 3b - 4$
    C. $b = 3l + 4$
    D. $l = \frac{b}{3} + 4$

12. Stacy is half as old as Adam, who is seven years older than Morgan. If Morgan is 15 years old, how old will Stacy be five years from now?
    A. 11 years old
    B. 16 years old
    C. 17 years old
    D. 22 years old

13. The equation $h = -16t^2 + 5t + 70$ gives the height h of a rock thrown up at time t seconds. What is the height of the rock when $t = 2$?

14. If $c = 6$, and $d = \frac{1}{6}$, then the value of c expressed in terms of d is
    A. $6d$
    B. $\frac{d}{36}$
    C. $\frac{d}{6}$
    D. $36d$

15. Justine spends $122 to create a lemonade stand. If she sells p cups of lemonade at $2.50 per cup, which of the following expressions represents her profits after expenses?

    A. $p + 122$
    B. $2.5 - p$
    C. $2.5p - 122$
    D. $p - 122$

16. What is the total value in dollars of x quarters (25 cents) and $x - 5$ dimes (10 cents)?

    A. $2x - 5$
    B. $35x - 50$
    C. $0.5x + 35$
    D. $0.35x - 0.5$

For problems 17 and 18 refer to the following definition:

For all real numbers a and b, let $\boldsymbol{a\#b} = \frac{a+b}{a-b}$

17. Find the value of 6#9.

18. If $5\#x$ is an integer, then which one of the following could be a possible value of x?

    A. 2
    B. 7
    C. 8
    D. 9

19. Three times a certain number p is four less than twice y. Which of the following shows the correct relationship between p and y?

    A. $3p - 2y = 4$
    B. $\frac{2y}{3p} = 4$
    C. $3p + 2y = 4$
    D. $2y - 3p = 4$

20. If $a = \frac{1}{3}, b = \frac{3}{5}$, and $c = \sqrt{5}$, find the value of $2c^2 + 15b - 21a$.

ALGEBRAIC WORD PROBLEMS Practice Set 2

1. Five times a certain number is 60. What is the number divided by 4?
    A. 3
    B. 4
    C. 5
    D. 12

2. Evan scored 122, 102, 160, and 154 on his first four throws in a darts game. How much does he need to score on his fifth throw to bring his average up to 136?

3. The square of a number is equal to the quotient of 175 and 7. What is the number?
    A. 4
    B. 5
    C. 7
    D. 15

4. If $\frac{2}{3} = \frac{18}{x}$, then what is the value of x?

5. If $\frac{1}{4}$ of a number is 36, then $\frac{1}{9}$ of the same number is?
    A. 4
    B. 12
    C. 16
    D. 18

6. The product of what number and 6 is equal to 20% of 180?

7. Allen is q years old. Dori is 5 years younger. What is the sum of their ages?
    A. $q - 5$
    B. $q + 5$
    C. $2q + 5$
    D. $2q - 5$

8. The quotient of 252 and a number equals $\frac{3}{5}$ of 60. What is the number?
    A. 7
    B. 12
    C. 36
    D. 212

9. If the average of 22 and m is equal to the average of 18, 15, and m, what is the value of m?
    A. 0
    B. 2
    C. 10
    D. 12

10. For all real numbers $a\Psi b = -b + a^2$. What is the value of $5\Psi 7$?

11. Lily has d dollars. Harry has 5 dollars less than twice the money that Lily has. If Harry gets $7 more, how much money will she have?
    A. $d + 7$
    B. $d - 5$
    C. $2d - 5$
    D. $2d + 2$

12. At La Entrada, there are three times as many students who play soccer as those who play tennis. If the number of tennis players is t, and the number of students playing soccer or tennis is 450, which of the following equations can be used to find the number of students that play tennis?
    A. $3t = 450$
    B. $4t = 450$
    C. $\frac{t}{3} = 450$
    D. $\frac{3}{t} = 450$

13. Dave is d years old and Andrew is a years old. If Dave is 3 more than half of Andrew's age, which of the following equations represents the relationship between Dave's and Andrew's ages?
    A. $d = a + 3$
    B. $a = \frac{1}{2}d$
    C. $d = \frac{1}{2}a + 3$
    D. $d = a - \frac{3}{2}$

14. If $x = 8$, and $y = \frac{1}{24}$, then the value of x in terms of y is?
    A. $3y$
    B. $8y$
    C. $24y$
    D. $192y$

15. The square root of $x - 1$ is equal to 3. What is the value of x?
    A. 3
    B. 9
    C. 10
    D. 12

16. The equation $A = \pi r^2 + 2\pi r$ gives the surface area of a cylinder. If $r = 4$, what is the surface area of the cylinder?
    A. 16π
    B. 24π
    C. 36π
    D. 64π

17. What is the value in dollars of p dimes and $p + 10$ pennies?
    - A. $2p + 10$
    - B. $0.2p + 1$
    - C. $0.11p + 0.1$
    - D. $0.11p + 10$

18. A baker sells c cupcakes at a cost of $1.25 each. If it cost $66 to buy all the ingredients to make the cupcakes, how much profit did the baker make?
    - A. $1.25c - 66$
    - B. $c - 66$
    - C. $1.25 - 66c$
    - D. $(1.25 - 66)c$

19. If $\frac{1}{2}$ of a number is 3 more than $\frac{1}{3}$ of the same number, what is the number?
    - A. 6
    - B. 12
    - C. 18
    - D. 24

20. $\frac{2}{5}$ of what number is equal to 4 less than 8 squared?
    - A. 120
    - B. 150
    - C. 180
    - D. 240

ALGEBRAIC WORD PROBLEMS Practice Set 3

1. Two-fifths of a certain number is equal to 24. What is the number?

2. If $\frac{1}{6}$ of a number is 45, then $\frac{2}{5}$ of the same number is?

3. To bring her average test score up to 89%, Melissa needs to score 95% on her fifth test in history. What was the total score for the first four tests she took?

4. The quotient of 32 and a number is equal to the product of 2 and 5. What is the number?
    A. 3.2
    B. 6
    C. 10.4
    D. 12

5. If $\frac{12}{b} = \frac{96}{40}$, then what is the number b?

6. The product of what number and 11 is equal to 15% of 440.

7. Duncan has p dollars. Damian has 7 dollars less than Duncan. How much money do they have all together?
    A. $p - 7$
    B. $2p$
    C. $2p + 7$
    D. $2p - 7$

8. The quotient of 110 and a number equals $\frac{1}{6}$ of 132. What is the number?
    A. 3
    B. 4
    C. 5
    D. 8

9. Chris is 4 years older than James. If James is x years old, what is the sum of their ages 5 years from now?
    A. $2x + 4$
    B. $2x + 5$
    C. $2x + 14$
    D. $2x + 16$

10. If the average of 15 and z is equal to the average of 13, 18, and z, what is the value of z?
    A. 5
    B. 9
    C. 16
    D. 17

11. Elliot has s shoes. Lydia has 3 more than twice the number of shoes that Elliot has. How many shoes do they have all together?

    A. $3s$

    B. $2s + 3$

    C. $3s + 9$

    D. $3s + 3$

12. There are r rooms at the Holiday Inn, and three times as many rooms at the Hilton Hotel. If the total number of rooms in the two hotels is 256, which of the following equations can be used to calculate the number of rooms at the Holiday Inn?

    A. $3r = 256$

    B. $\frac{r}{3} = 256$

    C. $4r = 256$

    D. $r = \frac{256}{3}$

13. Yvette is y years old, and Melissa is m years old. If Melissa is 3 years less than three times Yvette's age, which of the following shows the relationship between their ages?

    A. $m = 3y - 3$

    B. $y = 3m + 3$

    C. $m = \frac{y}{3} - 3$

    D. $3m = y - 3$

14. If $a = 2$ and $b = \frac{1}{16}$, the value of b in terms of a is?

    A. $2a$

    B. $4a$

    C. $\frac{a}{8}$

    D. $\frac{a}{32}$

15. The height h of a rock thrown vertically is given by the equation $h = -8t^2 + 10t + 85$ where t is time in seconds. What is the height of the rock when t is 3 seconds?

16. What is the total value in dollars of q quarters and $q - 3$ dimes?

    A. $2q - 3$

    B. $0.35q - 0.3$

    C. $0.25q - 3$

    D. $0.5q - 0.3$

17. The cube root of $a + 2$ equals to 2. What is a?

18. Sandra decides to start a lemonade stand. She sells c cups of lemonade at $1.50 a cup. If it cost her $22 to buy all the ingredients, how much in profit did she make?
    A. $1.5c - 22$
    B. $c - 22$
    C. $(22 - 1.5)c$
    D. $22 - \frac{1.5}{c}$

19. If $\frac{2}{5}$ of a number is 6 less than $\frac{3}{7}$ of the same number, what is the number?
    A. 180
    B. 200
    C. 210
    D. 240

20. $\frac{2}{9}$ of what number is equal to 5 less than 5 cubed?
    A. 125
    B. 300
    C. 480
    D. 540

ALGEBRAIC WORD PROBLEMS Practice Set 4

1. Three times what number is equal to 96?

2. If $\frac{1}{3}$ of a number is 22, then $\frac{1}{2}$ of the same number is?

3. To bring his average test score up to 85%, Cory needs to score 98% on his fourth test in English. What was the total score for the first three tests he took?

4. The product of what number and 7 is equal to $\frac{3}{4}$ of 84?

5. If $\frac{x}{9} = \frac{80}{180}$. What is the value of x?

6. There are c chairs in one classroom and 14 more chairs in another. What is the total number of chairs?
   A. $c + 14$
   B. $2c + 14$
   C. $15c$
   D. $c + \frac{c}{14}$

7. For real numbers, $t \emptyset s = 2t - s^2 + ts$. What is the $8 \emptyset 5$?

8. The quotient of 84 and what number is equal to 4% of 250?

9. If the average of 12 and y is equal to the average of 8, 14, and y, what is the value of y?
   A. 0
   B. 5
   C. 8
   D. 13

10. The SF Zoo has z animals. There are 6 less than twice the number of animals at the San Diego Zoo as there are at the SF Zoo. If 12 animals are added to the San Diego Zoo, how many animals are at the San Diego Zoo?
    A. $2z + 6$
    B. $2z - 6$
    C. $z + 12$
    D. $z - 6$

11. Stanford Stadium has s seats. Giants' stadium has 2,000 more seats. The number of seats in both stadiums is 102,000. What is the number of seats in Giants' stadium?
    A. 50,000 seats
    B. 52,000 seats
    C. 54,000 seats
    D. 56,000 seats

12. Jonathan is j years old, and Nicholas is n years old. Nicholas is 7 more than a third of Jonathan's age. Which equation shows the relationship between their ages?

    A. $j = 3n + 7$
    B. $n = 3j - 7$
    C. $n = \frac{j}{3} + 7$
    D. $j = \frac{n}{3} + 7$

13. If $m = \frac{1}{12}$ and $n = 36$, then the value of n expressed in terms of m is?

    A. $3m$
    B. $12m$
    C. $36m$
    D. $432m$

14. The distance s that a car travels is given by the equation $s = 8t + 8t^2$, where t is time in seconds. What is the distance travelled by the car in 0.5 minutes?

15. How many dollars is 6 quarters and $x - 3$ dimes?

    A. $0.1x + 1.2$
    B. $x + 1.5$
    C. $x + 1.8$
    D. $0.1x - 1.5$

16. If $\frac{1}{7}$ of a number is 4 less than $\frac{1}{5}$ of the same number, what is the number?

17. The cube root of $4 - b$ is equal to 3. What is b?

18. $\frac{2}{7}$ of what number is 18 more than 8 squared?

    A. 63
    B. 224
    C. 252
    D. 287

19. In the fraction $\frac{a}{ac}$ if the value of a and c are doubled, then the value of the fractions is?

    A. Doubled
    B. Halved
    C. Tripled
    D. Quadrupled

20. Machine A produces x toys a day. Machine B produces 120 less toys than Machine A. What is the average number of toys produced by the two machines in a day?

    A. $x - 120$
    B. $\frac{x}{2} - 120$
    C. $x - 60$
    D. $x + 120$

INEQUALITIES & ABSOLUTE VALUE Practice Set 1

1. What is the solution to the inequality $3x > 15$?
   A. $x > 3$
   B. $x > 5$
   C. $x < 5$
   D. $x > 12$

2. What is the solution to the inequality $2x - 3 > 11$?
   A. $x > 6$
   B. $x > 7$
   C. $x < 14$
   D. $x > 14$

3. What is the solution to the inequality $4x + 8 \geq 6x$?
   A. $x \geq 4$
   B. $x \leq 4$
   C. $x \geq 2$
   D. $x > 8$

4. What is the solution to the inequality $-3x - 8 \leq 10$?
   A. $x \leq -6$
   B. $x \geq -6$
   C. $x \geq 6$
   D. $x \leq 6$

5. What is the solution to the inequality $-13 \leq -10x + 7$?
   A. $x \geq 2$
   B. $x \leq 2$
   C. $x \geq -2$
   D. $x \leq -2$

6. Solve for x: $|x| = 8$
   A. 8
   B. ± 8
   C. -8
   D. ± 4

7. Solve for x: $|x + 5| = 11$
   A. ± 6
   B. 6 and -16
   C. 6
   D. 16

8. Solve for x: $|2x + 4| = 18$
   A. ± 7
   B. 7 and -11
   C. 7
   D. 11

9. Solve for x: $|-2x - 3| = 19$
   A. ± 11
   B. 8 and -11
   C. ± 8
   D. 11 and -8

10. Solve for x: $|x - 10| = -17$
    A. 7
    B. 27 and -7
    C. -7
    D. There is no solution for x.

11. Which solution set satisfies the absolute value
    function $|x + 5| \geq 7$?
    A. $x \geq 7$
    B. $x \geq 2$ or $x \leq -12$
    C. $x \geq 2$ or $x \geq -12$
    D. $x \geq 12$ or $x \geq 2$

12. Which solution set satisfies the absolute value
    function $|x - 3| \leq 1$?
    A. $x \leq 4$
    B. $2 \leq x \leq 4$
    C. $x \leq 2$ or $x \geq 4$
    D. $x \geq 2$ or $x \leq -2$

13. Which solution set satisfies the absolute value
    function $|x - 3| - 5 \leq 2$?
    A. $x \leq 10$
    B. $-4 \leq x \leq 10$
    C. $x \leq -4$ or $x \geq 10$
    D. $6 \leq x \leq 10$

14. Which solution set satisfies the inequality
    $10 < x + 2 < 20$?
    A. $8 > x > 18$
    B. $8 < x < 18$
    C. $12 < x < 22$
    D. $x > 22$ or $x < 12$

15. Which solution set satisfies the inequality
    $-2 < x - 3 < 5$?
    A. $-5 < x < 8$
    B. $1 < x < 8$
    C. $1 < x < 2$
    D. $x > 8$ or $x < -5$

16. What is the maximum value for b, if $b = 10x$ for
    $5 \leq x \leq 9$?
    A. 50
    B. 90
    C. 89
    D. 450

17. What is the maximum value for k, if $k = m^2$ for
    $3 \geq m \geq -11$?
    A. 9
    B. 121
    C. 64
    D. 0

18. What is the minimum value for z, if $z = 2y^3$ for
    $-2 \leq y \leq 3$?
    A. -54
    B. -16
    C. 0
    D. 8

19. A solution set is graphed on the number line shown.

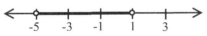

    A. $-5 > x > 1$
    B. $-5 < x < 1$
    C. $x < -5$ and $x > 1$
    D. $-5 \leq x \leq 1$

20. A solution set is graphed on the number line shown.

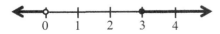

    A. $0 > x > 3$
    B. $0 \leq x < 3$
    C. $x \leq 3$ or $x > 0$
    D. $x \geq 3$ or $x < 0$

INEQUALITIES & ABSOLUTE VALUE Practice Set 2

1. True or false? $|-5| = 5$

2. True or false? $|-17| < 15$

3. Which of the following is correct?
   A. $|-11| = -11$
   B. $3 > |-2|$
   C. $-12 < -13$
   D. $|-22| < 22$

4. Which of the following is correct?
   A. $-7 > |-7|$
   B. $|3 - 2| > |2 - 3|$
   C. $-4 = -|-4|$
   D. $3 > |-9|$

5. Which of the following can be a solution to the absolute value $|x - 3| = 8$?
   A. -5
   B. -3
   C. 3
   D. 8

6. Which of the following can be a solution to the absolute value $|2x + 13| = 1$?
   A. -13
   B. -7
   C. 7
   D. 1

7. Which of the following can be a solution to the absolute value $|5x + 15| = 55$?
   A. -14
   B. -8
   C. 14
   D. 15

8. Which of the following does not satisfy the inequality $x < 4$?
   A. -4
   B. -1
   C. 3
   D. 4

9. Which of the following does not satisfy the inequality $x > -6$?
   A. -4
   B. -5
   C. -6
   D. -1

10. Which of the following does not satisfy the inequality $3x \leq 15$?
    A. -6
    B. 4
    C. 5
    D. 6

11. Which of the following does not satisfy the inequality $4x \geq 32$?
    A. 7
    B. 8
    C. 12
    D. 15

12. Which describes all values of x for which $|2x - 3| \geq 7$?
    A. $x \geq 10$
    B. $x \leq -2$
    C. $x \geq 5 \text{ or } x \leq -2$
    D. $x \leq 5 \text{ and } x \geq -2$

13. Which describes all values of x for which $|4x + 3| < 13$?

    A. $x > -4$ and $x < 2\frac{1}{2}$

    B. $x \geq -2\frac{1}{2}$ and $x \leq 4$

    C. $x < 4$ and $x > 2\frac{1}{2}$

    D. $x \geq 2\frac{1}{2}$ or $x \leq -4$

14. Which describes all values of x for which $|7 - x| > 2$?

    A. $x > 5$ or $x < 2$

    B. $x < -5$ or $x > 9$

    C. $x > 5$ and $x < 9$

    D. $x < 5$ or $x > 9$

15. Which describes all values of x for which $|6 - 2x| \leq 4$?

    A. $x \geq 1$ and $x \leq 5$

    B. $x \leq -1$ and $x \geq -5$

    C. $x \leq -1$ or $x \geq 5$

    D. $x \geq 1$ or $x \leq -5$

16. Which describes all values of x for which $|5 - 4x| \geq 27$?

    A. $x \leq 5\frac{1}{2}$ or $x \geq 8$

    B. $x \geq -5\frac{1}{2}$ and $x \leq 8$

    C. $x \leq 5\frac{1}{2}$ and $x \geq -8$

    D. $x \leq -5\frac{1}{2}$ or $x \geq 8$

17. Which solution set satisfies the inequality $-5 \leq 2x - 3 \leq 5$?

    A.
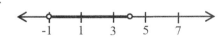

    B.
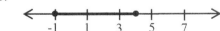

    C.

    D.
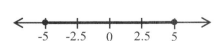

18. Which solution set satisfies the inequality $20 \leq 7x - 1 \leq 34$?

    A.

    B.

    C.
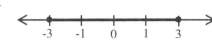

    D.

19. A solution set is graph on the number line shown.
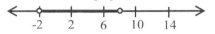

    A. $|x - 3| < 5$

    B. $|x + 5| > 9$

    C. $|x + 3| < 5$

    D. $|x + 2| > 6$

20. A solution set is graphed on the number line shown.

    A. $|x + 2| \geq 1$

    B. $|x + 3| \leq 1$

    C. $|x + 1| \leq 4$

    D. $|x + 4| \geq 1$

INEQUALITIES & ABSOLUTE VALUE Practice Set 3

1. True or false? $|-27| = -27$

2. Which of the following has the largest absolute value?
   - A. 4
   - B. 8
   - C. −9
   - D. −5

3. Which of the following is correct?
   - A. $-4 < |-5|$
   - B. $|7 - 5| > |5 - 7|$
   - C. $-9 = |-9|$
   - D. $11 < |-8|$

4. Which of the following is correct?
   - A. $|-13| = -13$
   - B. $5 < |-6|$
   - C. $12 < -13$
   - D. $|-88| < 88$

5. Which of the following can be a solution to the absolute value $|x + 1| = 7$?
   - A. −8
   - B. −6
   - C. 7
   - D. 8

6. Which of the following can be a solution to the absolute value $|3x + 6| = 9$?
   - A. −3
   - B. −1
   - C. 0
   - D. 1

7. Which of the following can be a solution to the absolute value $|4 - x| = 2$?
   - A. −2
   - B. −1
   - C. 6
   - D. 8

8. Which of the following does not satisfy the inequality $x < 9$?
   - A. −11
   - B. −8
   - C. 7
   - D. 9

9. Which of the following does not satisfy the inequality $x > -11$?
   - A. −13
   - B. −10
   - C. −6
   - D. 11

10. Which of the following does not satisfy the inequality $2x \leq 16$?
    - A. −2
    - B. 7
    - C. 11
    - D. 8

11. Which of the following does not satisfy the inequality $5x \geq 65$?
    - A. 15
    - B. 13
    - C. 16
    - D. 12

12. Which describes all values of x for which $|x - 1| \geq 9$?
    - A. $x \geq 10$
    - B. $x \leq -8 \text{ or } x \geq 10$
    - C. $x \geq -8 \text{ or } x \leq -10$
    - D. $x \leq 10 \text{ and } x \geq -8$

13. Which describes all values of x for which $|3x + 3| > 21$?

    A. $x > 6$ or $x < -8$

    B. $x \geq -8$ and $x \leq 6$

    C. $x < 6$ and $x > -8$

    D. $x \geq -8$ and $x \leq -6$

14. Which describes all values of x for which $|5 - x| > 7$?

    A. $x > 7$ and $x < 2$

    B. $x < -2$ or $x > 12$

    C. $x > 12$ or $x < 2$

    D. $x < 2$ and $x > -12$

15. Which describes all values of x for which $|10 - 5x| \leq 15$?

    A. $x \geq 1$ and $x \leq 5$

    B. $x \leq 1$ and $x \geq -5$

    C. $x \leq -1$ or $x \geq 5$

    D. $x \geq -1$ and $x \leq 5$

16. Which describes all values of x for which $|12 - 9x| \geq 6$?

    A. $x \leq \frac{2}{3}$ and $x \geq -2$

    B. $x \geq -\frac{2}{3}$ and $x \leq 2$

    C. $x \leq \frac{2}{3}$ or $x \geq 2$

    D. $x \leq -\frac{2}{3}$ or $x \geq 2$

17. Which solution set satisfies the inequality $-4 \leq 3x - 1 \leq 5$?

    A.

    B.

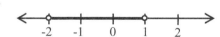

    C.

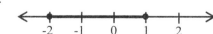

    D.

18. Which solution set satisfies the inequality $18 \leq 7x + 4 < 46$?

    A.

    B.

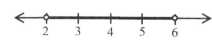

    C.

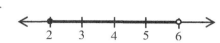

    D.

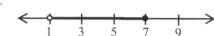

19. A solution set is graph on the number line shown.

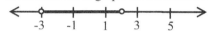

    A. $|x - 3| < 2$

    B. $|2x - 1| > 4$

    C. $|x + 2| < 3$

    D. $|2x + 1| < 5$

20. A solution set is graphed on the number line shown.

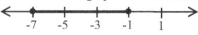

    A. $|x + 4| \geq -3$

    B. $|x + 3| \leq 4$

    C. $|x - 3| \geq -4$

    D. $|x + 1| \leq -6$

INEQUALITIES & ABSOLUTE VALUE Practice Set 4

1. What is the solution to the inequality $2x < 16$?
   - A. $x > 8$
   - B. $x > 14$
   - C. $x < 8$
   - D. $x < 18$

2. What is the solution to the inequality $5x + 1 > 16$?
   - A. $x > 3$
   - B. $x > 10$
   - C. $x < \frac{17}{5}$
   - D. $x > 85$

3. What is the solution to the inequality $x \geq 3x - 6$?
   - A. $x \geq -2$
   - B. $x \leq 2$
   - C. $x \geq -3$
   - D. $x \leq 3$

4. What is the solution to the inequality
   $-2x - 5 \leq 10 + 7$?
   - A. $x \geq -11$
   - B. $x \leq -11$
   - C. $x \geq 6$
   - D. $x \leq -6$

5. What is the solution to the inequality $-9 \leq -6x$?
   - A. $x \geq 3$
   - B. $x \leq -15$
   - C. $x \geq \frac{3}{2}$
   - D. $x \leq \frac{3}{2}$

6. Solve for x: $|x| = 20$
   - A. 20
   - B. -20
   - C. ± 20
   - D. $\sqrt{20}$

7. Solve for x: $|x - 3| = 5$
   - A. ± 8
   - B. 2 and 8
   - C. -2 and 8
   - D. 2 and -8

8. Solve for x: $|3x + 6| = 12$
   - A. ± 2
   - B. 2
   - C. 2 and 6
   - D. 2 and -6

9. Solve for x: $-4|-2x + 6| = -32$
   - A. 1 and -4
   - B. 2 and -6
   - C. -1 and 7
   - D. There is no solution for x.

10. Solve for x: $|x + 8| = -9$
    - A. $x = \pm 1$
    - B. $x = -17$ and $x = 1$
    - C. $x = -1$
    - D. There is no solution for x.

11. Which solution set satisfies the absolute value function $|x - 2| \geq 3$?
    - A. $x \geq 5$
    - B. $x \geq 5$ or $x \leq -1$
    - C. $x \geq -1$ and $x \leq 5$
    - D. $x \geq -5$ and $x \geq 1$

12. Which solution set satisfies the absolute value function $|x + 1| \leq 0$?
    - A. $x \leq 1$
    - B. $-1 \leq x \leq 1$
    - C. $x \leq -1$ or $x \geq 0$
    - D. $x = -1$

13. Which solution set satisfies the absolute value function $|x + 1| - 7 \leq 2$?
    - A. $x \leq 8$
    - B. $-10 \leq x \leq 8$
    - C. $x \leq -10$ or $x \geq 8$
    - D. $-8 \leq x \leq 10$

14. Which solution set satisfies the inequality
$5 < x - 3 < 11$?
    A. $8 < x < 14$
    B. $8 > x > 14$
    C. $2 < x < 8$
    D. $x > 8$ or $x < -8$

15. Which solution set satisfies the inequality
$-8 < x + 1 < -2$?
    A. $-9 < x < -3$
    B. $-7 < x < -1$
    C. $-9 < x < -1$
    D. $x > 7$ or $x < -3$

16. What is the maximum value for c, if $c = 3d^2$ for
$-4 \leq d \leq 5$?
    A. 0
    B. 48
    C. 75
    D. 243

17. What is the maximum value for x, if $x = y^2 - y$ for
$4 \geq y \geq -6$?
    A. -2
    B. 12
    C. 30
    D. 42

18. What is the minimum value for a, if $a = 2b^3 + 2$
for $-2 \leq b \leq 2$?
    A. -18
    B. -14
    C. 0
    D. 2

19. A solution set is graphed on the number line shown.
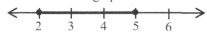
    A. $5 > x > 2$
    B. $5 < x < 2$
    C. $x \leq 2$ and $x \leq 5$
    D. $2 \leq x \leq 5$

20. A solution set is graphed on the number line shown.
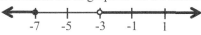
    A. $-7 > x > -3$
    B. $-7 \leq x < -3$
    C. $x \leq -7$ or $x > -3$
    D. $x > -7$ or $x \leq -3$

CHAPTER 11: WORD PROBLEMS

Experts in Test Prep, Tutoring, & Admissions Counseling

www.CardinalEducation.com

MEASUREMENT Practice Set 1

1. How many feet are in 2 miles?

2. How many ounces are in 3 pounds?

3. How many cups are in a gallon?

4. How many inches are in two yards?

5. How many centimeters are in a kilometer?

6. How many seconds are in one day?

7. 7,000 millimeters is how many meters?

8. 12,000 centimeters is how many meters?

9. 4.25 yards is how many inches?

10. 3.2 kilograms is how many milligrams?

11. 2.5 pints is how many ounces?

12. If Bruce spends 5 hours at the gym every week, how many hours will he spend at the gym in one year?

13. A recipe that feeds 1 person uses one cup of flour and one quart of water. If the same recipe is being used to feed 4 people, which of the following ingredient quantities is correct?
    A. 1 pint of flour and two quarts of water
    B. 1 pint of flour and one gallon of water
    C. 1 quart of flour and one gallon of water
    D. 2 quarts of flour and two gallons of water

14. If an adult fish weighs 3 kilograms and a baby fish weighs 10% of the adult fish, then how many grams does the baby fish weigh?

15. If mailing packages costs 25 cents for every ounce, what is the cost of mailing a package that weighs 2 pounds 8 ounces?

16. If steak costs $7.99 per pound, approximately how many ounces of steak could you buy for $25?
    A. 3 oz
    B. 33 oz
    C. 50 oz
    D. 200 oz

17. A professional athlete's salary is $2.4 million dollars per season. If a season has 100 games and the athlete plays 2 hours in every game, how much money is he paid each minute?

18. If there are 2.2 pounds in one kilogram, and Brett weighs 125 kilograms, how many pounds does he weigh?

19. If there are 1.6 kilometers in one mile, and Ben runs 10 kilometers, how many miles did he run?

20. Tommy can drive 1.5 miles in 90 seconds. How many kilometers can he drive in 1 hour?

MEASUREMENT Practice Set 2

1. How many pints are in 32 fl oz?

2. Which is the most reasonable unit to use when measuring the weight of a cell phone?
   A. Liters
   B. Ounces
   C. Centimeters
   D. Tons

3. A meter is what part of a kilometer?
   A. $\frac{1}{1,000}$
   B. $\frac{1}{100}$
   C. 10
   D. 1,000

4. How many liters are in 2 mL?

5. Change 350 minutes into hours. Leave your answer as a mixed fraction.

6. How many pounds are in 24 ounces?

7. How many grams are in 3.2 kg?

8. A running back in a football game runs for 167 yards. How many inches did he run for?

9. How many seconds are there in $\frac{1}{20}$ of a minute?
   A. 0.3 seconds
   B. 3 seconds
   C. 20 seconds
   D. 30 seconds

10. An adult whale shark can weigh up to 47,000 pounds. How many tons would such a whale shark weigh?
    A. 23.5 tons
    B. 47 tons
    C. 23.5 million tons
    D. 47 million tons

11. The ratio of 3 feet to 18 inches is?
    A. 1:6
    B. 1:9
    C. 2:1
    D. 3:1

12. What is the length in inches of 0.4 miles?

13. Patrick runs for 1.2 km on one day, 900 m the next day and 23,000 cm on the third day. What is the total distance in km that he ran on the three days?
    A. 2,3901.2 km
    B. 2.133 km
    C. 2.33 km
    D. 901.33 km

14. If $1 = 90 pesos, then $6.20 +200 pesos is equal to how many pesos?
    A. 200 pesos
    B. 490 pesos
    C. 558 pesos
    D. 758 pesos

15. A packet of eggs contains a dozen eggs, with each egg weighing 9 grams. What would be the weight in kilograms of 100 such packets?
    A. 10.8 kg
    B. 108 kg
    C. 1,080 kg
    D. 10,800 kg

16. Andrew spends 4.5 hours a week doing homework. How many seconds a week does Andrew spend doing homework?

17. $7\frac{1}{4}$ hours is how many more minutes than $6\frac{1}{3}$ hours?
    A. 50 minutes
    B. 55 minutes
    C. 56 minutes
    D. 58 minutes

18. A can of soda contains 200 mL of fluid. If cans are sold in six-packs, how many six-packs would contain 24 liters of fluid?
    A. 5 six-packs
    B. 10 six-packs
    C. 15 six-packs
    D. 20 six-packs

19. Which is the longest time?
    A. $2\frac{1}{2}$ hours
    B. $\frac{1}{12}$ of a day
    C. 300 minutes
    D. $\frac{1}{60}$ of a month

20. Wayne drives to a gas station and fills his car with 12.4 quarts of gas. If the price of gas is $3.50 per gallon, how much did Wayne pay?
    A. $8.50
    B. $10.50
    C. $10.85
    D. $43.40

MEASUREMENT Practice Set 3

1. How many millimeters are in 3.5 cm?

2. Which is the most reasonable unit for measuring the distance from Palo Alto to San Francisco?
   A. Inches
   B. Tons
   C. Miles
   D. Milliliters

3. A foot is what part of a yard?
   A. $\frac{1}{12}$
   B. $\frac{1}{3}$
   C. 3
   D. 12

4. How many quarts are in 27 pints?

5. Change 84 hours into days. Leave your answer as a mixed fraction.

6. How many tons are in 500 pounds?

7. How many minutes are there in $\frac{1}{15}$ of an hour?

8. An average soccer player runs for 6.2 miles in a game. What is the distance in feet?

9. How many kilograms are in 1,600 grams?

10. A regular soccer game last for 1.5 hrs. What is the duration of a game in seconds?

11. A male African elephant can weigh up to 25,000 lbs. How many tons would such an elephant weigh?

12. The ratio of 20 feet to 8 yards is?
    A. 4:2
    B. 5:4
    C. 2:3
    D. 5:6

13. What is the length in centimeters of 0.05 km?
    A. 0.0005 cm
    B. 500 cm
    C. 5,000 cm
    D. 50,000 cm

14. Joseph has three containers. The first container has 2.1 gallons of milk, the second contains 9 quarts of milk and the last has 30 pints of milk. What is the total amount of milk in gallons in the containers?
    A. 7.2 gallons
    B. 8.1 gallons
    C. 11.75 gallons
    D. 19.75 gallons

15. If $3 = 2 Euros, then $54 + 22 Euros is equal to how many dollars?
    A. $87
    B. $89
    C. $92
    D. $98

16. A ribbon $8\frac{1}{2}$ feet long can be cut into how many 3-inch pieces?
    A. 2 pieces
    B. 22 pieces
    C. 28 pieces
    D. 34 pieces

334

17. $4\frac{1}{4}$ feet is how many inches longer than $3\frac{2}{3}$ feet?
    A. 6 inches
    B. 7 inches
    C. 12 inches
    D. 35 inches

18. Which is the longest time?
    A. 400 minutes
    B. $\frac{1}{4}$ of a day
    C. $6\frac{1}{2}$ hours
    D. 3,600 seconds

19. A farmer wants to package 252 quarts of milk into 1.5-gallon containers. How many containers will he require?
    A. 34 containers
    B. 42 containers
    C. 63 containers
    D. 168 containers

20. Sergei goes to the store and buys 4.5 lbs of steak. If the price of steak is $0.80 per ounce, how much did Sergei pay for the steak?
    A. $3.6
    B. $36
    C. $57.60
    D. $62.50

MEASUREMENT Practice Set 4

1. How many feet are in 3 miles?

2. How many millimeters are in five meters?

3. How many cups are in a quart?

4. How many inches are in three yards?

5. How many ounces are in 2 pounds?

6. How many minutes are in one week?

7. 5,000 milliliters is how many liters?

8. 20,000 centimeters is how many meters?

9. 5 yards is how many inches?

10. 2 tons is how many ounces?

11. 5.75 grams is how many milligrams?

12. If Dylan goes to the movies twice every month, how many times will he go to the movies in three years?

13. A recipe that feeds 1 person uses 4 ounces of rice and 1 pint of water. If the same recipe is being used to feed 2 people, which quantities are correct?
    A. 1 cup of rice and one quart of water
    B. 1.5 cups of rice and two pints of water
    C. 2 cups of rice and one quart of water
    D. 1 pint of rice and a half gallon of water

14. If an adult hamster weighs 2 kilograms and a baby hamster weighs 25% of the adult hamster, then how many grams does the baby hamster weigh?

15. If mailing packages costs 50 cents for every ounce, what is the cost of mailing a package that weighs 1 pound 6 ounces?

16. If chicken costs $12 per kilogram, approximately how many grams of chicken could you buy for $3?
    A. 250 grams
    B. 333 grams
    C. 2,500 grams
    D. 3,600 grams

17. A professional athlete's salary is $9.6 million dollars per season. If a season has 50 games and the athlete plays 2 hours in every game, how much money is he paid each minute?

18. If there are 1.6 kilometers in one mile, and Andy runs 26.2 miles, how many kilometers did he run?

19. If there are 2.2 pounds in one kilogram, and Sarah weighs 242 pounds, how many kilograms does she weigh?

20. Jake can drive 100 kilometers in one hour. How many miles can he drive in 150 seconds? (1 kilometer = .6 miles)

RATIOS & PROPORTIONS Practice Set 1

1. A library lends out 60 books at the beginning of the month. At the end of the month, 16 books were lost and the rest were returned. In simplest terms, what is the ratio of returned books to lost books?
    - A. 15 to 4
    - B. 11 to 4
    - C. 4 to 15
    - D. 4 to 11

2. A 500-foot tower casts a shadow 125 feet long. How long is the shadow of a 20-foot tree if the tower and its shadow are in the same ratio as the tree and its shadow?
    - A. 3 feet
    - B. 4 feet
    - C. 5 feet
    - D. 80 feet

3. If one Twinkie weighs 5 grams, how many Twinkies are in a box weighing 32 kilograms? (1,000 grams = 1 kilogram)
    - A. 6,400 Twinkies
    - B. 8,400 Twinkies
    - C. 16,000 Twinkies
    - D. 32,000 Twinkies

4. The ratio of boys to girls in a certain school is 1 to 3. If there are 300 boys in the school, how many total students are in the school?
    - A. 600 students
    - B. 900 students
    - C. 1,200 students
    - D. 1,500 student

5. A dairy farmer is trying to package 50 gallons of milk into 1-quart containers. How many containers will the farmer need? (1 gallon = 4 quarts)
    - A. 50 containers
    - B. 100 containers
    - C. 150 containers
    - D. 200 containers

6. In a car factory, 3 out of 7 cars being assembled are hybrid cars. How many non-hybrid cars are assembled if the factory rolls out a total of 6,300 cars annually?
    - A. 2,700 non-hybrid cars
    - B. 3,600 non-hybrid cars
    - C. 4,500 non-hybrid cars
    - D. 4,900 non-hybrid cars

7. In a circus, there are 8 women for every 3 men. What is the ratio of the number of men to the entire circus?
    A. 8 to 3
    B. 3 to 8
    C. 8 to 11
    D. 3 to 11

8. In a survey of 60 people, three times as many people preferred vanilla ice cream to chocolate ice cream. If all people surveyed preferred either vanilla or chocolate ice cream, how many people preferred chocolate ice cream?
    A. 15 people
    B. 20 people
    C. 25 people
    D. 30 people

9. It costs $36 to buy 16 donuts. At the same rate, how many dollars will it cost to buy 24 donuts?
    A. $12
    B. $44
    C. $48
    D. $54

10. One kilometer is approximately 0.6 miles. How many kilometers are in 15 miles?
    A. 9 kilometers
    B. 12 kilometers
    C. 20 kilometers
    D. 25 kilometers

11. A rafting expedition costs $120 for 5 hours. At that rate, what would be the cost of a 14 hours rafting expedition?
    A. $336
    B. $372
    C. $402
    D. $480

12. Andrea has an orchard that is 20 feet by 12 feet. If she uses 1.5 kg of fertilizer per square foot, how many kg of fertilizer must she use for the entire orchard?
    A. 160 kilograms
    B. 240 kilograms
    C. 360 kilograms
    D. 400 kilograms

13. On a map, 1 cm = 33 km. $5\frac{1}{3}$ cm on the map equals to how many kilometers?
    A. 155 km
    B. 176 km
    C. 225 km
    D. 250 km

14. A recipe for 12 cupcakes requires 1.75 cups of sugar. How much sugar is required for 16 cupcakes?
    A. $2\frac{1}{6}$ cups
    B. $2\frac{1}{5}$ cups
    C. $2\frac{1}{4}$ cups
    D. $2\frac{1}{3}$ cups

15. To paint her room, Natalie mixes yellow, red, and white paint in a ratio of 4 to 3 to 1. If she requires 32 gallons of paint, how many gallons of white paint will she need?
    A. 2 gallons
    B. 4 gallons
    C. 12 gallons
    D. 16 gallons

16. Two negative whole numbers are in the ratio 4 to 5. If the larger of the numbers is -40, what is the average of the two numbers?
    A. -45
    B. -36
    C. -32
    D. -28

17. A fence post 3 meters high casts a shadow 12 meters long at the same time that a nearby tree casts a shadow 52 meters long. What is the height of the tree?
    A. 9 meters
    B. 12 meters
    C. 13 meters
    D. 15 meters

18. On a map 1 cm = 2.5 km. What would be the distance on a map for two cities that are 30 km from each other?
    A. 12 cm
    B. 13 cm
    C. 15 cm
    D. 18 cm

19. In a recycling plant, the ratio of plastic bottles to glass bottles is 1:5. If there are 1,800 bottles in one batch, how many glass bottles are there?
    A. 300 glass bottles
    B. 1,200 glass bottles
    C. 1,300 glass bottles
    D. 1,500 glass bottles

20. The height of a window on a blueprint measures 0.4 inches. If the actual window is 5 feet, what is the ratio of the blueprint dimensions to the house dimensions?
    A. 1:13
    B. 1:150
    C. 25:2
    D. 1:120

RATIOS & PROPORTIONS Practice Set 2

1. A jar of cookies contains 56 cookies. Over the course of two days, 14 of the cookies were eaten. In simplest terms, what is the ratio of cookies remaining to cookies eaten?
   A. 3 to 1
   B. 4 to 1
   C. 3 to 2
   D. 1 to 3

2. A baker is making 5 pans of cornbread and uses 15 cups of flour. If the baker is making 15 pans of cake and baking a cake requires the same ratio of flour as the cornbread, then how many cups of flour are required to bake the cake?
   A. 15 cups
   B. 25 cups
   C. 35 cups
   D. 45 cups

3. If one M&M weighs 0.5 grams, how many M&M's are in a package weighing 1.75 kilograms? (1,000 grams = 1 kilogram)
   A. 1,250 M&M's
   B. 2,500 M&M's
   C. 3,500 M&M's
   D. 45,000 M&M's

4. The ratio of offensive players to defensive players on a sports team is 3 to 5. If there are 35 defensive players on the team, how many total players are on the team?
   A. 21 players
   B. 35 players
   C. 45 players
   D. 56 players

5. The perimeter of a garden is 133 yards. If the gardener is trying to measure the garden with 1-foot rulers, how many rulers will he need? (1 yard = 3 feet)
   A. 600 rulers
   B. 399 rulers
   C. 109 rulers
   D. 33 rulers

6. In a greeting card store, 5 out of 9 cards being sold are birthday cards. If during a month the store sells 729 cards in total, how many are not birthday cards?
   A. 225 cards
   B. 324 cards
   C. 405 cards
   D. 630 cards

7. In a group of elephants there are 2 males to every 36 females. What is the ratio of females to the entire group?
    A. 18 to 19
    B. 1 to 18
    C. 18 to 1
    D. 19 to 18

8. At a party with 120 people, 4 times as many people preferred juice to soda. How many people preferred juice?
    A. 18 people
    B. 24 people
    C. 96 people
    D. 102 people

9. It costs $42 to buy 14 batteries. At the same rate, how many dollars will it cost to buy 35 batteries?
    A. $16.80
    B. $49
    C. $70
    D. $105

10. One inch is 2.54 cm. How many inches are in 381 cm?
    A. 968 inches
    B. 250 inches
    C. 150 inches
    D. 98 inches

11. A plane flight costs $300 for 4 hours in the air. At that rate, what would be the cost of a 14 hour flight?
    A. $3,000
    B. $1,050
    C. $900
    D. $450

12. Bart is building a patio that is 30 feet by 15 feet. If he uses 20 kg of concrete per square foot, how many kg of concrete must he use for the entire patio?
    A. 300 kilograms
    B. 600 kilograms
    C. 4,500 kilograms
    D. 9,000 kilograms

13. On a map 1 cm is 2.5 miles. How many miles is 66 cm?
    A. 165 miles
    B. 190 miles
    C. 250 miles
    D. 305 miles

14. A recipe for 8 loaves of bread requires 18.4 cups of flour. How much flour is required for 12 loaves of bread?
    A. 20.8 cups
    B. 27.6 cups
    C. 30.25 cups
    D. $36\frac{1}{3}$ cups

15. Sarah is trying to make the perfect color frosting. She mixes red, blue, and green food coloring in a ratio of 5 to 2 to 1. If she requires 48 drops of food coloring for the entire batch of frosting, then how many drops of blue coloring will she need?
    A. 12 drops
    B. 15 drops
    C. 25 drops
    D. 30 drops

16. A car dealer only sells three brands of cars – BMW, Lexus, and Mercedes Benz. He has them in a ratio of 1 to 3 to 3. If he has a total of 21 cars, how many BMW's does he have?
    A. 1
    B. 3
    C. 9
    D. 15

17. Half Dome is 1,440 meters high and at noon it casts a shadow 180 meters long at the same time that a nearby redwood tree casts a shadow 80 meters long. What is the height of the tree?
    A. 160 meters
    B. 420 meters
    C. 640 meters
    D. 720 meters

18. A motorboat requires a crew of 2 for every 8 passengers. If there is a cruise ship that can carry 3,600 passengers, and it has the same ratio of crew to passengers, how many crewmembers are on the cruise ship?
    A. 200 crewmembers
    B. 400 crewmembers
    C. 600 crewmembers
    D. 900 crewmembers

19. On a beach, the ratio of jellyfish to crabs is 4:15. If there are 195 crabs on a certain portion of beach, how many jellyfish are there?
    A. 26 jellyfish
    B. 52 jellyfish
    C. 78 jellyfish
    D. 92 jellyfish

20. On a topographic map, a series of closely spaced lines are proportional to distance on the ground. On the map the distance between these lines is 1/4 of a foot. If the actual distance on the ground is 5 feet, then what is the ratio of the distances?
    A. 1:5
    B. 1:15
    C. 15:2
    D. 1:20

RATIOS & PROPORTIONS Practice Set 3

1. A child is playing with blocks. There are 54 blocks total, 18 cylinders, and 36 triangular prisms. In simplest terms, what is the ratio of cylinders to prisms?
    A. 9 to 12
    B. 1 to 2
    C. 9 to 18
    D. 18 to 9

2. Marci is 5 feet tall, and her shadow is 8 feet long. How long is Mark's shadow if he is 6.25 feet tall and Marci and her shadow are in the same ratio as Mark and his shadow?
    A. 10 feet
    B. 16 feet
    C. 6.25 feet
    D. 12 feet

3. If each leg of a race is 500 meters and the entire race is 4.5 kilometers, how many legs are there in the race? (1 kilometer = 1,000 meters)
    A. 7 legs
    B. 12 legs
    C. 9 legs
    D. 8 legs

4. The ratio of cats to dogs in a certain animal shelter is 3 to 8. If there are 21 cats in the shelter, how many total animals are in the shelter?
    A. 81 animals
    B. 77 animals
    C. 56 animals
    D. 168 animals

5. A baker is trying to measure 40 oz of cream into a recipe, but she only has a container that measures in cups. How many cups of cream does the baker need to make up 40 oz? (1 cup = 16 oz)
    A. 50 cups
    B. 4.25 cups
    C. 16 cups
    D. 2.5 cups

6. In a car factory, 2 out of 3 cars being assembled are sedans. How many cars are assembled each year if the factory produces 2,300 sedans annually?
    A. 4,600 cars
    B. 4,200 cars
    C. 3,450 cars
    D. 6,900 cars

7. In a fish tank, there are 5 fish for every 2 hermit crabs. What is the ratio of the number of fish to the total number of animals in the tank?
    A. 7 to 5
    B. 5 to 7
    C. 5 to 2
    D. 9 to 5

8. In a survey done of 60 people, four times as many people preferred Halloween to Valentine's Day. If all people surveyed preferred either Halloween or Valentine's Day, how many people preferred Halloween?
    A. 48 people
    B. 50 people
    C. 12 people
    D. 32 people

9. It takes 45 minutes for Jim to catch 4 fish. At the same rate, how long will it take for him to catch 24 fish?
    A. 6.5 hours
    B. 8 hours
    C. 4.5 hours
    D. 6 hours

10. One package of nails weighs 30 grams. How many packages of nails are in a box weighing 4.5 kilograms? (1 kilogram = 1,000 grams)
    A. 30,000 packages
    B. 150 packages
    C. 4,500 packages
    D. 135 packages

11. A bus ride from Los Angeles to San Francisco costs $90 for a 450 mile trip. At that rate, what would be the cost of a 1,220 mile trip from Los Angeles to Seattle?
    A. $331
    B. $267
    C. $320
    D. $244

12. Dalia has a sandbox that is 5 feet by 4 feet. If she fills the sandbox with 4.25 kg of sand per square foot, how many kg of sand must she use to cover the entire sandbox?
    A. 85 kilograms
    B. 25 kilograms
    C. 105 kilograms
    D. 90 kilograms

13. A car drives at 70 kilometers per hour for 3.5 hours. How many miles has the car driven? (1 kilometer = 0.6 miles)
    A. 421 miles
    B. 147 miles
    C. 210 miles
    D. 273 miles

344

14. A recipe for 1 quart of limeade uses the juice from 5.5 limes. How many limes are used for 2 gallons of limeade?
    A. 20 lemons
    B. 18 lemons
    C. 22 lemons
    D. 44 lemons

15. To make a fruit salad, Emily mixes strawberries, raspberries, and blueberries in a ratio of 4 to 2 to 1. If she requires 14 cartons of fruit to make the salad, how many cartons of strawberries will she need?
    A. 6 cartons
    B. 10 cartons
    C. 5 cartons
    D. 8 cartons

16. Gene wants to paint a wall in front of his house. The wall measures 25 feet long by 12 feet tall, and each can of paints covers about 10 square feet. How many cans of paint does it take to paint the wall?
    A. 25 cans
    B. 30 cans
    C. 21 cans
    D. 32 cans

17. Anita is 64 inches tall and uses ski poles that are 42 inches long. If Peter is 72 inches tall and has the same height to pole ratio as Anita, how tall are his poles?
    A. 60 inches
    B. 37.3 inches
    C. 47.25 inches
    D. 49 inches

18. On a map, 1 cm = 3.5 miles. What would be the distance on the map for two cities that are 42 miles apart?
    A. 12 cm
    B. 13 cm
    C. 15 cm
    D. 18 cm

19. In a display case at a bakery, the ratio of vanilla cupcakes to chocolate cupcakes is 3 to 2. If there are 45 vanilla cupcakes in the case, how many total cupcakes are there?
    A. 67 cupcakes
    B. 30 cupcakes
    C. 75 cupcakes
    D. 82 cupcakes

20. A dairy cow can produce 4.5 gallons of milk a day. How many cows does a farm need if they want to fill 1,350 quart-sized bottles each day? (1 gallon = 4 quarts)
    A. 135 cows
    B. 63 cows
    C. 300 cows
    D. 75 cows

RATIOS & PROPORTIONS Practice Set 4

1. A family collection includes 63 different movies. There
   are 14 Blu-ray discs and 49 DVDs in the collection. What
   is the ratio of DVDs to Blu-ray discs?
   A. 2 to 7
   B. 7 to 2
   C. 14 to 9
   D. 14 to 4

2. Diane is 3 years old and has a total of 12 toys. Jeremy
   owns 20 toys. If Jeremy has the same ratio of age to toys
   as Diane, then how old is Jeremy?
   A. 1 year old
   B. 2 years old
   C. 4 years old
   D. 5 years old

3. Each block in Jenga is 2 centimeters tall. If the world
   record height for a Jenga tower is 1.2 meters tall, then
   how many Jenga blocks are there? (1 meter = 100 cm)
   A. 16 blocks
   B. 24 blocks
   C. 60 blocks
   D. 240 blocks

4. In a given classroom, the ratio of students who wear
   glasses to students with normal vision is 4 to 7. If there
   are 12 students who wear glasses, how many students are
   in the class?
   A. 33 students
   B. 22 students
   C. 21 students
   D. 14 students

5. At a soda factory, the recipe for a batch of cola requires
   86 quarts of syrup. If they can only measure in gallons,
   then how many gallons of syrup should they add to 2
   batches of cola? (1 gallon = 4 quarts)
   A. 172 gallons
   B. 90 gallons
   C. 43 gallons
   D. 24 gallons

6. A company produces red and blue pens. 4 out of every 5
   pens are blue. If the company produces 3,660 blue pens
   per year, then what is the total number of pens produced?
   A. 4,575 pens
   B. 4,225 pens
   C. 3,450 pens
   D. 6,750 pens

7. In the Serengeti, there are 2 lions for every 24 antelope. If there are 16 lions, then what is the ratio of antelope to total animals?
   A. 6 to 8
   B. 12 to 13
   C. 26 to 24
   D. 3 to 5

8. In a survey done of 75 people, four times as many people preferred cashews to peanuts. If all people surveyed preferred either cashews or peanuts, how many people preferred peanuts?
   A. 60 people
   B. 45 people
   C. 30 people
   D. 15 people

9. It takes Sam 3 hours to beat 4 levels of a video game. If the game has 56 total levels, then how many hours will it take him to complete the game?
   A. 12 hours
   B. 36 hours
   C. 42 hours
   D. 168 hours

10. One bale of hay weighs 30 kilograms. How many bales of hay are on a truck carrying 450 kilograms?
    A. 9 bales
    B. 15 bales
    C. 300 bales
    D. 13,500 bales

11. A boat ride from Los Angeles to Hawaii costs $402 for a 3,000 mile trip. At that rate, what would be the cost of a 500 mile trip from Los Angeles to Baja California?
    A. $2,412
    B. $201
    C. $150
    D. $67

12. Ricky is making a giant chessboard that is 8 feet by 8 feet. If he needs 14 kilograms of granite per square foot, then how many kilograms will the entire chessboard require?
    A. 64 kilograms
    B. 112 kilograms
    C. 896 kilograms
    D. 1,232 kilograms

13. A train travels 120 kilometers per hour for 5.4 hours. How many miles has the train gone? (1 kilometer = 0.6 miles)
    A. 388.8 miles
    B. 648 miles
    C. 845.5 miles
    D. 1,080 miles

14. A recipe for 2 quarts of dip needs 3 carrots. How many carrots are used to make 1.5 gallons of dip? (1 gal = 4 qt)
    A. 6 carrots
    B. 9 carrots
    C. 12 carrots
    D. 15 carrots

15. To make a parfait, Serena mixes strawberries, yogurt, and shortbread in a ratio of 1 to 4 to 3. If she requires 16 units total, how many units of yogurt does she need?
    A. 2 units
    B. 4 units
    C. 6 units
    D. 8 units

16. The Karate Kid wants to paint Mr. Miyagi's fence, which is 24 feet long by 6 feet tall. A can of paint covers 12 square feet. How many cans are needed to paint the wall?
    A. 3 cans
    B. 9 cans
    C. 12 cans
    D. 24 cans

17. Angela and Roy both broke their legs. Angela is 63 inches tall and uses crutches that are 42 inches tall. If Roy is 70 inches tall and has the same height to crutch ratio as Angela, then how tall are his crutches?
    A. 60 inches
    B. $46\frac{2}{3}$ inches
    C. 42.25 inches
    D. 39 inches

18. On a map 2 cm = 5 miles. What would be the distance on a map for two cities that are 55 miles from each other?
    A. 22 cm
    B. 18 cm
    C. 10 cm
    D. 5 cm

19. A sports store sells only baseballs and basketballs. The ratio of basketballs to baseballs is 2 to 9. If the store has 45 baseballs, how many total balls are in the store?
    A. 63 balls
    B. 55 balls
    C. 48 balls
    D. 45 balls

20. If a maple tree produces 8.5 gallons of maple syrup a day, how many trees are needed to fill 2,380 quarts a week?
    A. 10 maple trees
    B. 26 maple trees
    C. 54 maple trees
    D. 70 maple trees

348

PROBABILITY Practice Set 1

1. A 20-sided die is thrown. What is the probability that a 17 will come up?

2. There are 10 fish and 3 lobsters in a tank. If one sea creature is chosen at random, what is the probability that it will be a lobster?

3. There are 30 students in a class. 10 of them are boys. If the teacher randomly selects one student, what is the probability that it is a girl?

4. A toy chest has 5 green toys, 6 blue toys, and 4 red toys. If a toy is to be selected at random, what is the probability that it will be blue?

5. There are 3 goats, 4 cows, and 5 chickens on a farm. If one animal is chosen randomly, what is the probability that it has four legs?

6. A roulette wheel contains all of the numbers between 1 and 38, inclusive. The wheel has stopped on even numbers on the past 3 spins. What is the probability that the next spin will stop on an even number?

7. If a fair coin is tossed twice, what is the probability of getting two heads?

8. If two standard dice are rolled, what is the probability that the sum of the numbers landing face up is 2?

9. Harvey throws a dart at a dartboard with 20 equal sized spaces, numbered 1 through 20. Assuming his dart lands on the dartboard both times, what is the probability that his dart lands on number 11 both times?

10. The probability that the point guard on the Bears can make a wide open 3-point shot is 40%. What is the probability that the point guard on the Wildcats can make a wide open 3-point shot?
    A. 20%
    B. 40%
    C. 80%
    D. It cannot be determined from the information provided.

11. If one letter is randomly selected from the alphabet, and a coin is flipped, what is the probability that the letter will be Z and the coin will land on tails?

12. Kate has a box of 12 chocolates. Four of the chocolates have caramel on the inside. If Kate randomly selected one chocolate and then selected another chocolate, what is the probability that neither of the chocolates she chose had caramel on the inside?

13. Jim has 3 shirts, 2 pairs of pants, and 2 belts. If an outfit consists of one shirt, one pair of pants, and one belt, how many outfits does he have?

14. The probability that Ryan passes his history test is 0.65. What is the probability that he does not pass the test?

15. The only two ways for Shruthi and Debra to get home from school are to walk or ride bikes. There is a 0.25 chance that Shruthi will ride her bike, and a 0.4 chance that Debra will ride her bike. What is the probability that both Shruthi and Debra will walk home?

16. Sammy picks a card out of a deck of 52 cards and places it on the ground. He then picks another card from the same deck and places it on the ground. What is the chance that the first card he picked was the ace of spades and the second card was the ace of diamonds?

    A. $\dfrac{1}{52}$

    B. $\dfrac{1}{52} \times \dfrac{1}{52}$

    C. $\dfrac{1}{52} \times \dfrac{1}{51}$

    D. $\dfrac{1}{13} \times \dfrac{1}{4}$

17. There are 3 wood bats and 2 metal bats in the dugout. Barry randomly picks a bat and gives it to his teammate. Barry then randomly picks a second bat and keeps it. What is the probability that the first bat Barry picked was metal and the second was wood?

18. The probability that the Earthtrotters beat the Sentinels is $\dfrac{9}{10}$. If the two teams play each other 200 times, how many games will the Earthtrotters be expected to win?

19. The probability that it will not rain on any day in June is $\dfrac{7}{10}$. If there are 30 days in June, on how many days will it be expected to rain?

20. The probability that a red marble will be chosen from a bag of marbles is $\dfrac{3}{5}$. If there are 9 red marbles, how many total marbles are there?

PROBABILITY Practice Set 2

1. An ordinary dice is thrown. What is the probability that a 6 will come up?

2. There are 16 boys and 14 girls in a class. If one student is chosen at random, what is the probability that it will be a boy?

3. If a card is drawn from a standard deck of 52 cards, what is the probability it will be a 4?
   - A. $\frac{1}{52}$
   - B. $\frac{1}{13}$
   - C. $\frac{4}{13}$
   - D. $\frac{1}{4}$

4. In a bag, there are 8 red, 5 white, 6 green, and 5 blue marbles. If a marbles is to be selected at random, what is the probability that it will be green?

5. A fair coin is tossed twice, what is the probability of getting two tails?
   - A. $\frac{1}{4}$
   - B. $\frac{1}{2}$
   - C. $\frac{1}{3}$
   - D. $\frac{1}{8}$

6. There are 26 letters in the English alphabet. If one letter is chosen at random, what is the probability that it is a vowel? There are five vowels in the alphabet: a, e, i, o, u.
   - A. $\frac{5}{26}$
   - B. $\frac{5}{13}$
   - C. $\frac{21}{26}$
   - D. $\frac{25}{26}$

7. The probability that it will rain on Monday is 3 out of 10. What is the probability that it will rain on Tuesday?
   - A. $\frac{3}{10}$
   - B. $\frac{1}{2}$
   - C. $\frac{7}{10}$
   - D. It cannot be determined from the information provided.

8. A couple has two boys. If the couple is expecting a third child, what is the probability that the third child will also be a boy?

   A. $\frac{1}{8}$

   B. $\frac{1}{4}$

   C. $\frac{1}{3}$

   D. $\frac{1}{2}$

9. A lottery machine generates whole numbers from 1 to 12. What is the probability that the first two numbers generated are both odd numbers?

   A. $\frac{1}{12} \times \frac{1}{12}$

   B. $\frac{1}{2} \times \frac{1}{2}$

   C. $\frac{1}{12} + \frac{1}{12}$

   D. $\frac{1}{4} + \frac{1}{4}$

10. William is shooting arrows at a target 50 feet away. The probability that he hits bull's eye on the target is 0.55. What is the probability that he does not hit bull's eye?

    A. 0.45

    B. 0.5

    C. 0.55

    D. It cannot be determined from the information provided.

11. A cookie jar contains 6 chocolate chip cookies and 8 oatmeal raisin cookies. Mindy takes out and eats one chocolate chip cookie. If she selects a second cookie at random, what is the probability that it will be a chocolate chip cookie?

    A. $\frac{3}{7}$

    B. $\frac{4}{7}$

    C. $\frac{5}{13}$

    D. $\frac{5}{14}$

12. A fair coin is tossed three times, what is the probability of getting three heads?

    A. $\frac{3}{2}$

    B. $\frac{1}{2}$

    C. $\frac{1}{8}$

    D. $\frac{3}{8}$

13. A piggy bank contains 6 pennies, 10 dimes, 5 nickels, and 7 quarters. Alvin reaches in and takes out two coins. What is the probability that both coins are nickels?

    A. $\frac{5}{28} + \frac{4}{28}$

    B. $\frac{1}{28} \times \frac{1}{27}$

    C. $\frac{5}{28} \times \frac{4}{28}$

    D. $\frac{5}{28} \times \frac{4}{27}$

14. Diego has a bag of M&M's with different colors: red, yellow, brown, blue, and green. The probability of choosing a red M&M is 5 out of 12. Which combination of M&M's is possible?

    A. 5 red M&M's, 12 other colors M&M's

    B. 15 red M&M's, 21 other colors M&M's

    C. 20 red M&M's, 15 other colors M&M's

    D. 25 red M&M's, 30 other colors M&M's

15. Tony has 3 pairs of shoes, 5 pairs of pants, and 6 shirts. If he only has one pair of black shoes, one pair of black pants, and one black shirt, what is the probability that he is dressed in black shoes, black pants, and a black shirt?

    A. $\frac{3}{14} \times \frac{5}{14} \times \frac{6}{14}$

    B. $\frac{1}{3} \times \frac{1}{5} \times \frac{1}{6}$

    C. $\frac{1}{3} + \frac{1}{5} + \frac{1}{6}$

    D. $\frac{3}{14} + \frac{5}{14} + \frac{6}{14}$

16. Andrew and James are shooting free throws. The probability that Andrew makes his free throw is 3 out of 5 and the probability that James makes his free throws is 4 out of 7. If the both shoot one free throw each, what is the probability that they both make their free throws?

    A. $\frac{8}{35}$

    B. $\frac{3}{4}$

    C. $\frac{7}{12}$

    D. $\frac{12}{35}$

17. Ms. Monroe puts the names of all her students in a hat. The probability that she will pull out a girl's name at random is 4 out of 9. There are 25 boys in the class. How many girls are in Ms. Monroe's class?

    A. 5 girls

    B. 16 girls

    C. 18 girls

    D. 20 girls

18. Maxwell rolls an ordinary 6-sided dice and at the same time tosses a coin. What is the probability that an even number is rolled on the dice, and the coin lands heads up?

    A. $\frac{1}{4}$

    B. $\frac{1}{2}$

    C. $\frac{1}{12}$

    D. $\frac{3}{4}$

19. The probability that Diane is late for school is 2 out of 5. The probability that Katie is late for school is 4 out of 7. Which of the following events is most likely to happen on any school day?

    A. Diane is late for school.
    B. Katie is late for school.
    C. Diane is not late for school.
    D. Katie is not late for school.

20. In a math test, Jessie guesses on the last two problems. If each problem has 4 multiple choice answers, what is the probability that she gets both questions correct?

    A. $\frac{1}{16}$

    B. $\frac{1}{4}$

    C. $\frac{1}{2}$

    D. $\frac{1}{8}$

PROBABILITY Practice Set 3

1. There are 5 oranges and 4 apples in a fruit basket. If a fruit is picked at random, what is the probability that it will be an orange?

2. If a card is drawn from a standard deck of 52 cards, what is the probability that it will be a 10?
    A. $\frac{5}{26}$
    B. $\frac{1}{52}$
    C. $\frac{1}{13}$
    D. $\frac{2}{5}$

3. Eleanor picks a number between 1 and 10. What is the probability that the number she picks is prime?

4. The San Francisco 49ers are playing the New York Giants in an football game. If the chances that the 49ers win is 4 out of 7. What is the probability that the Giants win?
    A. $\frac{3}{7}$
    B. $\frac{4}{7}$
    C. $\frac{7}{3}$
    D. $\frac{7}{4}$

5. An ordinary dice is thrown. What is the probability that a 2 will come up?

6. A fair coin is tossed twice, what is the probability of getting two heads?

7. Adrian has 10 pairs of shoes. 3 pairs are white, 2 pairs are red, and the rest are black. What is the probability that on any particular day he wears black shoes?

8. There are 26 letters in the alphabet. If one letter is chosen at random, what is the probability that is an F or a Z?
    A. $\frac{1}{26}$
    B. $\frac{1}{13}$
    C. $\frac{2}{13}$
    D. $\frac{1}{2}$

9. The probability that it will be sunny on a Friday afternoon is 1 out of 3. What is the probability that it will not be sunny that Friday afternoon?

    A. $\frac{1}{3}$

    B. $\frac{2}{3}$

    C. $\frac{1}{2}$

    D. It cannot be determined from the information provided.

10. The weather forecast for Tahoe is a 60% chance that it will snow on Monday. What is the chance that it snows on Wednesday?

    A. $\frac{2}{5}$

    B. $\frac{3}{5}$

    C. $\frac{1}{2}$

    D. It cannot be determined from the information provided.

11. The probability that Serena Williams serves an ace in a tennis match is 0.84. What is the probability that she does not serve an ace?

    A. 0.04

    B. 0.26

    C. 0.16

    D. 0.48

12. An ordinary dice is rolled twice. What is the probability of rolling a 4 both times?

    A. $\frac{1}{6}$

    B. $\frac{1}{3}$

    C. $\frac{1}{36}$

    D. $\frac{1}{16}$

13. A computer program generates whole numbers from 0 to 14. What is the probability that the first two numbers generated are both even numbers?

    A. $\frac{8}{14} \times \frac{8}{14}$

    B. $\frac{1}{15} + \frac{1}{15}$

    C. $\frac{1}{14} + \frac{1}{14}$

    D. $\frac{8}{15} \times \frac{8}{15}$

14. There are cows, goats, sheep, chickens, and horses on a farm. If an animal is picked at random, the probability that it is a horse is 1 out of 8. Which of the following combinations of animals is possible?

    A. 4 horses and 28 other animals

    B. 2 horses and 16 other animals

    C. 5 horses and 25 other animals

    D. 7 horses and 32 other animals

15. Chris has 8 ties, 5 scarves, and 4 belts. He has one favorite tie, one favorite scarf, and one favorite belt. What is the probability that he wears his favorite tie, his favorite scarf, and his favorite belt at the same time?

    A. $\frac{1}{8} + \frac{1}{5} + \frac{1}{4}$

    B. $\frac{8}{17} \times \frac{5}{17} \times \frac{4}{17}$

    C. $\frac{8}{17} + \frac{5}{17} + \frac{4}{17}$

    D. $\frac{1}{8} \times \frac{1}{5} \times \frac{1}{4}$

16. Jonah and Brad are in the varsity soccer team. The probability that Jonah scores a goal in game is 2 out of 9, and the probability that Brad scores a goal is 1 out of 4. What is the probability that the both score goals?

    A. $\frac{2}{13}$

    B. $\frac{1}{18}$

    C. $\frac{17}{36}$

    D. $\frac{1}{6}$

17. Ms. Arreaga puts the names of all her students in a hat. The probability that she will pull out a boy's name at random is 3 out of 7. There are 32 girls in the class. How many boys are in Ms. Arreaga's class?

    A. 16 boys

    B. 18 boys

    C. 20 boys

    D. 24 boys

18. The probability that the Lakers win is 3 out of 5. The probability that the Warriors win is 1 out of 3. Which of the following events is most likely to happen?

    A. Warriors lose.

    B. Lakers win.

    C. Warriors win.

    D. Lakers lose.

19. In a history exam, Larry guesses on the last three problems. If each problem has two answer choices, what is the probability that he gets all three questions correct?

 A. $\frac{1}{3}$

 B. $\frac{1}{4}$

 C. $\frac{1}{8}$

 D. $\frac{1}{6}$

20. Marie has two types of books in her personal library: fiction and nonfiction. If she picks a book at random, the probability that it will be nonfiction is 7 out of 11. There are 36 fiction books on in her library. How many nonfiction books are in her library?

 A. 28 books

 B. 35 books

 C. 49 books

 D. 63 books

PROBABILITY Practice Set 4

1. A number between 1 and 15, inclusive, is chosen at random. What is the probability that it will be 13?

2. There are 5 basketballs and 3 volleyballs on a rack. If one ball is chosen at random, what is the probability that it will be a volleyball?

3. There are 15 models in a fashion show. 10 of them are women. If the choreographer randomly selects one model, what is the probability that it will be a man?

4. A buried treasure has 400 gold coins, 600 silver coins, and 2,000 bronze coins. If a coin is to be selected at random, what is the probability that it will be silver?

5. There are 10 bananas, 20 apples, and 30 oranges in a market. If one fruit is chosen randomly, what is the probability that it a round-shaped fruit?

6. A TV station has 10 different types of commercials it can play, and it chooses commercial randomly. The last two commercials played have been car commercials. What is the probability that the next commercial played will be a car commercial?

7. If a fair coin is tossed twice, what is the probability of getting heads on the first toss and tails on the second toss?

8. Each day, the director randomly selects one actor in the play to perform a solo monologue. If Jordan is one of 8 actors in the play, what is the probability that he will be chosen to give a monologue two days in a row?

9. The probability that Stephanie will pass her driving test is 0.3. What is the probability that she does not pass the test?

10. KC gets 75 television stations (#1-75). He has three favorite meals: burritos, burgers, and pizza. If KC randomly selects one television station and one meal, what is the probability that he will watch channel 33 and eat a burger?

11. A family wants to buy a dog, a cat, and a bird. The pet store has 5 breeds of dogs, 2 types of cats, and 4 types of birds. How many different combinations of 1 dog, 1 cat, and 1 bird are possible?

12. Greg has eight siblings. Two of his siblings are girls. Greg randomly selects one sibling to go to the concert with him, and then randomly selects another sibling to go to the concert with him. What is the probability that Greg will choose two of his brothers to go with him?

13. Bertha weighs 250 pounds and breaks 1 out of every 5 chairs that she sits on. If Oliver weighs 300 pounds, what is the probability that he will break a chair that he sits on?
    A. 1 out of every 6
    B. 20%
    C. 25%
    D. It cannot be determined from the information provided.

14. At a track meet, Ted is in the mile race and Sandy is in the 100-meter race. There is a 0.2 chance that Ted will win his race and a 0.5 chance that Sandy will win his race. What is the probability that neither will win?

15. Zeke picks two random numbers from 1-10 out of a hat. If the first number is even, what is the probability that the second number is odd?

16. In a building with 12 floors, Kenny gets into the elevator, closes his eyes, and randomly pushes the button to take him to some floor of the building. When he arrives there, he closes his eyes and again randomly pushes a button to take him to some floor of the building. What is the chance that the elevator will stay on its current floor?
    A. $\frac{1}{12}$
    B. $\frac{11}{12}$
    C. 1
    D. It cannot be determined from the information provided.

17. There are 6 blue plates and 3 white plates on the table. Max randomly picks two plates. What is the probability that the first plate was white and the second was blue?

18. If two standard dice are rolled, what is the probability that the sum of the numbers landing face up is 4?

19. The probability that the Michael scores more than 20 points in a game is $\frac{3}{4}$. If he plays 200 games, in how many games will he be expected to score more than 20 points?

20. The probability that a blue pen will be chosen from a box of pen is $\frac{5}{6}$. If there are 20 blue pens, how many non-blue pens are there?

RATE AND WORK Practice Set 1

1. Marion bikes to work every morning. If he bikes at a rate of 12 mph and it takes him 1.5 hours to get to work, how far does he bike?

2. Elliot can read 5 pages in 2 minutes. At this rate, how many pages will he read in 22 minutes?

3. Alex needs to be at a job interview in six hours. If he lives in a town 456 miles away from where his job interview is, how fast must he drive to get there in time?
   A. 72 mph
   B. 74 mph
   C. 76 mph
   D. 82 mph

4. It is raining at a rate of 0.75 inches per hour. If the rain is expected to continue for the next 3 days, what will be the total amount of rainfall over the course of the three days?

5. Diego can type 60 words per minute. Approximately how long will it take him to type a 2,500-word history essay?
   A. 40 minutes
   B. 42 minutes
   C. 51 minutes
   D. 53 minutes

6. Ron has a hybrid which gets 45 miles per gallon. James has a regular sedan which gets 32 miles per gallon. If they both drive from San Francisco to Las Vegas, a distance of 720 miles, how much more gas will James' car use than Ron's?
   A. 6.5 gallons
   B. 7.5 gallons
   C. 9 gallons
   D. 13 gallons

7. Kerry can read 30 pages in 10 minutes. How many pages can she read in one second?
   A. 0.02 pages
   B. 0.05 pages
   C. 3 pages
   D. 5 pages

8. There are 22 people in line waiting to use an ATM. If each person spends 4 minutes at the ATM, how long will it take all the people waiting in line to use the machine?
   A. 1 hour 8 minutes
   B. 1 hour 12 minutes
   C. 1 hour 14 minutes
   D. 1 hour 28 minutes

9. Ben and Ryan were driving at the same speed. If it takes Ben 10 minutes to drive 36 miles, how long would it take Ryan to drive 54 miles?
   A. 15 minutes
   B. 18 minutes
   C. 20 minutes
   D. 25 minutes

10. Meredith is kayaking down the Mississippi river. She travels a distance of 124 miles in $2\frac{1}{2}$ hours. What was her average speed?
   A. 46.6 mph
   B. 48.6 mph
   C. 48.8 mph
   D. 49.6 mph

11. Ruth earns $12 per hour delivering newspapers and $10 per hour shoveling snow. If she spends 3.5 hours delivering newspapers and 6 hours shoveling snow, how much did she earn?
   A. $92
   B. $98
   C. $102
   D. $106

12. At a certain factory, a machine can process 50 packages in 4 minutes. If on a certain day, 3,000 packages need to be processed, what fraction of the packages will be processed in one hour?
   A. $\frac{1}{60}$
   B. $\frac{1}{10}$
   C. $\frac{1}{4}$
   D. $\frac{1}{3}$

13. Timmy rides his scooter at a steady speed of 48 miles per hour. How far will he ride in 2 hours and 20 minutes?
   A. 96 miles
   B. 102 miles
   C. 106 miles
   D. 112 miles

14. If a waterfall delivers x gallons of water per minute, then the number of gallons delivered in two hours may be found by
   A. $2x$
   B. $\frac{x}{2}$
   C. $60x$
   D. $120x$

15. Alexis drives from Palo Alto to Sacramento, a distance of 252 miles. If she leaves at 1 pm and arrives in Sacramento at 4:30 pm, what was her average speed?
    A. 72 mph
    B. 76 mph
    C. 82 mph
    D. 84 mph

16. Elizabeth finished $\frac{1}{4}$ of her assignment between 5 pm and 5:30 pm. She needs to finish all her work by 10 pm, which is her bedtime. If she works at the same rate, what is the latest time that she can return to her homework?
    A. 5:30 pm
    B. 8:30 pm
    C. 9:00 pm
    D. 9:30 pm

17. On a recent road trip, Joan travelled 60 miles at an average speed of 80 mph. At this rate, she must have completed the journey in
    A. 45 minutes
    B. 48 minutes
    C. 60 minutes
    D. 80 minutes

18. A farmer purchases 3 cows at a cost of $450 per cow. Approximately how many gallons of milk must the farmer sell at $3.50 per gallon in order to cover the cost of purchasing the cows?
    A. 129 gallons
    B. 256 gallons
    C. 386 gallons
    D. 416 gallons

19. Mike can mow the lawn in 3 hours. His father can mow the lawn in 2 hours. How long will it take them if they decide to mow the lawn together?
    A. 5 hours
    B. 2.5 hours
    C. 1.5 hours
    D. 1.2 hours

20. Carlos leaves Los Angeles and travels towards San Francisco at 70 mph, a distance of 312 miles. At the same time, Ricardo leaves San Francisco and travels towards Los Angeles at 60 mph. How much time will elapse before they meet?
    A. 0.7 hours
    B. 2.1 hours
    C. 2.4 hours
    D. 4.5 hours

RATE AND WORK Practice Set 2

1. Alexei drives home from school every day at a rate of 32 mph. If it normally takes him takes him 0.75 hours to get home from school, how far does he drive?

2. Jonathon parachutes out of a plane near Fresno, CA. He jumps from 3.5 miles. If it takes him 0.1 hours to reach the ground, what is his average speed in miles per hour?

3. Brian works as a cook and makes $13 per hour. If he works the Saturday evening shift and makes $104, how many hours was he at work?

4. Usain Bolt can run the 100 yard dash in 9 seconds. If he can maintain the same pace for 63 seconds, how far will he run?

5. It is 8 pm and Taylor needs to finish a paper by midnight. If she has 9 pages left to write, how fast must she type in pages per hour?
    A. 1.75 pages per hour
    B. 2.0 pages per hour
    C. 2.25 pages per hour
    D. 2.5 pages per hour

6. A cuckoo clock is broken and chirps every 0.5 hour instead of every hour. How many times will it chirp in the next 2 days?

7. In Lake Tahoe it is snowing at a rate of 1.5 inches per hour. If there was no snow previously and skiing requires at least 12 inches, how long will it take before the ski resorts can open?
    A. 6 hours
    B. 8 hours
    C. 10 hours
    D. 12 hours

8. Benjamin and Robert are in a hot dog eating contest. Benjamin eats 2.5 hot dogs a minute while Robert eats 1.2 hot dogs per minute. If they both eat hot dogs for an hour, how many more hot dogs will Benjamin eat than Robert?
    A. 52 hot dogs
    B. 78 hot dogs
    C. 97 hot dogs
    D. 130 hot dogs

9. Anna can fold 12 paper cranes a minute. How many can she fold in one second?
    A. 0.05 cranes
    B. 0.1 cranes
    C. 0.2 cranes
    D. 5 cranes

10. There are 300 people in line waiting to ride Space Mountain. If each car can hold 4 people and takes 4 minutes, how long will it take for the last people to ride?
    A. 2 hours
    B. 3 hours
    C. 4 hours
    D. 5 hours

11. Rachel and Becca run together at the same speed. If it takes Rachel 20 minutes to run 4 miles, how long would it take Becca to run 16 miles?
    A. 40 minutes
    B. 1 hour
    C. 1 hour 20 minutes
    D. 1 hour 40 minutes

12. Blake is scuba diving in Hawaii at a depth of 30 meters. He checks his oxygen level and realizes he has only 8 minutes of oxygen left. How fast must he travel in order to make it to the top just as his oxygen runs out?
    A. 2.60 meters per minute
    B. 3.75 meters per minute
    C. 4.25 meters per minute
    D. 5.00 meters per minute

13. Dan is running a marathon (26 miles). If he runs for 1 hour at 8 miles per hour and 4 hours at 4 miles per hour, how many miles does he have left in the race?
    A. 0 miles
    B. 2 miles
    C. 14 miles
    D. 24 miles

14. At the mailroom in a particularly large building, the mailman can deliver 25 packages in 5 minutes. If on a certain day, 6,000 packages need to be processed, what fraction of the packages will be processed in two hours?
    A. $\frac{1}{120}$
    B. $\frac{1}{25}$
    C. $\frac{1}{10}$
    D. $\frac{1}{3}$

15. Jackie rides a horse at a steady speed of 15 miles per hour. How far will she ride in 3 hours and 12 minutes?

    A. 30 miles
    B. 45.2 miles
    C. 48 miles
    D. 60 miles

16. If a dog produces saliva at x ounces per minute, then the number of ounces delivered in 3 hours may be found by

    A. $3x$
    B. $\frac{x}{3}$
    C. $60x$
    D. $180x$

17. Amber finished $\frac{3}{5}$ her assignment between 3 pm and 4:30 pm. She needs to finish all her work by 10 pm, which is her bedtime. If she works at the same rate, what is the latest time that she can return to her homework?

    A. 4:30 pm
    B. 8:00 pm
    C. 8:30 pm
    D. 9:00 pm

18. A doctor purchases 3 stethoscopes at a cost of $250 each. Approximately how many patients must the doctor see at $12.50 per patient in order to cover the cost of purchasing the stethoscopes?

    A. 30 patients
    B. 40 patients
    C. 50 patients
    D. 60 patients

19. Sam can build a snowman in 4 hours. His brother can build a snowman in 2 hours. How long will it take them if they decide to build a snowman together?

    A. 6 hours
    B. 3 hours
    C. 1 hour 40 minutes
    D. 1 hour 20 minutes

20. Jenny leaves Los Angeles and travels towards San Francisco at 50 mph, a distance of 312 miles. At the same time, Ricardo leaves San Francisco and travels towards Los Angeles at 75 mph. Approximately how much time will elapse before they meet?

    A. 0.7 hours
    B. 2.0 hours
    C. 2.5 hours
    D. 4.3 hours

RATE AND WORK Practice Set 3

1. Josiah bikes to downtown Menlo Park from his house in Mountain View, a distance of 8 miles. If it normally takes him 0.5 hours, how fast is he traveling (in mph)?

2. Kristen can stay up on a wakeboard for 0.25 hours before she falls. If the boat is pulling her at 24 miles per hour, how far does she travel before she falls?

3. Michael Phelps holds the world record in the 400-meter individual medley. If he is swimming at an average speed of 1.6 meters per second, what is his time (__min __sec)?

4. Juan is running laps around a track. He can run one lap (0.25 miles) in 2 minutes. If he runs at the same pace for 2 hours, how far will he run?

5. It is 5 am, and Emily needs to get to swim practice by 7 am. If the pool is 120 miles away and it will take her 24 minutes to get ready to leave, how fast must she drive to arrive on time?
    A. 50 mph
    B. 60 mph
    C. 65mph
    D. 75 mph

6. Sharks off the coast of South Africa eat 15 fish in 0.75 hours. If they continue to eat at the same rate, how many fish will they eat over the next week?

7. At a certain bakery they produce chocolate chip cookies at a rate of 35 cookies per hour. If they have an order for 2,870 chocolate chip cookies, how many hours will it take them to complete the order?
    A. 35 hours
    B. 82 hours
    C. 107 hours
    D. 128 hours

8. Bear Grylls and Survivorman are hiking through the wilderness. Bear Grylls is traveling at 0.8 miles per hour while Survivorman is traveling at 1.2 miles per hour. If they both hike for 12 hours, how much farther will Survivorman go than Bear Grylls?
    A. 0.4 miles
    B. 1.5 miles
    C. 4.8 miles
    D. 6.2 miles

9. Joey works at a warehouse and can move 45 boxes of paper per hour. If he only has 15 minutes to work, how many boxes does he move?
    A. 3 boxes
    B. 5.5 boxes
    C. 8.25 boxes
    D. 11.25 boxes

10. Fifteen people are in line waiting to use the ATM. If there are 2 ATM machines and each person takes an average of 4 minutes at the ATM, how long will it take for the last person to use the machine?
    A. 30 minutes
    B. 40 minutes
    C. 50 minutes
    D. 1 hour

11. Bryan and Mark swim together at the pool at the same speed. If it takes Bryan 18 minutes to swim 10 laps, how long would it take Mark to swim 25 laps?
    A. 40 minutes
    B. 45 minutes
    C. 54 minutes
    D. 1 hour 18 minutes

12. Angela is out watching a movie at 2:30 pm when she remembers that her parents told her she has to be home by 3:15 pm. If she is currently 18 miles from home, how fast must she drive home in miles per hour?
    A. 24 mph
    B. 30 mph
    C. 44 mph
    D. 58 mph

13. Brett is driving across the country (3,000 miles). If he drives 12 hours a day for 2 days at 60 miles per hour and 3 days at 40 miles per hour, how many miles does he have left?
    A. 0 miles
    B. 60 miles
    C. 120 miles
    D. 180 miles

14. Avery responds to emails for the admissions department at her college. She can answer 3 emails in 8 minutes. If on a certain day, she needs to respond to 360 emails, what fraction of the emails can she respond to in 4 hours?
    A. $\frac{1}{120}$
    B. $\frac{1}{18}$
    C. $\frac{1}{8}$
    D. $\frac{1}{4}$

15. NASCARs drive at a steady speed of about 200 miles per hour. If the winner of a certain race finishes in 4 hours 15 minutes, how long was the race?
    A. 415 miles
    B. 725 miles
    C. 850 miles
    D. 1,000 miles

16. If a bee produces honey at x grams per minute, then the number of grams of honey produced in 4 hours 12 minutes may be found by
    A. $4.2x$
    B. $\frac{x}{252}$
    C. $25x$
    D. $252x$

17. Rachel finished $\frac{3}{4}$ of her homework between 3:00 pm and 6:00 pm. She needs to finish all her work by 10:00 pm, which is her bedtime. If she works at the same rate, how long can she stop to eat dinner for before returning to her homework?
    A. 1 hour
    B. 2 hours
    C. 3 hours
    D. 4 hours

18. A farmer purchases 4 pigs at a cost of $150 each. How much pork must the farmer sell at $6.00 per lb in order to cover the cost of purchasing the pigs?
    A. 20 lbs
    B. 100 lbs
    C. 150 lbs
    D. 600 lbs

19. Jake can build a sand castle in 2 hours. His younger brother can build a sand castle in 8 hours. How long will it take them if they decide to build a sand castle together?
    A. 1 hour
    B. 1 hour 36 minutes
    C. 1 hour 50 minutes
    D. 2 hours 12 minutes

20. Jesse leaves Los Angeles and travels towards Boston at 60 mph, a distance of 3,000 miles. At the same time, James leaves Boston and travels towards Los Angeles at 65 mph. Approximately how much time will elapse before they meet if they drive without stopping?
    A. 1 day
    B. 2 days
    C. 3 days
    D. 4 days

RATE AND WORK Practice Set 4

1. Abe runs the 2-mile race for his track and field team. If it normally takes him 0.2 hours, how fast is he traveling (in mph)?

2. A space ship can make it to the international space station in 9.5 hours. If the space ship is traveling at 1,000 miles per hour, how far does ship travel?

3. Jordanna shoots a bow and arrow at a target 150 yards away. If the arrow travels at 250 yards per second, how much time does it take for the arrow to reach the target?

4. Eric can eat 2 watermelons in 1.25 hours. If he eats watermelon for 5 hours, how many watermelons will he eat?

5. An actress has to be on the set, which is 21 miles away, at 7 am. If she wakes up at 5:30 am and does her make up for 48 minutes, how fast must she drive to arrive on time?
    A. 20 mph
    B. 30 mph
    C. 40 mph
    D. 50 mph

6. A certain employee makes $15 every 20 minutes. If the employee works a full work week (40 hours), how much money will she make?

7. It takes Carlo's bakery 24 minutes to make 2 layers of cake. If they have orders for 8 cakes with 5 layers each, how many hours will it take them to complete the order?
    A. 480 hours
    B. 192 hours
    C. 40 hours
    D. 8 hours

8. Whales and sharks are swimming in a certain part of the ocean. The sharks can swim at 50 miles per hour while the whales can swim at 30 miles per hour. If they both swim for 18 hours, how much farther will the sharks go than the whales?
    A. 20 miles
    B. 180 miles
    C. 360 miles
    D. 720 miles

9. Andy is a boxer and he can deliver 5 punches per second. If he can knock out his opponent at the end of the first round (10 minutes), how many punches will he have thrown?
   A. 50 punches
   B. 1,500 punches
   C. 3,000 punches
   D. 4,500 punches

10. There are 45 people waiting in line for the midnight opening of a movie. If they are letting in 3 people every 2 minutes, how long will it take for the last people in line to be seated?
    A. 20 minutes
    B. 30 minutes
    C. 40 minutes
    D. 1 hour

11. Elizabeth and Tracy work at a restaurant and they fold napkins at the same rate. If it takes Tracy 15 minutes to fold 8 napkins, how long would it take Elizabeth to fold 96 napkins?
    A. 1 hour 20 minutes
    B. 2 hours 10 minutes
    C. 3 hours
    D. 3 hours 20 minutes

12. Grace is at the park at 12:30 pm when she remembers that her parents told her she has to be home by 2:15 pm. If she is currently 35 miles from home, how fast must she drive home in miles per hour?
    A. 20 mph
    B. 30 mph
    C. 44 mph
    D. 58 mph

13. Louis is driving 3,000 miles to see his girlfriend. If he drives 18 hours a day for 2 days at 50 miles per hour and 1 day at 65 miles per hour, how many miles does he have left?
    A. 0 miles
    B. 30 miles
    C. 120 miles
    D. 180 miles

14. A caterer for a wedding can distribute 8 plates in 5 minutes. If at a certain wedding she needs to distribute 144 plates, what fraction of the plates can she distribute in 1 hour?
    A. $\frac{2}{3}$
    B. $\frac{2}{12}$
    C. $\frac{2}{6}$
    D. $\frac{2}{5}$

15. Cheetahs run at a speed of 65 miles per hour. If they can only run at that speed for 15 minutes, how far can they chase a gazelle?
    A. 16.25 miles
    B. 100.5 miles
    C. 65 miles
    D. 75.25 miles

16. If a spider can make x inches of web per second, then the length of web produced in 2 minutes 30 seconds may be found by
    A. $1.5x$
    B. $\frac{x}{150}$
    C. $150x$
    D. $2.5x$

17. Betsy climbed $\frac{3}{4}$ of a mountain between 8:00 am and 11:00 am. She needs to finish climbing up and down the mountain by 6:00 pm, so she can get down before dark. If she climbs at the same rate, how long can she stop to eat a meal and enjoy the view at the top?
    A. 1 hour
    B. 2 hours
    C. 3 hours
    D. 4 hours

18. A pet store purchases 8 dogs at a cost of $75 each. Approximately how much dog food must the pet store sell at $3.00 per lb in order to cover the cost of purchasing the dogs?
    A. 20 lbs
    B. 100 lbs
    C. 150 lbs
    D. 200 lbs

19. A toddler can build a Lego set in 10 hours. His older brother can build the same Lego set in 5 hours. How long will it take them to build the Lego set together?
    A. 3 hours 20 minutes
    B. 3 hour 45 minutes
    C. 6 hour 10 minutes
    D. 7 hours 30 minutes

20. Barbie leaves Beijing on an airplane and travels towards Paris at 500 mph, a distance of 5,000 miles. At the same time, Ken leaves Paris and travels towards Beijing at 500 mph. Approximately how much time will elapse before their planes pass each other?
    A. 12 hours 15 minutes
    B. 10 hours
    C. 8 hours 20 minutes
    D. 5 hours

CHAPTER 12: GEOMETRY

Experts in Test Prep, Tutoring, & Admissions Counseling

www.CardinalEducation.com

PERIMETER AND AREA Practice Set 1

1. The perimeter of the triangle below is 22 centimeters. The lengths of two of the sides are shown. What is the length of the third side?

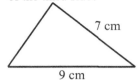

2. What is the area of the triangle below?

$$Area = \frac{Base \times Height}{2}$$

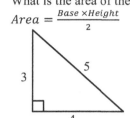

3. The perimeter of the rectangle below is 30 centimeters. What is the length of the top side of the rectangle?

4. The back and front walls of a classroom are each 15 feet long. The side walls are each 10 feet long. What is the area of the room?

5. What is the perimeter of a rectangle that has a length of 10 inches and a width of 6 inches?

6. The perimeter of a square is 28. What is the length of one side of the square?

7. The perimeter of an isosceles triangle is 24 inches. Each of the two equal sides has a length of 10. What is the length of the non-equal side?

8. The perimeter of a regular hexagon is 48. What is the length of one side of the hexagon?

9. The length of one side of a regular octagon is 7. What is the perimeter of the octagon?

10. The perimeter of a triangle is $19y$. One side of the triangle is $7y$. A second side of the triangle is $6y$. What is the third side of the triangle?

11. The area of a square is $9x^2$. What is the length of one side of the square?

12. The length of one side of a rectangle is 10. The length of the other side of the rectangle is a prime number between 20 and 25. What is the perimeter of the rectangle?

13. The lengths of two sides of a rectangle are 6 and 8. If all sides of the rectangle are increased by 2, the area of the rectangle will increase by how much?

14. An equilateral triangle has a perimeter of 2,400 inches. What is the length of one side of the triangle?

15. The area of a rectangle is 11 larger than its perimeter. Which of the following could be the lengths of the sides of the rectangle?
    A. 3 and 5
    B. 4 and 6
    C. 5 and 7
    D. 6 and 8

16. A window is 20 inches wide and 24 inches high. If the owner wants to make the window 8 inches shorter, by how many square inches will he need to decrease the total area of the window?

17. The base of a triangle is x meters. The height of the triangle is 7 meters. In terms of x, what is the area of the triangle?

18. The length of two sides of a rectangle are $x - 2$ and $x + 4$. What is the perimeter of the rectangle?

19. The width of a rectangle is 5. The perimeter of the rectangle is larger than its area. If the length of the rectangle must be an integer, what is one possible length for the rectangle?

20. A triangle and a square have the same base and the same height. What is the ratio of the area of the triangle to the area of the square?

PERIMETER AND AREA Practice Set 2

1. The lengths of the sides of a triangle are shown. What is the perimeter of the triangle?

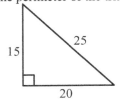

2. What is the area of the triangle below?

$Area = \frac{Base \times Height}{2}$

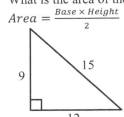

3. The area of the rectangle below is 42 inches. What is the length of the bottom side of the rectangle?

6 in

4. The front side of a rectangular fence is 40 feet long, and the other side is 20 feet long. What is the perimeter of the fence?

5. What is the area of a rectangle that has a length of 10 inches and a width of 6 inches?

6. The perimeter of a square is 52. What is the length of one side of the square?

7. The perimeter of a regular pentagon is 55. What is the length of one side of the pentagon?

8. The perimeter of an isosceles triangle is 50 cm. Each of the two equal sides has a length of x cm, and the length of the non-equal side is 20 cm. What is x?

9. The length of one side of a regular hexagon is 10. What is the perimeter of the hexagon?

10. The perimeter of a square is $20b$. What is the length of one side of the square?

376

11. The lengths of two sides of a rectangle are 5 and 10. If all sides of the rectangle are decreased by 3, the area of the rectangle will decrease by how much?

12. One side of an equilateral triangle is 18. What is the perimeter of the triangle?

13. The area of a rectangle is 8 larger than its perimeter. Which of the following could be the lengths of the sides of the rectangle?
    A. 5 and 6
    B. 2 and 10
    C. 3 and 8
    D. 4 and 11

14. The area of a rectangle is $40x^2$. If one side of the rectangle has a length of $8x$, what is the length of the other side of the rectangle?

15. The base of a triangle is 10. The height of the triangle is an even multiple of 7 between 20 and 30. What is the area of the triangle?

16. A wall is 17 feet wide and 10 feet high. If the wall is extended to the side by 8 additional feet, how many square feet of area need to be added to the wall?

17. The base of a triangle is $3p$ meters. The height of the triangle is $5p$ meters. In terms of p, what is the area of the triangle?

18. The length of two sides of a rectangle are $x + 1$ and $x + 2$. What is the area of the rectangle?

19. The area of a rectangle is 24, and all of its sides have lengths that are integers. If the perimeter of the rectangle is greater than the area, what could be the lengths of the sides of the rectangle?

20. A triangle and a rectangle each have a base of length 8. The height of the triangle is 20 and the height of the rectangle is 5. What is the ratio of the area of the triangle to the area of the rectangle?

GEOMETRIC CONCEPTS AND TERMS

ANGLES

- <u>Right angles</u> are 90°
- <u>Acute angles</u> are less than 90°
- <u>Obtuse angles</u> are greater than 90°
- Angles that form a line add up to 180°
- <u>Complementary angles</u> add up to 90°
- <u>Supplementary angles</u> add up to 180°

TRIANGLES

- The angles in a triangle always add up to 180°
- No side of a triangle can be longer than the sum of the other two sides
- <u>Isosceles triangle</u>: two sides are equal and the angles across from those sides are equal
- <u>Equilateral triangle</u>: all three sides of the triangle are equal and all three angles are 60°
- <u>Right triangle</u>
    - One angle is 90°
    - The other two angles add up to 90°
    - <u>Pythagorean Theorem</u>: $a^2 + b^2 = c^2$ when
- Area: $\frac{1}{2} \times base \times height$
- <u>Similar Triangles</u>: All sides are proportional, all angles are equal

RECTANGLES

- Area: $base \times height$
- Perimeter: $(2 \times base) + (2 \times height)$
- All angles in a rectangle are 90°

POLYGONS

- <u>Quadrilateral</u>: A 4-sided figure. All quadrilaterals have angles that add up to 360°
    - <u>Trapezoid</u>: A quadrilateral with one set of opposing sides parallel
    - <u>Parallelogram</u>: A quadrilateral with two sets of opposing sides parallel
    - <u>Rhombus</u>: A parallelogram in which all sides are the same length
- <u>Pentagon</u>: 5-sided figure
- <u>Hexagon</u>: 6-sided figure
- <u>Octagon</u>: 8-sided figure
- <u>Regular Polygon</u>: all sides and angles are equal

trapezoid

parallelogram

CIRCLES

- <u>Radius</u>: any line from the center of the circle to the edge of the circle, half the diameter
- <u>Diameter</u>: any line from edge of circle to the other edge of circle, passing through the center
- Area: πr^2
- Circumference: $2\pi r$

3-D FIGURES

- Cubes and rectangular prisms
    - Volume: $length \times width \times height$
    - Surface Area: Find the area of each side and add them all up

SLIDES, TURNS, AND REFLECTIONS

Slide/Translation:

Turn/Rotation:

Reflection/Flip:

ANGLES AND TRIANGLES Practice Set 1

1. Find the length of the missing side.

    A. 9
    B. 10
    C. 12
    D. 14

2. Given that line *AB* is parallel to *CD*, which of the following statements is true?

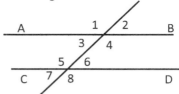

    A. ∠1 = ∠3
    B. ∠7 = ∠4
    C. ∠5 = ∠1
    D. ∠6 = ∠8

3. What is the perimeter of an equilateral triangle with sides 8 cm?

4. ∠MON = ∠NOQ. What is the measure of ∠NOP?

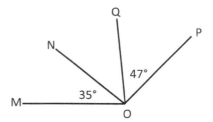

5. For the triangle shown below

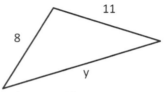

    A. $y = 19$
    B. $y > 19$
    C. $y < 19$
    D. $y = 20$

380

6. Find the measure of angle m.

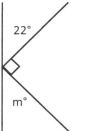

7. Three lines meet as shown in the diagram below. What is the value of $x + 3y$?

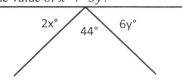

8. Find the value of y.

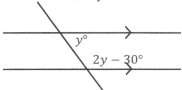

9. The three sides of a triangle are $4y - 2, 2y + 3$, and $3y - 7$. If the perimeter of the triangle is 48, what is the length of the largest side?
  A. 22
  B. 24
  C. 25
  D. 26

10. Find the value of x?

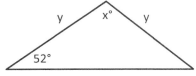

11. Find the area of triangle XYZ shown below.

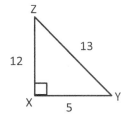

12. What is the value of angle m shown in the diagram below?

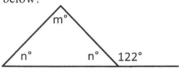

13. An equilateral triangle has sides of length $3x - 7$ and $x + 15$. What is the perimeter of the triangle?

14. Which of the following is equal to b?

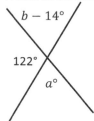

    A. $a°$
    B. $72°$
    C. $122°$
    D. $a - 14°$

15. The measure of side LM is

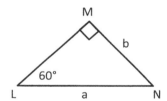

    A. $> a$
    B. $= b$
    C. $< b$
    D. $= a$

16. Which statement about triangle ABC is correct?

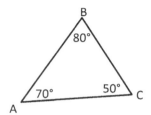

    A. $AC < BC$
    B. $AB > BC$
    C. $CB > CA$
    D. $BA < CB$

382

17. The diagonal distance of the square is $\sqrt{2}$. What is the length of one side of the square?

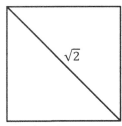

    A. 1
    B. 1.5
    C. 2
    D. 3

18. AB is perpendicular to BC. If $AB = 5$ and $BC = 8$, what is the shortest distance from A to C?

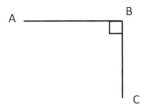

19. Find the area of the triangle shown below.

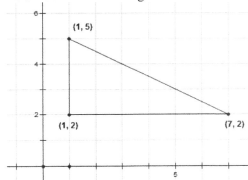

20. The base of an isosceles triangle is 3 times greater than the legs, and the perimeter of the triangle is 60. Find the length of one of the legs of the triangle.

    A. 12
    B. 15
    C. 20
    D. 30

ANGLES AND TRIANGLES Practice Set 2

1.   Which statement about the figure shown is false?

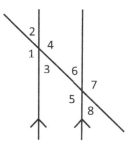

   A. $m\angle 2 = m\angle 3$
   B. $m\angle 1 = m\angle 5$
   C. $m\angle 6 + m\angle 4 = 180°$
   D. $m\angle 8 + m\angle 3 = 180°$

2.   Find the value of x.

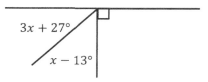

3.   Find the value of $x - y$.

      A.   21°
      B.   33°
      C.   63°
      D.   138°

4.   How much is b greater than a?

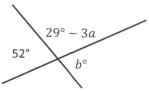

      A.   33°
      B.   52°
      C.   76°
      D.   85°

384

5. For the triangle shown below

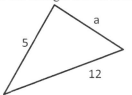

 A. $a < 17$
 B. $a = 17$
 C. $a > 17$
 D. $a < 18$

6. Lines m and n are parallel. Solve for x.

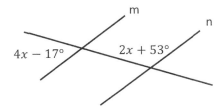

7. JK is perpendicular to KL. If JK = 5, and KL = 11, what is the shortest distance between points J and L?

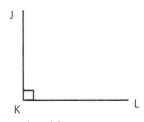

 A. 16
 B. $\sqrt{16}$
 C. $\sqrt{146}$
 D. 146

8. Find the value of x.

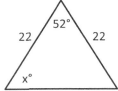

9. The three sides of a triangle are $3x - 8, x + 5$, and $26 - 3x$. If the perimeter of the triangle is 30, what is the length of the smallest side?
 A. 4
 B. 5
 C. 7
 D. 12

10. What is the area of the triangle shown below?

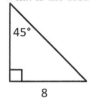

45°

8

11. An equilateral triangle has sides of length $15y - 27$ and $7y + 21$. What is the perimeter of the triangle?

12. The measure of side ST is

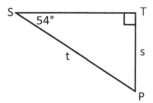

S 54° T
t
s
P

A. $> t$
B. $= s$
C. $> s$
D. $< t$

13. Which of the following statements about triangle WXY is correct?

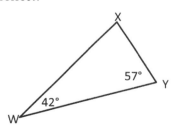

X
57° Y
42°
W

A. $WX > WY$
B. $XY > WY$
C. $XY < WX$
D. $WY < XW$

14. What is the length of the diagonal in the square below?

5

A. $\sqrt{10}$
B. 5
C. $5\sqrt{2}$
D. $2\sqrt{5}$

15. Find the value of x.

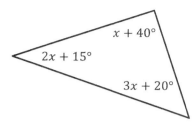

16. What is the value of $a + b$?

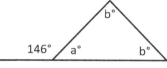

    A. 103°
    B. 107°
    C. 123°
    D. 146°

17. Find the area of the triangle shown below.

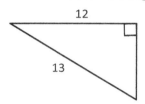

18. Roy leans a 20 foot ladder up against a wall. If the base of the ladder is 15 feet away from wall, how high up the wall does the ladder reach?

19. Find the area of triangle ABC shown in the coordinate system below.

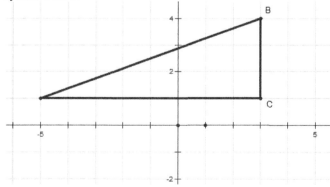

20. The base of an isosceles triangle is half the length of the legs of the triangle. If the perimeter of the triangle is 70, find the length of the base of the triangle.

ANGLES AND TRIANGLES Practice Set 3

1. One of the angles in an equilateral triangle is $2x - 24°$.
    What is the value of x?

2. Find the measure of angle n.

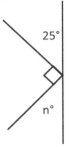

3. Find the perimeter of an equilateral triangle of sides 56.

4. Find the value of y.

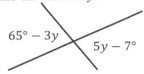

5. Find the value of x.

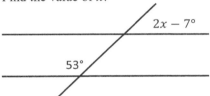

6. Find the perimeter of the triangle shown below.

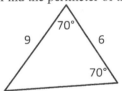

7. Find the measure of angle BCD

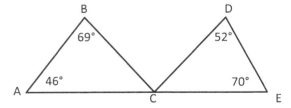

8. What is the value of $2x + 2y$?

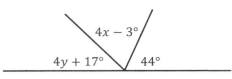

$4x - 3°$

$4y + 17°$ $44°$

    A.   61°
    B.   68°
    C.   122°
    D.   136°

9. What is the value of $y - x$?

113°

x°

38°   y°

10. A triangle has sides $2y - 5, 3y + 9$, and $5y - 7$. Find the length of the largest side if the perimeter is 87.

11. Which statement regarding triangle WAP is correct?

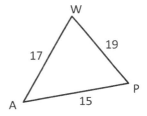

W

17   19

A   15   P

    A. $\angle WAP = \angle WPA$
    B. $\angle PAW > \angle AWP$
    C. $\angle PWA > \angle APW$
    D. $\angle WPA < \angle PWA$

12. The area of a triangle is 20 square units. Find its height if the base is 8 units.

13. Find the measure of the largest angle if the three angles in a triangle are $2m + 16, 60 - 3m$, and $80 - 5m$.

14. Line AB is perpendicular to line BC. If angle ABD is three times as large as angle DBC, find the value of ABD.

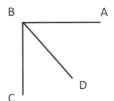

B   A

D

C

15. Find the perimeter of the rectangle shown below.

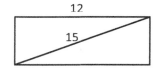

16. Which of the following statements is correct?

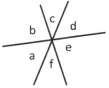

    A. $\angle a + \angle b = 180°$
    B. $\angle b = \angle f$
    C. $\angle e + \angle f + \angle a = 180°$
    D. $\angle c > \angle f$

17. Cory walks from his house 30 meters due east, then another 40 meters due south to the library. What is the shortest distance from the library to his house?

18. The perimeter of the triangle is how much less than the area?

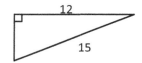

19. Triangle GFH is shown below. Which statement is true?

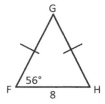

    A. $GH > GF$
    B. $GF = 8$
    C. $\angle GHF > \angle FGH$
    D. $GH < 8$

20. Find the area of triangle *DEF* below.

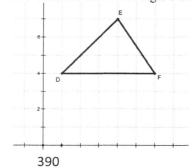

390

1. Given line PQ is parallel to ST, find the value of x.

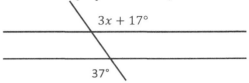

$3x + 17°$

$37°$

2. Which of the following statements is true?

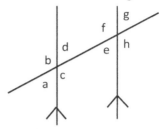

A. $\angle a > \angle g$
B. $\angle e + \angle b = 180°$
C. $\angle b + \angle g = 180°$
D. $\angle h = \angle d$

3. Line AB is perpendicular to line BC. What is the value of angle ABD?

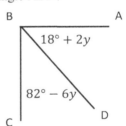

$18° + 2y$

$82° - 6y$

4. What is the value of m?

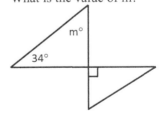

$m°$

$34°$

5. For the figure shown below

a

22   14

A. $a = 36$
B. $a = 37$
C. $a > 37$
D. $a < 36$

6. Find the perimeter of the triangle shown.

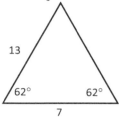

7. An equilateral triangle has sides of length $5x - 27$ and $3x - 11$. Find the perimeter of the triangle.

8. Find the value of a in the triangle shown below.

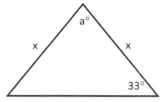

9. Which of the following statements regarding triangle CDE is correct?

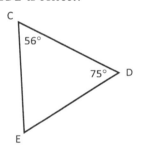

    A. $CD < ED$
    B. $DE > CE$
    C. $EC < DC$
    D. $CD > DE$

10. The measure of the acute angles in a right triangle are in a ratio of 4:1. The measure of the smaller acute angle is?

11. Find the value of a.

$$120° - 3a$$

$$14.5a + 15°$$

12. The figure shows three lines intersecting at a point. Find the value of $a + 2b$.

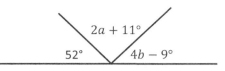

    A. 63°
    B. 64°
    C. 126°
    D. 128°

13. The area of triangle 2 is how much greater than the area of triangle 1?

    Triangle 1   Triangle 2

14. The measure of side RS is

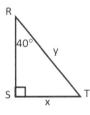

    A. $> y$
    B. $< x$
    C. $= x$
    D. $> x$

15. The diagonal of a square is $\sqrt{8}$. What is the length of one of the sides of the square?
    A. 1
    B. 2
    C. 3
    D. 4

16. What is the value of $2x + 2y$?

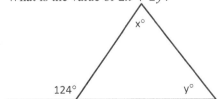

17. Find the area of triangle ABC shown in the coordinate system below.

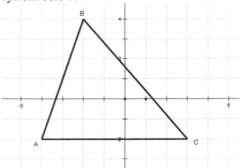

18. Jenna is standing 5 feet north of a sequoia tree. Her dog is 12 feet west of the same tree. What is the shortest distance between Jenna and her dog?
  A. 7 feet
  B. 13 feet
  C. 17 feet
  D. 19 feet

19. The area of the triangle is 28. What is the length of side *FH*?

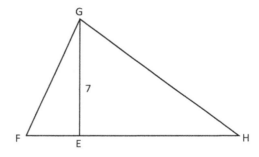

20. The legs of an isosceles triangle are 4 times the base. If the perimeter of the triangle is 63, what is the length of one of the legs of the triangle?

QUADRILATERALS AND CIRCLES Practice Set 1

1. A cube has edges that measure 6 cm. Find its volume.

2. If three central angles of a circle are 40°, 60°, and 90° as
    shown in the figure below, find the average of all four
    central angles on the circle.

    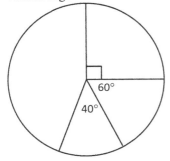

3. The area of a square is 169, find its perimeter.

4. Find the perimeter of the square shown below.

    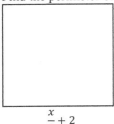

    $\frac{x}{8} + 2$

    A. $\frac{x}{8} + 8$
    B. $\frac{4x}{8} + 2$
    C. $\frac{x}{2} + 8$
    D. $\frac{x}{2} + 2$

5. What is the distance from A to D.

    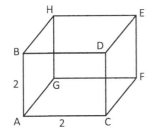

    A. 4
    B. $\sqrt{8}$
    C. $\sqrt{2}$
    D. 2

6. A box with dimensions $5 \times 6 \times 8$ has the same volume as a box with dimensions $2 \times 1 \times d$. What is the value of d?

7. A regular hexagon has a perimeter of 54. What is the length of one side of the hexagon?

8. A rectangular piece of cardboard has dimensions 6×12. If a 2×2 square piece of cardboard is cut out of every corner, what is the area of the remaining piece of cardboard?
   A. 16
   B. 40
   C. 52
   D. 56

9. The perimeter of a square is 68. Find its area.

10. If the circumference of a circle is 6.28, what is its radius? (Use $\pi = 3.14$)
    A. 0.25
    B. 0.5
    C. 1
    D. 2

11. The figure below shows a square. What is the area of the shaded region?

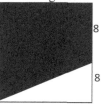

8

8

    A. 192
    B. 224
    C. 246
    D. 256

12. Rectangle MNOP has a perimeter of 24, find its area.

    A. 16
    B. 20
    C. 32
    D. It cannot be determined from the information provided.

13. Find the area of the shaded region if the radius of the outer circle is 9 and the radius of the inner circle is 6. (Use $\pi = 3.14$)

    A. 9.42
    B. 98.4
    C. 141.3
    D. 254.34

14. The length of the diagonal of a square with sides 5 inches is approximately?
    A. 6 inches
    B. 7 inches
    C. 9 inches
    D. 10 inches

15. In the figure below, $\angle XOY = 40°$. If O is the center of the circle, then minor arc XY is what part of the circumference of the circle?

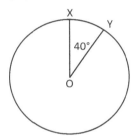

    A. $\frac{1}{9}$
    B. $\frac{1}{8}$
    C. $\frac{1}{4}$
    D. $\frac{1}{3}$

16. The figure below shows a circle inscribed in a square of length 8 cm. What is the area of the shaded region?

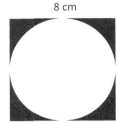

    A. $8 - 4\pi$ cm
    B. $8 - 8\pi$ cm
    C. $64 - 16\pi$ cm
    D. $64 - 64\pi$ cm

17. Joey's farm is in the form of a rectangle. The length of the farm is three times the width. If the width of the Joey's farm is w, what is the perimeter of the farm?

    A. $3 + 2w$
    B. $4w$
    C. $6 + 2w$
    D. $8w$

18. What is the ratio of the area of the shaded region to the area of the total region?

    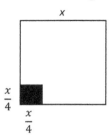

    A. $1 : 32$
    B. $1 : 16$
    C. $1 : 8$
    D. $1 : 4$

19. A rectangular pool with dimensions 90 ft × 40 ft × 10 ft is being filled with water by a pump. If the pump can fill the pool in 2 hours, at what rate is the pump pumping water into the pool?

    A. $300 \text{ ft}^3/\text{min}$
    B. $400 \text{ ft}^3/\text{min}$
    C. $500 \text{ ft}^3/\text{min}$
    D. $600 \text{ ft}^3/\text{min}$

20. The figure below represents a rectangular piece of cardboard with dimensions 12 cm × 8 cm. If 1 cm by 1 cm cuts are made on each corner as shown by the dotted lines, and the cardboard is folded to form a box with no lid, which of the following will be the volume of the box?

    A. 48 cm^3
    B. 60 cm^3
    C. 92 cm^3
    D. 96 cm^3

QUADRILATERALS AND CIRCLES Practice Set 2

1. Find the perimeter of a square whose area is 225 cm^2?

2. Find the circumference of a circle whose radius is 7 inches. (Use $\pi = 3.14$)

3. Andrew has just ordered a pizza that has slices that make a 45°, as shown below. Wow many slices are there?

4. The figure shows a circle with center O and four points, A, B, C, and D on its circumference. Which of the following statements about the figure shown is correct?

    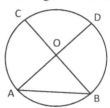

    A. $AD > CB$
    B. $DO < BO$
    C. $AO = CO$
    D. $AB > AD$

5. Below is a cube of sides 5. Find the distance from B to D.

    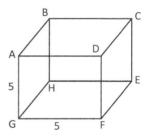

6. What is the perimeter of the quarter circle shown if its radius is 5? (Use $\pi = 3.14$)

7. A box with dimensions $2 \times 8 \times 12$ has the same volume as a box with dimensions $3 \times 4 \times h$. Find the value of h.

8. What is the total surface area of a cube with sides 7 cm?

9. Find the area of the shaded region?

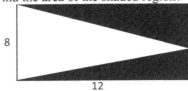

10. What is the area of a circle with diameter 34?
    A. 34π
    B. 68π
    C. 289π
    D. 1156π

11. Find the area of a square whose perimeter is 52.

12. The figure shows a square with sides $\frac{x}{12} + 5$. What is its perimeter?

$$\frac{x}{12} + 5$$

    A. $\frac{x}{12} + 20$
    B. $\frac{x}{3} + 20$
    C. $\frac{x}{3} + 5$
    D. $4x + 5$

13. Lauren is trying to place a new carpet in her living room which measures 20 feet by 14 feet. If the carpet she chooses costs $3.10 per square foot, how much will it cost her to carpet her entire living room?

14. A box has a base that measures 8 in by 6 in and a height of 5 in. Find its surface area if the box has an open top?

15. The parallelogram shown below has sides of length 20 in and 8 in and a height of 6 in. How much greater is the area than the perimeter?

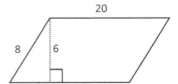

16. The swimming pool in Jasmine's house is four times as long as it is wide. If the length of the pool is p meters, what is the perimeter of the pool?

    A. $\frac{5}{4}p$ meters

    B. $\frac{5}{2}p$ meters

    C. $4p$ meters

    D. $10p$ meters

17. What is the ratio of the area of the shaded region to the total area?

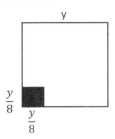

    A. 1:4

    B. 1:8

    C. 1:16

    D. 1:64

18. Find the area of the shaded region.

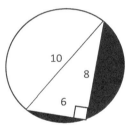

    A. $12.5\pi - 24$

    B. $25\pi - 24$

    C. $50\pi - 48$

    D. $50\pi - 24$

19. The figure below is a 20 by 14 piece of cardboard. If 2 in by 2 in cuts are made on each corner as shown by the dotted lines, and the cardboard is folded along the cuts to form a box with no lid, what is the volume of the box?

20. Tyrone jogged around a soccer field which measures 110 meters by 58 meters. He ran around the field 4 times at a speed of 2 meters/second. How long did he run for?

QUADRILATERALS AND CIRCLES Practice Set 3

1. Which of the following statements is correct?
    A. The diameter is half the radius.
    B. The area of a circle is always equal to its circumference.
    C. The circumference of a circle is its perimeter.
    D. The diameter is longer than the circumference.

2. Find the perimeter of a square whose area is 49 cm².

3. Which of the following statements about quadrilaterals is correct?
    A. A rectangle has four equal sides.
    B. Two angles of a rectangle are supplementary.
    C. The side of a square is longer than its diagonal.
    D. The angles in a rectangle are not equal.

4. What is the volume of a cube with sides 11 inches?

5. Jocelyn is baking an apple pie. If she decides to cut the pie into equal slices, each slice making a 60° as shown in the figure, how many slices are there?

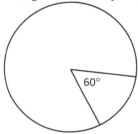

6. A box with dimensions $7 \times 8 \times 9$ has the same volume as a box with dimensions $4 \times 6 \times k$. Find the value of k.

7. The figure below shows a cube of sides 2. Which is the longest distance?

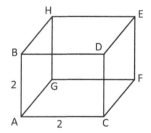

    A. HD
    B. BG
    C. DF
    D. GD

8. Find the circumference of a circle whose radius is 4.
    A. 2π
    B. 4π
    C. 8π
    D. 16π

9. A rectangle has a length that is four times as long as its width. If the width of the rectangle is w, what is the perimeter of the rectangle?
    A. $2w + 8$
    B. $10w$
    C. $4w^2$
    D. $4w + 8$

10. A regular pentagon is a five-sided figure. If the perimeter of a pentagon is 435 feet, what is the length of one side?

11. The length and width of a rectangle are increased by 50%. What would be the increase in the area of the rectangle?
    A. 50%
    B. 100%
    C. 125%
    D. 225%

12. The outer diameter of a pipe is 3.84 cm while the inner diameter is 1.74 cm. What is the thickness of the pipe?
    A. 0.87 cm
    B. 1.05 cm
    C. 1.94 cm
    D. 2.1 cm

13. Find the radius of a circle whose circumference is 80 cm.
    A. Divide 80 by 2π
    B. Divide 80 by π
    C. Multiply 40 by $\frac{\pi}{2}$
    D. Multiply 80 by 2π

14. The figure below shows a square. What is the area of the shaded region?

15. A rectangle has an area of 48 cm^2. What is its perimeter?
    A. 28 cm
    B. 31 cm
    C. 36 cm
    D. It cannot be determined using the information provided.

16. The perimeter of the rectangle shown below is 48. What is the value of $x + y$.

17. Find the perimeter of the square shown.

$$\frac{3x}{7} + 4$$

A. $\frac{12x}{7} + 16$

B. $\frac{3x}{28} + 16$

C. $\frac{12x}{7} + 4$

D. $\frac{3x}{7} + 16$

18. The radius of a circle is doubled, how much does the area increase?
   A. Decreases by half
   B. Doubles
   C. Triples
   D. Increases by a factor of 4

19. Jimmy is jogging around a football field which is 120 meters long and 60 meters wide. If he jogs at an average speed of 180 meters/hour, for 2 hours. How many laps did he run around the field?
   A. 1 lap
   B. 2 laps
   C. 3 laps
   D. 4 laps

20. What is the perimeter of the half circle shown below? (Use $\pi = 3.14$)

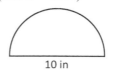

10 in

   A. 15.7 inches
   B. 25.7 inches
   C. 31.4 inches
   D. 41.4 inches

QUADRILATERALS AND CIRCLES Practice Set 4

1. What is the area of a square whose perimeter is 64?

2. ABCD is a rectangle. What is the value of x?

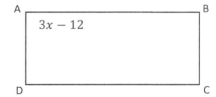

3. The diameter of a circle is halved. The circumference will
   A. Decrease by half
   B. Decrease by a third
   C. Double
   D. Triple

4. Which of the following statements about quadrilaterals is incorrect?
   A. A square has four equal sides.
   B. Opposite sides of a rectangle are parallel.
   C. The angles in a quadrilateral add up to 180°.
   D. Opposite angles of a rectangle are supplementary.

5. The circumference of a circle is 6.28. What is its radius? (Use $\pi = 3.14$)

6. If three central angles of a circle are 80°, 20°, and 70° as shown in the figure below, find the average of all four central angles of the circle.

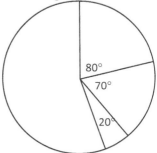

7. A regular octagon is an eight-sided figure. What is the perimeter of an octagon whose sides measures 37 inches?

8. Find the radius of a circle whose circumference is 70.
   A. Divide 70 by π
   B. Divide 35 by π
   C. Multiply 70 by 2π
   D. Multiply 35 by $\frac{\pi}{2}$

9. A rectangular piece of cardboard measures 27 by 18. If a 3 × 3 square piece of cardboard is cut out of each corner, what is the area of the remaining piece of cardboard?

10. The figure shows a circle with center O and four points A, B, C, and D on its circumference. Which of the following statements is false?

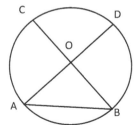

    A. AO = BO
    B. CB = 2OD
    C. 2OC = 2AB
    D. 2BO = AD

11. The outer radius of a pipe is 11.6 cm while inner radius of the pipe is 8.8 cm. What is the thickness of the pipe?
    A. 1.4 cm
    B. 2.8 cm
    C. 4.4 cm
    D. 5.6 cm

12. Find the volume of a cube whose sides measure 15 cm.

13. The area of the rectangle shown is 102. What is the value of xy?

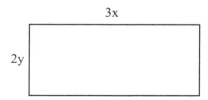

14. Grace has a rectangular garden in her backyard. The width of the garden is half its length. What is the perimeter of the garden if its length is l?
    A. $2l$
    B. $3l$
    C. $4l$
    D. $5l$

15. The length of the diagonal of a square with sides 7 is approximately?
    A. 7
    B. 8
    C. 10
    D. 14

16. The length and width of a rectangle are increased by 20%. What will be the percentage increase in its area?
    - A. 20%
    - B. 40%
    - C. 44%
    - D. 80%

17. Find the area of the shaded region.

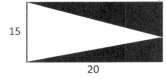

18. A water tank measuring 80 ft × 60 ft × 30 ft is being filled by two pumps that can fill the tank in 2 hours. If both pumps work at the same rate, how much water is being added to the tank by each pump every minute?
    - A. 400 ft³/min
    - B. 600 ft³/min
    - C. 900 ft³/min
    - D. 1,200 ft³/min

19. The figure shows a circle inscribed in a square of sides 10 cm. What is the area of the shaded region?

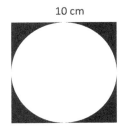

    - A. $10 - 10\pi$ cm
    - B. $10 - 25\pi$ cm
    - C. $100 - 10\pi$ cm
    - D. $100 - 25\pi$ cm

20. The figure below represents a rectangular piece of cardboard with dimensions 24 inches by 19 inches. If 1 inch by 1 inch cuts are made on each corner as shown by the dotted lines, and the cardboard is folded along the cuts to form a box with no lid, which of the following will be the volume of the box?

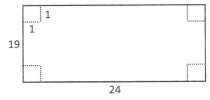

    - A. 374 in³
    - B. 414 in³
    - C. 448 in³
    - D. 458 in³

3-D FIGURES Practice Set 1

1. How many small cubes are being used to build the large prism?

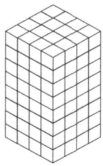

   A. 32 cubes
   B. 64 cubes
   C. 128 cubes
   D. 196 cubes

2. The figures show two cubes whose sides are proportional. What is the ratio of the volume of Figure 1 to the volume of Figure 2?

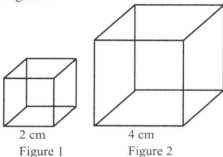

   2 cm   4 cm
   Figure 1   Figure 2

   A. 1 to 2
   B. 1 to 4
   C. 1 to 8
   D. 1 to 16

3. The height of the cylinder shown is 3 times its diameter. The formula used to find the volume of a cylinder is $V = \pi r^2 h$ where r is the radius of the cylinder and h is the height of the cylinder. If the diameter of the cylinder is 8 in, what is its volume?

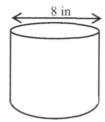

   8 in

   A. 384π in^3
   B. 432π in^3
   C. 576π in^3
   D. $1,536\pi$ in^3

4. Which figure cannot be drawn without lifting the pencil or retracing?

A.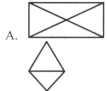

B.

C.

D.

5. Which of the following shapes shows a trapezoid?

A.

B.

C.

D.

6.

A.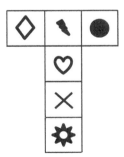

B.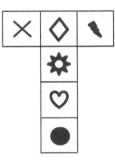

C.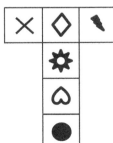

D.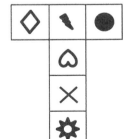

7.

A.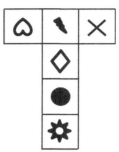

B.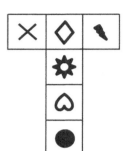

C.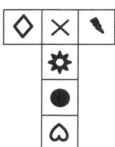

D.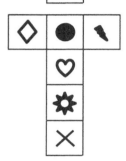

8.

A.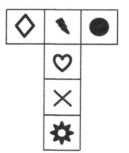

B.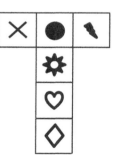

C.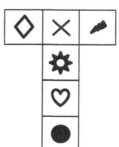

D.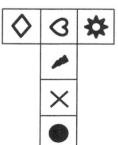

9.

A.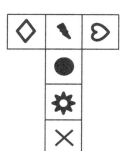

B.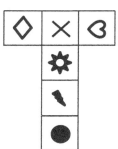

C.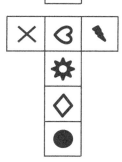

D.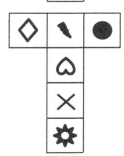

10.

A.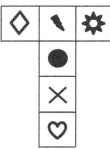

B.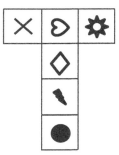

C.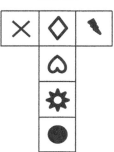

D.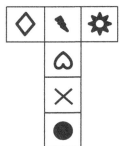

3-D FIGURES Practice Set 2

1. How many small cubes are being used to build the large prism?

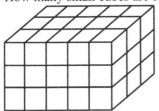

   A. 18 cubes
   B. 27 cubes
   C. 35 cubes
   D. 45 cubes

2. Which of the following shapes shows a hexagon?

   A.
   B.
   C.
   D.

3. Which figure cannot be drawn without lifting the pencil or retracing?

   A.

   B.

   C.

   D.

4. The volume of the small, shaded cube is 3 unit^3. What is the volume of the larger cube?

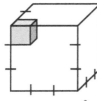

   A. 9 unit^3
   B. 21 unit^3
   C. 63 unit^3
   D. 81 unit^3

412

5. The height of the cone shown is 6 times its diameter. The formula used to find the volume of a cone is $V = \frac{1}{3}\pi r^2 h$ where r is the radius of the cone and h is the height of the cone. If the diameter of the cone is 6 in, what is its volume?

6 in

   A. 54π in^3
   B. 81π in^3
   C. 108π in^3
   D. 162π in^3

6.

A.

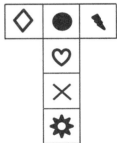

B.

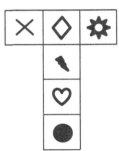

C.

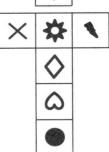

D.

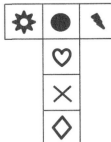

7.

A.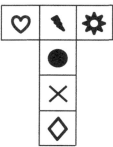

B.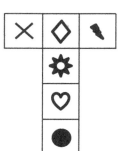

C.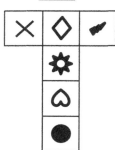

D.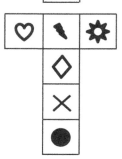

8.

A.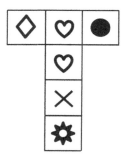

B.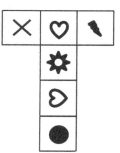

C.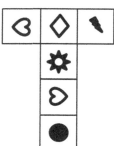

D.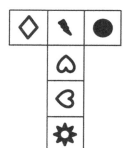

414

9.

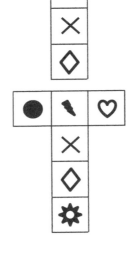

A.

B.

C.

D.

10.

A.

B.

C.

D.

COORDINATE GEOMETRY Practice Set 1

1. Write the equation of a line that has slope -2 and passes through $(-3, 4)$.
   - A. $y = -2x + 4$
   - B. $y = 3x - 2$
   - C. $y = -3x + 4$
   - D. $y = -2x - 2$

2. What are the coordinates of the point?

   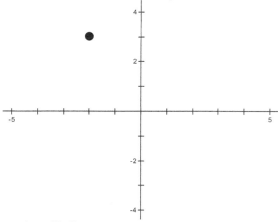

   - A. $(2, 3)$
   - B. $(3, 2)$
   - C. $(-2, 3)$
   - D. $(-3, 2)$

3. Points W and Y are two corners of rectangle $WXYZ$ in the coordinate plane. Which of the following could be the coordinates of points X and Z, if points X and Z complete rectangle $WXYZ$?

   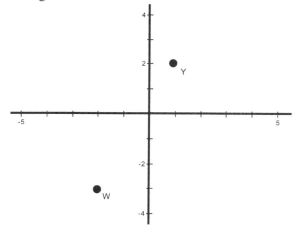

   - A. $X(-2, 2)$ and $Z(1, -3)$
   - B. $X(-2, 3)$ and $Z(-1, -3)$
   - C. $X(2, -3)$ and $Z(-2, 1)$
   - D. $X(-2, 2)$ and $Z(-1, -3)$

416

4. What is the slope of the line whose equation is
   $y = -5x + 7$?
   A. -5
   B. 5
   C. 5
   D. 7

5. What is the distance between the point A with coordinates
   $(3, 9)$ and point B with coordinates $(3, -4)$?
   A. 0
   B. 5
   C. 6
   D. 13

6. Points R, S, and T are three vertices of square $RSTU$ in
   the coordinate plane. Which of the following could be the
   coordinates of point U?

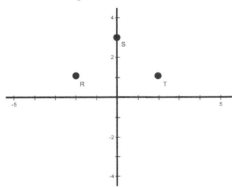

   A. $(0, 1)$
   B. $(0, -1)$
   C. $(0, 0)$
   D. $(2, -1)$

7. The grid shows three vertices of a parallelogram. Which
   of the following could be the coordinates of the fourth
   vertex of the parallelogram?

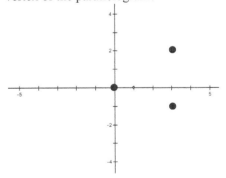

   A. $(0, -2)$
   B. $(0, 4)$
   C. $(7, 1)$
   D. $(0, -3)$

8. For which of the functions below does the y value increase at the greatest rate as the x value increases?

A.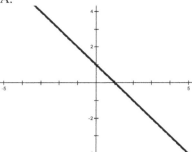

B.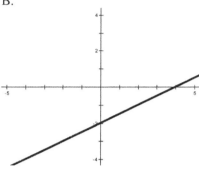

C.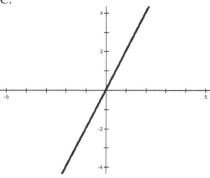

D.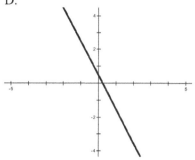

9. Which of the following is the graph of $y = x - 2$?

A.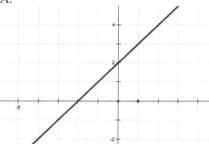

B.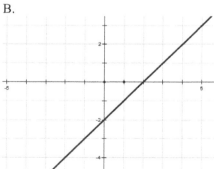

C.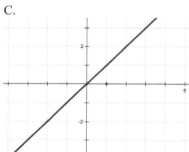

D.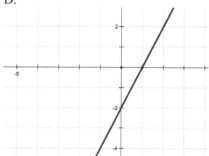

418

10. Find the midpoint of $(2, 7)$ and $(6, -1)$.

11. What is the slope of the line whose equation is $4x + 2y = 7$?

12. The equation of line f is $y = 3x - 4$. Line g is parallel to line f. What is the slope of line g?

13. What is the slope of the line below?

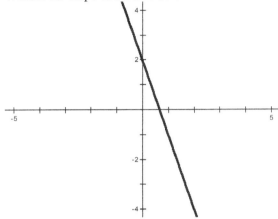

14. Express the relationship indicated in the table.

x	0	1	2	3
y	4	1	-2	-5

    A. $y = -3x + 4$
    B. $y = -2x + 4$
    C. $y = x - 4$
    D. $y = 4x$

15. Find the slope of the line that goes through the points $(1, -1)$ and $(4, 8)$.

COORDINATE GEOMETRY Practice Set 2

1. The equation of line d is $y = -2x + 7$. Line e is perpendicular to line d. What is the slope of line e?

2. Each square is 2 in^2, what is the area of the shaded region?

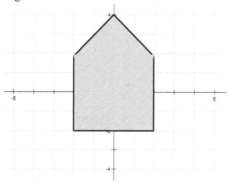

3. Which of the following points has coordinates $(4, -3)$?

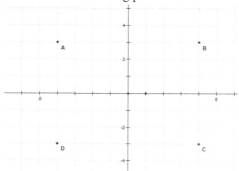

4. What is the slope of the line that goes through the points $(4, 7)$ and $(3, 10)$?

5. What are the coordinates of point F?

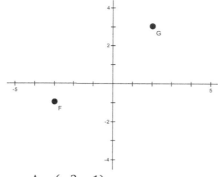

   A. $(-3, -1)$
   B. $(-1, -3)$
   C. $(2, 3)$
   D. $(3, 2)$

420

6. Points J and L are two corners of rectangle *JKLM* in the coordinate plane. Which of the following could be the coordinates of points K and M?

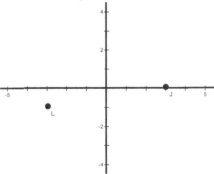

A. K(3, 1) and M(−3, 1)
B. K(1, 3) and M(−1, 3)
C. K(3, −1) and M(−3, 0)
D. K(3, 3) and M(−1, −3)

7. What is the distance between (−11, 5) and (3, 5)?

8. Points W, X, and Y are three vertices of square *WXYZ* in the coordinate plane. Which of the following could be the coordinates of point *Z*?

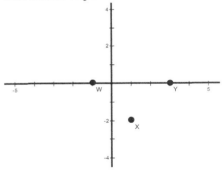

A. (0, 2)
B. (1, 2)
C. (0, 3)
D. (2, 1)

9. What is the slope of the line whose equation is
$y = 2x + 7$?

10. Find the midpoint of (3, 7) and (−1, 3).

A. (1, 5)
B. (2, 5)
C. (2, 4)
D. (1, 4)

11. Which equation supports the relationship in the table?

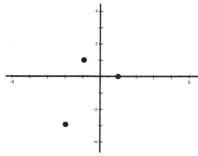

x	0	1	2	3
y	-3	-1	1	3

    A. $y = -x - 3$
    B. $y = 2x + 3$
    C. $y = 2x - 3$
    D. $y = -x + 4$

12. The grid shows three vertices of a parallelogram. Which could be the coordinates of the fourth vertex?

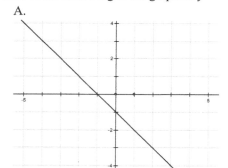

    A. $(-4, -2)$
    B. $(-3, -2)$
    C. $(1, 5)$
    D. $(0, -5)$

13. Which of the following is the graph of $y = -x - 1$?

A.

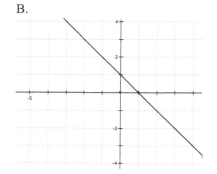

C.

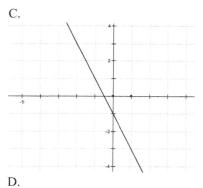

B.

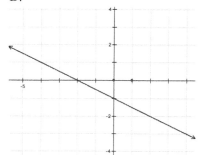

D.

14. For which of the functions below does the *y* value increase as the *x* value increases?

A.

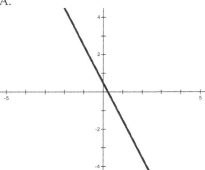

C.

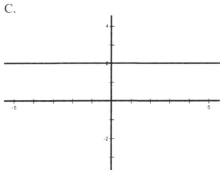

B.

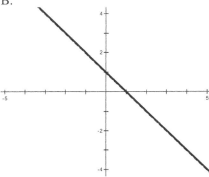

D.

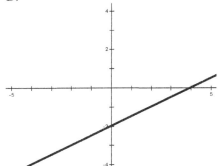

15. What is the slope of the line whose equation is $-3x - 3y = 10$?

COORDINATE GEOMETRY Practice Set 3

1. The equation of line m is $y = \frac{1}{2}x + 3$. Line p is parallel to line m. What is the slope of line p?

2. What is the slope of the line whose equation is $y + 3x = 7$?
    A. 3
    B. 7
    C. -1
    D. -3

3. What is the slope of the line below?

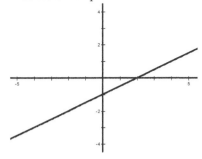

4. Find the coordinates of point P shown below.

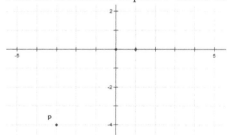

5. The equation of line r is $y = -3x - 1$. Line s is perpendicular to line r. What is the slope of line s?

6. If each square in the grid below is 3 in^2, what is the area of the shaded region?

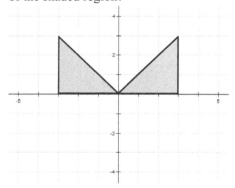

424

7. What are the coordinates of point K?

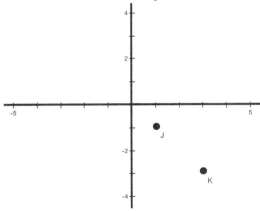

A. $(-3, 3)$
B. $(3, -3)$
C. $(1, -1)$
D. $(-1, 1)$

8. Find the midpoint of $(-2, -5)$ and $(4, -3)$.

A. $(2, 3)$
B. $(1, -4)$
C. $(1, -2)$
D. $(-1, -3)$

9. Points R and T are two corners of rectangle *RSTU* in the coordinate plane. Which of the following could be the coordinates of points S and U?

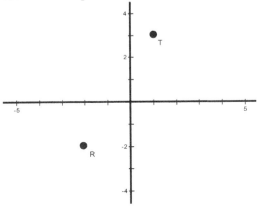

A. $S(2, 3)$ and $U(-1, -2)$
B. $S(-2, -3)$ and $U(1, 2)$
C. $S(-3, 2)$ and $U(-2, -1)$
D. $S(-2, 3)$ and $U(1, -2)$

10. For which function does y increase at the greatest rate?

A.

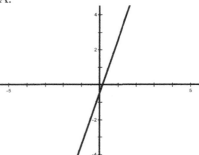

C.

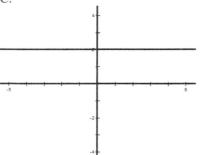

B.

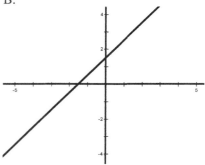

D.

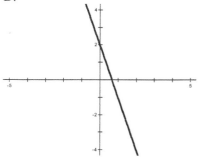

11. Which equation supports the relationship in the table?

x	-1	0	1	2
y	-10	-7	-4	-1

A. $y = -x - 9$
B. $y = -2x - 8$
C. $y = 3x - 7$
D. $y = -3x - 4$

12. What is the slope of the line whose equation is $5x - 2y = 5$?

13. Find the slope of the line that goes through the points $(3, 4)$ and $(-1, 5)$.

14. Point K has coordinates $(-2, 3)$. Point L is 7 units below Point K. What are the coordinates of Point L?

A. $(-2, 7)$
B. $(5, 3)$
C. $(-2, -4)$
D. $(-9, 3)$

15. In a coordinate system, how far from the origin is $(3, 4)$?

A. 3 units
B. 4 units
C. 4.5 units
D. 5 units

426

COORDINATE GEOMETRY Practice Set 4

1. The equation of line b is $y = -2x + 1$. Line c is parallel to line b. What is the slope of line c?

2. Which point has coordinates $(-2, 7)$?

    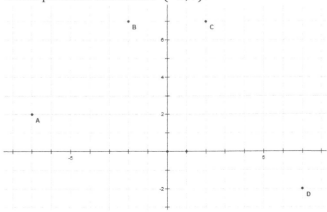

3. The distance between the points $(-3, -7)$ and $(5, -7)$ is?

4. What is the slope of the line $y - \frac{1}{2}x = 2$?

    A. $\frac{1}{2}$
    B. -2
    C. $-\frac{1}{2}$
    D. 2

5. What is the slope of the line below?

    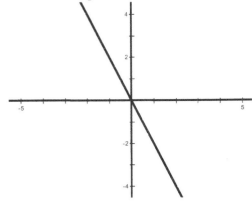

6. The equation of line g is $y = \frac{1}{3}x - 4$. Line h is perpendicular to line g. What is the slope of line h?

7. If each square in the grid below is 4 in^2, what is the area of the shaded region?

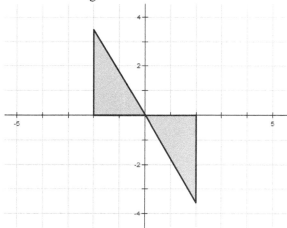

8. Find the midpoint of $(-1, 8)$ and $(5, 8)$.

9. Write the equation of a line with slope -3 that passes through the point $(2, 5)$.
   A. $y = -3x + 5$
   B. $y = -3x + 2$
   C. $y = -3x - 5$
   D. $y = -3x + 11$

10. The grid shows three vertices of a trapezoid. Which of the following could be NOT the coordinates of the fourth vertex of the trapezoid?

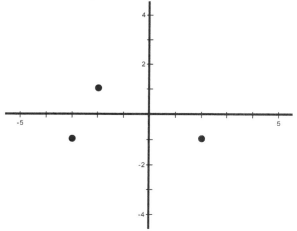

   A. $(0, 1)$
   B. $(1, 1)$
   C. $(2, 1)$
   D. $(1, 0)$

428

11. Express the relationship indicated in the table.

x	0	1	2	3
y	3	1	-1	-3

    A. $y = -3$

    B. $y = -2x + 3$

    C. $y = 2x + 1$

    D. $y = -3x + 2$

12. Find the slope of the line perpendicular to $5x - 3y = 4$.

13. Two points are on a coordinate system. Point M has coordinates $(-6, -3)$. Point N is to the 6 units to the left of point M. What are the coordinates of point N?

14. Find the slope of the line that goes through the points $\left(2, \frac{1}{2}\right)$ and $(4, 1)$.

    A. $\frac{1}{4}$

    B. $\frac{1}{2}$

    C. 2

    D. -4

15. In a coordinate system, how far from the origin is the point (6, 8)?

    A. 6 units

    B. 8 units

    C. 9 units

    D. 10 units

CHAPTER 13: STATISTICS, CHARTS, AND GRAPHS

Experts in Test Prep, Tutoring, & Admissions Counseling

www.CardinalEducation.com

STATISTICS Practice Set 1

1. What is the median of 26, 38, 11, 17, 102, 88, 33?

2. What is the mean of 7, 22, 19, 57, 38, 4, 84?

3. A basketball player averages 16.4 points per game in 25 games. How many total points did the player score?

Mr. Wade graded the tests for all the students in his class and calculated the following statistical measurements.

4. If the highest score was 96, what was the lowest score?
    - A. 10
    - B. 14
    - C. 43
    - D. 53

Measure	Value
Mean	82
Median	89
Mode	86
Range	43

5. Mr. Wade decided to add 5 points to every student's test scores, and then recalculate the statistical measures again. Which of the following statements is NOT true?
    - A. The mean score will be 87.
    - B. The range will not change.
    - C. The mode will not change.
    - D. The median will be 94.

The graph below shows the number of coffee drinks sold between 9 am and 10 am during a particular week.

6. What is the mode of the data?
    - A. 20 cups
    - B. 25 cups
    - C. 28 cups
    - D. 32 cups

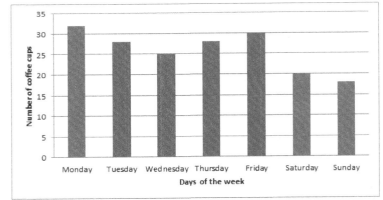

7. What is the median number of coffee cups sold?
    - A. 25 cups
    - B. 28 cups
    - C. 30 cups
    - D. 32 cups

8. In her chemistry class, Lisa has 88% in quizzes, 92% in homework, 98% in labs, and 84% in tests. If the test scores are counted twice, what will be her average grade?
    - A. 89.2%
    - B. 89.5%
    - C. 90.5%
    - D. 91%

The stem-and-leaf plot shown below represents the scores of 32 students in a history exam.

9. What is the mode of the data?
   A. 54
   B. 77
   C. 81
   D. 88

Stem	Leaf
5	3 4 4 5 6
6	2 3 6 8 9
7	0 4 5 7 8
8	1 1 1 2 2 4 5 5 7 8 8
9	4 5 7 8
10	0 0

10. What is the range of the data?
    A. 32
    B. 43
    C. 46
    D. 47

The box-and-whisker plot below represents Joey's quiz grades in math.

11. What is the median of the data?
    A. 84
    B. 88
    C. 90
    D. 94

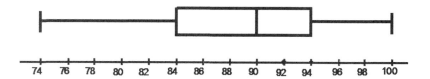

12. What is the range of the data?
    A. 10
    B. 24
    C. 26
    D. 36

Dennis conducts a survey on the number of cars owned by each household in his neighborhood. He compiles his data in the table shown below.

13. What is the mode of the data?
    A. 0 cars
    B. 2 cars
    C. 4 cars
    D. 21 households

Number of cars	Number of households
0	4
1	15
2	21
3	8
4	3

14. How many households have more than 1 car?
    A. 11 households
    B. 24 households
    C. 32 households
    D. 47 households

15. What is the median of the data?
    A. 2 cars
    B. 3 cars
    C. 4 households
    D. 8 households

16. What is the range of the data?
    - A. 4 cars
    - B. 5 cars
    - C. 13 households
    - D. 17 households

Lisa recorded the time that she spent studying and doing homework for five days of a week and recorded the data in the table below.

17. What was the average time that Lisa spent studying and doing homework during the five days?
    - A. 1 hour 36 minutes
    - B. 2 hours 21 minutes
    - C. 2 hours 24 minutes
    - D. 2 hours 48 minutes

Day of the week	Time spent
Monday	2 hours
Tuesday	2 hours 40 minutes
Wednesday	3 hours 20 minutes
Thursday	2 hours 15 minutes
Friday	1 hour 30 minutes

18. What was the range of the data?
    - A. 1 hour 10 minutes
    - B. 1 hour 20 minutes
    - C. 1 hour 40 minutes
    - D. 1 hour 50 minutes

19. If the average of x and y is 12. What is the average of x, y and 21?
    - A. 11
    - B. 15
    - C. 18
    - D. 21

20. Suarez scores 74, 77 and 92 in his first three algebra tests. What does he need to get on his fourth test to keep his average above 80%?
    - A. 77%
    - B. 78%
    - C. 80%
    - D. 84%

STATISTICS Practice Set 2

1. What is the mode of 1, 4, 7, 4, 18, 3, 11, 15, 3, 4?

2. What is the mean of 52, 12, 132, 400, 87, 61?

3. Jake averages 1.2 goals a game for his team. If there were
    15 games in the season, how many goals did he score?

Abby recorded the number of siblings each student in her class had in the table shown below.

4. What is the mode of the data?
    A. 1 sibling
    B. 2 siblings
    C. 1 and 2 siblings
    D. 11 students

Number of siblings	Number of students with that number of siblings
0	3
1	11
2	11
3	9
4	4

5. How many students have less than 2 siblings?
    A. 3 students
    B. 11 students
    C. 14 students
    D. 23 students

6. What is the average number of siblings?
    A. 1.5 siblings
    B. 2 siblings
    C. 2.5 siblings
    D. 3 siblings

The graph below shows the number of students who have watched different number of Harry Potter movies.

7. What is the mode of the data?
    A. 4 movies
    B. 7 movies
    C. 18 students
    D. 24 students

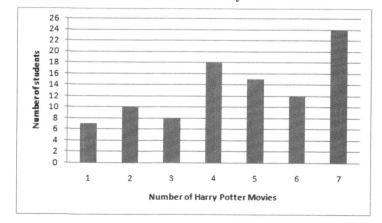

8. How many students have watched more than five
    Harry Potter movies?
    A. 12 students
    B. 13 students
    C. 24 students
    D. 36 students

9. What is the median of the data?
    A. 3 movies
    B. 4 movies
    C. 5 movies
    D. 6 movies

The stem-and-leaf plot below shows the number of home runs Babe Ruth hit in his 15 years with the New York Yankees, 1920 to 1934.

10. What is the least number of home runs Babe Ruth hit in any year?
    A. 15 home runs
    B. 22 home runs
    C. 25 home runs
    D. 34 home runs

Stem	Leaf
2	2 5
3	4 5
4	1 1 6 6 6 7 9
5	4 4 9
6	0

11. What is the median number of home runs?
    A. 41 home runs
    B. 46 home runs
    C. 47 home runs
    D. 54 home runs

12. What is the mode of the data?
    A. 46 home runs
    B. 47 home runs
    C. 54 home runs
    D. 59 home runs

The box-and-whisker plot shows the amount of sodium per slice (in milligrams) of several brands of cheese.

13. What is the median amount of sodium in cheese?
    A. 300 mg
    B. 320 mg
    C. 340 mg
    D. 360 mg

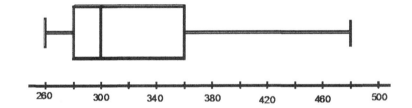

14. What is the range of the data?
    A. 180 mg
    B. 200 mg
    C. 210 mg
    D. 220 mg

After a night of bowling, Dana records all her scores and calculated the following statistical measurements

15. If her lowest score was 112, what was her highest score?

16. If Dana had scored 10 less points in every single game and then recalculated the statistical measures again, which of the following statements would NOT be true?
    A. The mean would be 122.
    B. The median would be 124.
    C. The range would be 53.
    D. The mode would be 116.

Measures	Value
Mean	132
Median	134
Mode	126
Range	63

17. Maureen has taken 4 tests so far in Algebra 1. Her scores are 88, 92, 87 and 90. The final exam will be counted three times in her mean. What is the lowest score she can get on her final exam and have a mean score of no less than 90?

    A. 90

    B. 91

    C. 92

    D. 93

18. If the average of w and z is 54. What is the average of w, z and 93?

    A. 49

    B. 67

    C. 73.5

    D. 74

19. If the average of 22 and m is equal to the average of 18, 15 and m, what is the value of m?

    A. 11

    B. 5

    C. 7

    D. 0

20. To bring her average test score up to 89%, Melissa needs to score 95% on her fifth test history. What was the total score for the first four tests that she took?

    A. 350

    B. 354

    C. 360

    D. 384

STATISTICS Practice Set 3

1. What is the mean of the following data?
   3.7, 8.4, 5, 12.3, 1.8, 2.7

2. What is the mode of the following data?
   0.04, 15, 3.8, 15, 0.04, 12.5, 0.04, 3.8

The table below shows the number of pets owned by different families in a certain neighborhood.

3. What is the mode of the data?
   - A. 1 pet
   - B. 2 pets
   - C. 4 families
   - D. 7 families

Number of pets	Families owning number of pets
0	5
1	8
2	7
3	2

4. How many families had at least 2 pets?
   - A. 2 families
   - B. 3 families
   - C. 9 families
   - D. 11 families

The number of appendectomies performed in a year by 15 different doctors at a certain hospital is represented by the stem-and-leaf plot below.

5. How many doctors performed less than 60 appendectomies in a year?
   - A. 8 doctors
   - B. 10 doctors
   - C. 11 doctors
   - D. 13 doctors

Stem	Leaf
2	0 5 5 7 8
3	1 3 4 6 7
4	4
5	0 9
6	
7	
8	5 6

6. What is the median number of appendectomies performed by doctors at the hospital?
   - A. 34 appendectomies
   - B. 37 appendectomies
   - C. 44 appendectomies
   - D. 50 appendectomies

7. What is the mode of the data?
   - A. 20 appendectomies
   - B. 25 appendectomies
   - C. 34 appendectomies
   - D. 44 appendectomies

The amount of rainfall in inches during one year in Palo Alto is represented by the box-and-whisker plot below.

8. How much rainfall was recorded in the driest month?
    A. 0 inches
    B. 1 inch
    C. 2 inches
    D. 3 inches

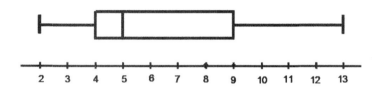

9. What is the median amount of rainfall?
    A. 2 inches
    B. 3 inches
    C. 4 inches
    D. 5 inches

10. The wettest month had how much more rainfall than the driest?
    A. 2 inches
    B. 7 inches
    C. 11 inches
    D. 13 inches

Mario records his scores for each round of darts he plays and calculates the following statistical measurements.

11. Mario multiplies each of his scores by 5 and recalculates
    the statistical measures. Which statement is true?
    A. The new median will be 50.
    B. The new range of the data will be 190.
    C. The mode of the data will not change.
    D. The new mean will be 46.

Measure	Value
Median	45
Mean	41
Range	38
Mode	52

12. If his lowest score was 28, what was his highest score?
    A. 40
    B. 42
    C. 64
    D. 66

The chart below shows the number of days that Mrs. Jensen has been out sick for the past 5 years.

13. Which of the following statements is true?
    A. The mode is greater than the mean.
    B. The median is less than the mode.
    C. The mean is greater than the median.
    D. The range of the data is greater than the mean.

14. Which of the following is a good prediction for the
    number of days that Mrs. Jensen will be out sick in
    2012?
    A. 4 days
    B. 5 days
    C. 7 days
    D. 11 days

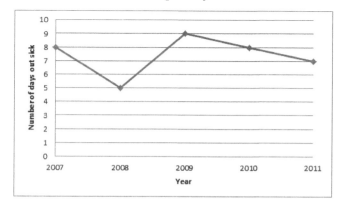

438

15. The difference between the mean and the range of the
    data is?
    A. 2.4 days
    B. 3.6 days
    C. 5 days
    D. 7.6 days

16. An adult seal weighs about 8,000 pounds while a baby
    seal weighs about 500 pounds. If there are 8 adult seals
    and 4 baby seals on sunbathing on a certain rock, what is
    the average weight of all the seals on the rock?
    A. 4,250 lbs
    B. 5,500 lbs
    C. 5,800 lbs
    D. 6,400 lbs

The stem-and-leaf plot shown represents the scores for 20 participants in a charity golf tournament.

17. What is the mode of the data?
    A. 3
    B. 72
    C. 83
    D. 92

Stem	Leaf
6	8 9 9
7	1 1 2 2 3 3 5
8	0 3 3 3 4
9	2 5 7
10	1 1

18. What is the range of the data?
    A. 4
    B. 23
    C. 28
    D. 33

19. If Ari, who was not participating in the golf tournament
    scores 79 playing in the same golf course, which of the
    following statement would be correct?
    A. Ari's score is less than the median of the data.
    B. Ari's score is less than the mode of the data.
    C. Ari's score is greater than the mode of the data.
    D. Ari's score is less than the range of the data.

20. The average of a, b, and c is 18. What is the average of a,
    b, c and 22?
    A. 16
    B. 18
    C. 19
    D. 20

STATISTICS Practice Set 4

1. What is the median 22, 212, 7, 85, 22, 189, 74, 104?

2. What is the mean of 0.2, 1.7. 3.3, 0.7, 5.9, 8.6?

3. The mean of 8 numbers is 12.6. What is the sum?

The stem-and-leaf plot shown below represents the people who attended the Watson's family reunion.

4. What is the age of the youngest person?

Stem	Leaf
0	3 4 7
1	2 7
2	1 2
3	3 5 7 7 9
4	2 3 4
5	0 1 3
6	1 3

5. What is the mean age of all the family members?
   - A. 22.4 years old
   - B. 27.8 years old
   - C. 30.3 years old
   - D. 33.7 years old

6. Which of the following statements is false?
   - A. The oldest is 60 years older than the youngest.
   - B. The mode age is 37 years.
   - C. The median age is 39 years.
   - D. There are more people over 50 than under 10.

7. There are 6 cows and 4 pigs. A pig weighs 250 lbs and a cow weighs twice as much. What is their average weight?

8. Doug and his four friends collect comics. They average 34.4 comics a person. If Doug has 54 comics, what is the average number of comics his friends have?
   - A. 29.5 comics
   - B. 30.4 comics
   - C. 30.6 comics
   - D. 32.5 comics

The table below shows the grade distribution of all the students in Mrs. Thompson's science class.

9. What is the mode of the data?
   - A. 7
   - B. A
   - C. 9
   - D. B

10. What is the median of the data?
    - A. A
    - B. 9
    - C. B
    - D. 7

Grade	Number of students
A	7
B	9
C	5
D	3
F	1

11. Christina received an 84, 78, 88, and 80 on her first four tests. The final exam will be counted twice towards her grade. What is the lowest score she can get on her final exam in order to have a mean score of no less than 86?

   A. 93
   B. 94
   C. 96
   D. 97

The box-and-whisker plot below shows the ages in years of twentieth century US Vice Presidents at inauguration.

12. The age of the oldest Vice President at inauguration is?

   A. 68 years old
   B. 70 years old
   C. 71 years old
   D. 72 years old

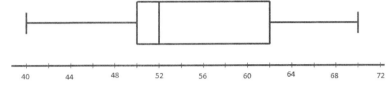

13. The median age for Vice Presidents at inauguration is?

   A. 40 years old
   B. 48 years old
   C. 50 years old
   D. 52 years old

14. Vice President Joe Biden was 67 at his inauguration. Which of the following statements is correct?

   A. At his inauguration, Joe Biden was 27 years older than the youngest Vice President.
   B. At his inauguration, Joe Biden was younger than the median age of Vice Presidents.
   C. Joe Biden was the oldest Vice President to be inaugurated.
   D. At his inauguration, Joe Biden was 4 years younger than the oldest Vice President.

The graph below shows the heights in inches of all the students in the St. Francis varsity swim team.

15. What is the range of the data?

   A. 0 swimmers
   B. 4 inches
   C. 5 swimmers
   D. 8 inches

16. What is the average height of the swimmers?

   A. 70.4 inches
   B. 71.7 inches
   C. 72.3 inches
   D. 72.7 inches

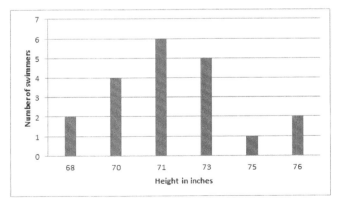

17. What is the median height of the swimmers?
    A. 68 inches
    B. 70 inches
    C. 71 inches
    D. 73 inches

18. One of the swimmers who is 76 inches tall leaves the team. Which of the following statements will not be true?
    A. The mean of the data will decrease.
    B. The median of the data will not change.
    C. The mode of the data will not change.
    D. The range of the data will decrease.

19. If the average of 4, s and t is 102. What is the average of s, t and 7?
    A. 103
    B. 104
    C. 107
    D. 109

20. To bring her average test score to 92%, Sammy needs to score 88% on her sixth and final exam. What was the average score for her other five tests?
    A. 90.4%
    B. 92.8%
    C. 94.4%
    D. 96.2%

CHARTS AND GRAPHS Practice Set 1

The following graph shows the average temperature in Woodside for the years 2006 – 2010.

1. Which was the hottest year in Woodside?
    - A. 2010
    - B. 2008
    - C. 2006
    - D. 2007

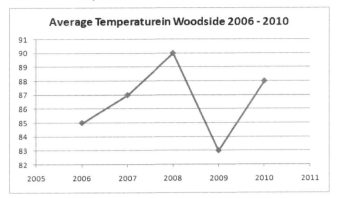

2. When did the greatest increase in temperature occur in Woodside?
    - A. 2007 – 2008
    - B. 2008 – 2009
    - C. 2009 – 2010
    - D. 2006 – 2007

The chart shows on average how Ashley spends her 24-hour day.

3. On average, how many hours did she spend on social and personal time?
    - A. 1.5 hours
    - B. 3.6 hours
    - C. 6 hours
    - D. 15 hours

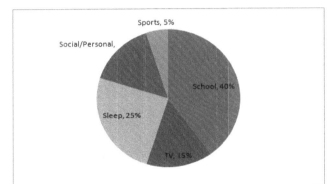

4. How many more hours did she spend on sleep than on watching TV?
    - A. 1.2 hours
    - B. 1.5 hours
    - C. 2.4 hours
    - D. 3.6 hours

5. The graph shows the number of days Jimmy spent rock climbing, skiing, or surfing in the last three years. Use the information provided in the graph to determine which of the following statements is true.
    - A. The number of days spent rock climbing in 2010 is less than the number of days spent skiing in 2008.
    - B. The number of days spent surfing in 2008 is greater than the number of days spent surfing in 2010.
    - C. The number of days spent skiing in 2010 is equal to the number of days spent rock climbing in 2009.
    - D. The number of days spent surfing in 2009 is less than the number of days spent rock climbing in 2008.

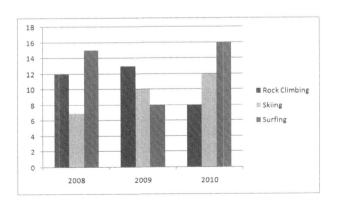

6. Tyler spends the first half of his trip driving on a rural road with a speed limit of 35mph. For the second half of his trip, he drives on the highway. Which graph most accurately shows Tyler's speed over the course of his trip?

A.

60 mph

30 mph

Time

B.

60 mph

30 mph

Time

C.

60 mph

30 mph

Time

D.

60 mph

30 mph

Time

7. The graph represents the percentage discount that a customer received at a store based on the total purchases that they make. What is the best estimate of the discount that a customer buying $1,900 worth of goods will receive?

   A. $150
   B. $250
   C. $300
   D. $400

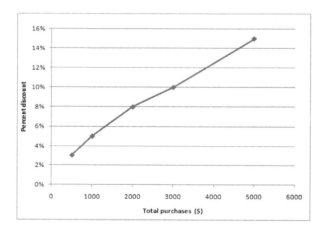

8. The local Starbucks sells coffee in three cup sizes: large, medium and small. If in the pie chart below 120 large cups of coffee were sold in a single day, how many medium cups of coffee were sold in the same time?

   A. 20 cups
   B. 40 cups
   C. 60 cups
   D. 80 cups

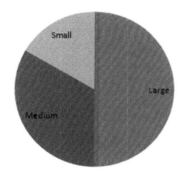

9. If each small cup coffee sells for $2.95, approximately how much was spent on small cup coffee?

   A. $120
   B. $210
   C. $270
   D. $360

444

Elizabeth kept a record of the total number of miles she ran each month for the past seven months.

10. On average, how many miles did she run each month?
    - A. 100 miles
    - B. 110 miles
    - C. 120 miles
    - D. 130 miles

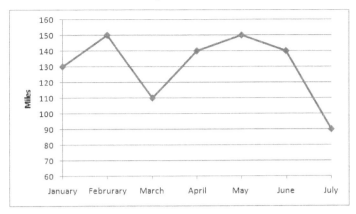

11. How many more miles did she run in May than she did in March?
    - A. 20 miles
    - B. 30 miles
    - C. 40 miles
    - D. 50 miles

300 students were asked what their favorite part of the Thanksgiving was. The results are in the pie chart.

12. If 10 students preferred, mashed potatoes, how many students preferred cranberry sauce?
    - A. 20 students
    - B. 30 students
    - C. 40 students
    - D. 50 students

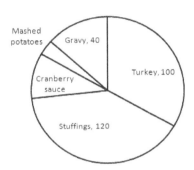

13. What percent of the students preferred turkey?
    - A. 25 %
    - B. 30%
    - C. $33\frac{1}{3}\%$
    - D. 40%

The price of Google stock over the past several years is shown in the graph.

14. When did the greatest increase in stock price occur?
    - A. 2007 to 2008
    - B. 2004 to 2005
    - C. 2009 to 2010
    - D. 2006 to 2007

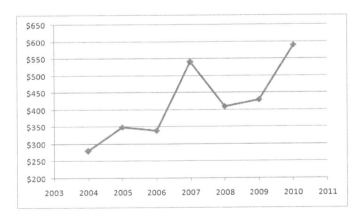

15. What is the approximate difference in the price of Google stock between 2006 and 2009?
    - A. $50
    - B. $80
    - C. $110
    - D. $120

16. The Venn diagram shows the results of a survey that was conducted to determine pizza toppings that the students in Mrs. Doubtfire's class prefer. How many more students prefer pepperoni & mushrooms than sausages & mushrooms?

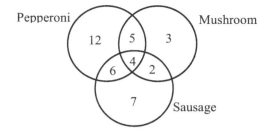

   A. 1 student
   B. 2 students
   C. 3 students
   D. 4 students

The chart shows Lisa's annual budget by percent of annual income. Lisa's annual income is $45,000.

17. How much of Lisa's income is budgeted for rent?
   A. $5,400
   B. $7,200
   C. $10,800
   D. $12,000

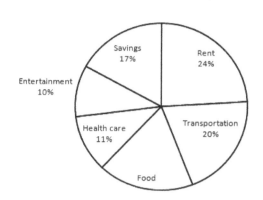

18. In how many of the categories is the annual income allocation less than $8,000?
   A. 2 categories
   B. 3 categories
   C. 4 categories
   D. 5 categories

The graph shows the amount of rainfall in San Francisco over the course of 5 months.

19. Select the correct answer
   A. January – December < 100
   B. October + February = 200
   C. February – November > 40
   D. January + October < 200

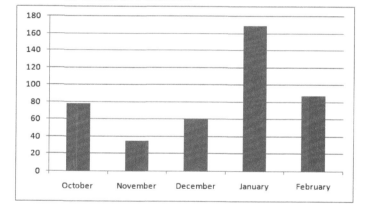

20. The Venn diagram shows three different sports that most students at an elementary school participate in. Which category is represented by the shade region?
   A. Students who play tennis only
   B. Students who play basketball only
   C. Students who play tennis and basketball
   D. Students who play tennis and soccer

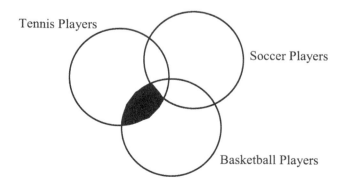

CHARTS AND GRAPHS Practice Set 2

The table shows the number of drinks sold at three different cafés, on a single day.

1. What was the total number of drinks sold at Happy Donuts on that day?
   - A. 48 drinks
   - B. 50 drinks
   - C. 52 drinks
   - D. 57 drinks

	Coffee	Tea	Mocha	Latte
Starbucks	22	14	18	7
Pete's Coffee	18	15	20	7
Happy Donuts	17	18	8	5

2. What was average amount of coffee sold in the three cafés?
   - A. 17 coffees
   - B. 18 coffees
   - C. 19 coffees
   - D. 20 coffees

3. The number of mochas sold at Pete's Coffee was what percent greater than the mochas sold at Starbucks?
   - A. 2%
   - B. 10%
   - C. 11%
   - D. 20%

The pie chart shows the percent distribution of ice cream flavors sold at an ice cream store.

4. What is the percent difference between the most favorite and least favorite ice cream flavors?
   - A. 14%
   - B. 22%
   - C. 24%
   - D. 26%

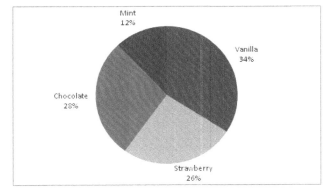

5. If 200 scoops of ice cream were sold, how many scoops of chocolate ice cream were sold?
   - A. 24 scoops
   - B. 36 scoops
   - C. 52 scoops
   - D. 56 scoops

6. If 65 scoops of strawberry ice cream were sold, how many scoops of vanilla were sold?
   - A. 70 scoops
   - B. 85 scoops
   - C. 95 scoops
   - D. 105 scoops

447

The bar graph shows the number of students that play five different sports at Palo Alto High School.

7. Which of the following statements is false?
   A. Cross-country is the least favorite sport.
   B. The number of students playing tennis and basketball is less than the number of students playing soccer.
   C. The difference between the number of students playing basketball and tennis is greater than the difference between the number of students playing lacrosse and cross-country.
   D. The number of students playing basketball, cross-country and lacrosse is greater than the number of students playing soccer.

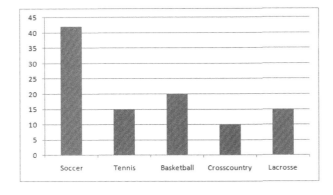

8. The average number of students playing tennis, basketball, and cross-country is?
   A. 15 students
   B. 18 students
   C. 19 students
   D. 20 students

9. The number of basketball players is what percent greater than the number of lacrosse players?
   A. 10%
   B. 20%
   C. 25%
   D. 33.3%

The graph shows number of whales seen during 5-day whale watching tour.

10. What was the total number of whales seen during the tour?
    A. 36 whales
    B. 38 whales
    C. 39 whales
    D. 41 whales

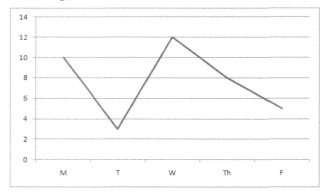

11. How many more whales were seen on Wednesday than on Friday?
    A. 4 whales
    B. 5 whales
    C. 6 whales
    D. 7 whales

12. The average number of whales seen during the tour was?
    A. 7.6 whales
    B. 7.8 whales
    C. 8.2 whales
    D. 8.1 whales

448

The pictogram shows the number of visitors to the Smithsonian during the first five months of the year.

13. Find the ratio of the number of visitors in March to the number of visitors in January.

    A. 3 to 1
    B. 9 to 4
    C. 8 to 3
    D. 7 to 2

Jan	▮▮▮▮
Feb	▮▮▮▮▮
Mar	▮▮▮▮▮▮▮▮
Apr	▮▮▮▮▮
May	▮▮▮▮▮▮▮

▮ = 500 visitors

14. The number of visitors in May was what percent greater than the number of visitors in April?

    A. 20%
    B. 25%
    C. 33.3%
    D. 50%

15. Which of the following statements is true?

    A. The month of April had the least number of visitors.
    B. The number of visitors in January and May was less than the number of visitors in February and March.
    C. There were 500 more visitors in May than in March.
    D. The average number of visitors for the five months was 2,000.

16. The Venn diagram shows the ice cream flavors sold by an ice cream vendor. How many people bought vanilla?

    A. 15 people
    B. 18 people
    C. 20 people
    D. 22 people

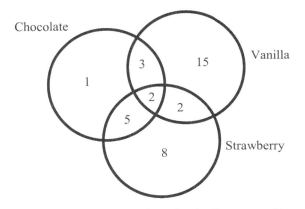

17. A skydiver jumps out of a plane flying at a height of 10,000 feet. At a height of 2,000 feet, the skydiver opens his parachute. Which graph best represents the height of the skydiver over time?

A.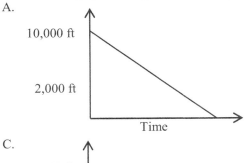

B.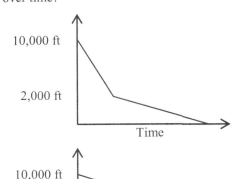

C.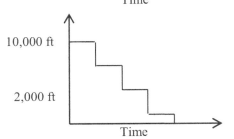

D.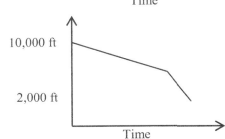

449

18. Use the Venn diagram below to answer the following question. Which of the following numbers is not represented by the shaded region?

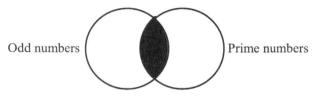

Odd numbers   Prime numbers

   A. 17
   B. 37
   C. 47
   D. 91

The pictogram shows the number of bottles James collected for recycling.

19. If he collected 90 bottles, how much does represent?
   A. 2 bottles
   B. 3 bottles
   C. 4 bottles
   D. 5 bottles

Green	▲ ▲ ▲ ▲ ▲ ▲ ▲
Brown	▲ ▲ ▲ ▲ ▲
Clear	▲ ▲ ▲ ▲ ▲ ▲

20. The number of clear bottles collected was what percent greater than the number of brown bottles collected?
   A. 16.7%
   B. 18%
   C. 20%
   D. 25%

CHARTS AND GRAPHS Practice Set 3

1. The Venn diagram shows the type and number of drinks ordered by customers at a restaurant. How many people ordered both water and wine?
   - A. 1 person
   - B. 3 people
   - C. 4 people
   - D. 8 people

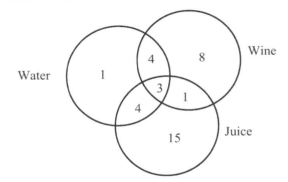

The pictogram shows the revenue collected by five different zoos over the course of an hour. $=$2, S=$1

2. How much was collected by the San Francisco Zoo?
   - A. $7.50
   - B. $15.00
   - C. $16.00
   - D. $19.50

Minnesota	$ $ $ $ $ $ $
Cleveland	$ $ $ $
San Francisco	$ $ $ $ $ $ $ S
Central Florida	$ $ $ $ $ S
Bronx	$ $ $ $ $ $ $ S

3. How much more revenue was collected by the Minnesota Zoo than by the Central Florida Zoo?
   - A. $2.50
   - B. $3.00
   - C. $4.50
   - D. $5.00

4. The average revenue collected by the five zoos was?
   - A. $12.50
   - B. $13.20
   - C. $13.40
   - D. $14.20

The pie chart shows the percentage distribution of the time Casey spent watching TV.

5. If on one day, Casey spent 8 hours watching TV, how many hours did she spend watching dramas?
   - A. 3.2 hours
   - B. 3.6 hours
   - C. 4 hours
   - D. 4.2 hours

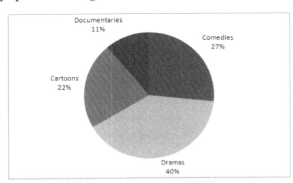

6. Which of the following statements is correct?
   - A. Casey spent a quarter of the time watching comedies.
   - B. Approximately half the time spent watching TV was spent watching dramas, and documentaries.
   - C. The time spent watching cartoons was greater than the time spent watching comedies.
   - D. Cartoons and comedies accounted for more than a half of the time spent watching TV.

7. The amount of time spent watching documentaries is approximately
    A. Half the amount of time spent watching dramas.
    B. Twice the amount spent watching cartoons.
    C. A third of the total time spent watching TV.
    D. A tenth of the total time spent watching TV.

The line graph shows the grades that Timothy got on the first his first 6 tests in Algebra 1.

8. When did the biggest change in grades occurred?
    A. Test 1 – Test 2
    B. Test 4 – Test 5
    C. Test 2 - Test 3
    D. Test 3 – Test 4

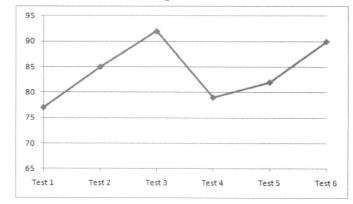

9. Which was his lowest grade?
    A. Test 4
    B. Test 1
    C. Test 5
    D. Test 2

10. In how many tests did he score more than 86%?
    A. 1 test
    B. 2 tests
    C. 3 tests
    D. 4 tests

The table shows the gallons of milk produced in one week by four different farms.

11. The average gallons of milk produced on Tuesday was
    A. 5.5 gallons
    B. 6 gallons
    C. 6.25 gallons
    D. 7 gallons

	M	T	W	Th	F	S	Su
Farm A	8	7	3	5	5	3	3
Farm B	4	4	2	3	6	2	4
Farm C	5	6	4	2	6	1	2
Farm D	7	8	8	1	7	5	4

12. Which of the following statement is true?
    A. Farm A produced more milk on Wednesday than Farm D did on Saturday.
    B. The greatest amount of milk produced by Farm B was 7 gallons.
    C. Farm B had the highest production on Friday.
    D. The least amount of milk was produced by Farm D on Thursday and Farm C on Saturday.

13. Farm D produced as many gallons on Friday as
    A. Farm A on Monday.
    B. Farm C on Friday.
    C. Farm B on Tuesday.
    D. Farm A on Tuesday.

The pictogram shows the number of 3rd graders playing 5 different sports. ● = 10 students.

14. Which of the following statements is correct?
    A. Soccer had twice as many students as football.
    B. Basketball had 10 more students than baseball.
    C. Football had 10 fewer students than hockey.
    D. Baseball had the highest number of students.

15. The number of students in baseball is what percent greater than the number of students in basketball?
    A. 10%
    B. 15%
    C. 20%
    D. 25%

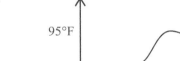

Baseball	● ● ● ● ●
Football	● ● ●
Soccer	● ● ● ● ● ●
Hockey	● ●
Basketball	● ● ● ●

16. The ratio of students playing soccer to hockey was?
    A. 3 to 1
    B. 3 to 2
    C. 6 to 1
    D. 6 to 5

17. In Philadelphia, the average daily temperature typically reaches a high of 95°F in July, and a low of 25°F in February. Starting at the beginning of the year, which of the following graphs could accurately represent the average daily temperature in Philadelphia over the course of a year (January - December)?

A.
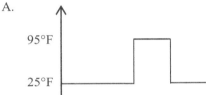

B.
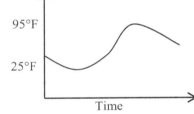

C.
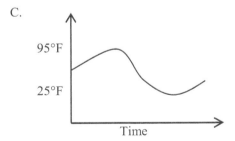

D.
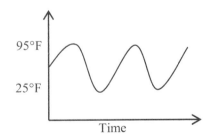

18. Use the Venn diagram to answer the following question. Which of the following numbers is not represented by the shaded region?
    A. 84
    B. 126
    C. 138
    D. 154

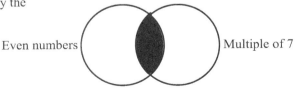

The bar graph shows the number of students at Woodside Elementary who have seen the new Harry Potter movie.

19. Select the correct answer.

    A. 8th graders $- 5^{th}$ graders > 40

    B. 6th graders $+ 7^{th}$ graders > 160

    C. 8th graders $- 7^{th}$ graders > 20

    D. 5th graders $- 6^{th}$ graders < 20

20. Approximately how many 7th graders and 5th graders have watched the new Harry Potter movie?

    A. 170 students

    B. 174 students

    C. 182 students

    D. 190 students

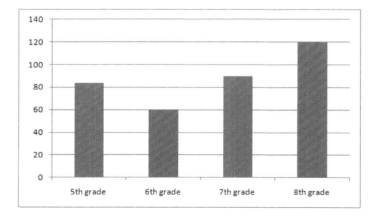

CHARTS AND GRAPHS Practice Set 4

The pictogram shows the number of toys that 5 different kids have. ☺ **represents 10 toys.**

1. What is the average number of toys that they have?
   - A. 10 toys
   - B. 20 toys
   - C. 25 toys
   - D. 30 toys

Name	Number of Toys
Adam	☺ ☺
Lily	☺ ☺ ☺ ☺
Sara	☺ ☺ ☺
Susan	☺ ☺ ☺ ☺ ☺
Sam	☺

2. The number of toys that Lily had was what percent greater than the number of toys that Sam had?
   - A. 75%
   - B. 150%
   - C. 300%
   - D. 400%

3. Which statement is incorrect?
   - A. Adam has twice as many toys as Sam.
   - B. Susan has as many toys as Adam and Sara combined.
   - C. Lily has as many toys as Sam and Adam combined.
   - D. Susan has $\frac{1}{3}$ of the total number of toys.

The table shows the number of calories consumed by Susan, Tim, Candy, and Taylor over the course of a week.

4. What is the total number of calories consumed by Candy during the week?
   - A. 14,500 calories
   - B. 14,800 calories
   - C. 15,400 calories
   - D. 15,600 calories

	M	T	W	Th	F	S	Su
Susan	1,200	1,500	1,800	1,700	1,800	1,700	1,400
Tim	1,800	2,000	1,800	2,200	2,000	1,900	1,700
Candy	2,000	2,100	1,900	2,300	2,100	2,400	2,000
Taylor	2,200	2,300	2,400	2,100	2,400	2,000	2,100

5. What is the average number of calories consumed on Friday?
   - A. 2,075 calories
   - B. 2,100 calories
   - C. 2,150 calories
   - D. 2,250 calories

6. Which of the following statement is correct?
   - A. Susan and Tim consumed as many calories on Tuesday as Candy and Taylor did on Friday.
   - B. Candy consumed 300 less calories on Saturday as she did on Tuesday.
   - C. Susan consumed more calories than Taylor during the whole week.
   - D. Tim consumed 400 more calories on Thursday as he did on Monday.

7. When Lauren runs a race, she starts slowly, reaches her top speed about ¼ of the way through the race, and then slows down slightly as fatigue sets in. If the race is close, she speeds up again at the end. Which graph best displays Lauren's speed over time in a close race?

A.
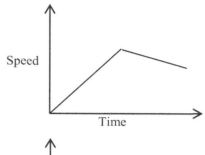

B.
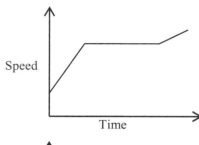

C.
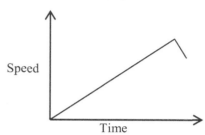

D.
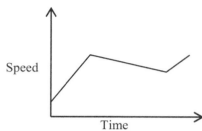

8. The Venn diagram shows the number of homes in a Woodside community that own three different kinds of pets. How many homes have a cat?
   A. 11 homes
   B. 18 homes
   C. 26 homes
   D. 32 homes

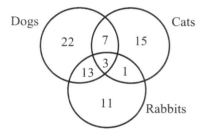

9. The Venn diagram shows the color preferences of students in an art class. Which statement is not correct?
   A. Red was the most preferred color.
   B. More students preferred blue than green
   C. More students preferred both red & blue than both red & green.
   D. No students preferred both green & blue.

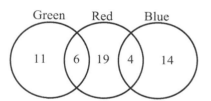

The bar graph shows the number of people ordering four different kinds of ice cream flavors at a particular store.

10. How many people ordered the two most popular flavors?
   A. 58 people
   B. 61 people
   C. 67 people
   D. 70 people

11. The number of people ordering strawberry is about what percent greater than those ordering mint?
   A. 15%
   B. 25%
   C. 50%
   D. 100%

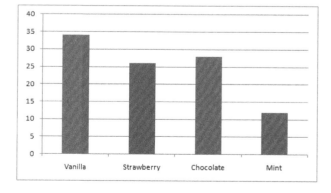

456

12. The number of people eating mint and chocolate was how many less than the number of people eating vanilla and strawberry?
    A. 10 people
    B. 15 people
    C. 20 people
    D. 30 people

The graph shows the amount of rainfall for five different months in Palo Alto.

13. What was the average rainfall in Palo Alto?
    A. 9.6 inches
    B. 9.9 inches
    C. 10.4 inches
    D. 10.8 inches

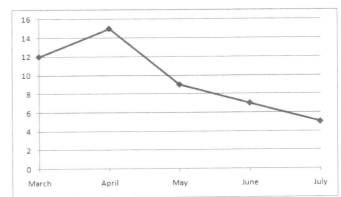

14. The greatest decrease in rainfall was between?
    A. June – July
    B. March – April
    C. April – May
    D. May – June

15. How much more rainfall fell in April than in June?
    A. 7 inches
    B. 8 inches
    C. 9 inches
    D. 10 inches

The pictogram shows the number of students earning A's in three different classes. ⭐⭐ **= 3 students.**

16. The number of students earning A's in Homeroom #2 was what percent greater than in Homeroom #1?
    A. 10%
    B. 15%
    C. 10%
    D. 25%

Homeroom #1	⭐ ⭐ ⭐ ⭐
Homeroom #2	⭐ ⭐ ⭐ ⭐ ⭐
Homeroom #3	⭐ ⭐ ⭐

The pie chart shows George's annual budget by percentages of annual income.

17. If George's annual income is $60,000, how much money was budgeted for health?
    - A. $1,500
    - B. $6,000
    - C. $9,000
    - D. $12,000

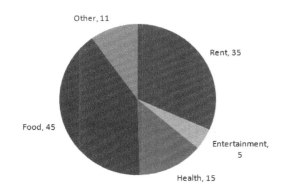

18. Which of the following statements is correct?
    - A. Less than one-third of the annual income was spent on rent.
    - B. $\frac{1}{5}$ of the annual income was spent on health and entertainment.
    - C. More than a half of the annual income was spent on food.
    - D. The amount spent on other expenses is four times the amount spent on food.

The bar graph shows the number of colleges in 6 different states.

19. Approximately how many colleges are in Texas and Pennsylvania combined?
    - A. 475 colleges
    - B. 505 colleges
    - C. 525 colleges
    - D. 635 colleges

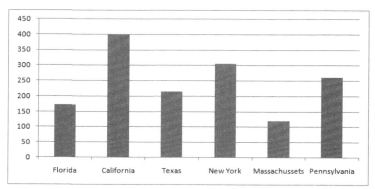

20. How many more colleges are in California than in New York?
    - A. 50 colleges
    - B. 60 colleges
    - C. 95 colleges
    - D. 105 colleges

458

CHAPTER 14: HSPT

Experts in Test Prep, Tutoring, & Admissions Counseling

www.CardinalEducation.com

SEQUENCES Practice Set 1

1. In the sequence: 80, 65, 50, 35, . . . , what number should come next?

2. In the sequence: 2,010; 2,003; 1,996; 1,989; . . . ; what number should come next?

3. In the sequence: 13.75, 12.25, 10.75, 9.25, . . . , what number should come next?

4. In the sequence: 23, 46, 69, 92, . . . , what number should come next?

5. In the sequence: 10, 4, -2, -8, . . . , what number should come next?

6. In the sequence: 3, -6, 12, -24, . . . , what number should come next?

7. In the sequence: 112, 56, 28, 14, . . . , what number should come next?

8. In the sequence: 46, 54, 61, 67, 72, . . . , what number should come next?

9. In the sequence: 25, 23, 20, 16, . . . , what number should come next?

10. In the sequence: 4,500; 900; 150; 30; 5; . . . ; what number should come next?

11. In the sequence: 5, 25, 20, 100, 95, . . . , what number should come next?

12. In the sequence: 5, 3, 12, 10, 40, . . . , what number should come next?

13. In the sequence: 40, 48, 42, __, 44, 52, 54, . . . , what number should fill the blank?

14. In the sequence: 14, 24, 21, 29, 24, 30, 23, . . . , what number should come next?

15. In the sequence: -3, 5, 3, 11, 8, 16, . . . , what number should come next?

16. In the sequence: 71, 64, 61, 58, 51, 48, 45, . . . , what number should come next?

17. In the sequence: 60, 5, 48, 4, 36, . . . , what number should come next?

18. In the sequence: 20, 5, 40, 10, 60, . . . , what number should come next?

19. In the sequence: 1, 1, 3, 27, 5, . . . , what number should come next?

20. In the sequence: 2, 4, 4, 16, 6, 36, 8, . . . , what number should come next?

SEQUENCES Practice Set 2

1. In the sequence: 132, 119, 106, 93, 80, . . . , what number should come next?

2. In the sequence: 1,454; 1,234; 1,014; 794; . . . ; what number should come next?

3. In the sequence: $\frac{5}{6}, \frac{2}{3}, \frac{1}{2}, \frac{1}{3}, \ldots$, what number should come next?

4. In the sequence: -40, -25, -10, 5, . . . , what number should come next?

5. In the sequence: 1, 4, 16, 64, . . . , what number should come next?

6. In the sequence: -2, 8, -16, 64, . . . , what number should come next?

7. In the sequence: 648, 216, 72, 24, . . . , what number should come next?

8. In the sequence: 12, 20, 29, 39, 50, . . . , what number should come next?

9. In the sequence: 90, 87, 82, 75, . . . , what number should come next?

10. In the sequence: 3, 6, 18, 72, . . . , what number should come next?

11. In the sequence: 3, 12, 8, 32, 28, . . . , what number should come next?

12. In the sequence: 240, 40, 60, 10, 30, . . . , what number should come next?

13. In the sequence: 25, 18, 28, __, 31, 24, 34, . . . , what number should fill the blank?

14. In the sequence: 4, 20, 11, 44, 37, 111, 106, . . . , what number should come next?

15. In the sequence: 30, 26, 22, 28, 24, 20, . . . , what number should come next?

16. In the sequence: 1, 3, 6, 8, 16, . . . , what number should come next?

17. In the sequence: 100, 5, 140, 7, 180, . . . , what number should come next?

18. In the sequence: 8, 48, 6, 36, 4, . . . , what number should come next?

19. In the sequence: 2, 4, 8, 3, 9, . . . , what number should come next?

20. In the sequence: 3, 27, 4, 64, 5, . . . , what number should come next?

SEQUENCES Practice Set 3

1. In the sequence: 450, 432, 414, 396, 378, . . . , what number should come next?

2. In the sequence: 12,000; 10,500; 9,000; 7,500; . . . ; what number should come next?

3. In the sequence: -3, -14, -25, -36, -47, . . . , what number should come next?

4. In the sequence: 17, 40, 63, 86, . . . , what number should come next?

5. In the sequence: -18, -13, -8, -3, . . . , what number should come next?

6. In the sequence: 2, 6, 18, 54, . . . , what number should come next?

7. In the sequence: -1, 5, -25, 125, . . . , what number should come next?

8. In the sequence: 5,000; -1,000; 200; -40; . . . ; what number should come next?

9. In the sequence: 4, 23, 43, 64, 86, . . . , what number should come next?

10. In the sequence: 45, 41, 35, 27, 17, . . . , what number should come next?

11. In the sequence: 1, 5, 10, 50, 100, . . . , what number should come next?

12. In the sequence: 20, 40, 30, 60, 50, . . . , what number should come next?

13. In the sequence: 50, 10, 100, __, 200, 40, 400, . . . , what number should fill the blank?

14. In the sequence: 3, 6, 12, 8, 16, 32, . . . , what number should come next?

15. In the sequence: 28, 16, 48, 36, 24, 72, . . . , what number should come next?

16. In the sequence: 3, 24, 4, 32, 5, . . . , what number should come next?

17. In the sequence: 5, 55, 6, 66, 7, 77, . . . , what number should come next?

18. In the sequence: 1, 1, 2, 4, 3, 9, 4, . . . , what number should come next?

19. In the sequence: 81, 9, 49, 7, 25, . . . , what number should come next?

20. In the sequence: 5, 5, 4, 16, 3, 27, 2, . . . , what number should come next?

462

SEQUENCES Practice Set 4

1. In the sequence: 812, 779, 746, 713, . . . , what number should come next?

2. In the sequence: 4,721; 4,611; 4,501; 4,391; . . . ; what number should come next?

3. In the sequence: -200, -150, -100, -50, . . . , what number should come next?

4. In the sequence: 14, 11.5, 9, 6.5, . . . , what number should come next?

5. In the sequence: 8, 25, 42, 59, . . . , what number should come next?

6. In the sequence: 6, 12, 24, 48, . . . , what number should come next?

7. In the sequence: -1, 3, -9, 27, . . . , what number should come next?

8. In the sequence: 64, -32, 16, -8, 4, . . . , what number should come next?

9. In the sequence: 17, 23, 30, 38, 47, . . . , what number should come next?

10. In the sequence: 200, 187, 173, 158, . . . , what number should come next?

11. In the sequence: 3,360; 420; 60; 10; . . . ; what number should come next?

12. In the sequence: 90, 15, 18, 3, 6, . . . , what number should come next?

13. In the sequence: 74, 80, 10, 16, 2, . . . , what number should come next?

14. In the sequence: 100, 50, 60, __, 40, 20, 30, . . . , what number should fill the blank?

15. In the sequence: 24, 15, 45, 35, 105, . . . , what number should come next?

16. In the sequence: 1,600; 800; 400; 500; 250; 125; . . . ; what number should come next?

17. In the sequence: 30, 5, 36, 6, 42, . . . , what number should come next?

18. In the sequence: 75, 15, 65, 13, 55, . . . , what number should come next?

19. In the sequence: 1, 8, 27, 64, . . . , what number should come next?

20. In the sequence: 27, 3, 64, 4, 125, . . . , what number should come next?

SEQUENCES: LETTERS & ROMAN NUMERALS Practice Set 1

1. In the sequence: 6A, 10B, 14C, 18D, . . . , what should come next?

2. In the sequence: H9, G11, F13, E15, . . . , what should come next?

3. In the sequence: 5H, 6J, 7L, 8N, . . . , what should come next?

4. In the sequence: 3A, 6D, 9G, 12J, . . . , what should come next?

5. In the sequence: 30S, 41P, 52M, 63J, . . . , what should come next?

6. In the sequence: Y4, W8, U16, S32, . . . , what should come next?

7. In the sequence: AK, BL, CM, DN, . . . , what letters should come next?

8. In the sequence: MP, KQ, IR, GS, . . . , what letters should come next?

9. In the sequence: YB, XE, WH, VK, . . . , what letters should come next?

10. In the sequence: SS, QT, OU, MV, . . . , what letters should come next?

11. In the sequence: AR, FS, KT, PU, . . . , what letters should come next?

12. In the sequence: BY, FU, JQ, NM, . . . , what letters should come next?

13. In the sequence: A, B, D, G, K, . . . , what letter should come next?

14. In the sequence: V, X, XV, XX, XXV, . . . , what numeral should come next?

15. In the sequence: I, II, III, IV, V, . . . , what numeral should come next?

16. In the sequence: XX, XXX, XL, L, . . . , what numeral should come next?

17. In the sequence: V, X, XX, XL, LXXX, . . . , what numeral should come next?

18. In the sequence: V, 12, XIX, 26, . . . , what should come next?

19. In the sequence: 5, X, 7, XIV, 11, XXII, 19, . . . , what should come next?

20. In the sequence: XIV, 24, XXXIII, 41, XLVIII, . . . , what should come next?

SEQUENCES: LETTERS & ROMAN NUMERALS Practice Set 2

1. In the sequence: 5J, 8K, 11L, 14M, . . . , what should come next?

2. In the sequence: T20, S18, R16, Q14, . . . , what should come next?

3. In the sequence: 20Z, 40X, 60V, 80T, . . . , what should come next?

4. In the sequence: 17L, 22O, 27R, 32U, . . . , what should come next?

5. In the sequence: 70B, 57F, 44J, 31N, . . . , what should come next?

6. In the sequence: T128, R64, P32, N16, . . . , what should come next?

7. In the sequence: DZ, EY, FX, GW, . . . , what letters should come next?

8. In the sequence: OJ, PH, QF, RD, . . . , what letters should come next?

9. In the sequence: XJ, UL, RN, OP, . . . , what letters should come next?

10. In the sequence: DP, EM, FJ, GG, . . . , what letters should come next?

11. In the sequence: ZZ, VX, RV, NT, . . . , what letters should come next?

12. In the sequence: HT, LP, PL, TH, . . . , what letters should come next?

13. In the sequence: A, C, D, F, G, I, J, . . . , what letter should come next?

14. In the sequence: XVII, XXII, XXVII, XXXII, . . . , what numeral should come next?

15. In the sequence: VI, VII, VIII, IX, . . . , what numeral should come next?

16. In the sequence: XL, C, CLX, CCXX, CCLXXX, . . . , what numeral should come next?

17. In the sequence: LXXXI, XXVII, IX, III, . . . , what numeral should come next?

18. In the sequence: 3, XII, 21, XXX, . . . , what should come next?

19. In the sequence: X, 7, XVII, 14, XXIV, 21, . . . , what should come next?

20. In the sequence: L, 45, XXXIX, 32, XXIV, . . . , what should come next?

SETTING UP EQUATIONS Practice Set 1

1. What number is 3 more than 5 times 12?
    A. 3
    B. 57
    C. 63
    D. 96

2. What number is 7 more than $\frac{1}{3}$ of 48?
    A. 19
    B. 23
    C. 31
    D. 151

3. What number is 6 less than $\frac{2}{3}$ of 24?
    A. 2
    B. 10
    C. 24
    D. 30

4. What number added to 12 equals the product of 7 and 5?
    A. 23
    B. 35
    C. 47
    D. 89

5. What number subtracted from 35 is the product of 7 and 4?
    A. 7
    B. 14
    C. 28
    D. 63

6. Four less than what number is the sum of 18 and 15?

7. Eight less than what number is $\frac{1}{3}$ of the product of 12 and 5?

8. What number divided by 2 leaves 20 less than 35?

9. What number divided by 6 leaves 5 more than $\frac{1}{3}$ of 12?

10. What number subtracted by $\frac{1}{4}$ of 20 leaves 7 less than 30?

11. What number subtracted by $\frac{5}{8}$ of 16 leaves 6 less than $\frac{1}{2}$ of 30?

466

12. 3 less than $\frac{1}{2}$ of 18 is 10% of what number?

13. 25% of what number is the difference between 82 and 67?

14. What number is $\frac{1}{4}$ of the square root of 64?

15. What number is $\frac{1}{2}$ of the cube root of 1,000?

16. $\frac{2}{3}$ of what number is 11 more than 5^2?

17. The product of 15 and what number is 60% of 5^3?

18. What number is 12 less than 3 times itself?
    A. 3
    B. 6
    C. 15
    D. 36

19. What number is 21 more than $\frac{1}{4}$ of itself?
    A. 7
    B. 24
    C. 28
    D. 56

20. The product of 3 and what number is 6 times the quotient
    of 60 and $\frac{1}{3}$ of 36?
    A. 3
    B. 5
    C. 6
    D. 10

SETTING UP EQUATIONS Practice Set 2

1. What number is 5 more than 3 times 11?
    A. 8
    B. 19
    C. 28
    D. 38

2. What number is 6 more than $\frac{1}{5}$ of 20?
    A. 4
    B. 10
    C. 16
    D. 106

3. What number is 8 less than $\frac{3}{4}$ of 40?
    A. 2
    B. 12
    C. 22
    D. 32

4. What number added to 23 equals the product of 4 and 8?
    A. 6
    B. 9
    C. 13
    D. 55

5. What number subtracted from 20 is the quotient of 60 and 4?
    A. 5
    B. 10
    C. 25
    D. 40

6. Ten less than what number is the sum of 19 and 27?

7. Fourteen less than what number is $\frac{1}{4}$ of the sum of 15 and 13?

8. What number divided by 4 leaves 10 more than 3?

9. What number divided by 2 leaves 2 less than $\frac{3}{4}$ of 16?

10. What number subtracted by $\frac{1}{7}$ of 56 leaves 10 less than 14?

11. What number divided by $\frac{2}{5}$ of 20 leaves 3 less than $\frac{1}{3}$ of 18?

12. 6 plus $\frac{1}{4}$ of 44 is 50% of what number?

13. 20% of what number is the difference between 21 and 12?

14. What number is three times the square root of 121?

15. What number is 10 more than the cube root of 27?

16. 3 times what number is 6 more than 9^2?

17. The quotient of 200 and what number is 12.5% of 2^4?

18. What number is 120 less than 5 times itself?
    A. 15
    B. 24
    C. 30
    D. 45

19. What number is 15 more than $\frac{1}{6}$ of itself?
    A. 6
    B. 18
    C. 36
    D. 72

20. The sum of 4 and what number is $\frac{1}{3}$ the product of 10 and $\frac{1}{4}$ of 12?
    A. 3
    B. 6
    C. 12
    D. 15

SETTING UP EQUATIONS Practice Set 3

1. What number is 8 more than 7 times 9?
   - A. 24
   - B. 55
   - C. 64
   - D. 71

2. What number is 12 more than $\frac{1}{4}$ of 32?
   - A. 8
   - B. 15
   - C. 20
   - D. 44

3. What number is 2 less than $\frac{1}{6}$ of 30?
   - A. 3
   - B. 5
   - C. 6
   - D. 7

4. What number added to 50 equals the product of 12 and 6?
   - A. 6
   - B. 10
   - C. 18
   - D. 22

5. What number subtracted by 6 is the quotient of 100 and 25?
   - A. 4
   - B. 6
   - C. 10
   - D. 14

6. Twenty less than what number is the product of 8 and 7?

7. Eleven less than what number is $\frac{2}{5}$ of the sum of 13 and 27?

8. What number divided by 5 leaves 6 less than 18?

9. What number divided by 8 leaves 2 more than $\frac{1}{8}$ of 40?

10. What number subtracted by $\frac{2}{7}$ of 49 leaves 3 less than 25?

11. What number subtracted by $\frac{2}{9}$ of 36 leaves 4 more than $\frac{1}{4}$ of 24?

12. 5 more than $\frac{2}{5}$ of 25 is 25% of what number?

13. 75% of what number is the difference between 43 and 28?

14. What number is $\frac{1}{5}$ of the square root of 225?

15. What number is 5 times the cube root of 8?

16. 80 divided by what number is 4 more than 6^2?

17. The product of 6 and what number is 75% of 4^3?

18. What number is 33 less than 4 times itself?
    A. 8
    B. 11
    C. 15
    D. 21

19. What number is 14 more than $\frac{1}{8}$ of itself?
    A. 8
    B. 16
    C. 32
    D. 40

20. The sum of 13 and what number is 4 times the quotient of 85 and $\frac{1}{2}$ of 34?
    A. 5
    B. 7
    C. 8
    D. 17

SETTING UP EQUATIONS Practice Set 4

1. What number is 10 more than 3 times 13?
   A. 0
   B. 6
   C. 29
   D. 49

2. What number is 11 more than $\frac{1}{2}$ of 68?
   A. 23
   B. 34
   C. 45
   D. 56

3. What number is 4 less than $\frac{4}{5}$ of 35?
   A. 3
   B. 14
   C. 24
   D. 32

4. What number added to 100 equals the product of 11 and 12?
   A. 21
   B. 32
   C. 44
   D. 45

5. What number subtracted by 2 is the quotient of 48 and 8?
   A. 6
   B. 8
   C. 24
   D. 42

6. Twelve less than what number is the product of 10 and 11?

7. Seventeen less than what number is $\frac{4}{5}$ of the product of 10 and 4?

8. What number divided by 3 leaves 8 more than 12?

9. What number divided by 4 leaves 9 more than $\frac{1}{6}$ of 42?

10. What number minus $\frac{3}{5}$ of 45 leaves 20 less than 55?

11. What number divided by $\frac{4}{5}$ of 25 leaves 7 less than $\frac{1}{5}$ of 60?

12. 13 more than $\frac{1}{7}$ of 63 is 50% of what number?

13. 60% of what number is the difference between 70 and 40?

14. What number is 5 less than the square root of 169?

15. What number is 3 less than the cube root of 125?

16. 7 times what number is 53 less than 12^2?

17. The quotient of 120 and what number is 10% of 20^2?

18. What number is 90 less than 3 times itself?
    A. 15
    B. 25
    C. 35
    D. 45

19. What number is 30 more than $\frac{1}{7}$ of itself?
    A. 35
    B. 49
    C. 56
    D. 70

20. The product of 3 and what number is 60% of the quotient of 1,900 and $\frac{1}{3}$ of 57?
    A. 15
    B. 20
    C. 60
    D. 180

HSPT COMPARISONS Practice Set 1

1. Examine (A), (B), and (C) and find the best answer.
   (A) $\frac{1}{2}$ of 12
   (B) $\frac{3}{4}$ of 8
   (C) $\frac{1}{3}$ of 24
   A. (A), (B), and (C) are all equal.
   B. (B) and (C) are equal and less than (A).
   C. (A) and (B) are equal and less than (C).
   D. (A) and (C) are equal and greater than (B).

2. Examine (A), (B), and (C) and find the best answer.
   (A) $\frac{3}{4}$ of 28
   (B) $\frac{1}{2}$ of 40
   (C) $\frac{2}{3}$ of 30
   A. (B) is greater than (A) or (C).
   B. (A) is greater than (B) and (C).
   C. (A) is equal to (C) and greater than (B).
   D. (A), (B), and (C) are all equal.

3. Examine (A), (B), and (C) and find the best answer.
   (A) $\frac{2}{5}$ of 35
   (B) $\frac{3}{4}$ of 16
   (C) $\frac{2}{7}$ of 56
   A. (B) is greater than either (A) or (C).
   B. (A) is greater than both (B) and (C).
   C. (A) is equal to (C) and less than (B).
   D. (C) is greater than either (A) or (B).

4. Examine (A), (B), and (C) and find the best answer.
   (A) $\frac{1}{4}$
   (B) 25%
   (C) 0.4
   A. (A), (B), and (C) are all equal.
   B. (B) and (C) are equal and less than (A).
   C. (A) and (B) are equal and less than (C).
   D. (A) and (C) are equal and greater than (B).

5. Examine (A), (B), and (C) and find the best answer.
   (A) 50%
   (B) $\frac{1}{5}$
   (C) 0.2
   A. (B) is greater than either (A) or (C).
   B. (A) is greater than both (B) and (C).
   C. (A) is equal to (C) and less than (B).
   D. (C) is greater than either (A) or (B).

474

6. Examine (A), (B), and (C) and find the best answer.
   (A) 3^3
   (B) 2^4
   (C) 4^2
   A. (B) and (C) are equal and less than (A).
   B. (A) and (B) are equal and less than (C).
   C. (A) and (C) are equal and greater than (B).
   D. (A) is less than (B) and (C).

7. Examine (A), (B), and (C) and find the best answer.
   (A) 45%
   (B) $4 \div 5$
   (C) $\frac{4}{5}$
   A. (A) is greater than either (B) or (C).
   B. (B) is greater than either (A) or (C).
   C. (A) is equal to (B) and less than (C).
   D. (A), (B), and (C) are all equal.

8. Examine (A), (B), and (C) and find the best answer.
   (A) 0.4×0.3
   (B) 0.6×2
   (C) 0.12
   A. (A) is greater than either (B) or (C).
   B. (B) is less than either (A) or (C).
   C. (A) is equal to (C) and less than (B).
   D. (A), (B), and (C) are all equal.

9. Examine (A), (B), and (C) and find the best answer.
   (A) $2 + 5(3 - 1)$
   (B) $7(3 - 1)$
   (C) $\frac{28}{2}$
   A. (A) is greater than either (B) or (C).
   B. (B) is equal to (C) and greater than (A).
   C. (A) is equal to (B) and less than (C).
   D. (A), (B), and (C) are all equal.

10. Examine (A), (B), and (C) and find the best answer.
    (A) $(5 - 3)^2$
    (B) $5^2 - 3^2$
    (C) 2^2
    A. (B) and (C) are equal and less than (A).
    B. (A) and (B) are equal and less than (C).
    C. (A) and (C) are equal and less than (B).
    D. (A) is greater than (B) and (C).

11. Examine (A), (B), and (C) and find the best answer.
    (A) $2x + 3$
    (B) $2(x + 3)$
    (C) $2x + 6$
    A. $(A) = (B) = (C)$
    B. $(A) = (B) \neq (C)$
    C. $(A) \neq (B) = (C)$
    D. $(A) \neq (B) \neq (C)$

12. Examine (A), (B), and (C) and find the best answer.
    (A) $3(x + y)$
    (B) $3x + 3y$
    (C) $3x + y$
    A. (A) = (B) = (C)
    B. (A) = (B) ≠ (C)
    C. (A) ≠ (B) = (C)
    D. (A) ≠ (B) ≠ (C)

13. Examine (A), (B), and (C) and find the best answer.
    (A) $4x^2$
    (B) $(2x)^2$
    (C) $2x^2$
    A. (A) ≠ (B) ≠ (C)
    B. (A) = (B) ≠ (C)
    C. (A) ≠ (B) = (C)
    D. (A) = (B) = (C)

14. Examine (A), (B), and (C) and find the best answer.

(A)

(B)

(C)

    A. (A) is more shaded than (B) and less shaded than (C).
    B. (A) is less shaded than (B) and more shaded than (C).
    C. (C) is less shaded than (A) and more shaded than (B).
    D. (A) and (C) are equally shaded.

476

15. Examine (A), (B), and (C) and find the best answer.

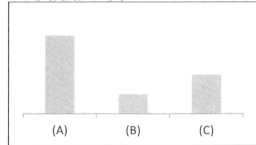

   A. (A) < (B) < (C)
   B. (A) > (B) > (C)
   C. (C) < (A) < (B)
   D. (A) > (C) > (B)

16. Examine (A), (B), and (C) and find the best answer.

   A. (A) < (B) < (C)
   B. (B) > (A) > (C)
   C. (C) < (B) > (A)
   D. (A) > (C) < (B)

17. Examine (A), (B), and (C) and find the best answer.

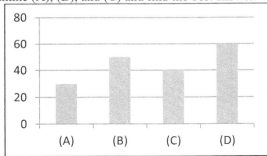

   A. (A) plus (C) equals (D).
   B. (D) minus (B) equals (C) minus (A).
   C. (C) plus (A) equals (B) plus (D).
   D. (D) plus (C) equals (A) plus (B).

18. Examine (A), (B), and (C) and find the best answer.

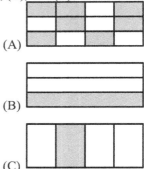

(A)

(B)

(C)

A. (C) is greater than (B).
B. (B) is equal to (C).
C. (A) is double (C).
D. (A) is the sum of (B) and (C).

19. Examine the diagram and find the best answer.

A. The area of the triangle is greater than the area of the square.
B. The perimeter of the triangle is equal to the perimeter of the square.
C. The area of the square is double the area of the triangle.
D. The perimeter of the triangle is 5 less than the perimeter of the square.

20. Examine the diagram and find the best answer.

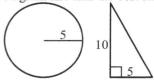

A. The area of the triangle is greater than the area of the circle.
B. The perimeter of the triangle is equal to its area.
C. The area of the triangle is less than the area of the circle.
D. The perimeter of the triangle is greater than the circumference of the circle.

1. Examine (A), (B), and (C) and pick the best answer.

    (A) $\frac{4}{5}$

    (B) $4 \div 5$

    (C) 0.45

    A. (A) = (C)
    B. (B) ≠ (C)
    C. (A) ≠ (B)
    D. (B) = (C)

2. Examine (A), (B), and (C) and pick the best answer.

    (A) $22 - 8 - 3$

    (B) $22 - (8 - 3)$

    (C) $(22 - 8) - 3$

    A. (A), (B) and (C) are all equal.
    B. (B) is greater than (A) which is less than (C).
    C. (B) is greater than (A) and (C).
    D. (A) is greater than (C) and less than (B).

3. Examine (A), (B), and (C) and find the best answer.

    (A) Two-thirds of 24

    (B) Four-fifths of 20

    (C) Half of 32

    A. (A), (B), and (C) are all equal.
    B. (B) and (C) are equal and less than (A).
    C. (A) and (B) are equal and less than (C).
    D. (A) and (C) are equal and greater than (B).

4. Examine (A), (B), and (C) and find the best answer.

    (A) Half of 10

    (B) One-sixth of 18

    (C) One-sixth of 30

    A. (B) is greater than (A) or (C).
    B. (A) is greater than (B) and (C).
    C. (A) is equal to (C) and greater than (B).
    D. (A), (B), and (C) are all equal.

5. Examine (A), (B), and (C) and find the best answer.

    (A) $\frac{2}{7}$ of 35

    (B) $\frac{3}{5}$ of 25

    (C) $\frac{5}{9}$ of 18

    A. (B) is less than either (A) or (C).
    B. (A) is greater than both (B) and (C).
    C. (A) is equal to (C) and less than (B).
    D. (C) is greater than either (A) or (B).

6. Examine (A), (B), and (C) and find the best answer.
(A) $\frac{1}{3}$
(B) 30%
(C) 0.3
   A. (A), (B), and (C) are all equal.
   B. (B) and (C) are equal and less than (A).
   C. (A) and (B) are equal and less than (C).
   D. (A) and (C) are equal and greater than (B).

7. Examine (A), (B), and (C) and find the best answer.
(A) 75%
(B) ¾
(C) 0.75
   A. (B) and (C) are equal and less than (A).
   B. (A) and (B) are equal and less than (C).
   C. (A) and (C) are equal and greater than (B).
   D. (A), (B), and (C) are all equal.

8. Examine (A), (B), and (C) and find the best answer.
(A) 5^2
(B) 2^5
(C) 3^3
   A. (A) and (B) are equal and greater than (C).
   B. (A) and (B) are equal and less than (C).
   C. (B) is greater than (A) and (C).
   D. (A) is greater than (B) and (C).

9. Examine (A), (B), and (C) and find the best answer.
(A) $1 \div 7$
(B) $\frac{1}{7}$
(C) 7%
   A. (A) is greater than (B) and (C).
   B. (B) is greater than either (A) or (C).
   C. (A) is equal to (B) and less than (C).
   D. (A), (B), and (C) are all equal.

10. Examine (A), (B), and (C) and pick the best answer.
(A) $3(y - 7)$
(B) $(y - 3)7$
(C) $3y - 21$
   A. $(A) = (B) \neq (C)$
   B. $(B) = (C) \neq (A)$
   C. $(A) \neq (B) \neq (C)$
   D. $(A) = (C) \neq (B)$

480

11. Examine (A), (B), and (C) and pick the best answer.

        (A) $(5 \times 8) + 7$

        (B) $13 + (7 \times 5)$

        (C) $(12 \times 4) - 3$

A. (A), (B), and (C) are all equal.

B. (B) is greater than (A) which is less than (C).

C. (C) is greater than (A) and (B).

D. (A) is greater than (C) and less than (B).

12. Examine (A), (B), and (C) and pick the best answer.

        (A) 2×0.03

        (B) 0.2×0.3

        (C) 0.6×0.1

A. (A), (B), and (C) are all equal.

B. (B) is greater than (A) which is less than (C).

C. (C) is greater than (A) and (B).

D. (A) is greater than (C) and less than (B).

13. Examine the graph and find the best answer.

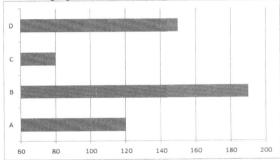

A. (D) minus (A) equals (C) plus (B).

B. (A) plus (D) equals (B) minus (C).

C. (D) minus (C) equals (B) minus (A).

D. (C) plus (D) equals (A) plus (B).

14. Examine (A), (B) and (C) and find the best possible answer.

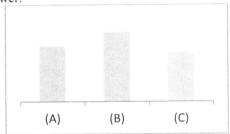

A. $(A) > (C) > (B)$

B. $(C) > (B) > (A)$

C. $(B) > (A) < (C)$

D. $(C) < (B) > (A)$

15. Examine (A), (B), and (C) and pick the best answer.

(A) $5(-x + 2y)$

(B) $x + 2(y - 3x)$

(C) $2y - 5x$

   A. (A) = (B) ≠ (C)

   B. (B) = (C) ≠ (A)

   C. (A) ≠ (B) ≠ (C)

   D. (A) = (C) = (B)

16. Examine (A), (B) and (C) and find the best answer.

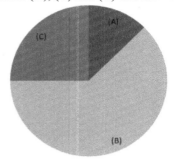

   A. (A) > (C) > (B)

   B. (C) > (B) > (A)

   C. (B) > (A) < (C)

   D. (C) < (A) < (B)

17. Examine (A), (B), and (C) and choose the correct answer.

(A) 5.04×10^4

(B) 50×10^3

(C) 66.3×10^1

   A. (A) is greater than (B) but less than (C).

   B. (C) is less than (B) but greater than (A).

   C. (B) is greater than (C) but less than (A).

   D. (A) is less than (B) but greater than (C).

18. Examine (A), (B), and (C) and choose the correct answer.

(A) 9 % of 80

(B) 12% of 70

(C) 7% of 108

   A. (A) is greater than (B) but less than (C).

   B. (C) is less than (B) but greater than (A).

   C. (B) is greater than (C) but less than (A).

   D. (A) is less than (B) but greater than (C).

19. Examine (A), (B), and (C) and choose the correct answer.

(A) 0.5×10^{-2}

(B) 1.2×10^{-3}

(C) 0.02×10^{-1}

   A. (C) is greater than (B) but less than (A).

   B. (A) is less than (B) but greater than (C).

   C. (B) is greater than (C) but less than (A).

   D. (A) is less than (B) but greater than (C).

20. Examine (A), (B), and (C) and find the best answer.

$$\text{(A)} \ \frac{1}{2}(6 - 7 \times 2) - 8$$
$$\text{(B)} \ -3(5 + 2 \times 4) + 6$$
$$\text{(C)} \ -\frac{2}{3}(8 \times 4 - 2) + 9$$

  A. (A) > (C) > (B)
  B. (C) > (B) > (A)
  C. (B) < (A) < (C)
  D. (C) < (A) < (B)

1. Examine (A), (B), and (C) and pick the best answer.

   (A) $\frac{7}{8}$

   (B) 0.78

   (C) $7 \div 8$

   A. (B) = (C)
   B. (A) ≠ (C)
   C. (A) = (B)
   D. (A) = (C)

2. Examine (A), (B), and (C) and pick the best answer.

   (A) $9 - (3 - 17)$

   (B) $17 - (9 - 3)$

   (C) $(3 - 9) - 17$

   A. (A), (B), and (C) are all equal.
   B. (B) is greater than (A) which is less than (C).
   C. (C) is greater than (A) and (B).
   D. (B) is greater than (C) and less than (A).

3. Examine (A), (B), and (C) and find the best answer.

   (A) $\frac{1}{3}$ of 30

   (B) $\frac{1}{5}$ of 45

   (C) $\frac{1}{4}$ of 36

   A. (A), (B), and (C) are all equal.
   B. (B) and (C) are equal and less than (A).
   C. (A) and (B) are equal and less than (C).
   D. (A) and (C) are equal and greater than (B).

4. Examine (A), (B), and (C) and find the best answer.

   (A) Half of 14

   (B) One-fourth of 36

   (C) One-fifth of 50

   A. (B) is greater than (A) or (C).
   B. (A) is greater than (B) and (C).
   C. (A) is equal to (C) and greater than (B).
   D. (A), (B), and (C) are all equal.

5. Examine (A), (B), and (C) and find the best answer.

   (A) $\frac{1}{6}$ of 36

   (B) $\frac{3}{8}$ of 16

   (C) $\frac{2}{9}$ of 36

   A. (B) is greater than either (A) or (C).
   B. (A) is greater than both (B) and (C).
   C. (A) is equal to (C) and less than (B).
   D. (C) is greater than either (A) or (B).

6. Examine (A), (B), and (C) and find the best answer.
    (A) 20%
    (B) 0.2
    (C) ½
    A. (A), (B), and (C) are all equal.
    B. (B) and (C) are equal and less than (A).
    C. (A) and (B) are equal and less than (C).
    D. (A) and (C) are equal and greater than (B).

7. Examine (A), (B), and (C) and find the best answer.
    (A) 9%
    (B) $\frac{1}{9}$
    (C) 0.9
    A. (C) is greater than either (A) or (B).
    B. (B) is greater than both (A) and (C).
    C. (A) is equal to (B) and less than (C).
    D. (B) is less than (A).

8. Examine (A), (B), and (C) and find the best answer.
    (A) 9^2
    (B) 3^4
    (C) 6^3
    A. (A) and (B) are equal and less than (C).
    B. (B) and (C) are both less than (A).
    C. (A) and (C) are equal and less than (B).
    D. (A), (B), and (C) are all equal.

9. Examine (A), (B), and (C) and find the best answer.
    (A) (0.4)(0.5)
    (B) 0.45
    (C) 45%
    A. (A) is greater than (B) and (C).
    B. (B) is less than (A) or (C).
    C. (A) is less than (B) or (C).
    D. (A), (B), and (C) are all equal.

10. Examine (A), (B), and (C) and pick the best answer.
    (A) $2(3 - 2x)$
    (B) $-2(2x - 3)$
    (C) $6x - 3$
    A. (A) = (B) ≠ (C)
    B. (B) = (C) ≠ (A)
    C. (A) ≠ (B) ≠ (C)
    D. (A) = (C) ≠ (B)

11. Examine (A), (B), and (C) and pick the best answer.
    (A) $(9 \times 9) + 2$
    (B) $19 + (2 \times 34)$
    (C) $(22 \times 6) - 47$
    A. (A), (B), and (C) are all equal.
    B. (B) is greater than (A) which is less than (C).
    C. (C) is greater than (A) and (B).
    D. (A) is greater than (C) and less than (B).

12. Examine (A), (B), and (C) and pick the best answer.

        (A) 8×0.3

        (B) 30×0.01

        (C) 4×0.1

  A. (A), (B), and (C) are all equal.

  B. (B) is greater than (A) which is greater than (C).

  C. (C) is greater than (A) and (B).

  D. (A) is greater than (C) and (B).

13. Examine the graph and find the best answer.

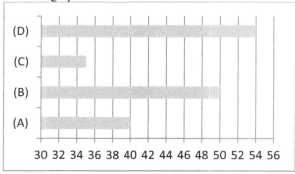

  A. (D) plus (B) equals (C) plus (A).

  B. (A) plus (D) equals (B) minus (C).

  C. (D) minus (C) equals (B) minus (A).

  D. (C) plus (D) equals (A) plus (B).

14. Examine (A), (B), and (C) and find the best possible answer.

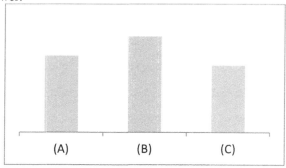

  A. $(A) > (C) > (B)$

  B. $(C) > (B) > (A)$

  C. $(B) > (A) < (C)$

  D. $(C) < (A) < (B)$

15. Examine (A), (B), and (C) and pick the best answer.

        (A) $4(2y - 5) - 5y$

        (B) $(y - 3)3 - 11$

        (C) $3y - 21$

  A. $(A) = (B) \neq (C)$

  B. $(B) = (C) \neq (A)$

  C. $(A) \neq (B) \neq (C)$

  D. $(A) = (C) \neq (B)$

16. Examine (A), (B), and (C) and find the best answer.

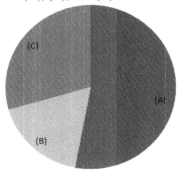

    A. (A) > (C) > (B)
    B. (C) > (B) > (A)
    C. (B) > (A) < (C)
    D. (C) < (A) < (B)

17. Examine (A), (B), and (C) and choose the correct answer.
        (A) 27×10^2
        (B) 2.66×10^4
        (C) 25.3×10^3
    A. (A) is greater than (B) but less than (C).
    B. (C) is less than (B) but greater than (A).
    C. (B) is greater than (C) but less than (A).
    D. (A) is less than (B) but greater than (C).

18. Examine (A), (B), and (C) and choose the correct answer.
        (A) 11% of 40
        (B) 6% of 78
        (C) 8% of 62
    A. (A) is greater than (B) but less than (C).
    B. (C) is less than (B) but greater than (A).
    C. (B) is greater than (C) but less than (A).
    D. (B) is less than (C) but greater than (A).

19. Examine (A), (B), and (C) and choose the correct answer.
        (A) 1.1×10^{-2}
        (B) 33×10^{-3}
        (C) 0.2×10^{-2}
    A. (A) is greater than (B) but less than (C).
    B. (C) is less than (B) but greater than (A).
    C. (B) is greater than (C) but less than (A).
    D. (A) is less than (B) but greater than (C).

20. Examine (A), (B), and (C) and find the best answer.
        (A) $(39 - 2 \times 9)\frac{1}{3} + 8$
        (B) $-\frac{3}{4}(14 - 6 \times 7) + 1$
        (C) $-2(4 - 3 \times 8) - 16$
    A. (A) > (C) > (B)
    B. (C) > (B) > (A)
    C. (A) > (B) < (C)
    D. (C) < (A) < (B)

1. Examine (A), (B), and (C) and find the best answer.
    - (A) $\frac{5}{6}$ of 30
    - (B) $\frac{1}{2}$ of 50
    - (C) $\frac{1}{5}$ of 75
    - A. (A), (B), and (C) are all equal.
    - B. (B) and (C) are equal and less than (A).
    - C. (A) and (B) are equal and greater than (C).
    - D. (A) and (C) are equal and greater than (B).

2. Examine (A), (B), and (C) and find the best answer.
    - (A) $\frac{1}{8}$ of 24
    - (B) $\frac{1}{4}$ of 12
    - (C) $\frac{1}{5}$ of 15
    - A. (B) is greater than (A) or (C).
    - B. (A) is greater than (B) and (C).
    - C. (A) is equal to (C) and greater than (B).
    - D. (A), (B), and (C) are all equal.

3. Examine (A), (B), and (C) and find the best answer.
    - (A) $\frac{3}{7}$ of 28
    - (B) $\frac{4}{5}$ of 20
    - (C) $\frac{1}{4}$ of 60
    - A. (B) is less than either (A) or (C).
    - B. (A) is greater than both (B) and (C).
    - C. (A) is equal to (C) and less than (B).
    - D. (C) is greater than either (A) or (B).

4. Examine (A), (B), and (C) and find the best answer.
    - (A) 60%
    - (B) $\frac{3}{5}$
    - (C) 0.6
    - A. (A), (B), and (C) are all equal.
    - B. (B) and (C) are equal and less than (A).
    - C. (A) and (B) are equal and less than (C).
    - D. (A) and (C) are equal and greater than (B).

5. Examine (A), (B), and (C) and find the best answer.
    - (A) 5%
    - (B) $\frac{1}{5}$
    - (C) 0.5
    - A. (A) is greater than either (B) or (C).
    - B. (B) is greater than either (A) or (C).
    - C. (A) is equal to (B) and less than (C).
    - D. (C) is less than either (A) or (B).

6. Examine (A), (B), and (C) and find the best answer.

   (A) 8^2

   (B) 4^3

   (C) 2^4

   A. (A) and (B) are equal and greater than (C).
   B. (B) and (C) are both less than (A).
   C. (A) and (C) are equal and less than (B).
   D. (A), (B), and (C) are all equal.

7. Examine (A), (B), and (C) and find the best answer.

   (A) 32%

   (B) 0.3×0.2

   (C) 0.32

   A. (A) is greater than (B) and (C).
   B. (B) is greater than either (A) or (C).
   C. (A) is equal to (C) and greater than (B).
   D. (A), (B), and (C) are all equal.

8. Examine (A), (B), and (C) and find the best answer.

   (A) 0.8×3

   (B) 4×0.6

   (C) 0.12×2

   A. (A), (B), and (C) are all equal.
   B. (A) is equal to (C) and less than (B).
   C. (A) is equal to (B) and greater than (C).
   D. (B) is less than either (A) or (C).

9. Examine (A), (B), and (C) and find the best answer.

   (A) $\frac{39}{3}$

   (B) $4 + 3(5 - 2)$

   (C) $7(8 - 5)$

   A. (A) is greater than either (B) or (C).
   B. (B) is greater than either (A) or (C).
   C. (A) is equal to (B) and less than (C).
   D. (A), (B), and (C) are all equal.

10. Examine (A), (B), and (C) and find the best answer.

    (A) 4^2

    (B) $(8 - 4)^2$

    (C) $8^2 - 4^2$

    A. (B) and (C) are equal and less than (A).
    B. (A) and (B) are equal and less than (C).
    C. (A) and (C) are equal and less than (B).
    D. (A) is greater than (B) and (C).

11. Examine (A), (B), and (C) and find the best answer.

    (A) $5(x - 1)$

    (B) $(x - 1) \times 5$

    (C) $5x - 5$

    A. $(A) \neq (B) \neq (C)$
    B. $(A) = (B) \neq (C)$
    C. $(A) \neq (B) = (C)$
    D. $(A) = (B) = (C)$

12. Examine (A), (B), and (C) and find the best answer.

(A) $4m + 4n$

(B) $4(m + n)$

(C) $4m + n$

A. (A) = (B) = (C)
B. (A) = (B) ≠ (C)
C. (A) ≠ (B) = (C)
D. (A) ≠ (B) ≠ (C)

13. Examine (A), (B), and (C) and find the best answer.

(A) $9x^2$

(B) $(3x)^2$

(C) $(1x)^3$

A. (A) ≠ (B) ≠ (C)
B. (A) = (B) ≠ (C)
C. (A) ≠ (B) = (C)
D. (A) = (B) = (C)

14. Examine (A), (B), and (C) and find the best answer.

(A)

(B)

(C)

A. (B) is more shaded than (A) and less shaded than (C).
B. (A) is less shaded than (B) and more shaded than (C).
C. (C) is less shaded than (A) and (B).
D. (A) and (C) are equally shaded.

15. Examine (A), (B), and (C) and find the best answer.

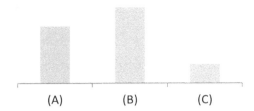

A. (A) < (B) < (C)
B. (A) > (B) > (C)
C. (C) < (A) < (B)
D. (A) > (C) > (B)

16. Examine (A), (B), and (C) and find the best answer.

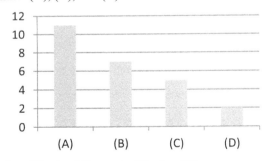

A. (A) > (B) < (C)
B. (B) > (A) > (C)
C. (C) < (B) > (A)
D. (A) < (C) < (B)

17. Examine (A), (B), and (C) and find the best answer.

A. (A) plus (C) equals (B) plus (D).
B. (B) minus (C) equals (A) minus (D).
C. (C) plus (B) equals (A) plus (D).
D. (B) minus (C) equals (D).

18. Examine (A), (B), and (C) and find the best answer.

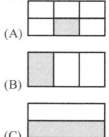

(A)

(B)

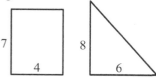

(C)

    A.   (A) is equal to (B).
    B.   (B) is greater than (C).
    C.   The sum of (A) and (B) is (C).
    D.   (A) minus (B) equals (C).

19. Examine the diagram and find the best answer.

    A.   The radius of the circle is 10.
    B.   The circumference of the circle is greater than
        the sum of the two diameters.
    C.   The circumference of the circle is greater than its
        area.
    D.   The area of the circle is 100π.

20. Examine the diagram and find the best answer.

    A.   The area of the triangle is greater than the area of
        the rectangle.
    B.   The perimeter of the triangle is equal to the
        perimeter of the rectangle.
    C.   The perimeter of the rectangle is greater than its
        area.
    D.   The area of the triangle is equal to its perimeter.

CHAPTER 15: QUANTITATIVE COMPARISON

Experts in Test Prep, Tutoring, & Admissions Counseling

www.CardinalEducation.com

BASIC COMPUTATION Practice Set 1

Directions: Using the information given in each question, compare the quantity in Column A to the quantity in Column B. All questions have these answer choices:

    (A) The quantity in Column A is greater.
    (B) The quantity in Column B is greater.
    (C) The two quantities are equal.
    (D) The relationship cannot be determined from the information given.

	Column A	Column B
1.	$3 + 2(8 - 3)$	18

	Column A	Column B
2.	$\frac{1}{3}$ of 66	$\frac{1}{4}$ of 200

	Column A	Column B
3.	0.2×0.3	$0.2 \div 0.3$

	Column A	Column B
4.	$(3 + 4)^2$	$3^2 + 4^2$

	Column A	Column B
5.	$(-5)^2$	-5^2

	Column A	Column B
6.	$\sqrt{36} + \sqrt{64}$	$\sqrt{36 + 64}$

$$k = 7m - 9$$

	Column A	Column B
7.	The value of k when $m = 2$	The value of m when $k = 26$

Chandler has 42 DVDs.

	Column A	Column B
8.	The number of DVDs Chandler will have remaining if he gives away ¾ of his DVDs.	25% of all of Chandler's DVDs.

Dan needs to go from LA to Vegas. The highway is 300 miles, and the back route is 200 miles.

	Column A	Column B
9.	The time it will take Dan to get from LA to Vegas if he takes the highway and travels at 60 mph.	The time it will take Dan to get from LA to Vegas if he takes the back road and travels at 50 mph.

On a science test, students earned these scores:

Justin	70
Lindsay	88
Jared	93
Lisa	85
Jenny	95

	Column A	Column B
10.	The average score of students whose names begin with the letter "J".	The average score of students whose names begin with the letter "L".

3, 4, 5, 7, 1, 5, 2

	Column A	Column B
11.	The median of the group of numbers above.	The mode of the group of numbers above

	Column A	Column B
12.	The slope of the line with the equation $x - 3y = 7$.	The slope of the line with the equation $y = -3x + 7$.

A clock chimes once at the half hour point of every hour (12:30, 1:30 etc.). On the hour, the clock chimes the number of times of that hour. For example, the clock chimes 3 times at 3:00.

Column A	Column B
13. Number of chimes between 2:15 and 4:15.	Number of chimes between 8:45 and 9:15.

Pieces of paper with the numbers 2-9 are put in a jar. Steve randomly picks a number from the jar.

Column A	Column B
14. Probability that Steve picks a prime number.	Probability that Steve picks an odd number.

Column A	Column B
15. The cost of a $20,000 car plus 8% sales tax.	The cost of a $21,000 car plus 4% sales tax

The temperature in Phoenix is 65° and increasing by 4° each day. The temperature in Dallas is 88° on Tuesday and decreasing by 3° each day.

Column A	Column B
16. The temperature it will be in Phoenix on Thursday.	The temperature it will be in Dallas on Saturday.

The sum of 3 consecutive odd integers is 51.

Column A	Column B
17. 18	The greatest of the three integers.

A store is selling t-shirts for $10.

Column A	Column B
18. Price of the t-shirts after a 50% discount, and then an additional 10% discount.	Price after a 60% discount.

Maggie has 16 quarters, 30 dimes, and 18 nickels.

Column A	Column B
19. The smallest number of coins she should use to make $5.00.	The largest number of coins she could use to make $1.50

Four athletes run a 100-m dash. The average time of their 4 runs is 12.6 seconds.

Column A	Column B
20. If a fifth runner runs the 100-meter dash in 13.1 seconds, the average time of all 5 runs.	12.8

BASIC COMPUTATION Practice Set 2

Directions: Using the information given in each question, compare the quantity in Column A to the quantity in Column B. All questions have these answer choices:

(A) The quantity in Column A is greater.
(B) The quantity in Column B is greater.
(C) The two quantities are equal.
(D) The relationship cannot be determined from the information given.

	Column A	Column B
1.	0.66	$\frac{4}{6}$

	Column A	Column B
2.	The number of integers between -12.1 and 9.2	The number of integers between 689 and 713.

	Column A	Column B
3.	16% of 18	18% of 16

	Column A	Column B
4.	-4^4	$(-4)^4$

	Column A	Column B
5.	3% of 8% of 13	24% of 13

	Column A	Column B
6.	$-2(3 - 4 \times 8 \div 16) - 17$	-20

	Column A	Column B
7.	$\sqrt{50} - \sqrt{37}$	2

	Column A	Column B
8.	$\sqrt{64 + 81}$	$\sqrt{64} + \sqrt{81}$

	Column A	Column B
9.	$\frac{17}{300}$	3.2×10^{-2}

	Column A	Column B
10.	The remainder when 284 is divided by 6.	The quotient when 384 is divided by 152.

	Column A	Column B
11.	$6 \div \frac{3}{4}$	$\frac{3}{4} \div 6$

	Column A	Column B
12.	0.78^{11}	0.78^9

	Column A	Column B
13.	The least common multiple of 18 and 54.	The greatest common factor of 18 and 54.

	Column A	Column B
14.	$\frac{2}{3} \div \frac{11}{2}$	$\frac{11}{2} \div \frac{2}{3}$

	Column A	Column B
15.	$\frac{1}{889}$	$\frac{1}{887} + \frac{1}{2}$

	Column A	Column B
16.	$\frac{2}{3} \times \frac{9}{14} \times \frac{7}{27}$	$\frac{2}{9}$

	Column A	Column B
17.	The number of distinct prime factors of 24.	2

	Column A	Column B
18.	9 yards.	24 feet

	Column A	Column B
19.	The average of 18, 17, and 16	17.5

	Column A	Column B
20.	$\lvert 387 - 267 \times 4 \div 3 \rvert$	$\lvert 33 \times 5 \div 2 - 25 \rvert$

ALGEBRAIC EXPRESSIONS Practice Set 1

Directions: Using the information given in each question, compare the quantity in Column A to the quantity in Column B. All questions have these answer choices:

(A) The quantity in Column A is greater.
(B) The quantity in Column B is greater.
(C) The two quantities are equal.
(D) The relationship cannot be determined from the information given.

$$\frac{2}{5} < m < \frac{4}{7}$$

Column A	Column B
1. m	$\frac{7}{11}$

$$0 < x < 1$$

Column A	Column B
2. x^2	x^3

$$x < y$$

Column A	Column B
3. $3x$	$-3y$

Column A	Column B
4. $5x + 7$	$5x - 3$

$$-1 < x < 0$$

Column A	Column B
5. x^7	x^8

$$y = -2x - 7$$

Column A	Column B
6. The value of x when $y = 9$.	The value of y when $x = 1$.

Column A	Column B
7. The slope of $5x - 3y = 12$.	The y-intercept of $3x + 5y = 2$

Column A	Column B
8. $(x - y)(x + y)$	$x^2 + y^2$

---

x represents a prime number greater than 10 and less than 20.
y represents an even number greater than 10 and less than 20.

Column A	Column B
9. $x - y$	$y - x$

$$2y - 7 = x + 3$$

Column A	Column B
10. $2y$	$x + 7$

---

x is a prime number. y is equal to $1{,}000x$

Column A	Column B
11. The sum of the digits of x.	The sum of the digits of y.

$$\frac{x - 3}{4x} = 0$$

Column A	Column B
12. x	0

$$\frac{x}{2} = \frac{y}{16}$$

Column A	Column B
13. x	y

The average of a and b is 52.

Column A	Column B
14. The sum of a and b.	102

A fair dice is tossed.

Column A	Column B
15. The probability that it lands a 4, 5, or 6.	The probability that it does not land an even number.

$$a < b < c < 1$$

Column A	Column B
16. bc	a

$$y = -2$$

Column A	Column B
17. $-y^3 + 3y^2 - 3y$	$y^3 - 3y^2 + 3y$

Column A	Column B
18. $3(8 - 3x)$	$24 - 3x$

Benjamin is x years old. Jonathan is three times as old as Benjamin.

Column A	Column B
19. The difference between Jonathan's and Benjamin's ages now.	The difference in their ages five years from now.

$$2(x + 3) > 14$$
$$4x - 2 < 18$$

Column A	Column B
20. 5	x

ALGEBRAIC EXPRESSIONS Practice Set 2

Directions: Using the information given in each question, compare the quantity in Column A to the quantity in Column B. All questions have these answer choices:

(A) The quantity in Column A is greater.
(B) The quantity in Column B is greater.
(C) The two quantities are equal.
(D) The relationship cannot be determined from the information given.

The base of a triangle is greater than its height.

Column A	Column B
1. Area of the triangle.	Perimeter of the triangle.

On the line below, G (not shown) is a point located to the right of F.

E ●———————● F ————————

Column A	Column B
2. The distance between E and G.	Two times the distance between F and G.

Column A	Column B
3. x	$-x$

Column A	Column B
4. h^2	h

$$j > k$$

Column A	Column B
5. $j - k$	$k - j$

$$m > p > 1$$

Column A	Column B
6. m^2	p^2

Column A	Column B
7. $x^2 - y^2$	$(x - y)(x + y)$

Square A has sides of length x. Rectangle B has length y and width x.

Column A	Column B
8. Area of Square A.	Area of rectangle B.

Column A	Column B
9. $4(n + 3)$	$4n + 3$

A bag contains equal numbers of green, red, and blue marbles.

Column A	Column B
10. If the first marble randomly drawn is red, the probability that the second marble randomly drawn will be red.	If the first marble randomly drawn is red, the probability that the second marble randomly drawn will be green.

x is a positive integer and y is a negative integer.

Column A	Column B
11. xy	$x - y$

$$8 \geq x \geq 5$$
$$2 \leq y \leq 5$$

Column A	Column B
12. x	y

500

Column A	Column B
13. x^3	$(x - 2)^3$

Column A	Column B
14. $xy - 10$	xy

P, Q, R, and S are points on a line, in that order. R is the midpoint of PS and Q is the midpoint of PR.

Column A	Column B
15. $PQ + QR$	RS

The average of x and y is 20.

Column A	Column B
16. The sum of x and y.	40

Neil has $2 in change.

Column A	Column B
17. The number of quarters that Neil has.	The number of dimes that Neil has.

Pat eats cheesesteaks at a constant rate. It takes him between 10 and 20 minutes to eat one cheesesteak.

Column A	Column B
18. The number of cheesesteaks Pat could eat in an hour.	7

Josh estimates that on his trip to Las Vegas he will spend no less than $300 and no more than $900.

Column A	Column B
19. The amount Josh will spend if he stays in Las Vegas for 3 days.	$200

$$x < 0$$
$$y > 0$$

Column A	Column B
20. $x + y$	$|x + y|$

PERIMETER AND AREA Practice Set 1

Directions: Using the information given in each question, compare the quantity in Column A to the quantity in Column B. All questions have these answer choices:

(A) The quantity in Column A is greater.
(B) The quantity in Column B is greater.
(C) The two quantities are equal.
(D) The relationship cannot be determined from the information given.

Quadrilateral EFGH has a perimeter of 68.

Column A	Column B
1. The area of the quadrilateral.	225

P ――― 23 ――― Q

R ――――― S

Quadrilateral PQRS has an area of 138.

Column A	Column B
2. Perimeter of PQRS.	59

A circle has radius of 2.

Column A	Column B
3. Circumference of the circle.	Area of the circle.

A square has sides of length 11.

Column A	Column B
4. Perimeter of the square.	Area of the square.

A circle has radius y.

Column A	Column B
5. The area of the circle.	The perimeter of the circle.

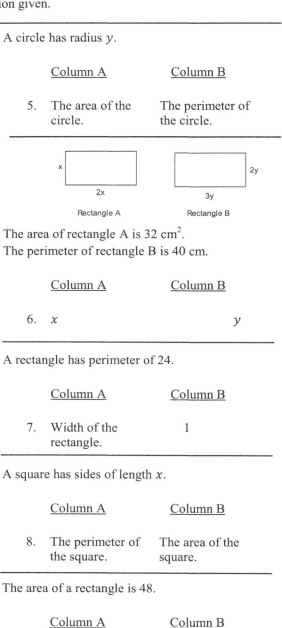

The area of rectangle A is 32 cm^2.
The perimeter of rectangle B is 40 cm.

Column A	Column B
6. x	y

A rectangle has perimeter of 24.

Column A	Column B
7. Width of the rectangle.	1

A square has sides of length x.

Column A	Column B
8. The perimeter of the square.	The area of the square.

The area of a rectangle is 48.

Column A	Column B
9. Perimeter of the rectangle.	48

Column A	Column B
10. The area of a square with sides x.	The area of a rectangle with side $2x$ and $\frac{1}{3}x$

A rectangle has length y and width $0.5y$.

Column A	Column B
11. Area of the rectangle.	Perimeter of the rectangle.

The area of a circle is 8π.

Column A	Column B
12. 3	Radius of the circle.

A triangle has two sides measuring 8 and 10 respectively.

Column A	Column B
13. 42	Greatest possible area of the triangle.

Column A	Column B
14. The volume of a cube with side length 4.	Surface area of a cube with side length 4.

Column A	Column B
15. Perimeter of a square with sides $\frac{1}{3}y$.	Perimeter of a rectangle with length $\frac{2}{5}y$ and width $\frac{1}{6}y$.

The area of a rectangle is 100.

Column A	Column B
16. 39	Perimeter of the rectangle.

A circle has radius 0.3

Column A	Column B
17. Circumference of the circle.	Area of the circle.

A triangle has two sides measuring 5 and 12.

Column A	Column B
18. Third side of the triangle.	17

The perimeter of a rectangle is 64.

Column A	Column B
19. The area of the rectangle.	36

A rectangle has length 7 and width 5.

Column A	Column B
20. The diagonal of the rectangle.	8

PERIMETER AND AREA Practice Set 2

Directions: Using the information given in each question, compare the quantity in Column A to the quantity in Column B. All questions have these answer choices:

(A) The quantity in Column A is greater.
(B) The quantity in Column B is greater.
(C) The two quantities are equal.
(D) The relationship cannot be determined from the information given.

The area of a rectangle is 36 cm^2.

Column A	Column B
1. The perimeter of the rectangle.	30 cm

The area of a rectangle is 20 in^2. All sides of the rectangle have integer lengths.

Column A	Column B
2. 43 in	The perimeter of the rectangle.

The area of a rectangle is 64 cm^2

Column A	Column B
3. The perimeter of the rectangle.	30 cm

The area of a rectangle is 48 cm^2

Column A	Column B
4. 28	The perimeter of the rectangle.

The area of a rectangle is 45 cm^2

Column A	Column B
5. 36 cm	The perimeter of the rectangle.

The perimeter of a rectangle is 20.

Column A	Column B
6. The area of the rectangle.	15

The perimeter of a rectangle is 40.

Column A	Column B
7. 100	The area of the rectangle.

The perimeter of a rectangle is 35.

Column A	Column B
8. The area of the rectangle.	81

The perimeter of a rectangle is 100. All sides of the rectangle have integer lengths.

Column A	Column B
9. The area of the rectangle.	48

The perimeter of a rectangle is 4. All sides of the rectangle have integer lengths.

Column A	Column B
10. The area of the rectangle.	1

The length of one side of a square is 7.

Column A	Column B
11. Area of the square.	Perimeter of the square.

The length of one side of a square is 4.

Column A	Column B
12. Area of the square.	Perimeter of the square.

The length of one side of a square is 1 ft^2.

Column A	Column B
13. Perimeter of the square in inches.	Area of the square in inches^2.

A rectangle has one side with length 6. The rectangle has a perimeter of 28.

Column A	Column B
14. The area of the rectangle.	48

Rectangle X has an area of 40. If each side of rectangle X is increased by 5, it creates rectangle Y.

Column A	Column B
15. Difference between the area of rectangle Y and the area of rectangle X.	Difference between the perimeter of rectangle Y and the perimeter of rectangle X.

Column A	Column B
16. Area of the square.	Area of the rectangle.

Rectangle R has one side with length 10, and a perimeter of 36. Rectangle S has one side with length 8, and a perimeter of 28.

Column A	Column B
17. The shortest side of rectangle R	The longest side of rectangle S

The area of rectangle G is 50 cm^2. The perimeter of square H is 20 cm.

Column A	Column B
18. x	y

The perimeter of rectangle L is 36 in^2.

Column A	Column B
19. The area of rectangle L.	The area of square M.

A rectangle and a triangle have the same base. The height of the triangle is half the height of the rectangle. The area of the rectangle is x.

Column A	Column B
20. The area of the triangle.	$\dfrac{x}{4}$

MIXED QUANTITATIVE COMPARISON Practice Set 1

Directions: Using the information given in each question, compare the quantity in Column A to the quantity in Column B. All questions have these answer choices:

(A) The quantity in Column A is greater.
(B) The quantity in Column B is greater.
(C) The two quantities are equal.
(D) The relationship cannot be determined from the information given.

	Column A	Column B
1.	0.7^3	0.6^2

	Column A	Column B
2.	$\frac{6}{9}$	$\frac{5}{8}$

	Column A	Column B
3.	100% of 8	8% of 100

	Column A	Column B
4.	x^4	x^5

	Column A	Column B
5.	$\sqrt{24}$	$2\sqrt{6}$

	Column A	Column B
6.	$\frac{1}{3}$	30%

	Column A	Column B
7.	90 inches	7.4 feet

	Column A	Column B
8.	Are of a square with sides 7.	Area of a triangle with base 8 and height 12.

	Column A	Column B
9.	The complement of 32°.	The supplement of 122°.

	Column A	Column B
10.	$3x + 4$	$8x + 4$

$$-5 \le x \le 0$$
$$-5 < y \le 7$$

	Column A	Column B
11.	x	y

	Column A	Column B
12.	$-4|-5|$	$4|-5|$

	Column A	Column B
13.	The greatest common factor of 24 and 64.	7

	Column A	Column B
14.	24% of 86	86% of 24

	Column A	Column B
15.	10% of 88	$\frac{1}{3}$ of 27.5

	Column A	Column B
16.	9^6	$\frac{3^{36}}{3^{24}}$

Column A	Column B
17. $6\frac{2}{5} + \frac{1}{100}$	6.4

Maria bakes x cookies, $33\frac{1}{3}\%$ of which are chocolate chip cookies.

Column A	Column B
18. Number of chocolate chip cookies.	Difference between other types of cookies and chocolate chip cookies.

Column A	Column B
19. $\sqrt{50}$	$\frac{100}{1} \times \frac{24}{400}$

The average of four numbers is 23.

Column A	Column B
20. Sum of the four numbers.	90

MIXED QUANTITATIVE COMPARISON Practice Set 2

Directions: Using the information given in each question, compare the quantity in Column A to the quantity in Column B. All questions have these answer choices:

(A) The quantity in Column A is greater.
(B) The quantity in Column B is greater.
(C) The two quantities are equal.
(D) The relationship cannot be determined from the information given.

	Column A	Column B
1.	The number of distinct prime factors of 176.	3

	Column A	Column B
2.	AC	$\sqrt{x^2 + y^2}$

	Column A	Column B
3.	The quotient of 355 and 17.	Ten more than a half of 20.

	Column A	Column B
4.	$200 - 8.6201$	$200 - 8.6199$

	Column A	Column B
5.	$\frac{1}{5}$ of 1,286	20% of 1,286

	Column A	Column B
6.	$5x + 10$	$5(x + 1)$

$$\frac{6}{7} > y > \frac{1}{4}$$

	Column A	Column B
7.	y	$\frac{3}{4}$

	Column A	Column B
8.	20	$\sqrt{420}$

	Column A	Column B
9.	The probability of getting heads from a coin toss.	The probability of rolling a 5 on a dice throw.

	Column A	Column B
10.	The median of 5, 6, 7, and 8.	The mean of 5, 6, 7, and 8.

	Column A	Column B
11.	The area of a circle.	The circumference of the same circle.

Figure 1   Figure 2

	Column A	Column B
12.	Surface area of Figure 1.	Surface area of Figure 2.

	Column A	Column B
13.	The area of a circle whose radius is x^2.	The area of a circle whose radius is $2x$.

	Column A	Column B
14.	The perimeter of a square with area 49.	The perimeter of a rectangle with area 48.

	Column A	Column B
15.	$\sqrt{25} + \sqrt{9}$	$\sqrt{36}$

$$3x - y = 4$$
$$x + y = 16$$

	Column A	Column B
16.	x	y

	Column A	Column B
17.	6^5	5^6

$$x < 0$$

	Column A	Column B
18.	x^2	x^3

$$(x - 2)(x + 2) = 0$$

	Column A	Column B
19.	x	2

	Column A	Column B
20.	Sum of the three smallest prime numbers.	Sum of the three smallest positive odd integers.

MIXED QUANTITATIVE COMPARISON Practice Set 3

Directions: Using the information given in each question, compare the quantity in Column A to the quantity in Column B. All questions have these answer choices:

(A) The quantity in Column A is greater.
(B) The quantity in Column B is greater.
(C) The two quantities are equal.
(D) The relationship cannot be determined from the information given.

Column A	Column B
1. 2^{15}	8^5

4

Column A	Column B
2. Volume of the cube.	Surface area of the cube.

In a school of 300 students, 40% of them are boys.

Column A	Column B
3. Half the number of boys.	Difference between the number of boys and the number of girls.

Column A	Column B
4. 20% of y	$\frac{1}{4}$ of y

1 mile is equal to 5,280 feet.

Column A	Column B
5. 3 miles	15,280 feet

Column A	Column B
6. The number of multiples of 5 between 1 and 63.	The number of multiples of 4 between 1 and 54.

Column A	Column B
7. $\frac{1}{998}$	$\frac{1}{997}$

Column A	Column B
8. $(0.12)^{14}$	$(0.12)^{13}$

Column A	Column B
9. $3(4x + 1)$	$12x + 12$

Column A	Column B
10. $10,000 - 7.6041$	$10,000 - 7.6401$

Column A	Column B
11. The area of a square with sides 6.	Area of a rectangle with length 9 and width 4.

Column A	Column B
12. The median of 18, 24, 36, 56.	The mean of 18, 24, 36, 56.

$$-3 < a < 10$$
$$0 \le b \le 7$$

Column A	Column B
13. a	b

$$\frac{x}{3} = \frac{40}{24} \qquad \frac{84}{60} = \frac{7}{y}$$

Column A	Column B
14. x	y

$$b = -1$$

Column A	Column B
15. $b^3 - b^2 + b - 1$	$-b^3 + b^2 - b + 1$

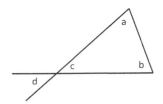

Column A	Column B
16. $180 - (a + b)$	d

Column A	Column B
17. $\sqrt{25} + \sqrt{36}$	$\sqrt{61}$

$$-3 \le x < 0$$
$$-3 > y \ge -5$$

Column A	Column B
18. x	y

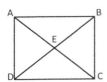

Column A	Column B
19. AD	EC + DE

Bethany is $1\frac{3}{7}$ of Amanda's age. Jenna is $\frac{7}{10}$ of Bethany's age.

Column A	Column B
20. Jenna's age.	Amanda's age.

MIXED QUANTITATIVE COMPARISON Practice Set 4

Directions: Using the information given in each question, compare the quantity in Column A to the quantity in Column B. All questions have these answer choices:

(A) The quantity in Column A is greater.
(B) The quantity in Column B is greater.
(C) The two quantities are equal.
(D) The relationship cannot be determined from the information given.

$$x + y = 7$$
$$-x + y = 11$$

Column A	Column B
1. x	y

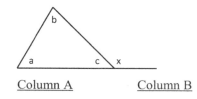

Column A	Column B
2. $a + b$	x

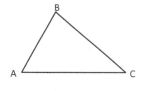

$$\angle CAB > \angle ABC$$

Column A	Column B
3. AC	BC

Column A	Column B
4. The greatest integer less than 12.	The least integer greater than 10.

Jon bought 3 KitKats and 4 Snickers for $8.20.

Column A	Column B
5. The price of one KitKat.	The price of one Snickers.

---

n represents an integer less than zero.

Column A	Column B
6. $12 - 2n$	$2n - 12$

$$(x - 4)(x + 4) = 0$$

Column A	Column B
7. x	4

Column A	Column B
8. The average of three smallest positive even integers.	The average of the three smallest prime numbers.

$$\frac{a + 3}{b + 3} = \frac{a}{b}$$

Column A	Column B
9. a	b

Column A	Column B
10. The cost of 9 oranges if the cost of 5 oranges is $2.50	$4.25

512

$$m > 5$$
$$n > 500$$

Column A	Column B
11. m	n

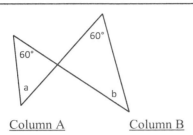

Column A	Column B
12. 0	$a - b$

Column A	Column B
13. 0.3^{21}	0.3^{22}

$$x < y < z < 0$$

Column A	Column B
14. y	$x + z$

Xavier lives 15 miles due south of his middle school. Cassandra lives 10 miles due east of the same middle school.

Column A	Column B
15. The shortest distance from Xavier's house to Cassandra's house.	25 miles

Column A	Column B
16. $\frac{8}{9}$ of $3.60	20% of 10% of $100.

Column A	Column B
17. $4a + 6$	$9a - 3$

Column A	Column B
18. The probability of getting a 5 on a toss of a dice.	$\frac{1}{5}$

Column A	Column B
19. $\frac{1}{3}$	The product of $\frac{3}{8}$ and $\frac{2}{5}$.

A bike costs $80. It goes on sale for 10% off. The next day the price is reduced by another 25%.

Column A	Column B
20. The final price of the bike.	$55

CHAPTER 16: SOLUTIONS

Experts in Test Prep, Tutoring, & Admissions Counseling

www.CardinalEducation.com

Chapter 1

Addition PS1 (17)
1. 165
2. 273
3. 341
4. 846
5. 932
6. 431
7. 622
8. 1,252
9. 921
10. 1,084
11. 29
12. 92
13. 169
14. 315
15. 94
16. 144
17. 138
18. 123
19. 261
20. 191
21. 200
22. 1,126
23. 3,158
24. 984
25. 8,082
26. 1,268
27. 10,665
28. 3,904
29. 11,480
30. 10,471

Addition PS2
1. 194
2. 303
3. 320
4. 636
5. 774
6. 801
7. 753
8. 1,176
9. 1,444
10. 1,211
11. 40
12. 69
13. 181
14. 243
15. 104
16. 151
17. 129
18. 110
19. 224
20. 186
21. 1,615
22. 3,317
23. 924
24. 4,129
25. 1,647
26. 10,950
27. 5,969
28. 4,312
29. 11,654
30. 13,798

Subtraction PS1 (21)
1. 16
2. 9
3. 52
4. 114
5. 79
6. 266
7. 447
8. 26
9. 378
10. 126
11. 24
12. 269
13. 446
14. 489
15. 2,687
16. 10,159
17. 7,786
18. 990
19. 7,438
20. 11,483
21. 879
22. 6,764
23. 1,888
24. 3,346
25. 4,191
26. 815
27. 3,474
28. 6,066
29. 216
30. 10,501

Subtraction PS2
1. 17
2. 48
3. 59
4. 85
5. 55
6. 208
7. 327
8. 29
9. 424
10. 147
11. 170
12. 482
13. 213
14. 246
15. 555
16. 1,491
17. 11,313
18. 3,052
19. 660
20. 3,363
21. 10,363
22. 619
23. 5,548
24. 7,001
25. 448
26. 28
27. 5,070
28. 8,530
29. 882
30. 11,920

Addition/Subtraction Missing
Digits PS1 (25)
1. 9
2. 6
3. 1
4. 5
5. 8
6. 9, 8
7. 0, 0, 3
8. 6
9. 1, 4, 8
10. 0, 0, 0

Addition/Subtraction Missing
Digits PS2
1. 0
2. 8
3. 5
4. 2
5. 0
6. 6
7. 8, 1, 2
8. 4, 8, 0, 2
9. 5, 8
10. 7, 2, 5

Multiplication PS1 (27)
1. 392
2. 702
3. 968
4. 1,505
5. 1,014
6. 308
7. 567
8. 444
9. 2,850
10. 4,928
11. 2,376
12. 3,390
13. 8,928
14. 15,466
15. 29,184
16. 80,352
17. 131,054
18. 60,916
19. 415,290
20. 502,660

Multiplication PS2
1. 192
2. 504
3. 1,323
4. 3,304
5. 2,968
6. 368
7. 544
8. 858
9. 1,632
10. 6,708
11. 4,879
12. 12,719
13. 17,050
14. 28,892
15. 31,824
16. 266,085
17. 89,046
18. 329,656
19. 334,642
20. 606,483

Multiplication PS3
1. 92
2. 234
3. 2,104
4. 4,644
5. 4,025
6. 476
7. 615
8. 1,012
9. 1,961
10. 4,731
11. 7,164
12. 8,502
13. 20,972
14. 20,562
15. 40,208

16. 112,488
17. 167,418
18. 400,649
19. 729,606
20. 325,556

Multiplication PS4
1. 72
2. 294
3. 1,820
4. 3,776
5. 2,296
6. 475
7. 434
8. 621
9. 767
10. 2,318
11. 7,733
12. 13,944
13. 23,577
14. 24,192
15. 20,886
16. 90,316
17. 374,740
18. 182,028
19. 490,941
20. 136,510

3 Number Multiplication PS1
(31)
1. 48
2. 84
3. 120
4. 144
5. 294
6. 132
7. 360
8. 208
9. 1,404
10. 1,694
11. 1,152
12. 1,820
13. 3,456
14. 2,904
15. 2,484
16. 7,548
17. 3,060
18. 5,720
19. 11,340
20. 16,016

3 Number Multiplication PS2
1. 112
2. 126
3. 360
4. 432
5. 182
6. 240
7. 204
8. 1,904
9. 1,482
10. 1,248
11. 812
12. 1,204
13. 2,440
14. 1,904
15. 1,890
16. 3,420
17. 20,664
18. 4,650
19. 3,520
20. 9,180

Multiplication Missing Digits
PS1 (33)
1. 7, 2
2. 3, 4
3. 6, 2
4. 6, 5
5. 2, 2, 3
6. 3, 3, 0, 8
7. 4, 4, 1, 2
8. 2, 6, 5, 3
9. 3, 4, 2, 6, 1
10. 5, 8, 4, 2, 8

Multiplication Missing Digits
PS2
1. 6, 0
2. 4, 4
3. 3, 4
4. 5, 4
5. 4, 4, 6
6. 5, 3, 9, 7
7. 8, 5, 1, 5
8. 5, 2, 5, 4
9. 4, 3, 4, 3, 1
10. 6, 2, 1, 2, 2

Division PS1 (35)
1. 15
2. 87
3. 41
4. 42
5. 9
6. 21
7. 7
8. 1
9. 11
10. 234
11. 725
12. 478
13. 581
14. 89
15. 54
16. undefined
17. 47
18. 12
19. 17
20. 26

Division PS2
1. 12
2. 44
3. 33
4. 37
5. 8
6. 1
7. 19
8. 7
9. 13
10. 196
11. 483
12. 688
13. 983
14. 81
15. 49
16. 29
17. 57
18. 0
19. 18
20. 23

Division PS3
1. 18
2. 47
3. 38
4. 41
5. 7
6. 18
7. 8
8. 14
9. 666
10. 0
11. 627
12. 979
13. 69
14. 58
15. 46
16. 66
17. 13
18. 19
19. 27
20. undefined

Division PS4
1. 13
2. 23
3. 1
4. 26
5. 6
6. 26
7. 9
8. 17
9. 234
10. 519
11. 777
12. 997
13. undefined
14. 39
15. 68
16. 43
17. 16
18. 14
19. 24
20. 13

Remainders PS1 (39)
1. 6 R 4
2. 19 R 2
3. 5 R 5
4. 6 R 8
5. 4 R 4
6. 26 R 4
7. 81 R 1
8. 28 R 5
9. 24 R 18
10. 15 R 46
11. 10 R 47
12. 3 R 93
13. 4 R 68
14. 3 R 185
15. 35 R 1
16. 67 R 75
17. 104 R 30
18. 27 R 54
19. 19 R 281
20. 9 R 152

Remainders PS2
1. 6 R 5
2. 18 R 2
3. 6 R 9
4. 6 R 7

5. 3 R 19
6. 28 R 4
7. 76 R 2
8. 48 R 7
9. 27 R 19
10. 14 R 11
11. 12 R 6
12. 3 R 89
13. 4 R 104
14. 7 R 36
15. 46 R 17
16. 62 R 21
17. 101 R 25
18. 17 R 216
19. 14 R 67
20. 9 R 716

Powers of 10 PS1 (41)
1. 220
2. 1,700
3. 13
4. 2,400
5. 35
6. 40
7. 200
8. 3,780
9. 160
10. 16,100
11. 800
12. 9,300
13. 45,000
14. 1,200
15. 13,200
16. 110
17. 160
18. 12,900
19. 1,200
20. 228,000

Powers of 10 PS2
1. 80
2. 1,200
3. 4
4. 1,400
5. 20
6. 20
7. 12
8. 3,630
9. 50
10. 12,000
11. 500
12. 2,200
13. 56,000
14. 200
15. 6,400
16. 130
17. 270
18. 7,500
19. 400
20. 242,000

Basic Order of Operations
PS1 (43)
1. 4
2. 9

3. 30
4. 1
5. 1
6. 69
7. 14
8. 32
9. 10
10. 20
11. 11
12. 80
13. 37
14. 12
15. 7
16. 10
17. 16
18. 6
19. 23
20. 41

Basic Order of Operations
PS2
1. 13
2. 8
3. 18
4. 5
5. 30
6. 15
7. 8
8. 12
9. 1
10. 26
11. 9
12. 130
13. 6
14. 24
15. 18
16. 28
17. 20
18. 4
19. 13
20. 17

Chapter 2
Basic Negative Number
Addition/Subtraction PS1
(46)
1. 4
2. 6
3. -8
4. 28
5. 52
6. 38
7. -19
8. 8
9. 21
10. 9
11. 9
12. -3
13. -11
14. -5
15. -23
16. -18
17. -33
18. -10
19. -38
20. -33

Basic Negative Number Addition/Subtraction PS2
1. -15
2. -8
3. -27
4. 9
5. 1
6. -11
7. 6
8. 22
9. 22
10. 27
11. 44
12. 6
13. -5
14. -35
15. -8
16. -44
17. -76
18. -16
19. -32
20. -32

Basic Negative Number Addition/Subtraction PS3
1. 41
2. 9
3. 30
4. 18
5. 14
6. -8
7. -9
8. -11
9. -2
10. 0
11. 5
12. -24
13. -6
14. 18
15. -30
16. -40
17. -45
18. -40
19. -43
20. -56

Basic Negative Number Addition/Subtraction PS4
1. 4
2. 7
3. -7
4. -32
5. -20
6. -40
7. -21
8. -41
9. -33
10. 24
11. 29
12. 61
13. -8
14. -14
15. 14
16. -18
17. -21
18. 16
19. -9
20. -19

Challenging Negative Number Addition/Subtraction PS1 (50)
1. 5,877
2. 10,467
3. 3,963
4. 940
5. 1,918
6. 9,487
7. 589
8. 1,965
9. -5,465
10. 1,899
11. 4,577
12. 2,173
13. 1,647
14. 4,434
15. -7,324
16. 555
17. -3,212
18. 10,432
19. -6,436
20. -8,298

Challenging Negative Number Addition/Subtraction PS2
1. 3,982
2. 12,587
3. 5,094
4. 980
5. 5,982
6. 9,485
7. 829
8. 4,037
9. -8,076
10. -963
11. 2,534
12. 1,189
13. 857
14. 5,385
15. 6,695
16. 213
17. -2,707
18. 14,312
19. -9,018
20. -11,483

Challenging Negative Number Addition/Subtraction PS3
1. 1,648
2. -7,449
3. 1,168
4. -334
5. 1,143
6. 325
7. -2,009
8. 1,606
9. -1,451
10. 930
11. -438
12. -5,670
13. -4,434
14. -1,604
15. -2,693
16. -3,490
17. -6,453
18. -8,545
19. -9,432
20. -7,161

Challenging Negative Number Addition/Subtraction PS4
1. 1,235
2. -5,564
3. 1,761
4. -262
5. 577
6. -922
7. 2,327
8. 1,813
9. -714
10. 139
11. -2,281
12. -6,694
13. -3,828
14. -3,146
15. -2,682
16. -2,710
17. -5,876
18. -6,586
19. -7,480
20. -7,999

Negative Number Multiplication/Division PS1 (54)
1. -32
2. 72
3. -5
4. -7
5. 4
6. -108
7. -13
8. 14
9. -90
10. -352
11. -936
12. 33
13. -1,044
14. 24
15. -80
16. 22,591
17. -2,775
18. -5
19. 39,424
20. 90

Negative Number Multiplication/Division PS2
1. -7
2. 36
3. -11
4. -42
5. 64
6. -12
7. -15
8. 391
9. -130
10. -7
11. -528
12. 13
13. -26
14. 128
15. -2,016
16. 4
17. -54
18. -1,820
19. -7
20. -14

Chapter 3
Addition/Subtraction Word Problems PS1 (57)
1. 1,515
2. 905
3. 5°C
4. 1,653 cans
5. 2,130
6. 6,423 seats
7. 10,303
8. 120 years
9. 10,388 competitors
10. 28,768 ft
11. $143
12. 3,190 newspapers
13. 27,770
14. D
15. 45 passengers
16. 1952
17. 36
18. 42
19. 21 years
20. -190

Addition/Subtraction Word Problems PS2
1. -221
2. $124,482
3. 210
4. 16,073 miles
5. 1,723
6. 1,674 pages
7. 3,110
8. 10,006
9. $28
10. -71
11. 4,885 buttons
12. 8,936 butterflies
13. 29
14. 65°F
15. 1857
16. 441,304 trees
17. 44
18. $241,576
19. 278 boxes
20. 58 points

Addition/Subtraction Word Problems PS3
1. 733
2. 231 people
3. 208
4. 1,764
5. 197,697 spectators
6. 14,362 songs
7. 3,021
8. 10,175
9. 681
10. 20
11. 8,654 lbs
12. 12°F
13. -196
14. 1839
15. 2,450 minutes
16. $18,606
17. 11,055 miles
18. -59
19. 3,554 butterflies
20. $1,536

Addition/Subtraction Word Problems PS4
1. 52
2. 3,576 miles
3. 22,354 trillion btu
4. 176
5. 2,035
6. 1,008
7. 4,403 words
8. 18
9. 2,111
10. 39 years old
11. 9,490
12. 37 mountains
13. 2,695 stitches
14. $187.50
15. 37 cans
16. 128 marbles
17. $54
18. 36,239 ft
19. -77
20. 637,722 copies

Multiplication/Division Word Problems PS1 (65)
1. 84
2. 12
3. D
4. 5
5. 3
6. C
7. A
8. B
9. B
10. 43
11. D
12. 3,780
13. C
14. 17 glasses
15. C
16. B
17. 4 buses
18. D
19. B
20. B

Multiplication/Division Word Problems PS2
1. 114
2. 54
3. B
4. 6
5. 4
6. C
7. C
8. D
9. D
10. 78
11. 3
12. C
13. B
14. 76
15. 16 packs
16. 22 scoops
17. C
18. D
19. A
20. D

Multiplication/Division Word Problems PS3
1. 6
2. 144
3. 16
4. 11
5. B
6. D
7. C
8. A
9. B
10. 5
11. 48
12. D
13. B
14. B
15. A
16. B
17. 65 pizzas
18. 315
19. 13 days
20. B

Multiplication/Division Word Problems PS4
1. 2
2. 9
3. 112
4. B
5. 72
6. C
7. 15
8. B
9. A
10. C
11. 56
12. 15 gallons
13. 143
14. C
15. C
16. B
17. C
18. A
19. 14 cat toys
20. B

Mixed Word Problems PS1 (77)
1. 8
2. $28
3. 81,334
4. 78,134
5. 7,653 members
6. -197
7. 4 bands
8. 187 players
9. 24 ounces
10. 220 words
11. 500 trees
12. 1,834
13. 18 pairs of shoes
14. 7 miles
15. 225 points
16. 1,404
17. 24 chaperones
18. 5 pencils
19. 457,311
20. C

Mixed Word Problems PS2
1. -7
2. 341,417
3. 34,074
4. 40 chocolates
5. 425,042 seeds
6. 7 people
7. 39 people
8. 1,536
9. 45°F
10. 48 sections
11. 126 meals
12. 59,162
13. 19 points
14. C
15. $36
16. 124
17. 10 dolphins
18. D
19. 100 years
20. 42,000 toys

Mixed Word Problems PS3
1. 219
2. 5 groups
3. 378,361 ants
4. 61,531
5. 40,426 points
6. $90
7. -14
8. $3
9. 593,114
10. 6 buses
11. 300,000 cookies
12. 707,601
13. 1,305,489
14. B
15. 19 cards
16. 2,280 people
17. 1,920,000 miles
18. 2,252 cars
19. A
20. D

Mixed Word Problems PS4
1. 6 groups
2. 427,656
3. 65,779
4. 696 hours
5. $15
6. 1,280 flies
7. $4,128
8. 310
9. $292
10. 78,134
11. $8
12. 16,784 miles
13. 53
14. B
15. 2,607 people
16. C
17. B
18. B
19. $4,497
20. 55°

Chapter 4
Rounding and Place Values PS1 (87)
1. C

2. Fifty thousand thirty-three
3. Ten thousands
4. Three million, five hundred sixty-four thousand, two hundred sixty-seven
5. B
6. 207,342
7. D
8. A
9. 2,043,603
10. C
11. 50
12. 27,000
13. 3,000
14. 7,000
15. 11,000
16. 101,000
17. 12,000
18. 1,020,000
19. 90,000
20. 3,280,000

Rounding and Place Values PS2
1. C
2. Twenty thousand, two hundred forty-four
3. Tens
4. Four million, one hundred nine thousand, two hundred thirty-four
5. A
6. A
7. A
8. C
9. A
10. C
11. 30
12. 7,090
13. 3,100
14. 38,900
15. 23,000
16. 680,000
17. 100,000
18. 3,020,000
19. 400,000
20. 4,860,000

Basic Number Properties PS1 (89)
1. A
2. D
3. -8, 0, 543
4. -4, 0
5. 2
6. -1, 9, 25
7. A
8. B
9. Multiplies of 5
10. Any 3: 1, 2, 3, 4, 6, 8, 12, 24
11. D
12. D
13. B
14. C
15. D
16. C
17. A
18. B

Basic Number Properties PS2
1. 8, 22, -20, 102
2. 3, 11
3. 13, 7, 101, -23
4. D
5. B
6. 2, 3, 5, 7
7. 2
8. D
9. 23, 29
10. True
11. 16
12. False
13. $2 \times 3 \times 5$
14. B
15. C
16. True
17. False
18. 1, 2, 3, 5, 6, 10, 15, 30
19. 98
20. $2 \times 2 \times 3 \times 3 \times 5$

Number Properties PS1 (91)
1. 8; 0; 2,002; 6; -72
2. 11, 13, 17, 19, 23, 29
3. 9
4. 6
5. 29, 17, 79
6. $2 \times 2 \times 2 \times 2 \times 3$
7. D
8. 23
9. 121
10. 7
11. 2
12. 60
13. 6
14. C
15. 6, 12, 18
16. B
17. 144
18. A
19. D
20. B

Number Properties PS2
1. 16, 0, 36
2. 2, 3, 5, 7, 11, 13, 17, 19, 23, 29, 31, 37
3. 9
4. 84
5. 37, 41, 83, 2
6. $2 \times 2 \times 3 \times 3$
7. B
8. 13
9. 61
10. 7
11. 3
12. 80
13. 16
14. C
15. 20, 40, 60
16. B
17. 288
18. B
19. D
20. A

Number Properties PS3
1. 10
2. D
3. C
4. B
5. 5
6. 3
7. 60
8. $7 \times 2 \times 2 \times 2$
9. 3
10. A
11. B
12. 12
13. 3, 11, 15, -9
14. 4
15. 12
16. A
17. 8
18. 2
19. 5
20. 5, -1

Number Properties PS4
1. 7
2. 5
3. 60
4. $2 \times 3 \times 11$
5. 13
6. A
7. C
8. 8
9. 6, 8, -6, -8
10. 4
11. 11
12. B
13. B
14. B
15. D
16. 10
17. 2
18. 7
19. -2, 4, 0, -6
20. 9

Challenging Number Properties PS1 (95)
1. 195
2. 13
3. C
4. C
5. 30
6. 240 seconds
7. 26
8. D
9. B
10. A
11. B
12. 32
13. C
14. D
15. 18
16. A
17. D
18. A
19. D
20. D

Challenging Number Properties PS2
1. C
2. D
3. C
4. C
5. B
6. A
7. C
8. Bobblehead
9. 12
10. 20
11. 14
12. B
13. A
14. C
15. C
16. 10 am
17. 7 pm
18. D
19. A
20. B

Patterns PS1 (99)
1. C
2. A
3. B
4. B
5. B
6. B
7. C
8. D
9. C
10. A

Patterns PS2
1. B
2. C
3. A
4. D
5. B
6. B
7. A
8. C
9. D
10. C

Patterns PS3
1. D
2. C
3. B
4. B
5. C
6. A
7. C
8. D
9. B
10. C

Patterns PS4
1. D
2. D
3. B
4. C
5. B
6. C
7. D
8. A
9. B
10. A

Chapter 5
Simplifying Fractions PS1 (108)
1. $\frac{1}{2}$
2. $\frac{1}{3}$
3. $\frac{1}{2}$
4. $\frac{1}{4}$
5. $\frac{1}{6}$
6. $\frac{1}{5}$
7. $-\frac{1}{7}$
8. $\frac{1}{10}$
9. $\frac{1}{9}$
10. $\frac{7}{2}$
11. $\frac{3}{2}$
12. $-\frac{7}{2}$
13. $\frac{5}{3}$
14. $\frac{7}{2}$
15. $\frac{2}{3}$
16. $-\frac{11}{12}$
17. $\frac{7}{5}$
18. $\frac{2}{15}$
19. $\frac{8}{5}$
20. $-\frac{9}{13}$

Simplifying Fractions PS2
1. $\frac{1}{2}$
2. $\frac{2}{3}$
3. $\frac{3}{5}$
4. $\frac{1}{2}$
5. $\frac{1}{5}$
6. $\frac{1}{3}$
7. $\frac{1}{8}$
8. $\frac{1}{7}$
9. $\frac{1}{8}$
10. $\frac{1}{9}$
11. $-\frac{3}{2}$
12. $\frac{5}{3}$
13. -3
14. $\frac{7}{3}$
15. $-\frac{13}{8}$
16. $\frac{8}{3}$
17. $-\frac{5}{2}$
18. $-\frac{20}{9}$
19. $\frac{18}{7}$
20. $-\frac{9}{5}$

Simplifying Fractions PS3
1. $\frac{1}{3}$
2. $\frac{1}{4}$
3. $\frac{2}{5}$
4. $\frac{3}{4}$
5. $\frac{1}{5}$
6. $\frac{1}{3}$
7. $\frac{1}{4}$
8. $\frac{1}{6}$
9. $\frac{1}{9}$
10. $\frac{1}{7}$
11. $-\frac{3}{2}$
12. $\frac{13}{3}$

13. −4
14. $\frac{5}{2}$
15. $-\frac{5}{2}$
16. $\frac{17}{6}$
17. $-\frac{9}{2}$
18. $\frac{19}{8}$
19. $-\frac{12}{7}$
20. $\frac{5}{3}$

Simplifying Fractions PS4
1. $\frac{1}{4}$
2. $\frac{4}{5}$
3. $\frac{1}{3}$
4. $\frac{3}{2}$
5. $\frac{1}{3}$
6. $\frac{1}{4}$
7. $\frac{1}{6}$
8. $\frac{7}{1}$
9. $\frac{1}{8}$
10. $\frac{1}{8}$
11. 4
12. $-\frac{11}{2}$
13. $\frac{13}{3}$
14. $-\frac{8}{3}$
15. $\frac{19}{6}$
16. $-\frac{9}{2}$
17. $-\frac{8}{3}$
18. $\frac{7}{3}$
19. $-\frac{3}{2}$
20. $\frac{17}{6}$

Conceptual Fractions PS1 (112)
1. C
2. B
3. D
4. C
5. B
6. B
7. A
8. B
9. A
10. A

Conceptual Fractions PS2
1. $\frac{1}{4}$
2. D
3. D
4. A
5. C
6. $\frac{2}{3}$
7. C
8. $\frac{3}{7}$
9. D
10. A

Mixed Numbers to Improper Fractions PS1 (114)
1. $\frac{5}{4}$
2. $\frac{5}{2}$
3. $\frac{8}{5}$
4. $\frac{13}{8}$
5. $\frac{9}{8}$
6. $\frac{17}{6}$
7. $\frac{29}{8}$
8. $\frac{35}{8}$
9. $\frac{60}{7}$
10. $\frac{101}{10}$
11. $\frac{5}{2}$
12. $\frac{13}{5}$
13. $\frac{24}{7}$
14. $\frac{17}{3}$
15. $\frac{43}{9}$
16. $\frac{9}{2}$
17. $\frac{38}{5}$
18. $\frac{21}{4}$
19. $\frac{26}{3}$
20. $\frac{28}{3}$

Mixed Numbers to Improper Fractions PS2
1. $\frac{4}{3}$
2. $\frac{9}{4}$
3. $\frac{7}{4}$
4. $\frac{13}{8}$
5. $\frac{13}{5}$
6. $\frac{16}{7}$
7. $\frac{23}{6}$
8. $\frac{38}{9}$
9. $\frac{43}{8}$
10. $\frac{50}{7}$
11. $\frac{8}{3}$
12. $\frac{19}{4}$
13. $\frac{10}{3}$
14. $\frac{14}{5}$
15. $\frac{44}{7}$
16. $\frac{28}{5}$
17. $\frac{23}{3}$
18. $\frac{52}{5}$
19. $\frac{42}{5}$
20. $\frac{37}{4}$

Improper Fractions to Mixed Numbers PS1 (116)
1. $1\frac{1}{4}$
2. $1\frac{1}{8}$
3. $2\frac{1}{2}$
4. $1\frac{2}{3}$
5. $3\frac{3}{4}$
6. $5\frac{1}{2}$
7. $8\frac{4}{7}$
8. $9\frac{7}{10}$
9. $10\frac{2}{5}$
10. $8\frac{5}{9}$
11. $2\frac{2}{5}$
12. $1\frac{1}{2}$
13. $2\frac{1}{5}$
14. $2\frac{3}{5}$
15. $4\frac{1}{2}$
16. $5\frac{2}{3}$
17. $10\frac{1}{2}$
18. $10\frac{4}{5}$
19. $9\frac{5}{7}$
20. $4\frac{4}{9}$

Improper Fractions to Mixed Numbers PS2
1. $1\frac{1}{2}$
2. $1\frac{1}{5}$
3. $2\frac{1}{3}$
4. $1\frac{2}{7}$
5. $4\frac{1}{3}$
6. $7\frac{2}{5}$
7. $8\frac{7}{8}$
8. $9\frac{1}{11}$
9. $10\frac{5}{6}$
10. $8\frac{8}{9}$
11. $4\frac{1}{2}$
12. $2\frac{2}{5}$
13. $2\frac{5}{7}$
14. $3\frac{1}{4}$
15. $6\frac{2}{3}$
16. $7\frac{1}{2}$
17. $12\frac{1}{2}$
18. $10\frac{2}{3}$
19. $9\frac{1}{8}$
20. $4\frac{1}{3}$

Addition/Subtraction of Fractions with Common Denominators PS1 (118)
1. $\frac{3}{4}$
2. $\frac{4}{1}$
3. $\frac{4}{5}$
4. $\frac{5}{5}$
5. $\frac{5}{6}$
6. $\frac{1}{5}$
7. $\frac{3}{7}$
8. $\frac{3}{5}$
9. $\frac{7}{8}$
10. $-\frac{1}{2}$
11. $\frac{8}{9}$
12. $\frac{1}{9}$
13. $\frac{7}{10}$
14. $-\frac{3}{5}$
15. $\frac{2}{3}$
16. $\frac{1}{4}$
17. $\frac{4}{3}$
18. $-\frac{1}{4}$
19. $\frac{7}{8}$
20. $\frac{1}{2}$

Addition/Subtraction of Fractions with Common Denominators PS2
1. $\frac{1}{2}$
2. $\frac{3}{2}$
3. $\frac{3}{2}$
4. $\frac{7}{5}$
5. $\frac{7}{2}$
6. $\frac{7}{3}$
7. $\frac{7}{2}$
8. $\frac{7}{3}$
9. $\frac{3}{4}$
10. $\frac{1}{8}$
11. $\frac{1}{2}$
12. $\frac{1}{7}$
13. $\frac{8}{3}$
14. $\frac{8}{5}$
15. $\frac{8}{9}$
16. $-\frac{1}{2}$
17. $\frac{7}{9}$
18. $\frac{4}{9}$
19. $\frac{2}{3}$
20. $-\frac{4}{9}$

Addition/Subtraction of Fractions with Different Denominators PS1 (120)
1. $\frac{3}{4}$
2. $\frac{1}{4}$
3. $\frac{2}{3}$
4. $\frac{1}{8}$
5. $\frac{7}{12}$
6. $\frac{2}{15}$
7. $\frac{9}{10}$
8. $\frac{1}{6}$
9. $\frac{2}{3}$
10. $\frac{3}{10}$

11. $\frac{11}{15}$
12. $\frac{1}{9}$
13. $\frac{4}{5}$
14. $\frac{1}{18}$
15. $\frac{23}{24}$
16. $\frac{13}{72}$
17. 1
18. $\frac{1}{5}$
19. $\frac{7}{8}$
20. $\frac{9}{14}$

Addition/Subtraction of Fractions with Different Denominators PS2

1. $\frac{3}{10}$
2. $\frac{1}{4}$
3. $\frac{5}{8}$
4. $\frac{1}{16}$
5. $\frac{10}{21}$
6. $\frac{1}{3}$
7. $\frac{17}{36}$
8. $\frac{1}{2}$
9. $\frac{23}{24}$
10. $\frac{7}{24}$
11. $\frac{43}{45}$
12. $\frac{1}{2}$
13. $\frac{5}{8}$
14. $\frac{11}{24}$
15. $\frac{19}{21}$
16. $\frac{25}{56}$
17. $\frac{5}{6}$
18. 0
19. $\frac{49}{60}$
20. $\frac{1}{6}$

Addition/Subtraction of Fractions with Different Denominators PS3

1. $\frac{1}{2}$
2. $\frac{3}{8}$
3. $\frac{3}{10}$
4. $\frac{1}{14}$
5. $\frac{7}{10}$
6. $\frac{1}{6}$
7. $\frac{13}{21}$
8. $\frac{3}{8}$
9. $\frac{8}{9}$
10. $\frac{5}{14}$
11. $\frac{5}{6}$
12. $\frac{1}{4}$
13. $\frac{3}{4}$
14. $\frac{5}{12}$
15. $\frac{45}{56}$

16. $\frac{43}{90}$
17. $\frac{1}{30}$
18. $\frac{29}{30}$
19. $\frac{1}{42}$
20. $\frac{4}{45}$

Addition/Subtraction of Fractions with Different Denominators PS4

1. $\frac{3}{8}$
2. $\frac{5}{6}$
3. $\frac{3}{5}$
4. $\frac{1}{18}$
5. $\frac{13}{36}$
6. $\frac{3}{28}$
7. $\frac{13}{15}$
8. $\frac{1}{4}$
9. $\frac{29}{35}$
10. $\frac{8}{45}$
11. $\frac{5}{6}$
12. $\frac{5}{24}$
13. 1
14. $\frac{7}{8}$
15. $\frac{1}{12}$
16. $\frac{15}{16}$
17. $\frac{9}{10}$
18. $\frac{1}{2}$
19. $\frac{47}{48}$
20. $\frac{3}{14}$

Addition/Subtraction of Mixed Numbers PS1 (128)

1. $1\frac{1}{2}$
2. $\frac{1}{2}$
3. $1\frac{1}{4}$
4. $\frac{1}{8}$
5. 3
6. $\frac{3}{5}$
7. $\frac{1}{2}$
8. $1\frac{4}{9}$
9. $4\frac{3}{8}$
10. $1\frac{1}{28}$
11. $2\frac{5}{6}$
12. $\frac{1}{4}$
13. $2\frac{1}{15}$
14. $1\frac{2}{15}$
15. $2\frac{9}{20}$
16. $1\frac{11}{12}$
17. $3\frac{2}{3}$
18. $\frac{1}{10}$
19. $3\frac{1}{2}$
20. $\frac{1}{6}$

Addition/Subtraction of Mixed Numbers PS2

1. $1\frac{1}{9}$
2. $1\frac{1}{10}$
3. $2\frac{1}{8}$
4. $\frac{8}{9}$
5. $2\frac{3}{8}$
6. $\frac{1}{8}$
7. $2\frac{3}{4}$
8. $1\frac{5}{12}$
9. $\frac{11}{15}$
10. $2\frac{1}{10}$
11. $\frac{17}{18}$
12. $2\frac{1}{24}$
13. $\frac{3}{28}$
14. $2\frac{7}{24}$
15. $\frac{2}{15}$
16. $3\frac{1}{6}$
17. $\frac{1}{12}$
18. $\frac{1}{18}$
19. $3\frac{11}{12}$
20. $\frac{5}{14}$

Addition/Subtraction of Mixed Numbers PS3

1. $1\frac{3}{8}$
2. $\frac{3}{4}$
3. $2\frac{1}{3}$
4. $\frac{2}{3}$
5. $2\frac{1}{3}$
6. $\frac{4}{9}$
7. 3
8. $1\frac{4}{15}$
9. $\frac{7}{10}$
10. $1\frac{17}{20}$
11. $\frac{11}{14}$
12. $2\frac{7}{12}$
13. $\frac{1}{15}$
14. $2\frac{19}{28}$
15. $\frac{1}{3}$
16. $3\frac{3}{20}$
17. $\frac{4}{15}$
18. $\frac{1}{28}$
19. $3\frac{19}{20}$
20. $\frac{11}{40}$

Addition/Subtraction of Mixed Numbers PS4

1. $1\frac{3}{10}$
2. $1\frac{3}{8}$
3. $2\frac{1}{6}$
4. $\frac{5}{6}$
5. $2\frac{2}{9}$

6. $\frac{3}{10}$
7. $2\frac{11}{12}$
8. $1\frac{3}{10}$
9. $1\frac{1}{6}$
10. $3\frac{1}{6}$
11. $\frac{17}{24}$
12. $1\frac{17}{35}$
13. $\frac{7}{15}$
14. $2\frac{13}{20}$
15. $\frac{1}{9}$
16. $2\frac{3}{4}$
17. $\frac{1}{24}$
18. $1\frac{33}{40}$
19. $2\frac{13}{15}$
20. $\frac{1}{15}$

Multiplication of Fractions PS1 (136)

1. $\frac{1}{20}$
2. $\frac{1}{54}$
3. $\frac{3}{70}$
4. $\frac{1}{25}$
5. $\frac{1}{12}$
6. $\frac{4}{21}$
7. $\frac{1}{9}$
8. $\frac{18}{35}$
9. $\frac{5}{27}$
10. $\frac{1}{3}$
11. $\frac{3}{10}$
12. $\frac{28}{45}$
13. $\frac{8}{15}$
14. $\frac{15}{28}$
15. $\frac{2}{7}$
16. $-\frac{5}{24}$
17. $\frac{1}{2}$
18. $\frac{1}{4}$
19. $-\frac{5}{18}$
20. $\frac{4}{7}$

Multiplication of Fractions PS2

1. $\frac{1}{28}$
2. $\frac{1}{16}$
3. $\frac{5}{8}$
4. $\frac{1}{18}$
5. $\frac{5}{12}$
6. $\frac{3}{2}$
7. $\frac{7}{8}$
8. $\frac{15}{12}$
9. $\frac{7}{12}$
10. $\frac{5}{27}$
11. $\frac{3}{10}$

12. $\frac{9}{40}$
13. $\frac{10}{21}$
14. $\frac{1}{6}$
15. $\frac{1}{9}$
16. $\frac{5}{12}$
17. $\frac{1}{4}$
18. $-\frac{8}{21}$
19. $-\frac{1}{3}$
20. $\frac{7}{18}$

Multiplication of Mixed/Improper/Whole PS1 (138)
1. $1\frac{1}{3}$
2. 6
3. $3\frac{3}{4}$
4. $3\frac{11}{18}$
5. $4\frac{4}{7}$
6. 8
7. $3\frac{61}{63}$
8. $16\frac{4}{5}$
9. $7\frac{13}{16}$
10. 4
11. $8\frac{1}{3}$
12. $9\frac{3}{8}$
13. $5\frac{5}{9}$
14. 4
15. $4\frac{16}{21}$
16. $4\frac{1}{2}$
17. 9
18. $11\frac{23}{32}$
19. $4\frac{1}{2}$
20. 13

Multiplication of Mixed/Improper/Whole PS2
1. $1\frac{7}{20}$
2. $3\frac{1}{2}$
3. $3\frac{1}{2}$
4. $3\frac{13}{25}$
5. $3\frac{5}{6}$
6. 16
7. $4\frac{1}{5}$
8. $5\frac{5}{6}$
9. $9\frac{4}{5}$
10. $5\frac{1}{7}$
11. $8\frac{5}{8}$
12. $9\frac{7}{9}$
13. $4\frac{11}{20}$
14. $3\frac{1}{3}$
15. $3\frac{23}{35}$
16. $2\frac{16}{25}$
17. 10

18. $12\frac{1}{2}$
19. $4\frac{3}{8}$
20. $19\frac{1}{5}$

Multiplication of Mixed/Improper/Whole PS3
1. $1\frac{1}{3}$
2. $2\frac{6}{7}$
3. $3\frac{1}{5}$
4. $3\frac{1}{2}$
5. $4\frac{1}{2}$
6. 8
7. $4\frac{13}{27}$
8. $4\frac{1}{5}$
9. $10\frac{2}{9}$
10. $4\frac{19}{24}$
11. $10\frac{5}{9}$
12. $7\frac{7}{8}$
13. $6\frac{1}{9}$
14. $4\frac{1}{8}$
15. $5\frac{5}{14}$
16. $2\frac{13}{16}$
17. 8
18. $11\frac{2}{3}$
19. 4
20. $12\frac{3}{4}$

Multiplication of Mixed/Improper/Whole PS4
1. 0
2. $3\frac{2}{5}$
3. $3\frac{1}{9}$
4. $3\frac{1}{8}$
5. 4
6. $7\frac{1}{5}$
7. 3
8. 6
9. $7\frac{5}{16}$
10. $4\frac{23}{24}$
11. $7\frac{1}{3}$
12. $7\frac{14}{25}$
13. $6\frac{7}{8}$
14. $3\frac{1}{40}$
15. $4\frac{4}{21}$
16. $3\frac{1}{9}$
17. $9\frac{3}{5}$
18. $11\frac{1}{5}$
19. $4\frac{1}{2}$
20. $15\frac{2}{3}$

Division of Fractions PS1 (146)
1. $1\frac{1}{2}$
2. $1\frac{2}{5}$

3. $\frac{9}{10}$
4. $1\frac{1}{3}$
5. $\frac{5}{8}$
6. 1
7. $\frac{10}{27}$
8. $\frac{5}{7}$
9. 3
10. $\frac{5}{12}$
11. $\frac{2}{3}$
12. 3
13. $\frac{5}{6}$
14. $1\frac{7}{8}$
15. $1\frac{1}{4}$
16. 1
17. $\frac{2}{25}$
18. $\frac{24}{25}$
19. $\frac{4}{5}$
20. $\frac{1}{2}$

Division of Fractions PS2
1. $1\frac{1}{2}$
2. $1\frac{2}{7}$
3. $\frac{3}{8}$
4. $2\frac{2}{5}$
5. $\frac{3}{7}$
6. $2\frac{1}{4}$
7. $\frac{5}{24}$
8. $1\frac{4}{21}$
9. $1\frac{4}{5}$
10. $1\frac{1}{2}$
11. $\frac{3}{5}$
12. $1\frac{1}{7}$
13. $\frac{7}{8}$
14. $2\frac{2}{5}$
15. $1\frac{5}{16}$
16. $\frac{9}{10}$
17. $2\frac{3}{5}$
18. $\frac{9}{16}$
19.
20. 1

Division of Mixed/Improper/Whole PS1 (148)
1. $6\frac{3}{4}$
2. $5\frac{3}{3}$
3. $1\frac{3}{4}$
4. 12
5. $\frac{4}{21}$
6. $1\frac{1}{9}$
7. $\frac{9}{35}$
8. $\frac{16}{21}$
9. $1\frac{13}{36}$

10. $\frac{81}{86}$
11. $14\frac{2}{5}$
12. $4\frac{9}{10}$
13. $\frac{2}{25}$
14. $\frac{2}{9}$
15. 16
16. 25
17. $6\frac{1}{4}$
18. 14
19. $28\frac{1}{2}$
20. $\frac{1}{49}$

Division of Mixed/Improper/Whole PS2
1. $\frac{1}{18}$
2. $\frac{1}{3}$
3. $4\frac{1}{2}$
4. $\frac{4}{25}$
5. $\frac{7}{30}$
6. $10\frac{2}{3}$
7. $3\frac{3}{7}$
8. $22\frac{1}{2}$
9. 12
10. $\frac{1}{14}$
11. $1\frac{7}{18}$
12. $1\frac{1}{8}$
13. $\frac{52}{55}$
14. $1\frac{1}{2}$
15. $16\frac{13}{14}$
16. $5\frac{1}{2}$
17. $1\frac{9}{14}$
18. 10
19. 12
20. $1\frac{33}{83}$

Division of Mixed/Improper/Whole PS3
1. $2\frac{1}{6}$
2. $3\frac{1}{9}$
3. $1\frac{7}{10}$
4. $1\frac{1}{4}$
5. $\frac{1}{9}$
6. $1\frac{3}{11}$
7. $\frac{3}{4}$
8. $\frac{5}{7}$
9. 1
10. $\frac{25}{72}$
11. $11\frac{1}{9}$
12. $5\frac{1}{3}$
13. $\frac{1}{6}$
14. $\frac{1}{54}$
15. 25
16. 30
17. 9

18. $13\frac{1}{3}$
19. $\frac{1}{81}$
20. 92

Division of Mixed/Improper/Whole PS4
1. $\frac{1}{8}$
2. $\frac{1}{12}$
3. $2\frac{2}{3}$
4. $\frac{3}{16}$
5. $\frac{5}{24}$
6. $7\frac{1}{7}$
7. $2\frac{1}{3}$
8. $18\frac{2}{3}$
9. 10
10. $\frac{1}{14}$
11. $\frac{35}{48}$
12. $1\frac{1}{2}$
13. $\frac{77}{80}$
14. 4
15. $8\frac{1}{2}$
16. 5
17. $1\frac{1}{2}$
18. 4
19. $5\frac{3}{5}$
20. $2\frac{1}{7}$

Comparing Fractions PS1 (156)
1. $\frac{1}{5}$
2. $\frac{3}{10}$
3. $\frac{4}{5}$
4. $\frac{6}{5}$
5. $\frac{7}{10}$
6. $\frac{3}{12}$
7. $\frac{3}{5}$
8. $\frac{5}{3}$
9. $1\frac{7}{8}$
10. $\frac{10}{6}$
11. $\frac{4}{3}$
12. $\frac{11}{5}$
13. $\frac{10}{8}$
14. $\frac{16}{5}$
15. $\frac{11}{9}$
16. $\frac{16}{7}$
17. $\frac{11}{2}$
18. $\frac{20}{6}$
19. $\frac{22}{18}$
20. $\frac{38}{7}$

Comparing Fractions PS2
1. $\frac{1}{4}$
2. $\frac{4}{3}$
3. $\frac{8}{5}$

4. $\frac{8}{9}$
5. $\frac{10}{12}$
6. $\frac{4}{14}$
7. $\frac{1}{7}$
8. $\frac{16}{9}$
9. $1\frac{5}{6}$
10. $\frac{17}{9}$
11. $1\frac{4}{6}$
12. $\frac{15}{8}$
13. $\frac{11}{8}$
14. $\frac{22}{7}$
15. $\frac{11}{8}$
16. $\frac{11}{8}$
17. $\frac{29}{6}$
18. $\frac{26}{7}$
19. $\frac{22}{12}$
20. $\frac{41}{7}$

Comparing Fractions PS3
1. $\frac{1}{7}$
2. $\frac{3}{12}$
3. $\frac{2}{3}$
4. $\frac{7}{8}$
5. $\frac{7}{9}$
6. $\frac{4}{15}$
7. $\frac{4}{3}$
8. $\frac{11}{6}$
9. $1\frac{9}{10}$
10. $\frac{12}{8}$
11. $\frac{7}{4}$
12. $2\frac{5}{6}$
13. $1\frac{1}{4}$
14. $\frac{19}{6}$
15. $\frac{10}{8}$
16. $\frac{9}{5}$
17. $\frac{3}{25}$
18. $\frac{26}{8}$
19. $\frac{14}{9}$
20. $\frac{53}{9}$

Comparing Fractions PS4
1. $\frac{1}{8}$
2. $\frac{3}{14}$
3. $\frac{3}{4}$
4. $\frac{5}{6}$
5. $\frac{5}{6}$
6. $\frac{6}{13}$
7. $\frac{5}{9}$
8. $1\frac{2}{3}$
9. $1\frac{8}{12}$
10. $\frac{13}{7}$

11. $1\frac{5}{9}$
12. $2\frac{7}{8}$
13. $\frac{6}{5}$
14. $\frac{25}{8}$
15. $\frac{6}{5}$
16. $\frac{11}{6}$
17. $\frac{21}{4}$
18. $\frac{27}{7}$
19. $\frac{28}{4}$
20. $\frac{45}{8}$

Ordering Fractions PS1 (160)
1. $\frac{1}{6},\frac{1}{2},\frac{2}{3},\frac{3}{4}$
2. $\frac{5}{8}$
3. $\frac{2}{9},\frac{5}{7},\frac{3}{10}$
4. $\frac{4}{6}$
5. $\frac{1}{3}$
6. C
7. $\frac{3}{10},\frac{2}{5},\frac{6}{8},\frac{8}{9}$
8. $\frac{11}{12}$
9. $\frac{4}{5},\frac{5}{6},\frac{6}{7},\frac{7}{8}$
10. $1\frac{1}{7}$
11. $2,\frac{21}{10},\frac{11}{5},2\frac{1}{4}$
12. $\frac{8}{9}$
13. $\frac{7}{3},\frac{22}{9},2\frac{5}{6},\frac{26}{9}$
14. $2\frac{3}{4}$
15. D
16. $4\frac{1}{3}$
17. $-\frac{23}{6},-\frac{34}{9},-3\frac{5}{8},-\frac{17}{5}$
18. $-\frac{17}{4}$
19. $5\frac{2}{9},\frac{43}{8},\frac{34}{6},5\frac{6}{7}$
20. $\frac{77}{10}$

Ordering Fractions PS2
1. $\frac{1}{4},\frac{1}{3},\frac{2}{5},\frac{1}{2}$
2. A
3. $\frac{4}{6}$
4. $\frac{1}{1}$
5. $\frac{2}{8},\frac{2}{6},\frac{3}{5},\frac{3}{4}$
6. $\frac{3}{9}$
7. $\frac{1}{5},\frac{2}{9},\frac{3}{8},\frac{1}{2}$
8. $\frac{1}{3}$
9. $\frac{3}{7},\frac{4}{8},\frac{3}{5},\frac{4}{6}$
10. $\frac{6}{5}$
11. $2,2\frac{1}{6},\frac{17}{9},\frac{11}{4}$
12. $-1\frac{2}{12}$
13. B
14. $2\frac{1}{9},\frac{18}{8},\frac{16}{6},2\frac{4}{5}$
15. $-\frac{11}{3},-3\frac{3}{5},-3\frac{2}{4},-\frac{19}{6}$
16. $4\frac{1}{4}$
17. $\frac{28}{9}$
18. $\frac{34}{8}$

19. $\frac{23}{4},5\frac{8}{10},\frac{35}{6},5\frac{7}{8}$
20. $7\frac{3}{8}$

Ordering Fractions PS3
1. $\frac{2}{5},\frac{3}{6},\frac{5}{7},\frac{3}{4}$
2. $\frac{5}{6}$
3. $\frac{3}{10},\frac{4}{8},\frac{6}{9},\frac{4}{5}$
4. $\frac{2}{2}$
5. $\frac{2}{6},\frac{4}{7},\frac{6}{8},\frac{4}{5}$
6. $\frac{4}{10}$
7. $\frac{2}{7},\frac{1}{3},\frac{3}{6},\frac{3}{4}$
8. $\frac{4}{9}$
9. A
10. $\frac{5}{4}$
11. $\frac{17}{9},2,2\frac{2}{8},\frac{14}{5}$
12. $1\frac{4}{10}$
13. C
14. $\frac{16}{6}$
15. $\frac{22}{7},3\frac{1}{5},\frac{13}{4},3\frac{5}{6}$
16. $4\frac{3}{8}$
17. $-\frac{15}{4},-3\frac{7}{10},-\frac{11}{3},-\frac{18}{5}$
18. $\frac{24}{6}$
19. $5\frac{3}{9},\frac{27}{5},\frac{38}{7},5\frac{2}{3}$
20. $-\frac{30}{4}$

Ordering Fractions PS4
1. $\frac{2}{6},\frac{1}{2},\frac{3}{5},\frac{3}{4}$
2. $\frac{1}{6}$
3. $\frac{1}{3},\frac{5}{9},\frac{3}{4},\frac{5}{6}$
4. $\frac{6}{8}$
5. C
6. $\frac{2}{6}$
7. $\frac{4}{10},\frac{2}{4},\frac{6}{8},\frac{7}{9}$
8. $\frac{9}{12}$
9. $\frac{4}{10},\frac{3}{7},\frac{5}{8},\frac{6}{9}$
10. $1\frac{1}{9}$
11. $\frac{14}{8},\frac{11}{6},2,\frac{19}{9}$
12. $\frac{11}{11}$
13. $\frac{13}{12},1\frac{4}{12},\frac{17}{8},\frac{13}{6}$
14. $2\frac{3}{5}$
15. C
16. $4\frac{3}{4}$
17. $\frac{10}{8},\frac{27}{5},\frac{17}{5},3\frac{3}{6}$
18. $4\frac{1}{7}$
19. $-5\frac{3}{8}$
20. $7\frac{4}{8},7\frac{6}{10},\frac{23}{3},\frac{39}{5}$

Fraction Applications PS1 (168)
1. B
2. D
3. A
4. $\frac{27}{20}$
5. C

6. $\frac{16}{35}$
7. A
8. C
9. $\frac{4}{3}$
10. $3\frac{23}{30}$ hours
11. D
12. $\frac{2}{21}$
13. B
14. A
15. A
16. C
17. 60 girls
18. D
19. B
20. C

Fraction Applications PS2
1. A
2. C
3. B
4. A
5. $1\frac{1}{7}$
6. C
7. $1\frac{1}{8}$
8. $\frac{9}{40}$
9. B
10. A
11. $1\frac{3}{26}$
12. $3\frac{17}{36}$ hours
13. B
14. B
15. 50 pretzels
16. B
17. C
18. A
19. B
20. D

Fraction Applications PS3
1. D
2. C
3. D
4. B
5. $1\frac{3}{4}$
6. $\frac{3}{20}$
7. $\frac{4}{5}$
8. B
9. C
10. C
11. $\frac{3}{32}$
12. $3\frac{23}{24}$ liters
13. A
14. 75 networks
15. C
16. C
17. D
18. B
19. B
20. A

Fraction Applications PS4
1. A
2. $1\frac{1}{6}$
3. B
4. D

5. C
6. B
7. $1\frac{5}{21}$
8. $\frac{8}{15}$
9. D
10. $\frac{8}{45}$
11. C
12. D
13. 105 widgets
14. $4\frac{4}{15}$ gallons
15. D
16. C
17. D
18. D
19. C
20. D

Chapter 6
Rounding Decimals PS1
(181)
1. 1.9
2. 12
3. 15.83
4. Tenths
5. 1.3659
6. 0.1
7. 3
8. Thousandths
9. 17
10. Hundredths
11. 6
12. 19.0
13. 0.010
14. 130.0
15. 1
16. Tens
17. Hundred thousandths
18. 100.897
19. 300.0
20. 0.9000

Rounding Decimals PS2
1. 0.3
2. 18.28
3. Ten thousandths
4. 122.5687
5. Ones/units
6. 0.1
7. 129
8. Thousandths
9. 0.1008
10. 18.0
11. 5,892.090
12. Hundredths
13. 30
14. 0.868
15. 0.1010
16. 60.80
17. 0
18. Tenths
19. 22.900
20. 300.0000

Addition of Decimals PS1
(183)
1. 6.8
2. 9.5
3. 21.3

4. 4.38
5. 24.23
6. 70.79
7. 9.307
8. 112.174
9. 49.172
10. 14.55
11. 116.61
12. 172.12
13. 91.668
14. 162.169
15. 849.231
16. 16.027
17. 78.169
18. 91.755
19. 211.808
20. 157.077

Addition of Decimals PS2
1. 6.5
2. 6.9
3. 20.1
4. 6.17
5. 25.14
6. 90.97
7. 8.482
8. 125.145
9. 40.137
10. 21.39
11. 115.65
12. 198.28
13. 88.448
14. 152.131
15. 831.163
16. 17.105
17. 68.612
18. 87.788
19. 201.904
20. 180.119

Subtraction of Decimals PS1
(185)
1. 3.3
2. 3.8
3. 26.7
4. 4.53
5. 5.37
6. 18.43
7. 0.81
8. 12.79
9. 0.45
10. 22.03
11. 13.417
12. 0.995
13. 3.482
14. -1.408
15. 6.983
16. 2.431
17. -0.783
18. 10.666
19. -13.545
20. 102.956

Subtraction of Decimals PS2
1. 3.8
2. 5.7
3. 48.6
4. 5.69
5. 8.88
6. 13.34
7. 0.85

8. 20.68
9. 0.29
10. 11.58
11. 13.776
12. 0.9
13. -8.912
14. 1.416
15. -4.981
16. 3.227
17. -0.345
18. 12.477
19. 14.449
20. -109.956

Subtraction of Decimals PS3
1. 4.8
2. 5.7
3. 26.9
4. 6.68
5. 6.53
6. 16.56
7. 0.66
8. 20.27
9. 0.69
10. 21.72
11. 10.885
12. 0.4
13. -4.464
14. 1.834
15. 6.989
16. -3.269
17. 0.176
18. -23.189
19. 13.446
20. -101.975

Subtraction of Decimals PS4
1. 3.8
2. 4.9
3. 11.8
4. 5.84
5. 7.65
6. 23.33
7. 0.85
8. 18.68
9. 0.57
10. 21.89
11. 12.868
12. 1.5
13. 3.646
14. -1.702
15. 8.982
16. 3.414
17. -0.539
18. 10.378
19. 5.496
20. -105.978

Multiplication of Decimals
PS1 (189)
1. 1.6
2. 0.42
3. 0.012
4. 6.75
5. 2.04
6. 0.192
7. 0.0224
8. 1.425
9. 10.989
10. 95.343
11. 0.0786

12. 0.000192
13. 5.9675
14. 23.005
15. 25.5
16. 116.688
17. 6.776
18. 0.375
19. 194.5736
20. 50.7791

Multiplication of Decimals PS2
1. 2.8
2. 0.45
3. 0.016
4. 10
5. 2.4
6. 0.318
7. 0.0328
8. 2.205
9. 14.652
10. 74.976
11. 0.1817
12. 0.000164
13. 6.7525
14. 4.399
15. 23.4
16. 115.814
17. 3.63
18. 1.0125
19. 225.2906
20. 42.5638

Multiplication of Decimals PS3
1. 1.8
2. 0.12
3. 0.054
4. 11.9
5. 2.66
6. 0.246
7. 0.0335
8. 0.975
9. 12.21
10. 113.197
11. 0.13875
12. 0.000222
13. 5.9125
14. 45.59
15. 30.15
16. 125.856
17. 1.815
18. 0.4375
19. 227.4702
20. 43.4076

Multiplication of Decimals PS4
1. 5
2. 0.64
3. 0.021
4. 6.6
5. 2.34
6. 0.252
7. 0.0216
8. 1.365
9. 29.304
10. 120.486
11. 0.1023
12. 0.000057
13. 5.805
14. 40.02
15. 24.08

16. 107.271
17. 6.534
18. 0.7875
19. 210.1344
20. 59.027

Division of Decimals PS1 (197)
1. 3
2. 3
3. 5
4. 3.8
5. 0.8
6. 2.1
7. 8
8. 18.75
9. 80
10. 0.8064
11. 0.112
12. 4.05
13. 7.7
14. 32
15. 20.72
16. 1.21
17. 8.16
18. 21.2
19. 17.5
20. 0.0084

Division of Decimals PS2
1. 0.4
2. 2
3. 3
4. 7
5. 2.7
6. 4.9
7. 40
8. 3.75
9. 40
10. 0.4156
11. 0.114
12. 1.775
13. 4.9
14. 50
15. 21.63
16. 2.13
17. 6.13
18. 22.7
19. 20.5
20. 0.005125

Division of Decimals PS3
1. 0.75
2. 1.2
3. 5
4. 4
5. 1.55
6. 4.3
7. 24
8. 8.125
9. 50
10. 0.6042
11. 0.164
12. 3.27
13. 6.6
14. 44
15. 15.83
16. 1.36
17. 12.73
18. 28.3
19. 22.5
20. 0.0065

Division of Decimals PS4
1. 0.6
2. 2
3. 3
4. 6
5. 3.1
6. 2.6
7. 16
8. 10.5
9. 90
10. 0.5043
11. 0.122
12. 4.72
13. 5.5
14. 42.5
15. 18.62
16. 1.89
17. 9.49
18. 13.4
19. 16.25
20. 0.0076

Decimal Word Problems PS1 (205)
1. B
2. $3,070.07
3. C
4. $1.84
5. B
6. D
7. A
8. $9.12
9. $3.85
10. D
11. 0.8
12. C
13. 221.3 lbs
14. A
15. −5.9°C
16. C
17. 0.27
18. B
19. $33
20. $148.85

Decimal Word Problems PS2
1. B
2. 17.38
3. $1.50
4. A
5. D
6. 22.3
7. D
8. B
9. D
10. $209.92
11. D
12. D
13. 4.88
14. B
15. 79 cakes
16. B
17. 13 days
18. 14 cars
19. 52.59 lbs
20. C

Decimal Word Problems PS3
1. C
2. 1.3
3. 210 apples
4. C
5. $16.05

6. B
7. $33.39
8. D
9. B
10. B
11. 15 miles
12. A
13. 0.25 minutes
14. B
15. D
16. C
17. $48.32
18. B
19. $1,105.48
20. $2,772.48

Decimal Word Problems PS4
1. B
2. A
3. 3.75
4. $50.82
5. 50.4 pages
6. $93.47
7. B
8. $1.65
9. C
10. 9.25 lbs
11. D
12. 2.25 inches
13. $1.96
14. B
15. $408.37
16. $9.68
17. D
18. $220.57
19. A
20. B

Chapter 7
Decimals to Fractions PS1 (218)
1. $\frac{1}{10}$
2. $\frac{1}{5}$
3. $\frac{1}{2}$
4. $\frac{4}{5}$
5. $1\frac{1}{4}$
6. $\frac{3}{100}$
7. $\frac{3}{50}$
8. $\frac{9}{100}$
9. $1\frac{11}{50}$
10. $\frac{8}{25}$
11. $\frac{1}{100}$
12. $\frac{3}{4}$
13. $\frac{1}{40}$
14. $\frac{7}{100}$
15. $\frac{19}{25}$
16. $12\frac{1}{2}$
17. $1\frac{21}{50}$
18. $4\frac{2}{25}$
19. $2\frac{1}{250}$
20. $\frac{11}{125}$

Decimals to Fractions PS2

1. $\frac{3}{10}$
2. $\frac{7}{10}$
3. $\frac{3}{25}$
4. $\frac{1}{50}$
5. $\frac{1}{20}$
6. $\frac{9}{20}$
7. $\frac{6}{25}$
8. $\frac{11}{50}$
9. $\frac{19}{50}$
10. $\frac{11}{20}$
11. $\frac{19}{25}$
12. $\frac{21}{25}$
13. $1\frac{13}{50}$
14. $\frac{3}{40}$
15. $\frac{9}{100}$
16. $20\frac{1}{2}$
17. $1\frac{17}{25}$
18. $4\frac{7}{100}$
19. $4\frac{1}{500}$
20. $\frac{11}{250}$

Fractions to Decimals PS1 (220)

1. 0.5
2. 0.25
3. $0.\overline{3}$
4. 0.2
5. 0.3
6. 0.4
7. 1.125
8. 2.6
9. 0.875
10. 1.8
11. 0.15
12. $0.\overline{6}$
13. 4.75
14. 0.95
15. 0.22
16. 6.3
17. 3.75
18. 1.68
19. 3.35
20. 5.3

Fractions to Decimals PS2

1. $0.\overline{6}$
2. $0.1\overline{6}$
3. 0.8
4. 0.75
5. 0.7
6. 0.625
7. $1.1\overline{6}$
8. 2.75
9. 1.375
10. 7.5
11. 0.2
12. 0.08
13. 0.75
14. 0.96
15. 0.34

16. 8.25
17. 2.375
18. 1.84
19. 3.7
20. 4.6

Decimals to Percents PS1 (224)

1. 10%
2. 50%
3. 40%
4. 70%
5. 3%
6. 8%
7. 25%
8. 0.6%
9. 0.08%
10. 10.5%
11. 78%
12. 8.6%
13. 2.2%
14. 186%
15. 205%
16. 907%
17. 300.2%
18. 2,230%
19. 1,788%
20. 2,000.5%

Decimals to Percents PS2

1. 20%
2. 80%
3. 70%
4. 1%
5. 4%
6. 13%
7. 22%
8. 0.5%
9. 0.06%
10. 11.2%
11. 64%
12. 7.7%
13. 4.5%
14. 124%
15. 209%
16. 888%
17. 400.3%
18. 2,150%
19. 1,579%
20. 3,000.3%

Percents to Decimals PS1 (226)

1. 0.2
2. 0.55
3. 0.04
4. 0.34
5. 0.09
6. 0.105
7. 0.972
8. 1.2
9. 2.14
10. 0.205
11. 0.0575
12. 1.228
13. $0.\overline{3}$
14. 0.005
15. 0.0006
16. 0.0107
17. $0.\overline{6}$

18. 0.7723
19. 0.0862
20. 0.00285

Percents to Decimals PS2

1. 0.1
2. 0.35
3. 0.03
4. 0.08
5. 0.26
6. 0.205
7. 0.245
8. 1.4
9. 2.41
10. 0.2525
11. $0.04\overline{6}$
12. 1.434
13. $0.8\overline{3}$
14. 0.008
15. 0.0005
16. 0.0606
17. 0.08375
18. 0.4178
19. 0.0593
20. 0.00123

Fractions to Percents PS1 (228)

1. 50%
2. 25%
3. 12.5%
4. $33\frac{1}{3}$%
5. 37.5%
6. 60%
7. 90%
8. 120%
9. 150%
10. 210%
11. $66\frac{2}{3}$%
12. 14%
13. 105%
14. 2.2%
15. 315%
16. 6%
17. 1.75%
18. 250%
19. $283\frac{1}{3}$%
20. 375%

Fractions to Percents PS2

1. 20%
2. $66\frac{2}{3}$%
3. 80%
4. 70%
5. 75%
6. 25%
7. $66\frac{2}{3}$%
8. 112.5%
9. $133\frac{1}{3}$%
10. 220%
11. $366\frac{2}{3}$%
12. 287.5%
13. 32%
14. 102%
15. 3.5%
16. 435%

17. 2.2%
18. 6.8%
19. 6.4%
20. 23.5%

Percents to Fractions PS1 (232)

1. $\frac{1}{5}$
2. $\frac{3}{5}$
3. $\frac{3}{4}$
4. $\frac{1}{20}$
5. $\frac{9}{100}$
6. $\frac{6}{5}$
7. $\frac{41}{200}$
8. $\frac{7}{200}$
9. $\frac{1}{3}$
10. $\frac{1}{125}$
11. $\frac{7}{1,000}$
12. $\frac{67}{5,000}$
13. $\frac{9}{4}$
14. $\frac{2}{3}$
15. $\frac{3}{2,500}$
16. $\frac{1}{400}$
17. $\frac{1}{40}$
18. $\frac{217}{800}$
19. $\frac{8}{125}$
20. $\frac{33}{400}$

Percents to Fractions PS2

1. $\frac{3}{10}$
2. $\frac{4}{5}$
3. $\frac{3}{4}$
4. $\frac{7}{100}$
5. $\frac{1}{50}$
6. $1\frac{2}{5}$
7. $\frac{13}{200}$
8. $\frac{2}{3}$
9. $\frac{1}{250}$
10. $\frac{9}{1,000}$
11. $\frac{27}{250}$
12. $2\frac{3}{4}$
13. $\frac{5}{9}$
14. $\frac{1}{625}$
15. $\frac{1}{200}$
16. $\frac{41}{2,500}$
17. $\frac{21}{400}$
18. $\frac{29}{500}$
19. $\frac{23}{160}$
20. $\frac{271}{400}$

	Fraction	Decimal	Percent
	$\frac{1}{4}$	0.25	25%
	$\frac{3}{5}$	0.6	60%
	$\frac{1}{5}$	0.2	20%
	$\frac{7}{10}$	0.7	70%
	$\frac{4}{5}$	0.8	80%
	$\frac{9}{20}$	0.45	45%
	$1\frac{2}{5}$	1.4	140%
	$\frac{19}{6}$	3.17	$316\frac{2}{3}\%$
	$\frac{1}{20}$	0.05	5%
	$\frac{1}{100}$	0.01	1%
	$\frac{12}{12}$	1	100%
	$\frac{21}{3}$	7	700%
	2	2	200%
	$2\frac{2}{25}$	2.08	208%
	$1\frac{3}{20}$	1.15	115%
$25 \div 4$	$6\frac{1}{4}$	6.25	625%
$14 \div 42$	$\frac{1}{3}$	0.33	$33\frac{1}{3}\%$
$104 \div 12$	$8\frac{2}{3}$	8.67	$866\frac{2}{3}\%$
$8 \div 36$	$\frac{2}{9}$	0.22	22.22%
$74 \div 7$	$10\frac{4}{7}$	10.57	1,057.14%

	Fraction	Decimal	Percent
	$\frac{2}{5}$	0.4	40%
	$\frac{1}{8}$	0.125	12.5%
	$\frac{3}{10}$	0.3	30%
	$\frac{3}{4}$	0.75	75%
	$\frac{9}{10}$	0.9	90%
	$\frac{17}{20}$	0.85	85%
	$1\frac{4}{5}$	1.8	180%
	$\frac{14}{3}$	4.67	$466\frac{2}{3}\%$
	$\frac{7}{100}$	0.07	7%
	$\frac{3}{100}$	0.03	3%
	$\frac{0}{11}$	0	0%
	$\frac{20}{5}$	4	400%
	1	1	100%
	$3\frac{18}{25}$	3.72	372%
	$2\frac{7}{20}$	2.35	235%
$27 \div 8$	$3\frac{3}{8}$	3.375	337.5%
$22 \div 3$	$\frac{2}{3}$	0.67	$66\frac{2}{3}\%$
$50 \div 6$	$8\frac{1}{3}$	8.33	$833\frac{1}{3}\%$
$35 \div 42$	$\frac{5}{6}$	.83	$83\frac{1}{3}\%$
$43 \div 9$	$4\frac{7}{9}$	4.78	477.78%

Conversion Chart PS3

	Fraction	Decimal	Percent
	$\frac{1}{4}$	**0.25**	**25%**
	$\frac{3}{5}$	0.6	**60%**
	$\frac{3}{25}$	**0.12**	12%
	$\frac{4}{5}$	0.8	**80%**
	$\frac{5}{8}$	**0.625**	**62.5%**
	$\frac{2}{25}$	**0.08**	8%
	$\frac{11}{40}$	0.275	**27.5%**
	$\frac{1}{3}$	**0.333**	$33\frac{1}{3}\%$
	$2\frac{1}{2}$	2.5	250%
	$\frac{9}{40}$	**0.225**	22.5%
	$\frac{17}{20}$	0.85	**85%**
	$1\frac{1}{5}$	**1.2**	120%
	$\frac{7}{2}$	3.5	350%
	$\frac{1}{50}$	0.02	2%
	$\frac{7}{4}$	1.75	175%
18 ÷ 4	$4\frac{1}{2}$	4.5	450%
34 ÷ 5	$6\frac{4}{5}$	6.8	680%
18 ÷ 24	$\frac{3}{4}$	0.75	75%
78 ÷ 60	$1\frac{3}{10}$	1.3	130%
9 ÷ 27	$\frac{1}{3}$	0.33	$33\frac{1}{3}\%$

Conversion Chart PS4

	Fraction	Decimal	Percent
	$\frac{3}{50}$	0.06	**6%**
	$\frac{1}{50}$	**0.02**	2%
	$\frac{13}{20}$	0.65	**65%**
	$\frac{4}{5}$	**0.8**	**80%**
	$\frac{9}{20}$	0.45	45%
	$\frac{1}{20}$	**0.05**	**5%**
	$1\frac{3}{5}$	1.6	**160%**
	$\frac{3}{8}$	0.375	**37.5%**
	$\frac{17}{200}$	0.085	8.5%
	$2\frac{4}{5}$	2.8	**280%**
	$\frac{3}{2,000}$	**0.0015**	0.15%
	$\frac{2}{3}$	0.67	$66\frac{2}{3}\%$
	$\frac{9}{500}$	0.018	**1.8%**
	$\frac{9}{4}$	**2.25**	**225%**
	$\frac{7}{8}$	0.875	87.5%
6 ÷ 5	$1\frac{1}{5}$	**1.2**	**120%**
26 ÷ 4	$6\frac{1}{2}$	**6.5**	**650%**
36 ÷ 48	$\frac{3}{4}$	0.75	**75%**
101 ÷ 10	$10\frac{1}{10}$	**10.1**	**1,010%**
49 ÷ 8	$6\frac{1}{8}$	**6.125**	**612.5%**

Chapter 8

Percentages PS1 (241)
1. 15 apples
2. 75 cars
3. 25%
4. 20%
5. 150
6. 5%
7. 108 people
8. 12.5%
9. 4.8
10. A
11. 400%
12. C
13. 15%
14. D
15. 82.5
16. B
17. A
18. 150%
19. 3,200
20. D

Percentages PS2
1. 16 dolls
2. $60
3. 20%
4. 25%
5. 50 crows
6. 4%
7. 152 trees
8. 12.5%
9. 18
10. B
11. 500%
12. B
13. 14%
14. D
15. 31.25
16. C
17. A
18. 300%
19. 1,600 airplanes
20. B

Percentages PS3
1. 27 ft
2. 35 golf balls
3. 37.5%
4. 25%
5. 75
6. 5%
7. 112 people
8. 16.67%
9. 43 oranges
10. B
11. 350%
12. B
13. 23%
14. D
15. 27.5
16. A
17. A
18. 500%
19. 2,500
20. C

Percentages PS4
1. 18 books
2. $48
3. 75%
4. 40%
5. 330 pencils
6. 5%
7. 144
8. 11.2%
9. 21
10. C
11. 275%
12. B
13. 18%
14. C
15. 25.4
16. B
17. A
18. 450%
19. 4,000 km
20. B

Percent Word Problems PS1 (245)
1. 25%
2. 22.5%
3. 24
4. 95
5. 25%
6. $12,720
7. 30.4
8. C
9. $247.5
10. A
11. D
12. $2,235
13. $1,062,500
14. B
15. C
16. A
17. $132,000
18. $7,920
19. B
20. C

Percent Word Problems PS2
1. 25%
2. 15%
3. $150
4. 279
5. 62.5%
6. $18,200
7. 31
8. B
9. $256
10. D
11. C
12. $1,264
13. 112.5 million jobs
14. C
15. D
16. B
17. $456,000
18. $2,750
19. C
20. C

Percent Word Problems PS3
1. 40%
2. 20%
3. $66\frac{2}{3}$%
4. 30%
5. 60
6. 73
7. 25%
8. $20,340
9. 48
10. D
11. $494.91
12. D
13. C
14. $2,530
15. 112.5 million jobs
16. B
17. C
18. A
19. $4,500
20. $4,347

Percent Word Problems PS4
1. 25%
2. 30%
3. 37.5%
4. 8%
5. 85
6. 89
7. 5%
8. $12,200
9. 41
10. C
11. $707.75
12. B
13. C
14. $3,400
15. 144 minutes
16. C
17. C
18. D
19. $5,400
20. $9,680

Comparing Fractions, Decimals, & Percents PS1 (253)
1. 27%
2. 1.18
3. $\frac{1}{3}$

4. 281%
5. 8.821
6. $\frac{3}{7}$
7. $\frac{2}{9}$
8. $29\%, 0.37, \frac{2}{5}, \frac{1}{2}$
9. $\frac{2}{8}, 31\%, \frac{1}{3}, 0.35$
10. $1.605, 165\%, \frac{5}{3}, \frac{9}{5}$
11. 2.604, 2.619, 2.64, 2.651
12. $0.357, 36\%, \frac{4}{11}, \frac{3}{8}$
13. 8.088, 819%, 8.3, 8.42
14. 6.012, 6.021, 6.102, 6.201
15. $0.209, 27\%, \frac{2}{7}, 29\%$
16. -3.360, -3.306, -3.063, -3.036
17. C
18. A
19. B
20. D

Comparing Fractions, Decimals, & Percents PS2
1. 85%
2. 3.39
3. $\frac{2}{3}$
4. 4.37
5. 7.485
6. $\frac{5}{8}$
7. 32%
8. $\frac{73}{8}$
9. $\frac{1}{8}, 13\%, 0.22, \frac{2}{9}$
10. $35\%, \frac{3}{8}, 0.44 \frac{3}{7}$
11. $1.41, \frac{10}{7}, 144\%, \frac{12}{8}$
12. 4.906, 493.1%, 496.1%, 4.963
13. $0.419, \frac{3}{7}, 49\%, \frac{5}{9}$
14. 6.116, 6.161, 6.616, 6.661
15. $\frac{21}{4}, 525.2\%, 5.282, \frac{37}{7}$
16. 75.557, 75.575, 75.757, 75.775
17. C
18. D
19. C
20. B

Comparing Fractions, Decimals, & Percents PS3
1. 0.34
2. 2.26
3. $\frac{1}{6}$
4. 3.94
5. 696.3%
6. $\frac{1}{7}$
7. $\frac{7}{9}$
8. $\frac{82}{9}$
9. $0.14, \frac{1}{6}, \frac{2}{10}, 21\%$
10. $\frac{1}{4}, 26\%, 0.33, \frac{1}{3}$
11. $\frac{12}{7}, 1.74, \frac{7}{4}, 177\%$
12. 3.505, 3.510, 3.525, 3.55
13. $\frac{5}{6}, 0.834, 91.5\%, \frac{11}{12}$

14. 9.011, 9.101, 9.110, 9.111
15. $862\% \frac{69}{8}, \frac{78}{9}, 8.67$
16. 10.001, 10.011, 10.101, 10.110
17. C
18. A
19. B
20. C

Comparing Fractions, Decimals, & Percents PS4
1. 67%
2. 4.46
3. $\frac{2}{9}$
4. 516%
5. 8.764
6. $\frac{5}{6}$
7. $\frac{7}{8}$
8. 915.2%
9. $19\%, \frac{1}{5}, \frac{2}{7}, 0.29$
10. $0.46, 49\%, \frac{4}{7}, \frac{3}{5}$
11. $\frac{10}{9}, 1.113, \frac{7}{6}, 116.9\%$
12. 5.201, 5.202, 5.212, 5.221
13. $30.9\%, 0.39, \frac{2}{5}, \frac{4}{9}$
14. 7.045, 7.054, 7.405, 7.504
15. $\frac{68}{9}, 755.6\%, 7.566, \frac{53}{7}$
16. 96.696, 96.699, 96.969, 96.996
17. B
18. C
19. D
20. D

Chapter 9
Basic Exponents PS1 (262)
1. 25
2. 225
3. 529
4. 64
5. 32
6. 45
7. 512
8. 49
9. -49
10. -125
11. 81
12. -8
13. 73
14. 17
15. -4
16. 144
17. 108
18. 25
19. 288
20. 400

Basic Exponents PS2
1. -1
2. 196
3. 343
4. 1,296
5. 1,000
6. 1
7. D
8. -1,331
9. -144

10. 100
11. -162
12. $-\frac{8}{27}$
13. 152
14. 40
15. $-\frac{11}{25}$
16. False
17. 135
18. 2,916
19. 27
20. 27

Basic Roots PS1 (264)
1. 7
2. 3
3. 1
4. 8
5. 11
6. 15
7. 13
8. 20
9. 30
10. 0
11. C
12. B
13. B
14. B
15. B
16. B
17. A
18. C
19. A
20. C

Basic Roots PS2
1. 0
2. 6
3. 4
4. 9
5. 15
6. 14
7. 12
8. 10
9. 25
10. B
11. C
12. 24
13. 25
14. C
15. False
16. 3
17. C
18. D
19. C
20. C

Challenging Exponents PS1 (266)
1. 1
2. $\frac{1}{125}$
3. $\frac{4}{9}$
4. 3,470
5. 12
6. C
7. 0.0018
8. B
9. C
10. C
11. A
12. C

13. C
14. 0
15. 48
16. 10
17. D
18. 2,740
19. 108
20. $-\frac{13}{3}$

Challenging Exponents PS2
1. 64
2. 343
3. 5.6
4. 128
5. C
6. 5,810,000
7. 0.0000072
8. C
9. C
10. C
11. D
12. D
13. B
14. 49
15. 96
16. 64
17. B
18. 30,140
19. $\frac{2}{75}$
20. 5,488

Challenging Exponents PS3
1. 1
2. 64
3. 162
4. C
5. C
6. 2
7. $\frac{8}{125}$
8. 0.000074
9. D
10. A
11. 625
12. A
13. C
14. 0
15. -512
16. 0.005
17. A
18. $32\frac{2}{5}$
19. 48,290
20. 1,024

Challenging Exponents PS4
1. $\frac{1}{625}$
2. 729
3. 100,000
4. 25,300
5. $\frac{3}{2}$
6. 0.00038
7. D
8. B
9. B
10. A
11. D
12. B
13. D

14. $\frac{3}{16}$
15. 0
16. $\frac{4}{25}$
17. 6,310
18. 256
19. A
20. 1

Challenging Roots PS1 (274)
1. $2\sqrt{3}$
2. $4\sqrt{2}$
3. $3\sqrt{3}$
4. $15\sqrt{7}$
5. $4\sqrt{5}$
6. $-2\sqrt{6}$
7. $2\sqrt{5}$
8. $11\sqrt{2} - 2\sqrt{3}$
9. $\sqrt{6} - 2\sqrt{7}$
10. $5\sqrt{13} - 7\sqrt{23}$
11. 5
12. $7\sqrt{7}$
13. 4
14. 300
15. C
16. $12\sqrt{3} - 12\sqrt{6}$
17. $2\sqrt{33}$
18. 36
19. C
20. 360

Challenging Roots PS2
1. $2\sqrt{7}$
2. $3\sqrt{11}$
3. $2\sqrt{6}$
4. $19\sqrt{3}$
5. $6\sqrt{5}$
6. $-15\sqrt{15}$
7. $-12\sqrt{6}$
8. $-2\sqrt{2} - 2\sqrt{3}$
9. $28\sqrt{11} - 34\sqrt{10}$
10. $7\sqrt{13} - 23\sqrt{17}$
11. 9
12. $7\sqrt{2}$
13. $\sqrt{21}$
14. $12\sqrt{15}$
15. B
16. 3
17. $5\sqrt{2} - 6\sqrt{7}$
18. $\frac{3}{2}$
19. 16
20. 24

Challenging Roots PS3
1. $2\sqrt{5}$
2. $6\sqrt{7}$
3. $3\sqrt{11}$
4. $6\sqrt{13}$
5. $4\sqrt{7}$
6. $-4\sqrt{22}$
7. $-7\sqrt{15}$
8. $6\sqrt{17} - 3\sqrt{6}$
9. $6\sqrt{5} + 3\sqrt{3}$
10. $-16\sqrt{19} - 13\sqrt{43}$
11. 16

12. $\sqrt{42}$
13. B
14. $6 - 4\sqrt{3}$
15. $15\sqrt{6}$
16. $10\sqrt{11} - 12\sqrt{17}$
17. 264
18. $\frac{5}{3}$
19. C
20. $\sqrt{93}$

Challenging Roots PS4
1. 6
2. $5\sqrt{14}$
3. $3\sqrt{11}$
4. $6\sqrt{22}$
5. $3\sqrt{19}$
6. $-16\sqrt{5}$
7. $5\sqrt{17}$
8. $19\sqrt{3} - 17\sqrt{7}$
9. $-9\sqrt{11} - 21\sqrt{22}$
10. $-9\sqrt{13} + 2\sqrt{31}$
11. $4\sqrt{2}$
12. 6
13. 4
14. $4\sqrt{7} - 2\sqrt{13}$
15. A
16. $3\sqrt{91}$
17. 6
18. 120
19. 48
20. C

Challenging Order of Operations PS1 (278)
1. 2
2. 20
3. -48
4. 80
5. -19
6. 39
7. 42
8. 99
9. 66
10. -24
11. 26
12. 203
13. 74
14. 48
15. 45
16. 11
17. 96
18. 49
19. 19
20. -49

Challenging Order of Operations PS2
1. 58
2. 45
3. 13
4. 11
5. -54
6. 55
7. -22
8. -6
9. -31
10. 4

11. 16
12. 50
13. -7
14. 20
15. -5
16. -28
17. 40
18. 48
19. -20
20. 42

Challenging Order of Operations PS3
1. 4
2. -6
3. 39
4. 0
5. -13
6. 6
7. 36
8. 21
9. 22
10. -13
11. 287
12. 8
13. 5
14. 28
15. -13
16. 86
17. 33
18. 17
19. -37
20. -52

Challenging Order of Operations PS4
1. -2
2. 17
3. -21
4. 28
5. 22
6. -13
7. 15
8. -9
9. 54
10. 23
11. -196
12. 32
13. 20
14. 14
15. 80
16. 48
17. -160
18. 101
19. 0
20. 25

Chapter 10
Conceptual Algebra PS1 (287)
1. $j - 5$
2. $30p$
3. $12 - y$
4. $\frac{200}{d}$
5. C
6. C
7. B
8. D
9. A
10. B

11. A
12. B
13. D
14. A
15. C
16. D
17. A
18. B
19. C
20. C

Conceptual Algebra PS2
1. $r + 4$
2. $5p$
3. $2 + m$
4. $\frac{500}{u}$
5. B
6. B
7. C
8. C
9. B
10. D
11. C
12. D
13. C
14. A
15. C
16. D
17. B
18. C
19. A
20. B

Conceptual Algebra PS3
1. $h + 10$
2. $31c$
3. $52 + k$
4. B
5. C
6. B
7. D
8. B
9. A
10. C
11. B
12. D
13. D
14. B
15. B
16. D
17. A
18. A
19. A
20. C

Conceptual Algebra PS4
1. $t + 2$
2. $12c$
3. $h + 4$
4. $18 - f$
5. C
6. D
7. B
8. A
9. C
10. B
11. A
12. D
13. C
14. B
15. A
16. D

17. C
18. B
19. D
20. A

Basic Algebra PS1 (299)
1. 12
2. 5
3. 18
4. 28
5. 6
6. 13
7. 6
8. 6
9. 30
10. 9
11. 4
12. 4
13. 1
14. 2
15. $6x - 3$
16. $6a + 1$
17. $a + 2b$
18. A
19. D
20. C

Basic Algebra PS2
1. 14
2. 11
3. 8
4. 12
5. 7
6. 16
7. 36
8. 3
9. 6
10. $2c$
11. 2
12. 0
13. -17
14. -1
15. $5xy - 7y$
16. $14b - 2a - 6ab$
17. $6m - 11n - 7mn$
18. B
19. D
20. A

Basic Algebra PS3
1. 4
2. 8
3. 10
4. 25
5. 2
6. 38
7. 24
8. 14
9. 5
10. 4
11. 8
12. 4
13. 2
14. 5
15. $3x + 4$
16. $5a + 2$
17. $5a - 2b$
18. B
19. B
20. A

Basic Algebra PS4
1. 7
2. 12
3. -2
4. 45
5. -6
6. 38
7. 7
8. 6
9. 8
10. 11
11. 28
12. 11
13. 13
14. $xy - 4x - 11y$
15.
16. $74mn - 25n - 20m$
17. D
18. B
19. B
20. C

Algebraic Expressions PS1 (303)
1. $4c^2 - c + 5$
2. $10a^2b - 12a^4b^2$
3. $3xy^4 - 7xy^3$
4. $19rst$
5. C
6. A
7. B
8. D
9. B
10. B
11. A
12. C
13. C
14. B
15. A
16. A
17. C
18. C
19. C
20. C

Algebraic Expressions PS2
1. $4 - 9x^2 - 12x$
2. $7a^4b^2 - 5a^2b^4$
3. $5m^3n^5 + 3m^2n^3$
4. $2xy^2z^3 - 11x^2y^3$
5. D
6. A
7. B
8. C
9. C
10. B
11. C
12. A
13. D
14. B
15. A
16. C
17. B
18. A
19. C
20. D

Algebraic Expressions PS3
1. $10a^2 + 2a - 11$
2. $4x^4y^2$
3. $-13p^2q^5 + 3pq^3$
4. $3r^2st^5 + 3rst^3$
5. D

6. C
7. B
8. A
9. C
10. B
11. A
12. D
13. B
14. A
15. A
16. C
17. C
18. D
19. B
20. D

Algebraic Expressions PS4
1. $c^2 - 11c + 2$
2. $-25a^4 - 5ab$
3. $7x^3y + 5xy$
4. $-12r^2st^3 - 4rst$
5. D
6. A
7. B
8. C
9. C
10. A
11. D
12. C
13. D
14. C
15. D
16. D
17. A
18. C
19. B
20. C

Algebraic Word Problems PS1 (311)
1. A
2. 77%
3. D
4. B
5. 12
6. A
7. D
8. A
9. C
10. A
11. C
12. B
13. 16
14. D
15. C
16. D
17. -5
18. B
19. D
20. 12

Algebraic Word Problems PS2
1. A
2. 142
3. B
4. 27
5. C
6. 6
7. D
8. A
9. A
10. 18

11. D
12. B
13. C
14. D
15. C
16. B
17. C
18. A
19. C
20. B

Algebraic Word Problems PS3
1. 60
2. 108
3. 350
4. A
5. 5
6. 6
7. D
8. C
9. C
10. D
11. D
12. C
13. A
14. D
15. 43
16. B
17. 6
18. A
19. C
20. D

Algebraic Word Problems PS4
1. 32
2. 33
3. 242
4. 9
5. 4
6. B
7. 31
8. 8.4
9. C
10. A
11. B
12. C
13. D
14. 7,440
15. A
16. 70
17. -23
18. D
19. B
20. C

Inequalities & Absolute Value PS1 (322)
1. B
2. B
3. B
4. B
5. B
6. B
7. B
8. B
9. B
10. D
11. B
12. B

13. B
14. B
15. B
16. B
17. B
18. B
19. B
20. D

Inequalities & Absolute Value PS2
1. True
2. False
3. B
4. C
5. A
6. B
7. A
8. D
9. C
10. D
11. A
12. C
13. A
14. D
15. A
16. D
17. B
18. B
19. A
20. C

Inequalities & Absolute Value PS3
1. False
2. C
3. A
4. B
5. A
6. D
7. C
8. D
9. A
10. C
11. D
12. B
13. A
14. B
15. D
16. C
17. D
18. C
19. D
20. A

Inequalities & Absolute Value PS4
1. C
2. A
3. D
4. A
5. D
6. C
7. C
8. D
9. C
10. D
11. B
12. D
13. B
14. A

15. A
16. C
17. D
18. B
19. D
20. C

Chapter 11
Measurement PS1 (331)
1. 10,560 ft
2. 48 oz
3. 16 cups
4. 72 in
5. 100,000 cm
6. 86,400 seconds
7. 7 m
8. 120 m
9. 153 in
10. 3,200 mg
11. 40 oz
12. 260 hours
13. C
14. 300 g
15. $10
16. C
17. $200
18. 275 lbs
19. 6.25 miles
20. 96 km

Measurement PS2
1. 2 pints
2. B
3. A
4. 0.002 L
5. $5\frac{5}{6}$ hrs
6. 1.5 lbs
7. 3,200 g
8. 6,012 in
9. B
10. A
11. C
12. 25,344 in
13. C
14. D
15. A
16. 16,200 seconds
17. B
18. D
19. D
20. C

Measurement PS3
1. 35 mm
2. C
3. B
4. 13.5 quarts
5. $3\frac{1}{2}$ days
6. 0.25 tons
7. 4 minutes
8. 32,736 ft
9. 1.6 kg
10. 5,400 seconds
11. 12.5 tons
12. D
13. C
14. B
15. A
16. D
17. B

18. A
19. B
20. C

Measurement PS4
1. 15,840 ft
2. 5,000 mm
3. 4 cups
4. 108 in
5. 32 oz
6. 10,080 minutes
7. 5 L
8. 200 m
9. 180 in
10. 64,000 oz
11. 5,750 mg
12. 72 times
13. A
14. 500 g
15. $11
16. A
17. $1,600
18. 41.92 km
19. 110 kg
20. 2.5 miles

Ratios and Proportions PS1 (337)
1. B
2. C
3. A
4. C
5. D
6. B
7. D
8. A
9. D
10. D
11. A
12. C
13. B
14. D
15. B
16. A
17. C
18. A
19. D
20. B

Ratios and Proportions PS2
1. A
2. D
3. C
4. D
5. B
6. B
7. A
8. C
9. D
10. C
11. B
12. D
13. A
14. B
15. A
16. B
17. C
18. D
19. B
20. D

Ratios and Proportions PS3
1. B
2. A
3. C
4. B
5. D
6. C
7. B
8. A
9. C
10. B
11. D
12. A
13. B
14. D
15. D
16. B
17. C
18. A
19. C
20. D

Ratios and Proportions PS4
1. B
2. D
3. C
4. A
5. C
6. A
7. B
8. D
9. C
10. B
11. D
12. C
13. A
14. B
15. D
16. C
17. B
18. A
19. B
20. A

Probability PS1 (349)
1. $\frac{1}{20}$
2. $\frac{3}{13}$
3. $\frac{2}{3}$
4. $\frac{2}{5}$
5. $\frac{7}{12}$
6. $\frac{1}{2}$
7. $\frac{1}{4}$
8. $\frac{1}{36}$
9. $\frac{1}{400}$
10. D
11. $\frac{1}{52}$
12. $\frac{14}{33}$
13. 12 outfits
14. 0.35
15. 0.45
16. C
17. $\frac{3}{10}$
18. 180 games
19. 9 days
20. 15 marbles

Probability PS2
1. $\frac{1}{6}$
2. $\frac{8}{15}$
3. B
4. $\frac{1}{4}$
5. A
6. A
7. D
8. D
9. B
10. A
11. C
12. C
13. D
14. B
15. B
16. D
17. D
18. A
19. C
20. A

Probability PS3
1. $\frac{4}{9}$
2. C
3. $\frac{2}{5}$
4. A
5. $\frac{1}{6}$
6. $\frac{1}{4}$
7. $\frac{1}{2}$
8. B
9. B
10. D
11. C
12. C
13. D
14. A
15. D
16. B
17. D
18. A
19. C
20. D

Probability PS4
1. $\frac{1}{15}$
2. $\frac{3}{8}$
3. $\frac{1}{3}$
4. $\frac{1}{5}$
5. $\frac{5}{6}$
6. $\frac{1}{10}$
7. $\frac{1}{4}$
8. $\frac{1}{64}$
9. 0.7
10. $\frac{1}{225}$
11. 40 combinations
12. $\frac{15}{28}$
13. D
14. 0.4
15. $\frac{5}{9}$
16. A
17. $\frac{1}{4}$
18. $\frac{1}{12}$

19. 150 games
20. 4 pens

Rate and Work PS1 (361)
1. 18 miles
2. 55 pages
3. C
4. 54 inches
5. B
6. A
7. B
8. D
9. A
10. D
11. C
12. C
13. D
14. D
15. A
16. B
17. A
18. C
19. D
20. C

Rate and Work PS2
1. 24 miles
2. 35 mph
3. 8 hours
4. 700 yards
5. C
6. 96 chirps
7. B
8. B
9. C
10. D
11. C
12. B
13. B
14. C
15. C
16. D
17. D
18. D
19. D
20. C

Rate and Work PS3
1. 16 mph
2. 6 miles
3. 4 minutes 10 seconds
4. 15 miles
5. D
6. 3,360 fish
7. B
8. C
9. D
10. A
11. B
12. A
13. C
14. D
15. C
16. D
17. C
18. B
19. B
20. A

Rate and Work PS4
1. 10 mph
2. 9,500 miles

3. 0.6 seconds
4. 8 watermelons
5. B
6. $1,800
7. D
8. C
9. C
10. B
11. C
12. A
13. B
14. A
15. A
16. C
17. B
18. D
19. A
20. D

Chapter 12
Perimeter and Area PS1 (374)
1. 6 cm
2. 6
3. 9 cm
4. 150 ft^2
5. 32 in
6. 7
7. 4 in
8. 8
9. 56
10. $6y$
11. $3x$
12. 66
13. 32
14. 800 in
15. C
16. 160 in^2
17. $\frac{7x}{2}$ m
18. $4x + 4$
19. 1, 2, or 3
20. 1:2

Perimeter and Area PS2
1. 60
2. 54
3. 7 in
4. 120 ft
5. 60 in^2
6. 13
7. 11
8. 15 cm
9. 60
10. $5b$
11. 36
12. 54
13. A
14. $5x$
15. 140
16. 80 ft^2
17. $\frac{15p^2}{2}$ m
18. $x^2 + 3x + 2$
19. 12 and 2 OR 24 and 1
20. 2:1

Angles and Triangles PS1 (380)
1. B
2. C
3. 24 cm
4. 82°

533

5. C
6. 68°
7. 68°
8. 70°
9. A
10. 76°
11. 30
12. 64°
13. 78
14. B
15. C
16. D
17. A
18. $\sqrt{89}$
19. 9
20. A

Angles and Triangles PS2
1. D
2. 19°
3. A
4. D
5. A
6. 24°
7. C
8. 64°
9. B
10. 32
11. 189
12. D
13. C
14. C
15. 17.5°
16. B
17. 30
18. $\sqrt{175}$ feet
19. 12
20. 14

Angles and Triangles PS3
1. 42°
2. 65°
3. 168
4. 9°
5. 67°
6. 24
7. 57°
8. A
9. 8°
10. 38
11. B
12. 5 units
13. 100°
14. 67.5°
15. 42
16. C
17. 50 m
18. 18
19. D
20. 7.5

Angles and Triangles PS4
1. $6\frac{2}{3}°$
2. C
3. 23°
4. 56°
5. D
6. 33
7. 39
8. 114°

9. A
10. 18°
11. 6°
12. A
13. 2.25
14. D
15. B
16. 248°
17. 21
18. B
19. 8
20. 28

Quadrilaterals and Circles
PS1 (395)
1. 216 m³
2. 90°
3. 52
4. C
5. B
6. 10
7. 9
8. D
9. 289
10. C
11. A
12. D
13. C
14. B
15. A
16. C
17. D
18. B
19. A
20. B

Quadrilaterals and Circles
PS2
1. 60 cm
2. 43.96 inches
3. 8 slices
4. C
5. $5\sqrt{2}$
6. 17.85
7. 16
8. 294 cm²
9. 48
10. C
11. 169
12. B
13. $868
14. 188 in²
15. 64
16. B
17. D
18. A
19. 320 in³
20. 672 seconds

Quadrilaterals and Circles
PS3
1. C
2. 28 cm
3. B
4. 1,331 in³
5. 6 slices
6. 21
7. D
8. C
9. B
10. 87 ft

11. C
12. B
13. A
14. 52
15. D
16. 24
17. A
18. D
19. A
20. B

Quadrilaterals and Circles
PS4
1. 256
2. 34°
3. A
4. C
5. 1
6. 90°
7. 296 inches
8. B
9. 450
10. C
11. B
12. 3,375 cm³
13. 17
14. B
15. C
16. C
17. 150
18. B
19. D
20. A

3-D Figures PS1 (408)
1. D
2. C
3. A
4. A
5. A
6. C
7. A
8. D
9. B
10. A

3-D Figures PS2
1. D
2. C
3. B
4. D
5. C
6. D
7. A
8. C
9. C
10. B

Coordinate Geometry PS1
(416)
1. D
2. C
3. A
4. A
5. D
6. B
7. D
8. C
9. B
10. (4, 3)

11. -2
12. 3
13. -3
14. A
15. 3

Coordinate Geometry PS2
1. $\frac{1}{2}$
2. 40 in²
3. C
4. −3
5. A
6. C
7. 14
8. B
9. 2
10. A
11. C
12. A
13. A
14. D
15. -1

Coordinate Geometry PS3
1. $\frac{1}{2}$
2. D
3. $\frac{1}{2}$
4. (−3, −4)
5. $\frac{1}{3}$
6. 27 in²
7. B
8. B
9. D
10. A
11. C
12. $\frac{5}{2}$
13. -4
14. C
15. D

Coordinate Geometry PS4
1. -2
2. B
3. 8
4. A
5. -2
6. -3
7. 28 in²
8. (2, 8)
9. D
10. D
11. B
12. $-\frac{3}{5}$
13. (−12, −3)
14. A
15. D

Chapter 13
Statistics PS1 (431)
1. 33
2. 33
3. 410 points
4. D
5. C
6. C
7. B
8. A

534

9. C
10. D
11. C
12. C
13. B
14. C
15. A
16. A
17. B
18. D
19. B
20. A

Statistics PS2
1. 4
2. 124
3. 18 goals
4. C
5. C
6. B
7. B
8. D
9. C
10. B
11. B
12. A
13. A
14. D
15. 175
16. C
17. B
18. B
19. D
20. A

Statistics PS3
1. 5.65
2. 0.04
3. A
4. C
5. D
6. A
7. B
8. C
9. D
10. C
11. B
12. D
13. A
14. C
15. A
16. B
17. C
18. D
19. B
20. C

Statistics PS4
1. 79.5
2. 3.4
3. 100.8
4. 3 years old
5. D
6. C
7. 400 lbs
8. A
9. D
10. C
11. A
12. B
13. D
14. A
15. D

16. B
17. C
18. D
19. A
20. B

Charts and Graphs PS1
(443)
1. B
2. C
3. B
4. C
5. D
6. A
7. A
8. D
9. A
10. D
11. C
12. B
13. C
14. D
15. B
16. C
17. C
18. B
19. C
20. C

Charts and Graphs PS2
1. A
2. C
3. C
4. B
5. D
6. B
7. C
8. A
9. D
10. B
11. D
12. A
13. B
14. C
15. B
16. D
17. B
18. D
19. D
20. C

Charts and Graphs PS3
1. C
2. B
3. D
4. C
5. A
6. B
7. D
8. D
9. B
10. B
11. C
12. D
13. D
14. A
15. D
16. A
17. B
18. C
19. C
20. B

Charts and Graphs PS4
1. D
2. C
3. C
4. B
5. A
6. D
7. D
8. C
9. C
10. B
11. D
12. C
13. A
14. C
15. B
16. D
17. C
18. B
19. A
20. C

Chapter 14
Sequences PS1 (460)
1. 20
2. 1,982
3. 7.75
4. 115
5. -14
6. 48
7. 7
8. 76
9. 11
10. 1
11. 475
12. 38
13. 50
14. 27
15. 12
16. 38
17. 3
18. 15
19. 125
20. 64

Sequences PS2
1. 67
2. 574
3. 1/6
4. 20
5. 256
6. -128
7. 8
8. 62
9. 66
10. 360
11. 112
12. 5
13. 21
14. 212
15. 26
16. 18
17. 9
18. 24
19. 27
20. 125

Sequences PS3
1. 360
2. 6,000
3. -58
4. 109

5. 2
6. 162
7. -625
8. 8
9. 109
10. 5
11. 500
12. 100
13. 20
14. 28
15. 60
16. 40
17. 8
18. 16
19. 5
20. 16

Sequences PS4
1. 680
2. 4,281
3. 0
4. 4
5. 76
6. 96
7. -81
8. -2
9. 57
10. 142
11. 2
12. 1
13. 8
14. 30
15. 94
16. 225
17. 7
18. 11
19. 125
20. 5

Sequences: Letters & Roman
Numerals PS1 (464)
1. 22E
2. D17
3. 9P
4. 15M
5. 74G
6. Q64
7. EO
8. ET
9. UN
10. KW
11. UV
12. RI
13. P
14. XXX
15. VI
16. LX
17. CLX
18. XXXIII
19. XXXVIII
20. 54

Sequences: Letters & Roman
Numerals PS2
1. 17N
2. P12
3. 100R
4. 37X
5. 18R
6. L8
7. HV
8. SB

9. LR
10. HD
11. JR
12. XD
13. L
14. XXXVII
15. X
16. CCCXL
17. I
18. 39
19. XXXI
20. 15

Setting Up Equations PS1
(466)
1. C
2. B
3. B
4. A
5. A
6. 37
7. 28
8. 30
9. 54
10. 28
11. 19
12. 60
13. 60
14. 2
15. 5
16. 54
17. 5
18. B
19. C
20. D

Setting Up Equations PS2
1. D
2. B
3. C
4. B
5. A
6. 56
7. 21
8. 52
9. 20
10. 12
11. 24
12. 34
13. 45
14. 33
15. 13
16. 29
17. 100
18. C
19. B
20. B

Setting Up Equations PS3
1. D
2. C
3. A
4. D
5. C
6. 76
7. 27
8. 60
9. 56
10. 36
11. 18
12. 60

13. 20
14. 3
15. 10
16. 2
17. 8
18. B
19. B
20. B

Setting Up Equations PS4
1. D
2. C
3. C
4. B
5. B
6. 122
7. 49
8. 60
9. 64
10. 62
11. 100
12. 44
13. 50
14. 8
15. 2
16. 13
17. 3
18. D
19. A
20. B

HSPT Comparisons PS1
(474)
1. C
2. B
3. D
4. C
5. B
6. A
7. B
8. C
9. B
10. C
11. C
12. B
13. B
14. A
15. D
16. C
17. B
18. D
19. C
20. C

HSPT Comparisons PS2
1. B
2. C
3. A
4. C
5. C
6. B
7. D
8. C
9. B
10. D
11. D
12. A
13. C
14. A
15. B
16. C

17. C
18. B
19. A
20. C

HSPT Comparisons PS3
1. D
2. D
3. B
4. A
5. D
6. C
7. A
8. A
9. C
10. A
11. B
12. D
13. A
14. D
15. A
16. A
17. B
18. D
19. D
20. B

HSPT Comparisons PS4
1. C
2. D
3. D
4. A
5. B
6. A
7. C
8. C
9. C
10. B
11. D
12. B
13. B
14. D
15. C
16. A
17. D
18. C
19. B
20. D

Chapter 15
Basic Computation PS1
(494)
1. B
2. B
3. B
4. A
5. A
6. A
7. C
8. C
9. A
10. B
11. B
12. A
13. C
14. C
15. B
16. A
17. B
18. A

19. A
20. B

Basic Computation PS2
1. B
2. B
3. C
4. B
5. B
6. A
7. B
8. A
9. A
10. C
11. A
12. B
13. A
14. B
15. B
16. B
17. C
18. A
19. B
20. A

Algebraic Expressions PS1
(498)
1. B
2. A
3. D
4. A
5. B
6. A
7. A
8. B
9. D
10. B
11. C
12. A
13. B
14. A
15. C
16. D
17. A
18. D
19. C
20. A

Algebraic Expressions PS2
1. D
2. D
3. D
4. D
5. A
6. A
7. C
8. B
9. A
10. B
11. B
12. D
13. A
14. B
15. C
16. C
17. D
18. B
19. A
20. D

Perimeter and Area PS1
(502)
1. C
2. B
3. C
4. B
5. D
6. C
7. D
8. D
9. D
10. A
11. D
12. A
13. B
14. B
15. A
16. B
17. A
18. B
19. D
20. A

Perimeter and Area PS2
1. D
2. A
3. A
4. D
5. D
6. D
7. D
8. B
9. A
10. C
11. A
12. C
13. B
14. C
15. A
16. D
17. C
18. C
19. B
20. C

Mixed Quantitative
Comparison PS1 (506)
1. B
2. A
3. C
4. D
5. C
6. A
7. A
8. A
9. C
10. D
11. D
12. B
13. A
14. C
15. B
16. C
17. A
18. C
19. A
20. A

Mixed Quantitative
Comparison PS2
1. B
2. C
3. C
4. B
5. C
6. A
7. D
8. B
9. A
10. C
11. D
12. A
13. D
14. D
15. A
16. B
17. B
18. A
19. D
20. A

Mixed Quantitative
Comparison PS3
1. C
2. B
3. C
4. B
5. A
6. B
7. B
8. B
9. B
10. A
11. C
12. A
13. D
14. C
15. B
16. C
17. A
18. A
19. B
20. C

Mixed Quantitative
Comparison PS4
1. B
2. C
3. B
4. C
5. D
6. A
7. D
8. A
9. C
10. A
11. D
12. C
13. A
14. A
15. B
16. A
17. D
18. B
19. B
20. B